HOOVER, ROOSEVELT, and the BRAINS TRUST

From Depression to New Deal

HOOVER, ROOSEVELT, and the BRAINS TRUST

From Depression to New Deal

Elliot A. Rosen

New York   Columbia University Press   *1977*

Library of Congress Cataloging in Publication Data
Rosen, Elliot A   1928–
Hoover, Roosevelt, and the Brains Trust.
Includes bibliographical references.
1. United States—Politics and government—1929–1933.
2. Presidents—United States—Election—1932.
3. Roosevelt, Franklin Delano, Pres. U.S., 1882–1945.
4. Hoover, Herbert Clark, Pres. U.S., 1874–1964.
I. Title.
E801.R65   320.9'73'0916   76-49976
ISBN 0-231-04172-1

Columbia University Press
New York   Guildford, Surrey
Copyright © 1977 Columbia University Press
Printed in the United States of America

To Carol Mendes Rosen

Preface

THE TEMPTATION is strong to rationalize a decision after the fact. My memory yields no distinct event which explains the origination of this work. Most likely, it took form in my mind as Raymond Moley and I shared his desk one day, as we so often did since I was in my teens, to consume our luncheon. He frequently marveled at the ethnicity of my wife's confection, I at the detail and richness of his recollection. Increasingly, I confess, I maneuvered the conversation to his reminiscence of the interplay between Franklin D. Roosevelt and his Brains Trust. Further, as we collaborated on *The First New Deal* (1966), the quantity and quality of documentation and memoranda he had retained in connection with the 1932 campaign scarcely escaped my attention. Our joint effort dealt with his brief public career. Would he object, I ventured, if I undertook an examination of the conceptualization of the New Deal by Roosevelt and his academic advisers? He signaled agreement in his uniquely restrained way.

My indebtedness to Raymond Moley defies adequate expression. His subjection to lengthy interviews, his provision of written recollections, then, before his passing, his encouragement of my interpretations as they parted substantially from his own, reflected the scholarly and kindly qualities of the man. When we last dined together in New York City thirty years after we first met, some months before his death, he observed that he remained convinced that Herbert Hoover originated the New Deal. Ailing from a debilitating stroke, aided by a cane and my arm, as we slowly walked on Madison Avenue, he puckishly mused that he could not see, however, that his reputation would suffer if I insisted on attributing the New Deal to him. He urged only fidelity to the sources and my own findings. This I have attempted to do.

Research began in the summer of 1963, the manuscript completed in the summer of 1976. Obligations accrued beyond my total recollection. Dr. Moley permitted examination of his vast manuscript holdings when they were in his possession. I should caution researchers that my citations are based on his original filing system, rather than that of the Hoover Institution on War, Revolution, and Peace, Stanford, California, where the Moley Papers now reside. Rexford Guy Tugwell graciously extended access to his personal papers and diaries, then helped to clarify my perception of the Brains Trusts' objectives, initially through correspondence, subsequently by offering his hospitality at his Santa Barbara home. James A. Farley, Jouett Shouse, Robert Jackson, and Adolf A. Berle shared their recollections, and Jackson generously offered the use of portions of his richly detailed diary.

In time, the task widened to an exploration of the setting in which the New Deal had been framed. Research into Herbert Hoover's response to the Great Depression scarcely corroborated conclusions reached by Hoover specialists. Examination of Democratic Party politics drew me into an investigation of the party's conservative coalition and its effort to check the inception of the interventionist state. Since neither Hoover nor Roosevelt confined himself to domestic considerations, I followed the interrelationship between domestic economic tides and diplomatic decisions. The task, which seemed endless at times, required thirteen years.

The completed work owes much to three readers. Henry Blumenthal, while a colleague at Rutgers-Newark, then in retirement, reflected upon and critiqued each chapter of the manuscript. I owe much to his unstinting editorial and intellectual suggestions, to his encouragement and wisdom. Frank Freidel offered valued editorial advice as the manuscript neared completion. In more ways than I can explain, both offered their support when the going seemed rough. Finally, Joan McQuary, Managing Editor at Columbia University Press, cheerfully gave her interested and informed assistance in bringing this work to its finished state.

Financial support derived from several sources, initially, when I was yet unpublished, from Henry Blumenthal's budget as Director of the Rutgers-Newark Social Sciences Division and from my wife's teaching income. The Rutgers Research Council and the Penrose Fund of the American Philosophical Society provided generous grants for research expenses at archives across the nation. Lucille and Donald Tuttle graciously offered their home as headquarters for much of my work at the Library of Congress. A Rutgers University Faculty Fellowship expedited completion of the manuscript.

My travels afforded contact with a magnificent group of professionals who facilitated my labors and gladly shared their expertise. Research at the Franklin D. Roosevelt Presidential Library commenced when Elizabeth Drewry served as its director and concluded when William Emerson assumed its leadership. I owe much to both for their hospitality and to their dedicated staff, especially William Stewart, Jerry Deyo, and Joseph Marshall. I am indebted also to the staff of the Manuscript Division of the Library of Congress, especially Dr. Paul T. Heffron, Assistant Chief; Mrs. Thomas R. Underwood of the University of Kentucky Library; Judith G. Schiff, Director of Historical Manuscripts, Yale University Library; Nancy Bressler, Assistant Curator of Manuscripts, Princeton University Library; Dwight Miller, Chief Archivist, Herbert Hoover Presidential Library; and the staffs of the University of Montana Library at Bozeman; the Alderman Library, University of Virginia; the Louisville Law School Library; the New York Public Library; the Houghton Library, Harvard University; the Bancroft Library, University of California, Berkeley; the Newark Public Library; the Columbia University Library Manuscript Division and Oral History Collection; the Eleutherian Mills Historical Library; the Connecticut College Library, New London; the Bennington College Library; and the Dana Library, Rutgers-Newark.

John L. Ely typed the original draft of this manuscript and Virginia Brown performed yoeman service in meeting my deadlines for the final two drafts.

This book is dedicated to Carol Mendes Rosen, who has given her affection and encouragement, accompanied me on several of my research trips, yet managed her own career as teacher and artist. She understood what I hoped to accomplish, sustained my spirit and energy when I tired, endured lonely hours as I scoured the archives and pieced this story together. Without her devotion I could not have undertaken so large a task.

Elliot A. Rosen
December 1976

Contents

HOOVER, ROOSEVELT, and the BRAINS TRUST

From Depression to New Deal

Introduction

THE GREAT DEPRESSION originated in a complex of circumstances, its roots extending back to the economic consequences of World War I. John Maynard Keynes warned as early as 1919 that the Versailles Treaty, especially the reparations intended to strangle Germany's economy, threatened Europe with economic dislocation. He urged in vain United States generosity in the treatment of the debts incurred by its former allies.

For a decade, the New Era it was called, prosperity seemed one of the permanent accoutrements of American life. Europe's problems seemed distant. For many the principal lesson to be derived from our involvement in the Great War was never again to become enmeshed in the perennial conflicts of the Old World. Yet, in the early 1930s our own economy, for a multitude of reasons, internal and external, very nearly ground to a halt. American farmers for a decade had produced more than the world market could absorb. Worldwide, distressingly low prices prevailed for most raw materials and the underdeveloped nations went under considerably before their creditors. In the advanced societies banking practices left much to be desired. Securities speculation created artificial prices bound to collapse. In this nation industry was able to produce more than consumers could absorb at prevailing levels of income. Millions of farmers were wiped out in the 1920s. By the early 1930s with millions of urban laborers unemployed, business and banking in jeopardy, awareness of the depression became acute. So intense was the experience that the generation that endured it never completely recovered from its trauma.

Traditionally, depressions had been permitted to run their course, the economic system allowed to cleanse itself. There were many in business, finance, and government who recalled approv-

ingly that the nation weathered the 1893–1898 crisis with a minimum of governmental intervention. The "wild men" of the nineties
✓ and their monetary panaceas, it could be argued, might have done
permanent damage. Instead Grover Cleveland clung to the gold
standard and a generation of prosperity ensued. Yet, government
management of the economy in World War I offered an alternative
course. As the depression deepened, the wartime experience of
successful overhead management was recalled and increasingly the
wartime metaphor evoked.

Divergent economic approaches were often reinforced or ratio-
nalized in political terms. Usually clothed as Jeffersonianism by
conservative Democrats, the notion of minimal government prevailed in a nation still chewing the cud of Spencerian dogma. Herbert Hoover elaborated his opposition to centralism as the American system, reliance on individualism, community effort, and upon
voluntary economic associations. Equation of modified laissez faire
doctrine with the retention of our political freedoms cut across
party lines. It dominated the Hoover administration's response to
the depression. In collaboration with Ogden L. Mills at Treasury,
Hoover focused on budget balance and maintenance of the United
States on the gold standard in 1932. The policy proved regressive.
Progressive Republicans pressed for rural and urban relief on a
scale opposed by the administration. Progressives could go elsewhere if dissatisfied. The chief executive regarded Congress as a
nuisance.

The bitterly divided minority party, legatee of the Jeffersonian
and Jacksonian tradition, was captured in 1928 by the heads of one
of the nation's great industrial empires. John J. Raskob maintained
✓ control of the Democratic Party for the Du Ponts even after Alfred
E. Smith's defeat. There seemed to this group precious little connection between the central government and the functioning of the
economy. Many congressional Democrats were similarly imbued
with the doctrine of passive government. Tame as the Roosevelt attitudes toward intervention, expenditures by government, and re-

form may appear to a later generation, they seemed threatening to the values of many in his own party.

Franklin D. Roosevelt was no ideologue. But his governorship of New York revealed progressive tendencies and the "wild men" of the Democratic party began to offer him their support in 1931. The Jeffersonian Democrats shuddered at the thought of another Bryan. Many believed Roosevelt to be weak, a vacuous country squire, capable of being swayed by radicals such as Burton K. Wheeler and Washington's Clarence C. Dill. In the years 1931 and 1932, the party's conservatives waged a major struggle for retention of control of its machinery for ideological reasons. And they fixed upon a candidate, Newton D. Baker of Ohio, more in harmony with their views.

However powerful and natural the desire to focus on our domestic problems, international issues intruded. Financial collapse in Central Europe, Great Britain's abandonment of the gold standard, threatened default in the payment of debts and reparations, intensification of trade warfare, were added in 1931 to the gnawing issues of disarmament and revision of the Versailles agreements. Internationalists were a distinct minority in this nation. But they tended to view the depression as caused by worldwide events and they feared above all intensification of nationalism and the potential of another major war. Fearful of a new round of bloodshed in Europe, Hoover's Secretary of State, Henry L. Stimson, and Senator Cordell Hull of Tennessee, a powerful Democratic spokesman, pressed for depression relief and prevention of conflict through a multinational approach.

It seems that the years 1931 and 1932 were pivotal in the interwar period in several areas that constitute a part of history's seamless web. The Hoover–Mills policies concentrated initially, in 1931, on the worldwide depression, then in response to popular political pressure shifted to an internal focus. Hoover's fear of centralization of control in the federal government and Mills's orthodox fiscal policies prevailed in 1932. The result was intensification of the downward spiral of collapse. It was not clear, until the Democratic National Convention of 1932, what alternatives might be offered. A coalition of conservative Jeffersonians fought the Roosevelt nomination and the potential of unorthodox measures. Calmly, behind the scenes, aware of his own limitations, the squire of Hyde Park gathered a group of economic advisers recruited from Columbia University for the purpose of elaboration of a synthesis. In broad outline the Brains Trust *—Raymond Moley, Rexford Tugwell, and Adolf A. Berle Jr.— gradually fashioned a program, one which required insulation of the nation's economy from world tides. Europe was left to fend for itself.

Although this study is concerned largely with the years 1931–1932, it does at times search for antecedents of problems, attitudes, and remedies. At times it glances ahead, for decisions made have their implications for the future. During those years Herbert Hoover and Franklin D. Roosevelt offered alternative visions of the nation's domestic priorities in substance and approach. The Republican President struggled for preservation of our decentralist past, for the maintenance of limited government, and reliance on individual, community, and voluntary solutions. Enlargement of the federal role was fraught with dangers, he argued passionately, to the political liberties treasured since the founding of the republic, a charge he would level at the New Deal the balance of his years.

Franklin D. Roosevelt and the Brains Trust offered the view that functions appropriate to government at the national level required expansion. Concentration of economic power in a relatively few private aggregates responsible to no one who represented the interests of the larger community, the massive collapse and disequilibrium of the period, dictated the evolution of a new constitutional

---

* The term "Brains Trust" was coined by *New York Times* reporter James Kieran on the eve of the 1932 campaign to describe the academicians who figured prominently in the Roosevelt entourage. Kieran used the term in the plural form and this work follows its original usage. In the years since it has been singularized and generally denotes presidential advisers.

order. These views and much of the New Deal depression program were elaborated in the 1932 campaign.

The relative virtues of centralism and decentralism are still debated in our own generation, and much of our government's exertion is expended in the avoidance of a repetition of the Great Depression. Interestingly, our society still wavers between the Hoover ethic, with its stress in individualism and voluntarism, and the desirability of interventionism and control at the federal level. The issue remains whether preservation of the marketplace and our political liberties are intertwined, whether either can withstand continued enlargement of government's economic and social role, or whether now we need to explore more radical alternatives. Perhaps a return to the origins of the debate preceding the New Deal will enlarge the dimension of our understanding.

1

Albany Days, Albany Advisers

FRANKLIN D. ROOSEVELT was convinced in 1928 that continued therapy at Warm Springs, Georgia, would permit him to regain use of his legs. Not that he and his intimate political adviser, Louis McHenry Howe, lacked aspirations to the White House. They nurtured such ambitions since they first met in the pre-Wilson years when the young Roosevelt represented Dutchess County in the New York State senate. They learned much under Josephus Daniels' tutelage at the Navy Department, then promoted their chance at the main prize by taking on a sacrificial role as vice-presidential nominee in the Cox campaign of 1920. Whatever the psychological blow when polio struck FDR at Campobello Island, Howe's devotion to the singular goal of placing Franklin in the presidency never wavered. In 1924 Roosevelt re-emerged with the "Happy Warrior" speech, placing Alfred E. Smith in nomination. Though supporters of Smith again in 1928, they anticipated his defeat and expected two terms for Herbert Hoover. They could bide their time.

But Alfred E. Smith determined otherwise. He needed the Roosevelt name and Protestant affiliation to carry New York in his contest with Hoover. The squire's identification with rural Dutchess County and fight against Tammany when he sat in the legislature had a particular appeal for upstate voters. It was hoped that Smith would benefit from Roosevelt's candidacy for the governorship in that part of the state where he was weakest. From the squire's perspective the proposition seemed less than alluring and he secreted himself at his Warm Springs retreat. Yet, he capitulated under an assortment of pressures. Smith's principal financial backer, now head of the Democratic National Committee, John J. Raskob, a Du Pont executive, offered to relieve Roosevelt of the financial burdens recently assumed in the creation of the Warm Springs Foundation. Herbert Lehman, member of a prominent New York banking family, agreed to assume sufficient of the burden of the governorship to allow Roosevelt ample time at Warm Springs. Even Eleanor Roosevelt was enlisted in the effort.

Franklin D. Roosevelt's capitulation proved a Pyrrhic victory for Alfred E. Smith and his backers. The former governor's failure to capture his home state in the presidential contest with Hoover and Roosevelt's slim victory over Albert Ottinger marked a turning point in their fortunes. The Happy Warrior and his coterie perceived the squire of Hyde Park as a custodian of their interests at Albany. Presumably Smith's experienced advisers, headed by Mrs. Belle Moskowitz, would remain at the state capital, prevent his successor from making blunders, and generally dominate his administration. In due course, they anticipated, they would have another crack at Hoover. But Roosevelt and Howe envisaged an alternative scenario.

Though Smith took up residence at Albany's Ten Eyck Hotel, he was left there to cool his heels. Ignored in his successor's preparations, he entrained for New York City. While Roosevelt did recruit the services of some of Smith's ablest appointees, including Frances Perkins and Samuel I. Rosenman, they quickly shifted their loyalty to the new governor. Howe assumed the role of *éminence grise* with Roosevelt's failure to retain the presence of Mrs. Moskowitz. Gradually they staked their own claim to the party's leadership by expansion of the political contacts built up in the 1920s and through the creation of a progressive record in the management of the state's affairs.

Roosevelt spelled out his formula for a Democratic resurgence in 1924. In a letter to the delegates who had attended the bitterly divided national convention torn by urban/rural rivalry, and following the defeat of Wall Street attorney John W. Davis by Calvin

Coolidge, Roosevelt urged the necessity for unity and a progressive image. It was not without coincidence that he could fill the bill. Unlike Smith, he was scarcely a creature of Tammany politics, anathema to the party's rural wing. Always understood was the political magic of the Roosevelt name and its potential for reaching across party lines. The governorship offered a chance to recast the image of weakness and indecision and create a functioning base of power. The intensity of his campaign for office demonstrated his physical mobility. In time the depression would make Herbert Hoover vulnerable and the Democratic presidential nomination in 1932 a coveted prize.[1]

THE FIRST GUBERNATORIAL TERM, spanning the years 1929 and 1930, was still part of the decade of normalcy, and Roosevelt forged a record in the mold of the Smith governorship. Relentlessly, using the radio in frequent appeals to his constituents over the heads of a conservative Republican-dominated state legislature, he pressed for modernization of the state's administrative machinery, penal and judicial reform, state development of the waterpower potential of the St. Lawrence River, stricter regulation of utilities, expansion and improvement of workmen's compensation coverage, greater protection of women and children in industry, and exploration of the possibility of unemployment insurance and old-age pensions under state law. In one area, agricultural relief, Roosevelt transcended Smith's interests and developed a comprehensive program which enhanced the normal political appeal of a New Yorker.

Several of these issues won Roosevelt national attention and a broad party following, even Progressive Republican support. Development of St. Lawrence power meshed with the larger issue fought for a decade between Republican presidents and Senator George W. Norris of Nebraska over development of the nation's waterpower reserves located largely in the public domain. Public power progressives favored federal development and transmission of the electricity that might be generated and stymied efforts to sell the Muscle Shoals complex to private enterprise. Norris and his allies questioned the willingness or ability of private utilities to provide reasonable service at low rates. Many operating companies were burdened by a maze of holding companies built up by the Insulls and J. P. Morgan and Company. And their rates seemed extortionate when compared with those charged by the publicly owned Ontario power facility in Canada. The issue was social as well as economic. Cheap electricity was viewed as basic to a better standard of living. The winning of progressive support in those areas of the country that stood to benefit from cheap public power depended on an appropriate stance on the issue.

Although he never went the whole way with Norris' "gas and waterworks socialism," Roosevelt gradually formulated a set of procedures for St. Lawrence power development that won over the advocates of public ownership. His experience in the field would serve him well in the 1932 campaign. Initially, the newly inaugurated governor proposed New York State development of the power site and issuance of long-term leases for transmission and sale. This procedure scarcely satisfied the public power group, since the decisive issue was transmission and prices beyond the bus bars. A series of critical editorials in the *New York World* prodded the governor, who turned to Julius Henry Cohen, a Smith adviser, on the subject. A formula was struck for state control of rates and profits, one that avoided ownership of transmission lines. It hinged upon creation by the legislature of a corporate body to develop and manage St. Lawrence power and to negotiate contracts for the sale of electricity allowing only a reasonable rate of return on original investment. The capstone of Roosevelt's efforts as governor in the power field came on April 7, 1931, early in his second term, with creation of the St. Lawrence Power Authority along the lines he had advocated. Included in the legislation, at his insistence, was a birch rod, as he put it. In the event the governor disapproved the contract, the trustees could propose a plan for state construction of transmission facilities.

The basic issue was cheaper electricity. And Roosevelt waged a parallel struggle for that end with the state's Public Service Commission (PSC). Created during the Progressive ferment as a regulatory body, it transmuted itself into an adjudicatory forum in which complainants were pitted against the expert legal talent retained by the utilities. For all intents and purposes the PSC had devolved into a rubber-stamp operation for the utilities which, Roosevelt concluded, were mulcting the public. Investigation of the agency by a Public Service Survey Commission, created jointly by Roosevelt and the state legislature, culminated in the chairman's resignation and Roosevelt's appointment of the highly regarded Milo R. Maltbie as chairman of the PSC.

Roosevelt's dogged pursuit of the PSC, his warfare with the Morgan-dominated Niagara-Mohawk Corporation, an upstate utility, his enlistment as advisers and appointees of respected utilities experts anxious for reform, including Frank P. Walsh, New York labor attorney, Morris L. Cooke, a utilities engineer associated with Gifford Pinchot, and Columbia University's specialist, James C. Bonbright; above all creation of the St. Lawrence Power Authority won kudos from progressives such as Josephus Daniels, Daniel C. Roper, and Norris. True, the Republican Senator from Nebraska had wanted more, especially the granting of direct authority for the St. Lawrence trustees to construct transmission lines without the need to secure legislative approval. But it was a better record than Hoover's opposition to Norris' proposals for public development of Muscle Shoals, and the Norris–Roosevelt relationship warmed.

In April 1930, Roosevelt endorsed Muscle Shoals' development by the federal government in a private communication to Edward Keating, editor of *Labor*. To Norris' disappointment, Roosevelt refused to be quoted directly, part of an overall strategy of avoidance of public discussion of national and international questions until 1932. But he permitted Keating's paper to attribute to him approval "of the government development of the big plant at Muscle Shoals." Roosevelt's private assurances sufficed for Norris and Judson King's National Popular Government League, a rallying ground for the issue, until the public statement of his views in the 1932 campaign.[2]

No issue touched Roosevelt more deeply than the plight of the agrarian.[3] Rural poverty surrounded him in the Hudson Valley and struck him as suffocating in rural Georgia, his second home. As governor, later as President, he concerned himself much with the amelioration of the drab and discouraging lot of farmers. Particularly helpful in this area during the governorship period were the services of a neighboring Dutchess County gentleman farmer and publisher of *The American Agriculturalist*, Henry Morgenthau Jr.

Soon after the 1928 election, at Roosevelt's request, Morgenthau gathered an Agricultural Advisory Commission. Within a matter of weeks it offered a program which became the substance of the governor's Albany effort for the New York State farm community. Its initial proposal, creation of a permanent agricultural commission, was quickly adopted, with Morgenthau appointed as its head. With farm taxation at ruinous levels, the group, made up largely of rural Republicans, urged state assumption of highway construction costs, payment by the state or railroads for elimination of grade crossings, and state funding of the minimum salary of rural schoolteachers. Other concerns included the general problems of farm marketing, paucity of educational opportunities for farm youngsters, rural health, control of animal diseases, and abandonment or conversion of marginal land to forestry and other conservation uses.[4] As his first term in office drew to a close, Roosevelt could claim enactment into law of a farm program of considerable breadth including all of the recommendations placed before him by the Morgenthau group.

On July 2, 1931, as an aspiring nominee to still higher office, Roosevelt detailed his undertakings for the farmer before the Conference of Governors at French Lick, Indiana. It was a tactical coup. The governor of one of the most urbanized states in the Union advanced a comprehensive program including scientific planning for agriculture, better utilization of farm acreage, and cheaper electricity. But at this juncture his farm policies could

scarcely be differentiated from those of Herbert Hoover. Unless
farmers in the staple-producing areas of the country could be induced to accept crop restriction and police it effectively, and a
means discovered to finance the program, farm income in the staple crop regions would remain at depressed levels.[5]

Roosevelt's interest in social welfare, another route pursued during the governorship period, could be realized in only limited ways
in those years. He explored the concept of insurance against temporary, involuntary unemployment, also of old-age pensions, ably
abetted by Frances Perkins, his industrial commissioner. But the
conservative state legislature balked on these issues, and with the
deepening of the depression in his second term at Albany, the governor's emphasis shifted from long-range planning to immediate
relief. When it became obvious by 1931 that private philanthropy
could no longer cope with relief requirements, he recommended
creation of the Temporary Emergency Relief Administration under
the chairmanship of Jesse Isidor Straus, head of New York City's
Macy's department store. Straus, in turn, secured the services of
Harry L. Hopkins as executive director of TERA.

The Hopkins effort hardly matched the scale of relief spending
achieved during the New Deal years. A fiscal conservative, Roosevelt proposed the spending of only $20 million for relief in 1931.
Pressed by the legislature and the harsh realities of the bitter
winter of 1931–1932, he turned to the inadequate device of a state
bond issue in March 1932. Up to that point, the aspiring candidate
for the presidency had neither a basic comprehension of the depression's major causes or its remedies.[6]

ON THE HEELS of Roosevelt's smashing victory in the 1930 gubernatorial campaign—a margin of some 700,000 votes over
Charles H. Tuttle—the principal thrust of his energies shifted per-
ceptibly. Clearly the Democratic party's leading contender, he
required a political organization capable of securing the two-thirds
vote needed for the presidential nomination. Although many of the

substantive issues of the first gubernatorial term continued to be advanced, the Republican legislature became increasingly uncooperative for philosophic as well as political reasons. Moreover, as the depression took on worldwide dimensions, the problems of any governor's constituency seemed approachable only at the federal level. Cities and states quickly exhausted their limited resources. As the urgency for relief became more pressing, leaders at every level of government were equally troubled by the specter of bankruptcy as revenues declined. The burden seemed Herbert Hoover's and, for a time, during 1931, the President's reputation largely intact, he suffered little criticism. Roosevelt's formula of avoidance of discussion of national and international questions allowed for the expenditure of energy in the building of a political team.

As a generalization, some reassessment needs to be offered of the coterie assembled at Albany in 1931. For in the course of more than a year of pre-convention maneuvering the Roosevelt candidacy was nearly run onto a siding—not for lack of dedication or effort, but for lack of insight into the economic philosophy of the anti-Roosevelt coalition. Political and economic understanding were compartmentalized, in the depression's context, only at a candidate's peril. Yet, the Albany advisers, with the exception of Colonel Edward M. House, were purely politically oriented. The potential for emergence of a substantial philosophically cohesive ✓ antistatist bloc within the Democratic party, opposed to Roosevelt's nomination, scarcely struck the group around the governor.

By virtue of seniority and sheer raw power, Louis McHenry Howe dominated the Albany group. He was hardly interested in economic issues and no architect of the New Deal.[7] Comfortable only with the old party "pros," distrustful of those who managed to come too close to Franklin, Howe, so the legend has been built, shielded the squire from egregious political blunders. But an alternative view may be proposed. The old Wilsonians had scant regard for Howe's political acumen. The record of his pursuit of pivotal state delegations is strewn with blunders. It is tempting to speculate, to carry the argument one step further, that the Howe legend is sustained in part by the squire thesis, also open to question. Contemporaries of Roosevelt's, later some historians, have been convinced that the squire of Hyde Park was intellectually shallow, too eager to please, unable to grasp the complexity of events which surrounded him in the quest for the presidency. As events unfolded, however, the record suggests that Roosevelt rescued his candidacy from the brink of extinction to which he was led by the Albany advisers.[8]

Virtually as long as Howe lived, to 1936, every adviser in the Roosevelt camp reckoned with him by affording appropriate obeisance. But because of shortcomings of health and stamina, as well as an unkempt physical appearance, the necessity arose for an alter ego, a message bearer to the faithful, and recruiter of waverers. Upon the declination of Edward J. Flynn, boss of the Bronx, the task befell James A. Farley. Genial, voluble, irrepressibly optimistic, Farley emerged as a king-maker in the public's eye, in the later recounting of Roosevelt's march to the White House. His willingness to grant interviews to writers and historians, his frequent rendition of his exploits, added even greater luster to the record of one of the twentieth century's legendary political teams, the Albany advisers. The story has been related so often that it scarcely bears repetition.[9] Perhaps, instead, it requires some critical scrutiny. For like messengers of old, Farley bore only pleasing tidings to his principals. His frequent predictions of a first ballot victory by Roosevelt, while intended to foster a bandwagon psychology, if taken too seriously, as they were through much of 1931, could have culminated in a disaster.

Indicative of the double-edged quality of Farley's optimism is the frequently heralded Elks trip of June and July 1931, his maiden venture on Roosevelt's behalf. It was intended to promote Farley's personal contacts with politicians he would need to know at the 1932 conclave, also, to gage and promote the governor's chances for the nomination. "If I continue to find the same sentiment in the other states that I have found already," Farley reported from Seattle on July 6, "I will probably reach New York so enthusiastic that I will make a statement and those who read it believe I am a fit candidate for an insane asylum."

Farley was misled. Most of the states traversed en route to the National Elks Convention at Seattle—Washington, the Dakotas, Montana, Oregon, Utah, Nebraska, and Kansas—could be anticipated as Roosevelt states. The New Yorker was conceded a convention majority from the outset. But it was not clear that he could muster a two-thirds vote by overcoming a combination of "favorite son" candidacies, the loyal following built up by Smith in the urban-Catholic states, and the conviction held by many, promoted by Walter Lippmann and Bernard Baruch, that FDR was a "boy scout."

The genuine test of Farley's sophistication occurred in Indiana and California. The Hoosier state's convention delegation, he reported to Howe, "will go for the Governor," the situation there "O.K. in every respect." In reality Indiana's delegation was divided from the outset and through the first three ballots at Chicago. Upon surveying the California scene, Farley reported that Justus Wardell of San Francisco, a one-time Smith supporter, had the situation well in hand. William Gibbs McAdoo and his fellow drys appeared insufficiently strong to challenge Roosevelt's lead. Later, following Farley's return home, Wardell offered further assurances of a Roosevelt victory in the California primary. Subsequently, Roosevelt was trounced in that primary by a combination of McAdoo, William Randolph Hearst, and John Nance Garner. In short, Farley had not accomplished the heading off of uninstructed and "favorite son" candidacies in two pivotal states, a task regarded as critical. It was an ill omen.[10]

Colonel Edward M. House, a former Wilson adviser, now well into his seventies, completed the Albany triumvirate. Eccentric, his role limited by age, the claim that he was simply used by Howe seems exaggerated, at least until March 1932, when he was replaced by the Brains Trust. His inability to deliver the Texas delegation to Roosevelt has been stressed at the expense of his more

positive contributions, a political *savoir faire* unmatched by Howe
and Farley, and a wide range of contacts among the old Wilsonians. In the gaging of New England politics, Smith's political
stronghold, House's judgments proved soundly based. When he was
ignored by Howe and Farley, it was at Roosevelt's political peril.
He was at his weakest as an adviser on national and international
questions, his ear tuned to the requirements of an earlier era.

The House–Roosevelt friendship originated in the Wilson administration. In 1925 House indicated warm support for Roosevelt's stillborn proposition that a Democratic conference be held to
heal the wounds of the 1924 convention and to move the party in
the direction of progressive principles. "The Party is thinking of
you," House wrote in rather patronizing fashion, "as one of our
principal assets." When House congratulated Roosevelt on his nomination for the governorship in 1928, the New Yorker replied that
"I would rather have your approval than that of almost any other
man I know." The stunning gubernatorial victory of 1930 brought
House's prediction of election to the presidency two years later and
ushered in the Colonel's activities in that cause.[11]

With the collaboration of Robert Woolley, long active in Democratic politics and a mutual friend of House and Roosevelt, the
former Wilson adviser undertook the recruitment of key party figures. Initially, the Albany advisers hoped, they might contest
Smith's and Raskob's complete domination of the party's machinery. Eventually, they intended to forge a coalition of Southern
and Western Democrats for domination of the 1932 convention.
The most difficult task would be the attempt to cut into Smith
strongholds in the urban Northeastern states.[12]

The Colonel's maiden effort in this direction, an attempt to enlist
William Gibbs McAdoo, met with a rebuff. McAdoo appealed to
the party's fundamentalist, dry wing, a substantial rural constituency strewn across middle and southern America, once devoted to
William Jennings Bryan. Despite his move to Los Angeles in the
early 1920s to head a lucrative law practice in the Transamerica
building, Wilson's son-in-law lost little of his former following. He

was uncompromisingly nationalistic, bone dry, a paradigm of Bible Belt distrust of the iniquitous East. Particularly onerous were the financial interests of Wall Street and Gotham's Tammany Hall. Although usually exceptionally cautious in his political correspondence with former associates of the Wilson days such as Baruch, Baker, and House, McAdoo revealed his own ambitions when he rejected House's efforts early in 1931 to recruit him in Roosevelt's cause.

> Replying to your questions about 1932 I can't see Roosevelt or any other New Yorker, at the moment. . . . If Baker had run for the Senate in Ohio and had kept off the Wickersham Commission, he probably would have presented a formidable candidacy. I don't knów why it is but Baker seems to have no large popular following. He has never appealed to the rank and file of his party, nor to the masses of the people. . . . Who, of all men on our side now being mentioned, has any popular hold upon the imagination or the interest of the American people? Without meaning to be vain [he was a man of enormous vanity], but speaking merely of the fact, I think I had a very strong hold upon the masses.

House cleverly backed off with flattery. McAdoo was assured that he had no more ardent admirer and that he would have been a worthy successor to Wilson in the White House, in his popular appeal "another Jackson." If the Democrats were to be stalemated again in 1932, "that would be the chance for your friends to spring your name upon the Convention." In a lengthy correspondence agreement was reached to challenge jointly the Smith–Raskob dominance of the party machinery, but McAdoo clung otherwise to his insistence that the party shun another New Yorker as nominee. "Tammany and the bosses" had chosen Cox in 1920, Davis in 1924, when McAdoo, with Klan support, had a majority but could not obtain the needed two-thirds vote, and Smith in 1928. "Each time disastrous defeat resulted." [13] In all likelihood McAdoo hoped for a replay of the 1924 convention, a stalemate in 1932, only this time with a reversal of the wheel of fortune, which he believed had cheated him of the Democratic nomination.

Elsewhere House's efforts and the news that he gathered appeared more promising in the early months of 1931. Scott Bullitt of Seattle, brother of William C. Bullitt, affirmed Roosevelt's popularity in the Northwest. Breckinridge Long, another of the old Wilsonians, enlisted in Roosevelt's cause. Senator Henry F. Ashurst of Arizona, a Catholic, ventured that Roosevelt could command 3 million more votes west of the Mississippi than any other Democrat, and Daniel C. Roper, a North Carolina businessman and former McAdoo ally, affirmed his endorsement of Roosevelt.

These and other developments, reported to House in March 1931, were relayed to Farley. It seems that the confluence of House's messages, the famous polls taken by Jesse Isidor Straus, which presumed to show businessmen's endorsement of Roosevelt (two to one over Owen Young), then the support offered to Farley as he made his own canvass, led him to assume the relative ease of a first-ballot victory. House was less sanguine and urged that Newton D. Baker's candidacy be taken more seriously. "I have a letter from a close friend," House did not reveal the source to Roosevelt, ". . . close to Newton Baker—as close to him as to me," indicating that the Ohioan had not eliminated himself from the race.[14]

The initial major strategy session for contesting Smith in New England, the area of his strongest support, was held at a Roosevelt–House luncheon at Beverly Farms, Massachusetts, on June 13, 1931. The object was to bring together House's candidate and the Democratic leadership of the Bay State: Senators David I. Walsh and Marcus A. Coolidge and Boston's Mayor James M. Curley. Invited, too, were some of the Wilsonian intellectuals, including the *Atlantic Monthly's* Ellery Sedgwick, known to be less than enthusiastic about the possibility of a Roosevelt nomination.

Although it is generally believed that House's attempt to play kingmaker to another President was a failure, there is nothing in the record to substantiate the view that he played the fool. On the contrary, the meeting was a resounding success. As the group disbanded, Senator Walsh explained to newspaper reporters that if Smith wanted the nomination, Massachusetts would support him.

Then, significantly, "Next to Smith, of course, I am for Roosevelt."

It was not at all a bad day's work for House. Walsh's position was eminently satisfactory, since Smith deserved a first ballot Massachusetts vote if he wished it. Unfortunately Roosevelt had met Boston's Mayor Curley on the train before the meeting and was taken in by Curley's blandishments. Curley, anxious to recoup a loss he had suffered to Walsh and Governor Joseph B. Ely in the 1930 fight for control of the state's Democratic organization, saw the Roosevelt candidacy as his steppingstone. Apparently he convinced Roosevelt that an alliance between them would sweep Ely and Walsh aside and place Massachusetts directly in the Roosevelt column. The decision to fight for the Massachusetts delegation, a horrendous blunder, was not of the Colonel's making.[15] Smith swept the 1932 primary contest in the Bay State by a three-to-one margin over Roosevelt, a major defeat for the front-runner.

House's recommendations at the 1931 Beverly Farms luncheon included the recruitment of Robert Jackson as manager of Roosevelt's effort to win the New Hampshire primary. Jackson could not attend the gathering and chose to meet Roosevelt at Boston's Hotel Statler instead. There they agreed on the strategy to be followed as well as the urgency of winning that contest. That bucolic New England locale had been the graveyard of more than one candidacy for national leadership. For Roosevelt, New Hampshire's primary took on special significance in 1932, since the Protestant squire needed to demonstrate that he could capture a significant portion of the new immigrant vote so clearly identified with Smith in 1928.

Jackson, long active in Democratic politics, was a successful New England businessman whose political acquaintances included some of the nation's most powerful Democrats, among them Cordell Hull, Bernard Baruch, and Joseph P. Kennedy. His principal asset was his intimacy with New England politics and politicians. Born and bred in New Hampshire, educated at Dartmouth, he was an influential figure in that state's small Democratic party. Roosevelt and Jackson first met when the New Yorker served as Assistant Secretary of the Navy under Josephus Daniels and Jackson was a shipbuilder in the Wilson era. They conferred at Roosevelt's request for four hours on the evening of June 11, 1931.

It was not unusual for Roosevelt, then or in later years, to engage in casual banter before broaching a serious subject. Perhaps it was to put his visitor at ease, perhaps a habit developed as a defensive and exploratory mechanism. The governor described sailing visits to Rye Beach, New Hampshire, the location of Jackson's summer home, during Harvard vacations, and recalled navigating the Isles of Shoals, tying up at Newcastle. Few professional mariners, Jackson mused, knew the New England coast as well. The conversation drifted to a mutual friend linked with the suicide of a beautiful young woman, they believed unfairly, and the end thereby of a promising political career. "A wholly innocent man," Roosevelt suggested, "is better off to say nothing because a denial or explanation will be received with disbelief by many. Such ordeals are the occupational hazard of a conspicuous personality. One must ignore the clamor; it will be the sooner forgotten." Only gradually, at that with Jackson's prodding, did the conversation get around to the New Hampshire primary, more than half a year distant.

When they recalled that a dozen years earlier Jackson had introduced the youthful New Yorker at a state convention at Concord as a future president, Roosevelt's face brightened. What were his chances of carrying the New Hampshire primary in the face of a likely contest with Smith? Jackson explained that while at least half of that state's registered Democrats were Catholic, they were split down the middle into Irish and French-Canadian factions. French Canadians resented their treatment by the Irish church hierarchy and would not necessarily vote for a candidate idolized by the Irish. Other factors would aid Roosevelt in a primary contest. The primary date coincided with Town Meeting Day and local issues such as appropriations for education would result in a large turnout in rural Protestant areas. Urban Catholic areas had no such meetings and the primary ballot presented them usually contained a lengthy and confusing list of delegate names. Jackson urged the virtue of immediate organization. The Roosevelt slate, he advised, should consist of a mix of Irish and French-Canadian names, for Protestant voters preferred an Anglo-Saxon nominee in any event.

Jackson wanted assurance that Roosevelt was a presidential candidate and received it. Again the conversation drifted, to Roosevelt's chances in other states and finally to his opinion of Herbert Hoover and Ogden Mills. Roosevelt credited the President with organizing ability, but put Hoover's political skill at a minimum. Hoover would defeat himself in 1932. For reasons unknown to Jackson, Roosevelt expressed contempt for Mills, then emerging as a principal figure in the Hoover administration. "Little Oggie," Roosevelt insisted in cutting references to the Acting Secretary of the Treasury, in what "was more sneer than accusation." Jackson was astonished at the quick abandonment of the governor's previously jubilant mood. Roosevelt and Mills had known one another since their youth. They were Dutchess County neighbors, had a common background of wealth and social position, attended the same schools, joined the same clubs. "Perhaps in that background," Jackson mused in his diary, "is to be found the explanation." Roosevelt never explained.

At well past eleven at night Eleanor Roosevelt interrupted. "Franklin, you have a hard day tomorrow. You should get a good night's rest." Jackson took his leave and soon took charge of Roosevelt's critical contest for the New Hampshire vote.[16]

THE HOUSE–ROOSEVELT RELATIONSHIP extended to national and international questions Roosevelt believed he would need to consider the following year in the campaign. In June 1931, they exchanged letters on the Hoover Moratorium. The governor relayed Bernard Baruch's request (Baruch had just conferred with Hoover) that he "say nothing and do nothing to block the president's plan for some kind of financial intervention in Europe's troubles." Roosevelt indicated that he had no knowledge of the specifics of Hoover's plan, but he did know that Washington was disturbed by conditions, especially in Germany, and was groping for a solution. House advised, in reply, that no impediment be placed in Hoover's path because of the deteriorating financial situation in Europe. Roosevelt never did in fact comment on the Moratorium.[17]

The following month, in July, Roosevelt and House initiated correspondence on the question of the party's platform and the governor's future approach toward national problems. At the prodding of Daniel C. Roper, Roosevelt's initial concern turned to the credit situation. He reached several tentative conclusions. First, he decided, the Federal Reserve System had fallen too much under the sway of a small group of New York financiers. Second, he was convinced that small businessmen and manufacturers were unable to get sufficient credit. Also, general control of the banking system needed revision and reorganization. It was a perceptive analysis of some of the principal weaknesses of the nation's banking system made possible, one suspects, by his own background in banking. As yet, Roosevelt observed, he had no firm policy. He and House would need to consult their friends and "talk things out between now and next winter."

The mood remained basically optimistic in the summer and autumn months of 1931. House negotiated for Roosevelt on the troublesome Prohibition question, doing all he could to reconcile differences in the party. The Straus poll, House's intelligence, including a trip through the South and West made by Robert Field, paid for by Louis Howe through the Democratic State Committee, Farley's Elks trip—fed the mood of euphoria and led to House's decision that the controversial issues should be avoided. "It is better," he advised Roosevelt, "to leave things as they are."

In a meeting with Roosevelt in late September, House took an even more conservative tone. Economic conditions were growing increasingly desperate and the aging adviser could see the possibility of labor troubles and riots. In such an instance, he intoned, Roosevelt, as governor of New York, would need to summon the militia. Though there is no evidence of Roosevelt's reaction, one wonders if House's attitude evoked Roosevelt's realization that the Colonel was of another era and offered him the sort of advice that Hoover received.[18]

Whatever Roosevelt's thoughts, House had the impression that he was the key man in Roosevelt's circle of advisers. "There is no 'Roosevelt organization,'" he wrote Woolley. "So far we have succeeded in getting along with Howe and four stenographers." He profferred advice to Howe and Farley, as when he asked Louis to caution Farley that repetition of his belief that Roosevelt could write his own platform would only cause trouble with the party's drys. He dealt with some of the nation's most influential Democrats on the issues and questions of delegate support, among them Cordell Hull, Daniel C. Roper, Joseph Guffey of Pennsylvania, and Robert W. Bingham, publisher of the Louisville *Courier-Journal*. House, in fact, was responsible particularly for the recruitment of Bingham, to Roosevelt's delight. Bingham became an avid supporter and substantial contributor to the New Yorker's candidacy and later was awarded with the ambassadorship to Great Britain.[19]

Some of the old Wilsonian group in Washington, especially Cordell Hull and Robert Woolley, were less sanguine than Roosevelt and House. Perhaps their discontent reflected Hull's normal pessimism or Woolley's emotional bent. But the Washington group had wandered in the wilderness for nearly a dozen years and had seen the party riven to shreds by the internal strife of the twenties, particularly at the conventions of 1924 and 1928. They believed themselves more experienced in Democratic affairs than the Albany group, Woolley being long active in the party and Hull serving as National Chairman from 1921 to 1924. Woolley warned Roosevelt and House in separate letters, in September 1931, that they lived in a fool's paradise. The "Power crowd" and the American Expeditionary Force were booming Baker, and with Owen Young out of the picture the Smith–Raskob group had also turned to Wilson's Secretary of War. The Roosevelt boom, Hull and Woolley were convinced, had peaked.

Hull went further. Howe and Farley were botching the Roosevelt candidacy with overoptimism. Unless there was an effort to
nail down delegations, Hull warned, "Roosevelt is liable to be
blown up and landed on the northeast corner of the moon." Woolley and Hull wanted more experienced management than Howe
and Farley could offer on the national level, someone from outside
New York or New England. They may also have desired greater
control for the old Wilsonian group of Roosevelt as nominee.[20]

House disagreed. "I talked to him [Roosevelt] a good deal along
the lines that Cordell Hull talked to you," he wrote Woolley in
reply, minimizing the Baker candidacy and the threat of favorite
sons to deadlock the convention. He made no mention of Hull's
desire that Howe and Farley be superseded. Instead he focused
on the growing deterioration of the nation's economy.[21]

Woolley would not be put off. The searching out of the principal
obstacle to Roosevelt's nomination was initially his work and as a
matter of fact began with a dinner he had at Jouett Shouse's Washington home in March 1931. Shouse, chairman of the party's National Executive Committee, unusually candid, conceded that Al
Smith was the only major Democrat who could not defeat Hoover
in 1932. Despite Shouse's assertion of neutrality, Woolley surmised
that he favored Owen D. Young. When Young, for personal reasons, indicated that summer that he would not enter the contest,
Woolley learned, the Smith–Baker coalition was forged.[22]

Although House occasionally noted Baker's willingness to entertain a draft in his own correspondence with Roosevelt, it was only
in November that Woolley convinced both House and Roosevelt
that a stop-Roosevelt coalition had been formed. It was believed
that Baruch and Raskob furnished the money and that Jouett
Shouse had been employed to do the legwork. In view of these developments, Roosevelt summoned Woolley to Albany for a meeting
on December 10, 1931, to discuss political strategy. The governor,
in high spirits, jested about the ancient Albany mansion with its
Victorian exterior and "early Pullman " interior. (Woolley's mind
flashed back to the previous time he saw Roosevelt, at his East

Sixty-Fifth Street residence in New York City in October 1922, his legs in plaster casts, his face pale and drawn, apparently a dying man.) Once down to business, Woolley received the assignment of recruiting Alben Barkley of Kentucky and the powerful Harry F. Byrd of Virginia. Both states were potential sources of support for a Baker try at the nomination and Byrd was rumored to have aspirations of his own.[23]

To his dismay, Roosevelt's emissary learned at the meeting of the Democratic National Committee in Washington, on January 9, 1932, that Byrd was committed to a Baker–Byrd ticket. Baker's nomination, Woolley learned from an intimate of the Virginia governor, assured Byrd of the vice-presidency. Roosevelt would turn to the West for a running mate. Alarmed, Woolley and the experienced Daniel C. Roper, manager of Wilson's 1916 campaign, communicated with Roosevelt. In a lengthy document they outlined miscalculations which might lead to Roosevelt's defeat and estimated his first ballot strength at 550 votes, more than 200 short of the required two-thirds. They had been down the same path with McAdoo in 1924 and lost out to a dark horse. Al Smith, they warned, would turn to anyone capable of checking Roosevelt's candidacy.[24]

The sharp tone of the Woolley–Roper admonition reflected a second conclusion pressed by the old Wilsonians. They wanted one of their number included in the Albany group. The issue was debated behind the scenes at the Democratic National Committee meeting. Robert Jackson, newly appointed secretary of the committee, a concession by Raskob to the Roosevelt forces, lectured Farley privately on the Albany group's lack of organization. Roper and Woolley, joined by Homer Cummings, entreated with Howe for the addition of one of the Washington group to Roosevelt's entourage. Howe refused. For the time being Farley and Howe remained in command and the Smith–Baker coalition the exclusive concern of the old Wilsonians.[25]

2

Stop Roosevelt Stage 1:
The Democratic
Conservative Coalition

WHEREAS ROOSEVELT AND HOWE made the state house at Albany their base of power, Alfred E. Smith and John J. Raskob literally owned the Democratic party and its machinery at the national level. They met in 1926, when Smith required funds for his gubernatorial campaign against the wealthy Ogden L. Mills. Raskob functioned as a conduit between Smith and the Du Pont–General Motors millionaires who financed his political ambitions beginning in 1928. Upon the Happy Warrior's nomination for the presidency at Houston, he offered the chairmanship of the national committee to Raskob, until then a Republican.[1]

Smith's 1928 presidential campaign is traditionally considered a landmark in its appeal to the urban masses, the laboring class, minorities, and Catholics, the new immigrants who had previously avoided identification with either major party. And it has been argued, further, that his defeat in 1928, rather than Roosevelt's 1932 victory over Hoover, "marked off the arena in which today's politics are being fought." The urban revolt of the underprivileged and the laboring minorities climaxed, according to this view, in Roosevelt's 1936 landslide and the modern Democratic majority. Yet, the thesis seems incomplete and contains contradictions. From its inception, the Smith–Raskob coalition represented a protest against the contemporary journey toward the interventionist state. And it appears questionable, in retrospect, that the Democratic party would have acquired majority status without the occurrence of the depression and the New Deal. From this perspective the 1932 contest seems basic in its portent for the nation's future.[2]

Differing approaches toward domestic and international economic policies lay at the root of the contest. But its articulation, in typically American fashion, was clothed in political terms. The Smith group formulated its position in 1928 and never wavered despite the depression. The conservative coalition required in 1932 a candidate amenable to its philosophy and more acceptable to the South and West than the Happy Warrior. Roosevelt's progressive instincts remained ill defined until the *mise en scène* of a Brains Trust in 1932. On this score, the conservative coalition enjoyed a second distinct advantage in addition to its control of the party apparatus.

THE RASKOB–DU PONT–SMITH ALLIANCE of 1928 stemmed basically from the thinking of Pierre S. du Pont, president of E. I. du Pont de Nemours & Co., who determined during World War I to wage a fight against Woodrow Wilson's decision to levy heavy taxes on corporations and incomes. Du Pont opposed taxation of the productive sector of the American economy and preferred that the burden of taxation should be borne by the lower classes, not by those who created the jobs. Some time in the ensuing decade—the exact time cannot be established from the evidence available— Pierre du Pont decided, as did John J. Raskob, a key executive in the Du Pont company, Christiana Securities, and General Motors, that the solution lay in the legalization of beer.[3] When, in November 1927, Voluntary Committee No. 28 of the Association Against the Prohibition Amendment (AAPA) maintained in a report that a tax on beer, dependent on Prohibition repeal, would yield $1.3 billions, permitting a 50 percent reduction in income and corporate taxes, Raskob and the Du Ponts arrived at two major decisions. They financed the AAPA with half a million dollars annually beginning in 1927 in order to bring about Prohibition repeal. Then, they captured control of the bankrupt Democratic party, which had been thrashed in 1924, and envisaged it as a conservative instrument in national affairs.[4]

By early 1928 a number of extraordinarily wealthy and powerful members of the business community had been recruited for membership on the Board of Directors of the AAPA. In addition to Pierre S., Lammot, and Irénée du Pont of E. I. du Pont de Nemours & Co., and Raskob, there were Charles Sabin, chairman of the board of New York Guaranty, Intercontinental Rubber, and the Mechanics and Metals National Bank, and nearly seventy others—heads of major banks, businesses, and insurance companies.[5] Many of the same individuals, principally Raskob, less discernibly Pierre S. du Pont and Charles Sabin, undertook to manage the finances and the future of the Democratic party.[6] Smith agreed, after his nomination in 1928, with Raskob and Irénée du Pont that our society required a reduction of government interference in big business. Raskob interpolated to Du Pont that this meant the protection of business and wage earners through high tariffs and reduction of Interstate Commerce Commission controls over the management and operation of railroads. The only difference between the two major parties, Raskob concluded, was the wet and dry question.[7]

Raskob remained undaunted despite Smith's loss to Herbert Hoover in 1928. He continued to finance the party, reduced its debt, and employed as chairman of the party's National Executive Committee, Jouett Shouse, for the sum of $200,000 for the years 1929 through 1932.[8] Experienced in the ways of the business world, tough, and urbane, they proved more sophisticated than their Rooseveltian counterparts, Howe and Farley. Moreover, Raskob and Smith had a clearly defined point of view.

Fundamentally, Raskob subscribed to the Jeffersonian concept of limited central government with a minimum of interference in the affairs of the business community, to voluntarism, to extreme frugality in government expenditures, and to a return of authority to the states. The Prohibition issue functioned as a smokescreen in reality for an economic program that advocated:

1. A five-day week for workingmen to stimulate leisure and consumption, the one feature designed to attract working-class support for the balance of the Raskob program.

2. The empowering of the Federal Trade Commission to grant immunity from antitrust prosecution in cases where it decided that a given combination or merger was not inimical to the public interest. And in general a liberalization of regulatory legislation to allow trade practices aimed at elimination of destructive competition.

3. Elimination of capital gains and losses taxation to encourage speculation and investment.

4. Tariff protection for U.S. industries because of the high wages attained by labor during the Wilson years. Specifically Raskob urged the creation of a bipartisan Tariff Commission which would determine the differences in costs of production of domestic articles and foreign goods.

5. Return of liquor control to the states and collection of liquor taxes in order to abolish or reduce the income tax and corporate taxation.

6. Private operation of public utilities under "fair" (minimal) public regulation and the leasing to private industry ("not public operation") of Muscle Shoals.[9]

Initially Raskob looked favorably on Franklin D. Roosevelt's political ambitions, since they meshed with Alfred E. Smith's goals in 1928. One of the factors which served to induce Roosevelt to accept the 1928 New York gubernatorial nomination was Raskob's offer of $25,000 outright and an additional $125,000 as a guarantee, if the latter sum could not be raised elsewhere, to meet certain obligations of the Georgia Warm Springs Foundation which fell due in February 1929.[10] During the course of the ensuing four years, the two men maintained a perfectly proper relationship on the surface, but in reality each became the leader of opposite wings of Democratic thought regarding the future orientation of the nation.

IMMEDIATELY FOLLOWING the strong showing made by the Democratic party in the November 1930 congressional elections,

Raskob seized upon the tactic of using the National Committee as a vehicle for launching a conservative platform and a conservative nominee. After correspondence and dinner meetings with allies in the House and Senate, with the three surviving former presidential nominees, also traditionalist in outlook, James Cox (1920), an Ohio newspaper publisher, John W. Davis (1924), and Smith, as well as Joe Tumulty, Wilson's private secretary, Raskob decided upon a convocation of the National Committee in Washington, D.C., on March 5, 1931. He proposed as its principal purpose unequivocal endorsement of Prohibition repeal.[11]

Considerable pressure was exerted on Raskob to alter his course. Party spokesmen, including Cordell Hull, Bernard Baruch, and William Gibbs McAdoo, viewed the procedure as a usurpation of authority. Tactically they deemed it unwise to saddle the nominee with a platform fifteen months in advance of the national convention. The Prohibition issue seemed moot to some who believed the depression required priority, and dangerous to others, calculated simply to reopen the old urban/rural split that tore the party to shreds in 1924 and yielded the Southern defection of 1928. The possibility loomed, further, of an open clash between Cordell Hull's free trade views and Raskob's advocacy of a high tariff system. As the meeting approached, the entire affair threatened to become a shambles. Even Raskob's most intimate associates, Shouse and DNC publicity director Charles Michelson, came to question the wisdom of forcing the issue of Prohibition repeal. To no avail.

Raskob persisted in airing his views at the March 5 meeting. Southern and Western Democrats, drys, and low tariff advocates vented their disagreement with Raskob's tactics and definition of issues. Cordell Hull and Senator Joseph T. Robinson of Arkansas dominated the proceedings. Roosevelt and Howe won the initial contest with the Smith group by steering clear of the entire affair. Raskob feigned surprise at the level of dissent he generated, beat a hasty retreat, and withdrew the repeal proposal for consideration at a later date. A clumsy performance, it scarcely proved fatal. The conservative coalition remained intact and formulated a new strategy.[12]

Raskob determined, after the blustery March 5, 1931, Democratic National Committee meeting, upon two objectives: first to open a dialogue with Southern conservatives to find those issues that would provide an intellectual meeting ground, and second to settle on a mutually satisfactory candidate. In private correspondence in those days, early in 1931, he indicated a willingness to lose the South if it would secure the urban-industrial North and East for the party. But this point can be overemphasized. Raskob and his able lieutenant, Jouett Shouse, who had powerful ties in Kentucky, wanted instead, if possible, a reconciliation with Byrd and Glass of Virginia, Robinson of Arkansas, and Garner of Texas.[13]

Of particular importance was Raskob's exchange of ideas with Governor Harry Flood Byrd of Virginia. Raskob argued that the National Convention was too cumbersome a mechanism to write a platform and that the smaller National Committee should act as an instrument of continuous thought and action, much like the directors of a corporation. Raskob explained his call of the National Committee on the grounds that he sensed serious trouble for the party in the 1932 campaign if the North and South could not in some way reach agreement on the Prohibition issue. He wanted particularly a reconciliation of views among himself, Byrd, Hull, and Robinson, not outright repeal but a "Home Rule Plan" which respected local prerogatives in the matter of liquor "regulation."

Byrd responded that the Democratic party could hardly be equated with a corporation. Its candidate, chosen once in four years, not the platform was of principal importance, and it was as inappropriate to recommend a platform as it was for the Committee to nominate a candidate. Further, the current Committee went out of business before the next campaign and therefore could hardly bind a candidate. Equally important, he feared another revolt in the South.[14]

The Raskob–Byrd correspondence, supplemented by secret discussions in New York, broadened by the summer of 1931 into a search for issues and a candidate they could agree upon and then present not only to Southern but other sectional party leaders. A second Smith candidacy was ruled out. The risk of raising the religious issue once more, Smith's identification with Tammany, and his blatant opposition to Prohibition in the twenties seemed a combination of liabilities which represented too much of a gamble. As the depression intensified, in fact, the consensus view surfaced in the party, even among the Smith group, that he was the only Democrat capable of losing to Hoover in 1932. Owen D. Young, widely believed to be the conservative coalition's first choice, declined, and the Smith–Raskob–Shouse group quickly settled upon Newton D. Baker as a satisfactory alternative.[15]

Raskob initiated correspondence with Newton Baker in late July 1931, and the two conferred in New York in early August. An exchange of ideas on the key issues that needed to be broached in the 1932 campaign appeared harmonious enough to justify further negotiations between Jouett Shouse, on behalf of Raskob, and Ralph Hayes, Baker's "Louis Howe." [16] Shouse received authorization to promise that if Baker "would consent to be supported, [Smith] will not only eliminate himself but throw to you every particle of strength he can muster." Raskob, in turn, offered to free Baker of any obligation to him in the event of his nomination and election, going so far as to offer his resignation as head of the Democratic National Committee.[17]

Baker traveled to Washington in mid-September for a meeting with Jouett Shouse and Ralph Hayes at the Willard Hotel. He convinced Shouse that he would not actively seek the nomination and would consent to run only if drafted. (Josephus Daniels and John Stewart Bryan, prominent Southern newspaper editors who also favored a Baker candidacy, had the same understanding.) But the Smith–Raskob group never gave up and had no reason to do so. Baker, who had suffered a heart attack in 1928, submitted to a physical examination, as did Roosevelt, was pronounced fit enough for a limited campaign, and negotiated for months with the Smith entourage behind the scenes.[18]

At a series of meetings held at New York and Washington in the late summer and early autumn of 1931, Raskob, Smith, Shouse, Hayes, and Baker determined upon the strategy that became the keystone of the stop-Roosevelt movement.

1. They and their allies encouraged an open convention made up of uninstructed and native-son delegations and bound by the two-thirds rule.*

2. Aware that open endorsement by Smith of Baker would be tantamount to a kiss of death, Smith shrewdly decided to take as much of the delegate strength of the Northeast for himself as he could muster into the convention. This strategy, he hoped, would eventually enable him to enter into an agreement with the other stop-Roosevelt leaders and with native sons on the selection of a third person.

3. This third person would be a conservative, yet capable of binding up the wounds in the party.

Walter Lippmann, who had access to Smith, came to this same conclusion shortly after Smith's announcement of his candidacy early in 1932. "It is impossible to believe," he wrote, "that Smith, who is a great realist . . . expects to be nominated. He had no illusions about his election in 1928 and he can hardly have any now about the party's willingness to go again through an ordeal by fire. But that he does not wish to be ignored, that he believes he represents a political force, that he intends to be consulted on the candidate and the platform is now evident." Lippmann concluded that Smith's followers could do no more than deadlock the convention and nominate someone other than Smith or Roosevelt. That candidate, he predicted, would be Newton D. Baker.[19]

Baker emerged as the logical choice for the conservative coalition. Identified with the Progressive movement in Cleveland, respected as a dedicated internationalist, many regarded him as the heir apparent of Woodrow Wilson. Yet, upon his return to Cleve-

* Native-son delegations offered secondary candidates, usually a governor or a senator, a chance at the vice-presidential nomination or the potential of a dark horse candidacy in the event of a convention stalemate. The opportunity to swing the convention at a pivotal point to one or another leading contender was also tempting. In short, they were not necessarily conspiratorial. Texas' commitment to Garner is illustrative.

land after serving as Wilson's Secretary of War, Baker had increasingly associated himself with conservative positions and with the business community. Although Baker lacked Roosevelt's charisma, he nevertheless possessed eloquence as an extemporaneous public speaker and built a reputation as a first-rate intellect and for his integrity of character.

Baker's political star began its ascent in Cleveland, Ohio, where he became intimately connected with one of the luminaries of the Progressive era, reform Mayor Tom L. Johnson. As Cleveland's city solicitor, from 1902 to 1912, he served as one of Johnson's key aides in the famous street railway controversy, which had as its goals municipal control and lower fares. Baker aided also in the effort to secure additional municipal revenues by reassessment of railroads and utilities. As mayor of Cleveland, from 1912 to 1916, after the death of Johnson, Baker won the admiration of Progressives for his personal integrity and the maintenance of Cleveland's reputation as the nation's best-governed city. Particularly appealing to the radical progressives was Baker's establishment of a municipally owned power plant.

When Woodrow Wilson's Secretary of War, Lindley M. Garrison, resigned early in 1916, as a consequence of the President's concessions to the Congress in the famous preparedness controversy, Wilson tapped his former Johns Hopkins student for the post. In the course of five years' service, until 1921, Baker, who came to Washington with a reputation as a progressive pacifist, made the same reputation as Secretary of War for efficiency and integrity that he had enjoyed in Cleveland. In the process he also emerged as one of Wilson's most trusted advisers.

Baker returned to Cleveland in 1921 to head the distinguished law firm of Baker, Hostetler, and Sidlo. Throughout the twenties he crusaded for American commitment to the League of Nations as the best hope to forestall another world war. Particularly well known was his moving speech before the Democratic National Convention of 1924 in which he attempted without success to secure endorsement by the party of Wilson's advocacy of U.S. membership in the League. Though he lost the battle, his emotional appeal in behalf of those, including Wilson, who had died for a principle enhanced his stature and shaped his image as heir apparent to the mantle of the former President.

Byron R. Newton summed up the feelings of much of the old Wilsonian group when he wrote Baker in March 1931:

> Few men are born nine feet tall, and few men are born with the breadth and strength to sacrifice themselves to the advantages of the great cause or the betterment of their fellow men. Usually these chaps died in childbirth or were burned at the stake quite early in their career, but when they do survive the burning and the childbirth they leave history and milestones behind them, because, like yourself, they have no illusions, no vanities, no fears—just a steadfast gaze at the road ahead.
>
> That was the one quality in Woodrow Wilson that in my eyes lifted him above all other men. In my life I had seen much of other men whom the world called great, but Wilson was the only one of them all, who if he thought necessary to the achievement of some great end, would sacrifice himself and his political future to the betterment of mankind. Such men are nine feet tall, very scarce, but in the great plan of human life it seems necessary for one to appear now and again to wallop the floundering mob into shape.

For Byron R. Newton and many other of the old Wilsonians, Baker, too, was "nine feet tall" and would have made an excellent candidate for the presidency. No less a personage than the former President's widow expressed her complete accord.[20]

Yet, some people contended that the once-progressive disciple of Tom Johnson and Woodrow Wilson had grown conservative. They observed that his Cleveland law firm became associated with a large corporate law practice, sometimes as a representative for utilities. And when he served a term as president of Cleveland's Chamber of Commerce, he favored the open shop.[21] Actually, Baker and Al Smith were cut of the same cloth. Both were administrative progressives, proponents of efficiency and economy in government, administrative reorganization, judicial and penal reform, and of humane social legislation such as workmen's compensation. But neither accepted the statist premises of the advanced progressives. Neither leopard had changed his spots. A "gas and waterworks socialist" in his younger years and a disciple of some of the thinking of Henry George, once Cleveland's street railways and utilities were properly assessed and a public lighting plant had been built, Baker remained content. Fundamentally, like Alfred E. Smith of New York, Baker never adhered to radical progressive notions.[22]

The possibility of a Baker candidacy in 1932 seemed particularly attractive to the Eastern business and financial community, which hewed to conservatism in its domestic outlook and to internationalism because of overseas economic commitments. Also, it appealed to the moderate and conservative press and to a large segment of the academic community. Among the Eastern conservatives in business and banking who expressed support for Baker candidacy were A. Lincoln Filene of Boston; Owen Young, president of General Electric; John W. Davis and Frank Polk; Thomas Lamont of J. P. Morgan & Co.; Lee Olwell, vice-president of the National City Bank of New York; Melvin Traylor, a Chicago banker; Robert Woodruff, president of Coca Cola; Nathan Straus and B. Howell Griswold of Alex Brown & Sons, Baltimore bankers; Eugene Untermeyer of Guggenheim, Untermeyer, and Marshall; and Norman Davis, also a member of the international banking community. The philosophy of this group seemed perhaps best typified by David F. Houston, Woodrow Wilson's Secretary of Agriculture and in 1932 president of Mutual Life Insurance. Houston decried increasing dependence of the people on the federal treasury, nor did he sympathize with efforts in Washington aimed at relief of the farmer.[23]

In the field of news media an imposing array of writers and editors, in addition to Walter Lippmann, supported Baker's candidacy. These included James Cox, the 1920 nominee and publisher of a number of newspapers in Ohio and Florida; John Stewart Bryan, editor of the *Richmond News Leader;* Mark Watson, Mark Sullivan, and Fred I. Kent of the *Baltimore Sun;* Roy

Howard of the Scripps-Howard chain; Julius Mason, editor of the conservative *New York Evening Post;* the *Cleveland Plain Dealer;* the *Cincinnati Enquirer;* the *Des Moines Register-Tribune;* and H. V. Kaltenborn and George Creel. If some did not openly endorse Baker, as in the instance of the *Baltimore Sun* and the Scripps-Howard papers, endorsement of Alfred E. Smith served as a "cover" until the propitious moment.[24]

Despite the wide range of his support, Baker appeared particularly vulnerable on two counts: one was the identification of his law firm with the railroads and power interests; the other his advocacy of U.S. membership in the League of Nations, hardly a popular cause in the post-Versailles years.[25] In January 1932, Baker took the necessary step to divorce himself from the League issue. The question seemed academic anyway given American disillusionment with the continental powers and the world organization.

CAMPAIGN STRATEGIES for the opposing Democratic camps seemed evident enough as the convention year opened. The conservative coalition intended to block Roosevelt's access to a two-thirds vote through several ballots, then unveil its alternative. Baker's appeal was sufficiently wide to win as a compromise candidate in the apparent contest between Roosevelt and Smith.

Roosevelt planned to forge one of those typically successful coalitions modeled on Wilson's 1912 effort. The requirement of a two-thirds vote dictated not only command of the South and West, but the ability to cut into Smith's Eastern strongholds as well. It proved a difficult task. The old Wilsonians tended to be conservative and internationalist in viewpoint. The Middle West sought tariff protection for the farmer and tended to be progressive in its instincts. Holding Cordell Hull and Senator Burton K. Wheeler, an inveterate isolationist, under one umbrella required the talents of a juggler. But there were precedents and Roosevelt proved a political artist.

The unknown quantity, as the 1932 contest opened, was the

depression. For a time Democratic contenders remained content to allow the Great Engineer considerable leeway. For one thing few understood the faltering economy. For another it seemed good politics to let Hoover stew in his own juice. As the year 1931 unfolded, the collapse assumed an enduring hue. It refused to dissipate. Instead, whenever a ray of hope appeared, the calamity broadened. Hoover grew increasingly vulnerable, an easy political target. But what of his views? A Democratic successor in office would be obliged either to accept or reject them. They could not be totally ignored.

During the opening stages of the contest for control of the Democratic party, the international marketplace and its financial underpinnings went awry: Germany's banking system collapsed; Great Britain, economically weakened, abandoned its traditional role as mainstay of the world's eco-system. Suddenly new demands were thrust at the United States. What role should it properly assume in respect to the collapsing European economic and political system?

By dint of his presidential responsibilities, the task of formulating an initial analysis and an appropriate response befell Herbert Clark Hoover. He interpreted the depression as rooted in the economic dislocations brought on by the Great War, and his initial response reflected this nation's status as a major economic power capable of pressing for remedy through a series of international arrangements. To many it seemed an appropriate, if politically unpopular, course. In a matter of months, however, he lost his nerve, retreated from his commitment to the internationalist prescriptions he originated, and pursued a nationalist approach in deference to domestic political considerations.

3

Hoover: First of the New Presidents?
or Last of the Old?

> This campaign is more than a contest between two men. It is more than a contest between two parties. It is a contest between two philosophies of government.
>
> We are told by the opposition that we must have a new deal. It is not the change that comes from normal development of national life to which I object, but the proposal to alter the whole foundations of our national life which have been builded through generations of testing and struggle, and of the principles upon which we have builded the nation. . . . They are proposing changes and so-called new deals which would destroy the very foundations of our American system.
>
> —HERBERT C. HOOVER *

IT SEEMED AN IDEA whose time had come when, in 1963, Professor Carl Degler suggested in an essay in *The Yale Review* that Herbert Hoover, one of the most castigated of the nation's former chief executives, deserved the reappraisal of historians. "In the history books," he noted, "his administration is usually depicted as cold-hearted, when not pictured as totally devoid of heart, inept or actionless in the face of the Great Depression." Degler contended in a suggestive but undocumented article that there never existed two Herbert Hoovers, the progressive sought out by liberal Wilsonians, including Franklin D. Roosevelt, as a potential Democratic nominee in 1920, as opposed to the presumed

* "Text of President's . . . Speech Calling for Preservation of the American System," *New York Herald Tribune*, November 1, 1932.

reactionary who refused to respond to the initial shockwaves of economic depression. "The notion . . . should have never grown up; his life and views were too consistent for that."

Coincidentally, a widely used college textbook of that time, John D. Hicks's *The American Nation*, struck the same theme even more forcefully. The inauguration of the modern interventionist state, it suggested, reflected primarily the work of the Hoover administration. Hicks judged as precedent-shattering in magnitude the activities of the Federal Farm Board; the conferences of bankers, industrialists, railroad magnates, agricultural spokesmen, and labor leaders held at the White House; public works programs amounting to some $2 billion and offering employment to a million men; the creation of the Reconstruction Finance Corporation; and the passage of the Home Loan Bank Act of July 22, 1932. All were proposed by Hoover. Despite some dissimilarity in approach, both inquiries challenged accepted dogma which stressed the New Deal's departure from Hoover's policies and pointed instead to the progressive qualities of the Hoover presidency and its anticipation of the Roosevelt program.[1]

Since that time, efforts at reinterpretation of the Hoover era have attempted to refurbish the thirty-first President's once-tarnished image. The tendency is to view him as a progenitor of the modern era.[2] Herbert Hoover was no progressive. Nor was he a precursor of the interventionist policies of the New Deal. His depression measures were designed to preserve existing institutional relationships, not to alter them. As Hoover stated in the 1932 campaign, he opposed interventionist policies that violated existing relationships among the central, state, and local governments. As he viewed the programs unfolded in the New Deal era in 1936, the former Republican President labeled them manifestations of socialism and fascism, ideologies that had come to infest much of the Western World and which needed to be kept from our shores.[3] Indeed, the United States was unique under his tutelage in the era following the Great War in its avoidance of direct social and economic intervention and the adoption of a set of principles under the hubris of voluntarism. It remained inviolate until challenged by Roosevelt and the Brains Trust in the 1932 campaign.

It needs to be ventured, further, that Herbert Hoover was no innocent bystander in the unfolding of the Great Depression, which began in this nation with the postwar collapse of agricultural prices. As a principal, whose authority extended well beyond the Commerce Department, in the administrations of his two predecessors in the presidency, he adopted specific stances that promoted the depression. He elaborated a set of doctrines, viewed as progressive by some of today's revisionist historians, which in reality proved stultifying through the tragic winter of 1932–1933, when the crisis sank to its nadir.

These assertions are best understood by a review of the philosophy Hoover offered in 1922, which subsequently guided his response to economic issues. Although more formally structured, Hoover's views replicated those of the Democratic party's conservative coalition. Despite a progressive gloss, such views were anchored in nineteenth-century strictures. Had the Smith–Baker coalition defeated Roosevelt in the contest for control of the Democratic party, it is likely (one can only guess) that the Hoover ethic might have survived the depression years. There was no inevitability in the fundamental changes instituted by Roosevelt and the Brains Trust.

THE SPAN from 1922 to 1932 is more meaningful as the "Hoover decade" than terms more commonly used, such as "Normalcy" or the "New Era." The latter are vacuous expressions and should be abandoned by historians in search of a *geist* that might explain the age of jazz and Fitzgerald in its economic and political manifestations. Government-business-agricultural relationships (labor remained a minor force) were spelled out in a set of maxims with the precision and certitude of an engineer. In *American Individualism* (1922), the nation's most prominent self-made man imprinted his ethos and personal experience upon an era. The Hoover presidency and its approach toward the Great Depression is intelligible only in that larger context.

American Individualism framed Hoover's views on the role of central, state, and local government in American society, of the individual, of cooperation among individuals, even his diplomatic attitudes. The essence of Hoover's presentation can be distilled into several simple precepts: individualism; voluntarism or cooperation by organized groups of citizens with the encouragement of the central government; the absence of direct federal intervention for social or economic ends; and American diplomatic participation in the economic affairs of the world in pursuit of its own interests and as a balance wheel, but avoidance of entanglements or alliances or stances that would involve us in Europe's quarrels, its totalitarian and class-oriented mentality, and its periodic warfare. The Great Engineer viewed American society and its economic system as unique and distinct from that of Europe and presented in 1922 what might be termed a theology which governed his actions throughout his life and dominated the Harding and Coolidge presidencies as well as his own.

Hoover's 1922 essay, in many respects a reflection of the dominant ethic and trends of his times, needs to be understood, also, in the context of his several years' relief work during World War I in Europe, as head of the Belgian Relief Commission, which fed, clothed, and sheltered hapless children, women, and men devastated by war. Subconsciously, perhaps consciously, these associations of Europe with poverty, hunger, and fear, with its rigid class structure, its inhibiting ideologies, led to a contrast with his own emergence in the United States from orphaned poverty to recognition as "the Great Engineer" by the time he reached his thirties. Unquestionably as he toured continental Europe his mind must have reverted to the hopes nurtured at Stanford University and fulfilled in an open and fluid society within a brief span of years in the late nineteenth and early twentieth centuries.

Hoover's statement of elemental principles served as more than a personal credo. It suited admirably a generation tired of progressive reformers, anxious to proceed along the lines of Social Darwinism, modified by what appeared to be a civilized set of ground rules for a competitive era. The hatred for Hoover, displayed in the 1932 campaign, when he rarely left the sanctuary of the White House, bitter, deep, full of emotion, reserved by Americans for relatively few of their Chief Executives, was the enmity visited upon a prophet of an era whose visions had proven hollow. In that sense, the depression generation judged the thirty-first President more meaningfully, if less charitably, than the current generation of historians which, contrary to his policies and attitudes, has attempted to saddle him with the philosophy and outlook of the New Deal.

Warren G. Harding's Secretary of Commerce described himself, in 1922, as "an unabashed individualist" who rejected, however, extreme forms of competitive behavior that culminated in excess and injustice. American individualism was explained as "equality of opportunity," a credo that fitted Woodrow Wilson's views on the subject of progressivism, essentially retrogressive in nature, the keeping of avenues open for advancement in the nation's economic mainstream. As Hoover defined the term:

> Our individualism differs from all others because it embraces these great ideals: that while we build our society upon the attainment of the individual, we shall safeguard to every individual an equality of opportunity to take that position in the community to which his intelligence, character, ability, and ambition entitle him; that we keep the social solution free from frozen strata of classes; that we shall stimulate effort of each individual to achievement; . . . while he in turn stand up to the emery wheel of competition.

Despite Hoover's contention that his interpretation of individualism posited an abandonment of eighteenth-century laissez faire attitudes, it represented in reality the enshrinement of nineteenth-century Social Darwinism meliorated by certain civilized ground rules under the umbrella of voluntarism, or competition within structured interest groups. He accounted neither for the disappearance of competition in certain of the nation's largest industries, nor for the huge capital outlay required for entry into the marketplace in the postwar era, nor for the apparent emergence of an underclass that only theoretically enjoyed equality of advantage in WASP America. The Iowa-born Quaker turned a deaf ear to Theodore Roosevelt's assertions, beginning at Osawatomie, Kansas, in 1910, reasserted by his cousin Franklin in the "Forgotten Man" speech in 1932, that the disadvantaged substrata of American society required governmental assistance in the form of social minima in order to participate and become eventually part of the mainstream.

Certain generalizations offered by the Commerce Secretary in 1922, again in his 1928 quest for the nation's highest office, might have led historians in recent years, as part of a quest to rehabilitate the Hoover reputation, to conclude that he was a progressive in a conservative era. Hoover frequently asserted that he favored the promotion of social and economic justice through legislation, "a fair division of the product" of our economy, and "certain restrictions on the strong and dominant." But he scarcely believed in the utilization of the federal government as an instrumentality to gain these ends.

To achieve a better balance or distribution of goods, Hoover proposed the elimination of waste; reliance on taxation (though he scarcely indicated disagreement with Treasury Secretary Andrew W. Mellon's proposals for steep reduction of taxes levied on individual incomes, estates, and corporations), and the control of economic concentration by private corporations through antitrust legislation. Legislative provisions against corporate concentration and restraint of trade, a keystone of the Wilson administration, the Sherman–Clayton approach favored by the Commerce Secretary, was a demonstrable failure. Concentration of control increased in the 1920s as huge aggregates grew larger and more powerful. Yet, Hoover insisted on an outmoded approach which limited government's function to that of an "umpire" in the elimination of unfair trade practices.

Superficially innovative, actually a recognition of what had already developed in American life, was the Commerce Secretary's encouragement of private economic cooperation by groups exempted from antitrust strictures. Naively he insisted that organized interest groups could be restrained from price-fixing and other forms of behavior prohibited by the antitrust laws. He dubbed the concept "voluntarism," the hallmark of the Hoover era. It favored incorporation of individual initiative within a framework of voluntary economic cooperation by groups of like interests. As if it were an article of religious faith, the author of *American Individualism* equated voluntarism with "spiritual individualism." He explained:

> The vast multiplication of voluntary organizations for altruistic purposes are themselves proof of the ferment of spirituality, service, and mutual responsibility. These associations for advancement of public welfare . . . represent something moving at a far greater depth than "joining." They represent the widespread aspiration for mutual advancement, self-expression, and neighborly helpfulness.

Hoover lauded organizations such as "the chambers of commerce, trade associations, labor unions, bankers, farmers, propaganda associations, and what not." They represented, he wrote approvingly, a fusion of altruism and self-interest. Within these voluntary associational groupings individuals could discover opportunities for self-advancement. His model was the trade association, which emerged in the late nineteenth and early twentieth centuries, flourished under wartime pressure for an organized economic effort, and functioned in the 1920s under the aegis of the Commerce Department. "Today," Hoover wrote in 1922, "business organization is moving toward cooperation. There are in the cooperative great hopes that we can even gain in individuality, equality of opportunity, and an enlarged field for initiative." Voluntarism would result in the elimination of waste, the furtherance of individualism, the promise of economic expansion, and the avoidance of the cancer of socialism which had proven a "ghastly failure" in Russia. As Hoover testified, voluntarism was a progressive philosophy for conservatives:

We in America have had too much experience of life to fool ourselves into pretending that all men are equal in ability, in character,
in intelligence, in ambition. That was part of the claptrap of the
French Revolution. We have grown to understand that all we can
hope to assure to the individual through government is liberty, justice, intellectual welfare, equality of opportunity, and stimulation to
service.[4]

American Individualism, at least implicitly, contained important
elements of Hoover's economic diplomacy as Secretary of Commerce and President. The abhorrence of Europe's inhibiting ideologies and rigid class structure served as a sharp contrast to the
chauvinistic portrait of his native land. Like other Wilsonians,
among them Franklin D. Roosevelt, Hoover shifted from advocacy
of League membership to a more nationalistic stance in the 1920s.
He insisted on repayment of the wartime debts and wavered only
in the face of the international economic collapse of 1931. Hoover,
further, advocated high, protective tariffs, promoted U.S. business
entry in areas of vital economic interest, especially where he believed foreign governments or cartels dominated raw materials
needed by American industry, yet as President demurred when
France sought political guarantees as a quid pro quo for reduction
of German reparations. He was a genuine Wilsonian in his conviction that American economic advancement and its technology, if
carried abroad, as he himself had functioned as a world-famous
trouble-shooter mining engineer, might well extend the American
system beyond our boundaries. In the process, however, while he
generally favored U.S. economic participation to our advantage, he
wanted no political commitments or entanglements that bound us
to a course in advance of specific situations, a course, in other
words, that might involve us in one of Europe's periodic imbrog-
lios.[5]

Herbert Hoover's economic policies and attitudes as Commerce
Secretary and President of the United States reflected the impera-
tives of his 1922 essay. Regardless of changing tides, he never
swerved from the course set forth in *American Individualism*, im-

printed his principles on other agencies of the government and generally on key economic policies in the course of the Harding and Coolidge administrations. He took over Commerce at Warren G. Harding's request when it was very nearly moribund, attracted funds from an otherwise niggardly Congress and talent from the business community, and infused into the situation his own enormous energy and his philosophy. S. Parker Gilbert's quip that Hoover was "Secretary of Commerce and Undersecretary of all other departments" understated the matter.[6]

As Secretary of Commerce, Hoover promoted cooperative arrangements, especially in the form of pools, under the Webb-Pomerene Act of 1918. These facilitated entry by U.S. firms into markets and raw materials producing areas hitherto dominated by European cartels. The large and effective Commerce Department staff, stationed partly overseas, provided American firms with data and at times with needed diplomatic clout. For all practical purposes, Commerce under Hoover appropriated the normal functions of a static State Department for itself—not without an occasional jurisdictional fight but, more often than not, State concentrated on the paper treaties that banished war, proclaimed battleship ratios, and offered sterile definitions of offensive and defensive weaponry that most cynical observers regarded as worthless in the long run.

Where it benefited American industrial entrepreneurs who sought entry into world markets and raw-materials producing areas, Hoover proved himself an internationalist by his advocacy of free trade and the concept of "comparative advantage," nineteenth-century doctrines. Yet he could be a nationalist, particularly through his insistence on the maintenance of high tariffs on imports as a means of maintaining our prosperity at Europe's expense. The consequence of these policies was a fatal imbalance of trade between the United States and the Western European nations, the most important outlet for our agricultural and industrial surplus. It constituted one of the fundamental causes of the international economic and financial collapse that greeted his presidency. In this respect, as in other vital areas, Hoover's hegemony and broad range of responsibility for economic policies that proved disastrous well antedated his presidency. [7]

In the domestic arena the Commerce Secretary nurtured the trade association as the exemplar of voluntarism. Some 2,000 cooperative organizations of businessmen engaged in the exchange of information on production, sales, purchasing, and prices when he took office in 1921. Markets were often divided and prices "stabilized." Although adverse Supreme Court decisions hampered such activity in the early years of the decade, the nation's highest court took a more relaxed view of trade association practices in *Maple Flooring Manufacturers Association et al. v. United States* in 1925. Commerce became a clearing house and an umpire in the exchange of business information, assuring smaller enterprises the expertise acquired by larger units. It was voluntarism in its finest hour. [8] As Hoover explained the procedure:

> . . . We enlisted the different trade associations in creation of codes of business practice and ethics that would eliminate abuses and make for higher standards. I set up a staff in the Department to work them out. After agreement with each association on a "code" we submitted it to the Department of Justice and the Federal Trade Commission; and, to establish confidence in the "code," the Trade Commission promulgated it as a standard of fair practice. . . . They were solely voluntary. By degrees many standards in these codes became embodied in the business custom of the country.

Interestingly, despite agreement by economists and historians that trade association practices, codified under the auspices of the Commerce Department, often led to the elimination of price competition, Hoover denied this in his *Memoirs*. Yet, control of production, division of markets, and price agreements characterized numerous industries, particularly those that prospered, and led agrarian economists, such as Rexford Tugwell and M. L. Wilson, to insist that a depressed agriculture be permitted the same economic advantage as an escape from the looming shadow of peasantry. But it would have necessitated government intervention, and Hoover, based on his advocacy of voluntarism, took a pivotal position that

connected him to the agrarian collapse of the twenties, the depression's major domestic source.

Hoover's attitude toward proposals for agricultural relief reflected the intellectually subtle but formidable distinction he drew between the activity of the trade associations and the New Deal's National Industrial Recovery Act. Both involved price-fixing and production controls. But in the Hoover era government functioned exclusively as a conduit for the exchange of information, as a passive umpire for trade association activity. What he really opposed was not industrial cooperation, but direct government participation and supervision as a partner in the process, which he later labeled "sheer economic fascism." Government intervention stood at the nub of the matter. In this respect he correctly argued in his *Memoirs* that the New Deal's efforts at federal participation in the economy, interventionism, thrust at the heart of his American system.[9] Voluntarism guided as well Hoover's insistent and successful resistance to McNary-Haugenism,* when he served as Commerce Secretary, and later his opposition to domestic allotment, when he served as President.

Hoover's talent for public promotion of his doctrinal views and successful political infighting determined many, perhaps most, of the critical economic choices made in the course of the Harding and Coolidge presidencies. This was true of the farm question, despite his nominal post as head of the Commerce Department. Shy, retiring, overtly no political partisan, regarded as a masterful economic technician, disliked by the Old Guard and many of the party regulars, the Iowa-born Quaker won a formidable victory over Henry Cantwell Wallace and the farm bloc Republicans when they insisted on direct government intervention to resolve the farmers' depression. The consequence was not simply economic but, over the long run, political as well. For it fragmented the party, weakened it at its geographic center, alienated the progres-

---

* For all of its complicated mechanisms, McNary-Haugenism, at its core, would have rid the United States of its agricultural surplus by dumping it abroad. Domestic allotment featured acreage controls. Either scheme required federal intervention.

sives, and condemned the Republicans to minority status in the post-Hoover era. Appropriately, the trotting out of the author of *American Individualism* at convention after convention beginning in 1936, into the 1950s, constituted a symbol of conservative abhorrence of the New Deal.

Henry C. Wallace, Harding's Secretary of Agriculture, like Hoover, was an empire builder with a mission. Comparable to Hoover's reliance on Dr. Julius Klein's Bureau of Foreign and Domestic Commerce, Wallace created the Bureau of Agricultural Economics as a research-oriented and data-gathering agency intended to provide a solution for agriculture's growing economic dilemma in the twenties. Wallace recognized the need for political clout required to enact a program and participated in the formation of the American Farm Bureau Federation, the largest and most powerful grouping of farmers in the nation. And he counted, also, on the assistance of the Farm Bloc, formed by farm-state legislators. He failed, however, to anticipate the effective veto of his cabinet counterpart, who not only guided the nation's domestic and overseas business activity but insisted on the application of the strictures of voluntarism to agriculture as well.

The massive surveys of the Bureau of Agricultural Economics (BAE), guided by Henry C. Taylor as its chief, provided the statistical basis for McNary-Haugenism, agrarian America's frustrated hope in the decade of Hoover's hegemony. When it became apparent to the Commerce Secretary that it camouflaged a dumping scheme which required federal intervention in the marketplace, he proved its most effective opponent. As early as 1921, Hoover, categorized the Norris Export Plan, the forerunner of McNary-Haugenism, as a "vicious" plan that would reintroduce federal intervention into the private sector. He abhorred the use of wartime precedents in the 1921 depression and again after 1929, despite his later use of the wartime metaphor to exhort the nation in the direction of self-help and local group effort. He would not countenance a proposal that required the federal government's interference with the normal processes of supply and demand. McNary-Haugenism,

evolved within the BAE, sponsored by Republican legislators, was dubbed "Socialism," for Hoover a term of consummate opprobrium.

The Secretary of Commerce insisted on the resolution of the farm problem through the mechanisms of the marketplace and upon the utilization of farm cooperatives to control and standardize output, for he regarded the farm cooperative movement as a development that should parallel the trade association. His agricultural expertise, severely limited, rested upon his acquaintance with California citrus cooperatives. That millions of wheat producers could not cooperate effectively in control of quality and quantity of production, considering the vast geographical scope of grain production and the international dimension of competition and markets, seemed of little moment.[10]

Hoover's shortsighted attitude toward agricultural overproduction and declining farm prices found expression in a memorandum prepared for use in connection with the 1924 Republican national platform. The statement reveals both the range of his power in the Harding and Coolidge administrations and the strictures that voluntarism required. He conceded the need for farm relief since we were, particularly in grains and hogs, undersold by Canada and Australia on world markets. He understood, also, that domestic prices, as matters stood, could not rise above world market prices; further, that we lacked foreign customers for our output. Yet, he conceded no possibility of government remedy. "We cannot by legislative fiat raise the price of wheat or hogs above the level established by world competition in a world market. We cannot suspend the operation of economic law by legislative mandate." Hoover elaborated in nineteenth-century terms:

> The distress of the wheat farmer is the distress that inheres in over-production. Artificial price fixing or subsidies from the government would stimulate production and aggravate the evil we are asked to cure. . . . The economic hurt of over-production is self healing. . . . Nature when given a chance corrects a lopsided economic situation.

The Republican party cannot in candor and honesty approve of governmental subsidies to overbuilt industries. . . . Government subsidy to business is a two-edged sword, at once stimulating over-activity where economic law demands curtailment and at the same time taking money out of one man's pocket to put in the business of another. In like measure governmental price fixing [is defendable] only in times of military emergencies [and] is at best a counsel of des-peration quite contrary to the genius and character of a self reliant, resourceful, independent people.[11]

Hoover never wavered in his opposition to government inter-vention for the purpose of "price fixing" or the accomplishment of a balance of supply and demand. McNary-Haugenism was unaccept-able to him, and it is generally believed that he authored Calvin Coolidge's two successful vetoes of the scheme. Support, on the other hand, of the Cooperative Marketing Act of 1926 is explained by the fact that the newly created Division of Cooperative Market-ing could provide no explicit federal assistance. The American sys-tem remained inviolate in the 1920s, and the cooperative move-ment became the keystone of Hoover's agricultural policies as trade associations flourished on the urban-industrial scene.[12]

It is generally believed, but remains unsubstantiated, that Calvin Coolidge was something less than firm, as his first full term came to an end, in his earlier resolve that he did not choose to run again for office in the 1928 presidential election. The surprising state-ment had been uttered when on a fishing vacation in North Da-kota's Black Hills following the death in 1927 of his son, Calvin Jr. Coolidge had been struck a deep psychological blow. Reporters and supporters wondered, as the 1928 Republican National Con-vention approached, whether he had had a change of heart. But "Silent Cal" never elaborated upon his 1927 renunciation of a sec-ond full term. Whatever change of heart Coolidge might have had by 1928, as some suspected he did, Herbert Hoover was the choice of the party's rank and file. One is tempted to suggest that, by 1928, the Great Engineer had so imprinted himself and his values on the "New Era" and, in turn, so reflected the attitudes of the postwar period, that even the popular Coolidge could not have checkmated the steamroller that gave the Commerce Secretary 837 of 1,084 votes cast on the convention's first ballot. It is interesting that despite rumors that Coolidge would submit to a draft, the incumbent kept his silence. Perhaps Harding's successor in office simply recognized that his hard-driving Secretary of Commerce had become, de facto, the nation's chief executive.[13]

THE CAUSES of the depression were too complex to be attributed exclusively to Herbert Hoover or his implementation of his economic philosophy. But it seems equitable to assert that Hoover's policies as Secretary of Commerce and President stimulated the Great Depression and subsequently accelerated the downward economic spiral. When the financial machinery of the Western nations foundered—as he saw it, following the Creditanstalt debacle in April 1931—he argued that the depression grew out of the Great War and the dislocations that followed: the excessive flotation of foreign securities of dubious value in American markets by greedy New York bankers, the excess of credit made available by lax Federal Reserve policies, and the low margin requirements for stock purchases. He contended that he had checked domestic deflationary tides through voluntary cooperation under government auspices, but could not cope with worldwide financial dislocations once they surfaced in 1931. Overall Hoover's explanation of the calamity focused too narrowly on financial markets and mechanisms. Consequently, his approach was equally delimited, almost literally myopic.[14]

Hoover's responses to the shockwaves of the depression were at best inadequate and belated, at worst restrained by voluntarism, calculated to avoid the creation of governmental mechanisms that would outlast the duration of the immediate crisis and alter existing institutional relationships. The result, more often than not, meant avoidance of what Rexford Tugwell described as conjuncture, the meeting of a crisis situation by remedies unhampered by previous intellectual commitments. Illustrative of the constraints he im-

posed on critical situations was Hoover's approach to the crisis in
American agriculture that had taken shape after the war's termination, a condition he acknowledged in his campaign for the presidency, against Alfred E. Smith, in 1928.

In his St. Louis speech, as part of a program that he dubbed "the
New Day," the Republican candidate acknowledged the existence
of a "depression" that had affected one-third of the nation's population. Earlier, in his acceptance statement of August 11, 1928,
Hoover conceded that low farm prices, the result of a glut of commodities in the marketplace, needed to be resolved "if we are to
bring prosperity and contentment" to the farm community directly
and "to all of our people indirectly." The remedies he proposed
were in part traditional, such as the improvement of the nation's
inland waterway system, and anchored in the old Populist demand
for cheaper and more competitive transportation rates than the
railroads had proven willing to offer. The promise of "an adequate
tariff," which took shape as the Smoot-Hawley Act of 1930, protected manufacturers rather than agriculturalists who were ex-
porters and subject to world market prices. Worse still, Smoot-
Hawley dislocated world trade and fostered economic nationalism
in the form of tariff warfare and currency restrictions, an egregious
blunder in the context of 1930–1931. Innovative, however, and the
most important measure of what Hoover was willing and unwilling
to do in the face of the depression can be discerned in his sponsorship of a federal farm board, enacted in to law by the Agricultural Marketing Act of June 15, 1929.

The Farm Board proposal and its ramifications, like the later
Reconstruction Finance Corporation (RFC), placed the credit of
the United States behind cooperative and individual effort in the
private sector, promoted cooperative ventures as an inherent good,
and assumed the generative qualities of the American system were
such that the status quo ante would soon reappear. It studiously
avoided production controls by government, the only realistic solution, for fear that American individualism would be undermined.
Hoover explained the objectives and limitations of his agricultural

program in 1928, as follows: "The whole foundation and hope of our nation is the maintained individualism of our people. Farming is and must continue to be, an individualistic business of small units and independent ownership. . . . No solution that makes for consolidation into large farms and mechanized production can fit into our national hopes and ideals." [15]

Experienced students of agriculture expressed skepticism, for they knew that nineteenth-century techniques and overproduction constituted the core of the problem. But Hoover had won the 1928 contest with Smith by one of history's most formidable landslides, cracked open the solid Democratic South, and rode the tide of technocracy as "the Great Engineer," presumably the best technician of them all. The Agricultural Marketing Act of 1929, passed by a special session of Congress summoned for the purpose of securing relief for the farm community, and its creation of a Federal Farm Board bore Hoover's stamp. It was executive legislation.

The allocation by Congress of a revolving fund of $500 million for loans to agricultural cooperatives and for the operations of commodity stabilization corporations seemed huge for its time, particularly since it supplemented credit available from normal sources such as commercial banks and insurance companies and the federal intermediate credit bank system. Superficially, in terms of willingness to venture federal funds, the Agricultural Marketing Act, like the later RFC law, appeared innovative. Yet, the essence of this sort of legislation, characteristic of the Hoover approach toward the depression, really was the preservation of the institutional status quo, the prevention of fundamental change. When it became evident that the Federal Farm Board, despite huge outlays and losses, could not stem ruinous declines in farm prices, Hoover refused to take the next logical step—production controls instituted by the federal government. He would not violate the tenets of voluntarism. He never did as President, regardless of the severity of the crisis he faced. Likely, psychologically, he could not.

The failure of cooperatives and commodity stabilization corporations to check declining farm prices, especially after the stock market collapse of autumn 1929, became apparent. The Farm Board, under Alexander Legge's administration (Legge was president of International Harvester), then resorted to crop loans. These, too, could not stem the collapse of farm prices as the tide of depression widened. The example of wheat prices is important. For despite huge expenditures and losses by the Farmers National Grain Corporation and the Grain Stabilization Corporation, prices fell below the cost of production and the prospect of large-scale economic ruin led to the demand for acreage allotment.

The Farmers National Grain Corporation, headed by Clarence E. Huff of the Farmers Union, represents the quintessence of voluntarism for agriculture in its federation of local and regional grain cooperatives by the Farm Board for the purpose of fact-finding and the offering of remedies. Similar national cooperatives marketed cotton, wool, pecans, beans, livestock, and other products. When surpluses of any commodity became unmanageable, the Farm Board created a stabilization corporation for that particular product. Wheat prices peaked at $1.18 a bushel in October 1929. By June 1930, despite huge purchases by Farmers National and loans by the Grain Stabilization Corporation, involving the expenditure of $90 million, wheat had collapsed to 33 cents a bushel. One year later, during June 1931, after an investment of $169 million and the accumulation of 275 million bushels of wheat in storage, which overhung the market and served as a price depressant, wheat prices had been pushed up to 81 cents.

But government tax revenues were in decline. Ogden L. Mills began, as we shall see, to press Hoover for matching outgo with income for fear that the credit of the United States was endangered; and the Farm Board had exhausted its financial resources. No longer inclined to throw good money after bad, aware that huge purchases of wheat and cotton had simply stimulated unwanted production, the Federal Farm Board indicated its desire in late June and early July 1931, to liquidate. With wheat no longer supported by Corporation purchases, and with the Farm Board anxious to liquidate its own huge holdings, prices collapsed in July 1931, to the 30–40–cent range.

In its liquidation of wheat stocks, accomplished by April 29, 1933, the Grain Stabilization Corporation traded 25 million bushels for 1 million bags of Brazilian coffee; sold 15 million bushels to China on credit for $9 million, and half that amount to Germany, also on credit, for $4 million; turned over 85 million bushels to the Red Cross for relief; and sold the rest on domestic and world markets. The Cotton Stabilization Corporation and cotton prices suffered a similar experience. Despite huge expenditures and accumulations, prices declined from 18 cents a pound in September 1929, to 12 cents in July 1930, to 8.5 cents in July 1931, to 4.6 cents in 1932. When the losses were toted in 1933, it was discovered that the Farm Board's revolving fund of $500 million had been diminished by $344 million. In the meantime, prices in key areas, such as the grains and cottons, had fallen below the cost of production.[16]

In Keynesian or perhaps neo-populist terms it can be argued that the failure of Hoover's effort can be attributed to the inadequacy of the level of expenditures. Yet, it is questionable that an expenditure by the Farm Board equal to the entire national budget, which would have wrecked the nation's financial system in an era when the balanced budget served as the test of national credibility, would have accomplished more than the simple rendering of cash to the farmer, whose product commanded a price lower than his cost of production.

The availability of federal cash alone, in any conceivable quantity, offered no permanent solution. The cash expended by the Farm Board as "loans" to cooperatives and stabilization corporations—advances of $1.148 billion against repayment of $777—on the contrary, papered over the fundamentals of the situation and constituted a means of avoidance of the central issue, the requirement of production controls. Nor is it accurate to argue, as did Harris G. Warren in the earliest full-scale effort by a historian to

rehabilitate Hoover as depression President, that the administration was too preoccupied with the collapse of 1931–1932 to give
heed to M. L. Wilson's proposals. As Warren conceded, Hoover
would have vetoed domestic allotment if it had been passed by the
Congress. More than likely, he was fully apprized of the scheme
for acreage control by the Federal Farm Board and by his Secretary of Agriculture and of its portent for the demise of voluntarism.[17]

Agrarian experts realized by the summer of 1931, when the Federal Farm Board conceded the failure of its efforts at maintenance
of crop prices, that the Hoover agricultural program had stimulated
production when it should have curtailed it. Producers of staple
crops in the United States had lost their largest foreign market,
that of Great Britain and the empire, through trade and currency
restrictions that were formalized in the Ottawa Agreements of
1932.[18] Generally, the world market for our agricultural exports
evaporated and agrarian specialists agreed that the export-deben-
ture and equalization fee proposals favored by farm organizations
and most farmers offered no solution since they relied on dumping.

When M. L. Wilson, professor of Agrarian Economics at the
Montana State College, Bozeman, decided upon acreage allotment
as the only immediate way to save the nation's wheat farmers from
extinction, he initially approached the Hoover administration, not
Roosevelt and the Brains Trust. This was natural, for he was a
Republican and the people he knew in farm circles and in Washington were of his own party. Rejection, more accurately the deliberate avoidance of his proposals by Hoover, cannot be explained by
Wilson's academic obscurity. Wilson's experiments in the 1920s at
determining the ideal size and capitalization for successful wheat
farming were funded by the Rockefeller Foundation. His work
earned kudos from John D. Black at Harvard and Rexford Tugwell
at Columbia as well as the Rockefeller foundation economist,
Beardsley Ruml. Further, Wilson was known to that segment of
the business community concerned with agriculture's problems,
including Henry I. Harriman, the New England utilities magnate,

and Alexander Legge of International Harvester, who presided over the Federal Farm Board as long as it remained a hopeful experiment. Knowledgeable and respected in the agrarian community, M. L. Wilson knew, as he focused his energies on the securing of acreage allotment in the winter of 1931–1932, its accomplishment would meet resistance from many quarters: grain millers, who selfishly preferred low commodity prices to government interference in the marketplace; farmers, pridefully independent and wary of government bureaucrats who might tell them how much they could plant, always sanguine that somehow next year things might be better; heads of the powerful farm organizations, which had fought for a decade for the export debenture and equalization fee proposals and were, therefore, wedded to them and their reliance on world markets; and the President himself, the principal foe of McNary-Haugenism since its emergence as a concept.[19]

The tracing of Wilson's thinking on agriculture's problems needs to be completed in the frame of Roosevelt's campaign for the presidency, where domestic allotment found acceptance. But his initial approaches on the subject, which required the abandonment of voluntarism, were made to farm bloc Republicans and the Hoover administration. Like the Swope Plan in industry, domestic allotment in agriculture is the appropriate test of continuity between Hoover and Roosevelt, not levels of federal expenditures or budget balancing which were of relatively minor institutional or long-run economic significance as a measure of interventionism. Put another way, the New Deal should not be judged an exercise in public works and relief, which were tangential to the long-run goals of Roosevelt and the Brains Trust. Nor is it accurate, as historians are wont to do, to depict the New Deal as the welfare state. Welfare, whether in the form of public works, relief, or the modern version, hardly represented its principal aim or accomplishment.

Anxious to win over the powerful Federal Farm Board to the voluntary domestic allotment program, Wilson broached the subject with its chairman, James C. Stone, Legge's successor, in the spring of 1932, some nine months after the Farm Board conceded its failure by announcing the liquidation of its holdings. "A movement is developing here in the Northwest which I think would be of interest to you," Wilson suggested. "My attitude toward the Board has always been one of extreme friendliness and a sympathetic desire to assist and support it whenever I could." Old McNary-Haugenites, Wilson explained, now favored domestic allotment. There would be a meeting at Chicago's La Salle Hotel on April 19, to frame an allotment proposal for introduction into the Congress as well as an accompanying land use measure. Participants and supporters included: Henry Agard Wallace (son of Henry Cantwell), Chester Davis, Frank O. Lowden (former Illinois Republican governor, years earlier favored by farm state Republicans as a presidential nominee), Henry I. Harriman (president of the Boston Chamber of Commerce), Orlando Webber of Allied Chemical and Dye, and Beardsley Ruml.

Fishermen describe the procedure as chumming, the throwing overboard of bait in order to land the big ones. The Chicago conference, Wilson assured the Farm Board chairman, was not intended for propaganda purposes. The allotment idea was originated by John D. Black of Harvard, an economist long associated with the Farm Board and Hoover administration farm policies. The allotment scheme would "decentralize things" under farmer-controlled state and county committees. Acreage restrictions could be introduced only after 70 percent of the farmers involved voted them. The package included a land repurchase program, long favored by Hoover. Three bills were likely to emerge, Wilson predicted: "an allotment bill specifically to apply to wheat and possibly to cotton, an agricultural planning bill somewhat on the order of the Christgau bill, and a land policy bill."

Aware that agricultural proposals would need to be filtered through the Farm Board—the Hoover administration, like Commerce, functioned on the staff principle, unlike Roosevelt's helter-skelter tendencies as an administrator—Wilson suggested to Stone his willingness to travel from Chicago to Washington to discuss the proposals with the Board. "I think I could do this in a quiet personal way," the shrewd Montana agrarian economist reassured Stone, "through which there would be no publicity and perhaps as a result of such conference the proposals could be made more agreeable to the Board." The Montana professor did not denigrate cooperative marketing, Hoover's hallmark, but it was a "long slow pathway. . . . Something must be done immediately . . . to bring about fundamental adjustments in production." Stone took the bait. "Come to Washington our expense," he telegraphed, "to discuss plan with Board." [20]

Toward the end of April 1932, Wilson argued the merits of domestic allotment before the Federal Farm Board, also with Hoover's personal secretary, Walter Newton, and the Secretary of Agriculture, Arthur M. Hyde. He regarded his reception as courteous and attentive, but noncommital. In May, Chairman Stone instructed Mordecai Ezekiel, a Farm Board economist, to examine the proposal for its feasibility. In a series of memoranda Ezekiel gave domestic allotment his blessing. "The plan," he concluded, "is a promising one, and offers real possibilities of improving the position of farmers, both immediately and in the long run." It would result, Ezekiel estimated, in an immediate benefit of $524 million to farmers, or a 25 percent increase in their income on exportable products. It had further advantages: it avoided the need for government expenditures; it would not stimulate production; administration would be decentralized and the plan was voluntary; without resorting to price fixing, domestic allotment offered effective tariff protection on exportable commodities; and by avoidance of dumping it would not invite foreign retaliation, McNary-Haugenism's principal defect. [21]

Despite the vital endorsement by Alexander Legge, who had executed the Farm Board operations in earlier, more sanguine days, Wilson's proposals drew no response from the administration. Versions of domestic allotment were introduced in the House as the Fulmer and Hope bills and by Senator Peter Norbeck of South Dakota in the upper chamber. This transpired in June and July.

Yet, probably because of Hoover's opposition, only following Roosevelt's election, actually in a special report to Congress on December 7, 1932, did the Farm Board express approval. Even then there was little hope for its enactment.[22]

"Confidentially," M. L. Wilson wrote Mordecai Ezekiel on January 11, 1933, as a drifting, angry, leaderless Congress haggled over the details of agricultural legislation, "Tugwell and H. A. Wallace think, and I agree, that the bill is not going to pass at this session nor if it did pass would it be signed by President Hoover." Wilson's assumptions proved correct. Agreement could not be secured in the 72d Congress. Earlier, as the outgoing President and the President-elect conferred privately for a few minutes following their White House meeting of November 22, 1932, in the absence of their economic advisers, Ogden Mills and Raymond Moley, Roosevelt inquired if Hoover could support domestic allotment legislation, bogged down in the Congress. Hoover refused. "No power on earth," he had claimed in his acceptance of the Republican nomination on August 11, 1932, "can restore prices except by restoration of general recovery and markets. . . . There is no relief to the farmer by extending government bureaucracy to control his production and thus curtail his liberties. . . . I shall oppose them."[23] The tenets of *American Individualism* remained inviolate to the bitter end.

Actually many of the specifics of M. L. Wilson's proposals for agricultural relief in 1932 emulated previous efforts by industry to rationalize production and prices. Proposals for economic rationalization were widespread in the twenties and trumpeted with even greater vehemence as the depression broke. Influenced by technocracy, the work of the institutional economists, the activity of the trade associations, the emergence of planning in the Soviet Union and the corporative state under Mussolini, various stabilization plans surfaced. More radical schemes, such as those offered by George Soule in *The New Republic* and by Rexford Guy Tugwell, represented genuine national planning, for they would be dominated really by a civil service bureaucracy under policy controls laid down by the President and the Congress. More conservative proposals, which emanated from the business community, although similar in their structure, were rooted in corporate and trade association experience and when examined closely would be essentially guided by the trade associations. Whatever the source, however, Hoover rejected stabilization proposals as an unacceptable violation of the American system.[24]

Gerard Swope, president of the General Electric Company, presented his scheme for stabilization of industry and employment in September 1931, privately to the President and then publicly before a dinner meeting of the National Electrical Manufacturers Association. It was summarized for Hoover by his Acting Attorney General, Thomas D. Thacher, as follows:

> (1) All industrial and commercial companies with fifty or more employees, and doing an interstate business, shall be required to accept or adopt for the benefit of all their employees (a) a uniform workmen's compensation act, (b) life and disability insurance, (c) old age pensions and (d) unemployment insurance. The insurance and pension systems are to be maintained by contributions from the companies subject to the Plan and their employees.
>
> (2) All such companies shall be required to adopt standardized accounting systems, uniform in each industry. All companies having twenty-five or more stockholders, and living in more than one state, shall be required to furnish their stockholders with quarterly statements of earnings and an annual balance sheet and statement of earnings.
>
> (3) The foregoing measures are to be supervised by a Federal supervisory body, and by trade associations, which all companies within the scope of the Plan are required to join.
>
> (4) The antitrust laws are to be liberalized.[25]

Hoover recoiled in horror at the Swope proposals, which he labeled as an unconstitutional violation of the Sherman and Clayton Laws and later on as nascent Socialism or Fascism. But he suspected, incorrectly, that he would "have to meet [it] . . . in the Congress" and recruited the assistance of conservative Senator Felix Hebert of Rhode Island, a member of the Senate Judiciary Committee and an insurance company executive. Hebert took to the hustings declaiming that it was an illegal price-fixing scheme that would serve to expand the federal bureaucracy. There were already too many "uplift movements," Hebert confided to the President. Hoover regretted only that Hebert's sentiments failed to attract sufficient publicity.[26]

The President secured an opinion from the Acting Attorney General that the federal government could not use the Commerce clause as a basis for the regulation of industry in interstate commerce. Swope's proposal that corporate agreements be supervised at the initial stage by trade associations, then at the national level by the Federal Trade Commission and Justice Department, was held an unwarranted extension of congressional power under the Constitution. Further, provisions requiring workmen's compensation, old age pensions, and unemployment insurance of employers, again through the device of the Commerce clause, were held to be prohibited by the Supreme Court in Hammer v. Dagenhart, 247 U.S. 251 (1918).[27]

Pressure for economic rationalization continued. When, in December 1931, the United States Chamber of Commerce circulated a modified version of the Swope Plan among its membership, and secured endorsement, Hoover countered that it would lead to monopoly, worse yet, he later argued, to Socialism or Fascism. Then, in April 1932, Herbert Bayard Swope, former publisher of The World and brother of Gerard Swope, the plan's progenitor, Bernard Baruch, and Owen Young, a governor of the Federal Reserve Board and officer of the General Electric Company and RCA, urged a national planning board on Ogden L. Mills. All were intimates of Hoover's principal economic adviser, and the Treasury Secretary seemed somewhat interested. Yet, he concluded the matter with the observation that "For better or worse it looks as if we would have to fight it out on the old lines." Evidently, the President had the last word.[28]

HERBERT HOOVER'S APPROACH toward the economic crisis of the early 1930s underwent three stages. Initially, his efforts were largely hortatory, from the 1929 stock market crash to the collapse of the Creditanstalt in the spring of 1931. The first stage requires no elaboration. For it is generally agreed that the innumerable conclaves of leaders of the business, banking, labor, and agricultural communities reflected the President's abiding faith in the generative ability of voluntary, group effort. These conferences proved barren in their results.

The picture changed in 1931, drastically so, with the collapse of Europe's financial system. For a time, Hoover and his principal adviser, Ogden L. Mills at Treasury, pursued a policy of U.S. leadership in minimizing the shock waves of the international crisis. Much of what they attempted, while worthwhile, was limiting in its focus on financial measures. Perhaps their stress on international causes and remedies reflected a calculated effort at deflection of the charge, now widespread, that the policies of Andrew Mellon and Herbert Hoover contributed to the growing domestic crisis. Whatever the motives and limitations of the international approach, however, it offered possibilities as a start. At the close of 1931, Hoover abandoned the international quest. Manifestly it appeared too risky in the political climate of the era. Later he would revive the course he initiated and urged it on Franklin D. Roosevelt in the 1932–1933 interregnum in a final, desperate effort to head off the New Deal.

The third stage of the Hoover–Mills response to the depression, adopted in the winter of 1931–1932, concentrated on the maintenance of this nation on the gold standard. The policy proved regressive. Scarcely a harbinger of the modern era, it exacerbated the downward economic spiral and resulted in disaster.

4

The Disharmony of
International Cooperation

THE EARLY 1930s marked the final test in determining whether Versailles might develop as a genuine step toward peace in Europe or serve merely as a truce between two wars. It was in 1931, particularly, as Henry L. Stimson recalled in later years in his memoirs, that "the peace of 1919 was challenged and found wanting." [1] The Creditanstalt, Austria's leading private bank, collapsed in the late spring of that year and, subsequently, also much of the banking and economic fabric of Central Europe. This development deepened the depression, which entered a new international phase further endangering political and economic stability in the world. The rise of Hitler loomed as an imminent possibility in the wake of the financial prostration of Germany. Japanese troops marched into Manchuria in late 1931 and the postwar arrangements in the Far East hung in the balance.

The initial response of the Hoover administration, pressed particularly in 1931 and again in the 1932–1933 interregnum, pointed toward promotion of international cooperation and the reduction of tensions in Europe which threatened to make a shambles of the Versailles agreements. But Hoover failed to act on his assumptions. The collapse of the world marketplace remained untouched as a subject for direct action. Our high tariff system was treated as inviolate. The Hoover–Mills policies stressed instead a purely financial approach on the assumption that confidence would then be restored elsewhere. Attention was limited to the temporary abatement of intergovernmental financial obligations (the debts and reparations), maintenance of the gold standard, the balancing of national budgets, avoidance of the collapse of private financial institutions—in general, maintenance of national economic solvency and thereby restoration of confidence in the advanced nations of the world.[2] Hoover's approach failed by late 1931 because of its inadequacy, extreme nationalism, and the intrusion of a tangle of international political questions which stifled every sincere effort at checking the trend toward autarchy. But it failed, too, because of timidity in its financial undertakings and an avoidance of the fundamentals.

IN HIS *Memoirs* Herbert Hoover attributed the Great Depression to foreign collapse. Although he took a vigorous swipe at Federal Reserve Board policies which, at the behest of European bankers, inflated credit before the crash, essentially he saw our own economic misfortunes as a product of the disintegration of the European economic and financial structure. The European debacle, in turn, was a delayed consequence of economic dislocations in trade and finance caused by World War I, the Versailles agreements, and the profligate spending policies of European nations especially for armaments. It culminated, he later decided, in the dread hand of Communism, Fascism, and World War II.

The specific point of departure for Hoover occurred in the late spring and early summer of 1931 when Europe's central banks, and the German government, appeared on the verge of collapse. Until then, in his view, the United States was on its way out of the depression.[3] On May 11, 1931, the Austrian government announced that the nation's principal private bank, the Creditanstalt für Handel und Gewerbe, had suffered losses during 1930 very nearly equal to its capital and reserves. Although the Creditanstalt did not close its doors (the government, the Austrian central bank, the Nationalbank, and the president of the Creditanstalt, Baron Louis de Rothschild, came to the rescue with loans and credits), the shock shattered confidence in other European banking institutions. Germany was already weakened by an outflow of funds following the September 1930 national elections when the Nazis and Communists scored sharp gains, then by the international crisis following her announcement in March 1931 of an intended customs union with Austria, but she was shaken more directly when subjected to an outflow of funds generally as well as withdrawal of Austrian balances with the Creditanstalt collapse.

The German financial crisis of the late spring and early summer, 1931, culminating with the closing of her principal banks in July, stemmed from factors even more basic than the Creditanstalt collapse. The depression reduced German overseas trade and thereby caused severe unemployment as well as the loss of overseas earnings. The reparations burden amounted to more than the German government could sustain, it claimed, in the face of the decline in overseas income. Moreover, the government in response to these developments felt compelled to introduce an austerity budget, which intensified deflation. And it pursued a revisionist diplomacy which, in order to secure changes in the Versailles and reparations agreements, exaggerated its economic plight, causing a loss of overseas confidence in its ability or willingness to meet its obligations. The result was acceleration of the downward spiral of Germany's economic depression. The Creditanstalt crisis merely precipitated the collapse of Germany's already tottering financial structure.[4]

The Hoover Moratorium was intended to save the German financial structure and that of the western nations from the domino-like deflationary tides of 1931. A general German default, the inability of its government and banking institutions to meet current obligations, would not have left the United States untouched. U.S. holdings in German securities, particularly in the form of short-term bank credits, were estimated at $500 million to upwards of $1.7 billion. These were held principally by the New York banks, and if the German banks defaulted the major New York institutions would themselves be in dire straits. The Chase Bank and the Guaranty Trust Company of New York, for instance, had committed nearly half their capital to these loans because of the attraction of high interest rates as well as the lack of domestic outlets for their funds.[5]

Beginning in May 1931, when U.S. Ambassador to Germany Frederic M. Sackett called on Hoover in Washington and brought the gravity of the German banking and political situation to the President's attention, Hoover determined upon two priorities. The crisis could be ameliorated, he believed, by relief from the burdens of intergovernmental debts and reparations and, second, by additional relief of European budgets through reduction in expenditures for land armaments. In his diary, on June 5, 1931, Hoover elaborated the significance of his maneuvers on the international scene. He believed, he recorded, that a one-year moratorium on the payment of intergovernmental obligations would give the nations of the world the opportunity to right their domestic economies and recover from the depression. Nothing, Hoover ventured, would contribute more to restore employment and business activity. During the moratorium year, he hoped, action by the proposed disarmament conference in the form of reduction of land armaments would lift the economic burden even more substantially. In addition, Hoover told Ambassador Sackett before his return to Germany in June, "the whole reparations and debt complex could well be temporarily reviewed in the light of capacity to pay under depression conditions." [6]

Hoover's conclusion that relief from debt and reparations payments and reduction of armaments expenditures lay at the very core of restoration of national and international solvency needs to be challenged on the grounds that the economic causes of the depression ran deeper and wider than he seemed prepared to acknowledge. But even in the narrower frame in which he was willing to act, there was little chance of attainment of his objectives in the existing climate of intense nationalism and mutual distrust. Europe, Edward W. Bennett observed in his definitive study of Germany's financial crisis, required a Bismarck or a Talleyrand and he might well have added a Castlereagh. Instead, it had Heinrich

Brüning, Pierre Laval, and Ramsay MacDonald, wavering heads of shaky governments. Unstable, minority governments talked international cooperation, but their leadership, like Hoover, fearful of defeat at the polls, never acted on their own assertions or assumptions.

Thomas W. Lamont of J. P. Morgan & Co. claimed, when the moratorium was declared, that the greatest economic danger lay in the political attitude of the Germans themselves. Germany's Chancellor Brüning had argued national bankruptcy so effectively (to get reparations reduction) that his own nationals and industries shifted funds to Switzerland, Holland, and the United States. As a further deterrent to Franco-German cooperation, the Brüning government, because of its need to broaden its minority support into a larger constituency, appeased Germany's nationalistic aspirations by demands for revision of the Versailles agreements. German proposals for a customs union with Austria and for military parity with France created political uncertainties and stimulated French suspicions to such an extent that the benefits of the moratorium were dissipated at its very inception.[7]

British Prime Minister J. Ramsay MacDonald broached the complicated political tensions that choked efforts at economic cooperation in a lengthy and confidential discussion with the U.S. Chargé d'Affaires in London, Ray Atherton, early in June 1931. The European situation, he concluded since his recent talks at Chequers with Germany's Chancellor Heinrich Brüning and Foreign Minister Julius Curtius, was moving in a dangerous direction politically as well as economically. Curtius warned MacDonald that the collapse of the Brüning government would result in the coming to power of either the Communists or Hitlerites. The economic plight of the German people disposed them against those whom they, rightly or wrongly, held responsible for high taxes, unemployment, and reduced relief measures. MacDonald feared a wider Communist revolution, with Soviet support, which would engulf Germany, Poland, and all of Eastern Europe. Did MacDonald fear war, Atherton inquired? He replied, "No, revolution." The British Prime Minister feared an alternative danger to Europe, that of French domination. "Nationalistic considerations dominated French finance and French policy," MacDonald asserted, and "French loans to Czechoslovakia, Rumania, Poland, and Yugoslavia were based on French aggrandizement and it was idle to expect an international character of French banking or diplomacy." [8]

The discussion was followed up by a personal letter from Laborite MacDonald to Secretary of State Henry L. Stimson. The Nazis and Communists, he warned, might well crush the middle parties between an upper and a nether millstone and if Germany became submerged politically and economically the revolution and economic crisis that would follow could not be contained. The specific economic causes of Germany's collapse he attributed to shortage of capital, unemployment, high taxes, bankruptcy of the Reich, and reparations. MacDonald, keenly conscious of the Hoover administration's difficulties with the Congress on involvement in European problems, suggested to Stimson that he bill his forthcoming trip to Europe as one concerning disarmament rather than economic and financial matters. [9]

As warnings mounted concerning the increasing flight of capital from Germany, Hoover canvassed congressional opinion on a proposal to suspend for one year all intergovernmental payments of debts and reparations. He consulted with Simeon D. Fess and James E. Watson, key Senate Republicans, then with Ambassador to England Charles G. Dawes on a trip to Indianapolis. On June 18, in Washington, he conferred with Democratic leaders of the House and Senate. Joseph T. Robinson of Arkansas and John Nance Garner of Texas refused to endorse the proposed moratorium but agreed not to make any statement in opposition until Congress convened. [10] On June 20, 1931, Hoover announced his proposal, subject to ratification by Congress, for a one-year moratorium on payments of intergovernmental obligations. The President's statement reaffirmed the traditional U.S. view that no connection existed between German reparations and the debts owed us by our wartime allies. Pointedly, he asserted his opposition to cancellation of the debts. [11]

The proposed moratorium, approved quickly by the other nations involved, ran into difficulty when the French balked. France, like the United States, was a major creditor nation and her leaders bridled at Hoover's failure to consult them in advance. French resentment heightened when Hoover threatened to enter into agreements with other nations, bypassing France. France's leaders, moreover, feared German military and economic resurgence and wanted an assortment of guarantees, particularly Germany's abandonment of the proposed customs union with Austria and planned construction of a second pocket battleship in the *Deutschland* class. (Germany's Reichstag voted the funds on March 20, 1931.) The depression shattered the illusion of Versailles as a permanent political settlement, and of the Young Plan as a permanent economic settlement of the reparation problem. Germany sought revision of both agreements; France wanted political and economic assurances in exchange. England became increasingly neutral in the controversy, perhaps even inclined toward Germany's favor—and most Americans cared little if at all about Europe's affairs.

France yielded on the moratorium question only after enormous diplomatic pressure from Washington. She was willing, Premier Pierre Laval explained to Walter Edge, to dispense with conditional annuities due her from Germany, but not with unconditional annuities used for rehabilitation of war-damaged regions. Laval questioned the wisdom of relieving Germany of all its outpayments also on the grounds that the funds retained would be utilized for armaments and the dumping of German goods abroad. If the French government made concessions on the issue, he maintained, it would fall.[12]

Ogden Mills and Henry L. Stimson replied for the Hoover administration that the unconditional payments,[13] which were substantial, could not be excluded from the moratorium without defeating its intent. Moreover, Ambassador Edge informed the French Premier of Senator Borah's warning in a telegram to Hoover that he would not support the moratorium if Germany alone was compelled to make payments, whatever their nature. Without Borah's support the plan would fail in the Senate, Germany's economy would collapse, and France would be isolated in her efforts to resolve the reparations problem.[14]

In essence the difference between the Hoover administration and that of the Laval administration was Washington's attempt, on the one hand, to provide economic relief, and Paris' desire to attach needed political conditions to such relief. Laval and France's moderate Foreign Minister Aristide Briand, the latter a pan-Europeanist, needed concessions from Germany to satisfy nationalistic pressures in the French Assembly. France had her own "Borahs." The French conditions were outlined to Edge as follows: "(One) Disarmament (Briand referred yesterday to the abandonment of the construction of the German *Ersatz Praussen* class which would he said enable France to reduce her naval program and thus help both security and the budgets); (Two) The abandonment of the Austro-German Customs Union project; and (Three) The cessations [sic] by Germany in the French spheres of influence in Central Europe and the Balkans." [15]

Laval and Briand wanted Germany's Chancellor Brüning and Foreign Minister Curtius to visit Paris for negotiations on these questions, but the German leaders argued that they could not do so without exacerbating their own internal political situation. To negotiate with the French for reparations relief in exchange for political concessions, Brüning and Curtius argued with U.S. Ambassador Sackett, would be political suicide.[16] In an official statement Curtius and Staatsskretär Bernard von Bülow (the chief permanent official of the German Foreign Ministry) contended that Germany would be better off invoking her right to a moratorium under provisions of the Young Plan than by making political concessions. Yet they softened the threat by adding that any funds saved under the Hoover proposal would be used exclusively for relief of German finances and not for armaments. Then, on June 30, 1931, the next day, Brüning threatened that if France did not acquiesce to the Hoover moratorium he would be compelled to declare a moratorium unilaterally effective July 14.[17]

Beset on two sides, by German leaders who were making dour

predictions to our Ambassador concerning imminent economic collapse and a Hitlerite or Communist *putsch* and by the French who kept imposing political conditions on their consent, Hoover became increasingly testy towards the Laval government. Brüning's ominous warnings of German financial collapse and a radical debacle of either right or left political militants reached a crescendo on the evening of July 2, 1931. "The Chancellor told me tonight," Ambassador Sackett cabled, "that his only reliance . . . lay in the army. . . . He felt sure that any public declaration made by the Government which involved any derogation of the meager rights granted Germany under the Treaty of Versailles, particularly with respect to the right to building cruisers in replacement of . . . superannuated vessels," would arouse so much passion as to impair the loyalty of the army, particularly the younger officers. Sackett regarded Brüning's pessimistic declamation as honest. Since the Chancellor's moderate government had only minority support, Brüning, he believed, could not take a firm stand against the "Nationalist extremists, no matter how unreasonable their opposition may intrinsically be." [18]

By July 5, 1931, negotiations with France brought Hoover to the point of outrage. The French raised eight new points with Ambassador Edge and Treasury Secretary Andrew Mellon, Hoover noted in his diary, "all impossible of acceptance." The deadlock was broken in part by Brüning's public announcement of his hitherto private assurances that his nation would not use funds released by the Hoover plan to increase its military budget; and in part by Hoover's threats to bypass France which would be blamed for the consequences stemming from failure to reach an agreement. [19]

American and French negotiators arrived at a moratorium agreement on July 6, 1931: 1) the payment of intergovernmental debts was postponed from July 1, 1931, to July 1, 1932; 2) Germany would meet the unconditional annuity payment by deposit of railway bonds with the Bank for International Settlements (BIS); 3) all suspended payments, spread over ten years, would be resumed on July 1, 1933; 4) the BIS and the major Central Banks would render assistance to the countries of Eastern Europe; 5) a committee of experts would resolve the issue of deliveries in kind (some $20 million) in the spirit of the Hoover moratorium; 6) France reserved the right to request German assurance that the sums freed from the Reich budget would not be utilized for armaments.[20]

THE HOOVER MORATORIUM, approved by Congress on December 23, 1931, often regarded as Hoover's most statesmanlike accomplishment, proved an illusion. It gave the appearance that payment of intergovernmental debts and reparations, postponed for one year, would be resumed on December 15, 1932. Actually more sophisticated government officials and observers of the international economic and political scene knew that Germany would in all likelihood never again be willing or able to meet her reparations obligations. Further, that our principal debtors had no intention of continuing their payments in full if at all. Little doubt existed in the summer of 1931 that resumption of debts and reparations payments a year later was more of a political football than an economic reality.[21]

The most disappointing feature of the moratorium was its inadequacy in the face of the international financial crisis. The closing of Germany's banks in mid-July and the abandonment of the gold standard by Great Britain in September 1931 can be grasped only by an understanding of the origins of the financial collapse, basically a crisis of liquidity, followed by a desire in a panic to convert long-term assets and then even short-term assets into cash and gold.

Huge expenditures during World War I were followed by heavy postwar investment in industrial and agricultural recovery. Western European banks, heavily invested in industrial expansion, found themselves in a relatively illiquid position. When production and profits declined, banks could not meet demands for cash without calling in industrial loans.

Outside of Europe, in South America, Canada, Australia, India, and the United States, huge agricultural surpluses built up in the 1920s. Heavy wartime and immediate postwar demand, mechanization, and expansion of acreage was followed by a decline in demand in the mid- and late twenties caused by dietary changes away from the grains and by European efforts at self-sufficiency. Private finance as well as semi-public agencies, such as Hoover's Federal Farm Loan Board, poured hundreds of millions of dollars into holding operations designed to keep agricultural produce off the world market until demand and supply were more nearly matched. But to no avail, for agricultural prices collapsed in 1930 and 1931 as stored commodities overhung the marketplace.

The sharp decline in worldwide agricultural prices, which ushered in the farm depression in the United States nearly a decade before the stock market collapse, struck entire raw-materials-producing nations in South America and Asia also before 1929. The underdeveloped nations, traditionally debtor countries, received inadequate financial assistance in the period 1927–1929 because of heavy investment in industrial and financial activities, and received even less aid from their traditional creditor sources in Europe when the depression broke.[22]

By 1930, the international economic picture deteriorated sharply. Gold flowed from the debtor raw-materials countries to the world financial centers. Canada went off gold early in 1929, then Argentina and Uruguay later that year. In 1930, four additional Latin American nations abandoned gold, as did Australia and New Zealand. The ramifications resembled the whorls of a whirl-pool with everything in sight sucked under. Exports of advanced nations declined since underdeveloped countries could neither sell nor borrow adequately abroad. Prices and production fell, as a result, leading to excess capacity, deflation, and unemployment.

As the general economic crisis deepened, international credit shriveled. France, customarily a creditor nation, experienced a net import of capital in 1929 and 1930. Great Britain and the United States maintained foreign lending, but at a reduced rate disproportionate to the need of the traditional debtor countries.

Bank failures in France and the United States exacerbated the crisis and led to a growing insistence on liquidity in the face of feared insolvency. The French demand for gold, a response to fears for German political and financial stability, heightened late in 1930 with the failure of the Banque Oustric, the Banque National de Crédit, a major Paris institution, and a dozen provincial banks. It led to French gold withdrawals and liquidation of short-term loans and credits in Central and Eastern Europe. In the United States, 1,345 banks closed in 1930 and 687 in the first half of 1931, because of the agricultural depression and because of inadequacies in capital, liquidity, and regulation.[23]

This background of worldwide agricultural depression, bank closings, cash and then gold hoarding, unemployment, deflation, shortage of credit, declining industrial production and trade, and increasing vulnerability of major fiduciary institutions formed the basis for the three major financial jolts of 1931. These were the closing of Austria's Creditanstalt in May, then of Germany's banks in July, and finally Great Britain's abandonment of gold in September.

Every national crisis had its own peculiar features. Austria's Creditanstalt collapsed because it had been forced in November 1929 to absorb the unsound Boden Credit-Anstalt and because it became too deeply mixed in Austrian and East European manufacturing enterprises which went bankrupt in the depression. When the psychological tide toward withdrawals developed, it found itself in an illiquid position. French withdrawals of credits merely exposed an untidy situation to say the least.[24]

Germany's banking system was subjected to the usual panic withdrawals and the inability of banks to meet them in late June and July. But unique to Germany was the government's own statements of imminent bankruptcy in the face of reparations demands. Such predictions hardly inspired confidence in German fiduciary institutions. The Brüning government, desirous of precipitating a crisis to prove its point on reparations, discovered by mid-July, when the German banks closed their doors, that it had been all too successful.[25]

Before the collapse of the German banks, President Hoover

applied pressure on Governor George Harrison of the New York Federal Reserve Bank to extend and enlarge credits to the Reichsbank. Harrison demurred. The principal defense of the mark, he argued, should be made by the Reichsbank through adoption of a firmer credit policy and restriction of the flight of capital. Harrison would not support extension of additional credit by the New York Federal Reserve Bank until its German counterpart had done all it could to save its own situation.[26]

The French adopted a similar position. In Paris, on July 11, Hans Luther, who headed the Reichsbank, secured from Governor Clément Moret of the Bank of France, Finance Minister Pierre-Etienne Flandin, and French bankers a three-month extension of the existing $100 million credit. But Luther needed more. The French insisted on abandonment of the proposed customs union with Austria. Luther contended that he was President of the Reichsbank, not a politician. The French refused additional credits. (Very shortly the German-Austrian Customs Union proposal was dropped anyway.) [27]

In Berlin, also on July 11, the weekend before the key Darmstädter und Nationalbank (Danat) closed its doors, the German leadership indicated to U.S. Ambassador Sackett a belated willingness to go to Paris for political discussions. Sackett conferred with Staatssekretär von Bülow, Chancellor Brüning, and the vice-president of the Reichsbank. Our ambassador learned: "The very last resources are being thrown in tomorrow, . . . but at the very latest these cannot carry beyond Monday noon, after which a panic was considered inevitable. . . . Closing of banks, the failure on the part of industries to meet payrolls, and people being thrown into the streets would result from this. They declared that actual revolution is implied."

Sackett reported to Washington the inability of Brüning's minority government (he tended to be sympathetic with its plight and was perhaps to a point taken in) to make concessions in the form of renunciation of the Customs Union and battleship construction. Brüning, he believed, faced desertion by key members of the Cabinet if he conceded these points. But Brüning was willing to go to Paris for political discussions in late July or early August if the Reichsbank received additional credits from the Federal Reserve Bank, the French and English Central Banks, and the Bank for International Settlements. Sackett concluded that substantial political concessions to the French would bring Brüning's government down, also that the French were willing to take the risk of a new government in Germany "even if the Extremist Right were in control." [28]

Hoover sought advice in the crisis from Acting Secretary of the Treasury Ogden Mills and Acting Secretary of State William Castle, both nationalists. [29] They maintained that Germany's financial difficulties should be resolved by the heads of principal Central Banks, scheduled to meet at Basle on July 13. Further, they argued, the United States government lacked resources for the relief of German banking institutions. [30] Repeated requests from Europe for some sort of U.S.-Franco-British intergovernmental loan to head off the German banking crisis resulted in negative responses from both the United States and Britain.

On July 13, 1931, the Darmstädter und Nationalbank (Danat) closed and the following day all German banks shut down. The German banking system finally succumbed. Some 6 billion reichsmarks were immobilized, exchange controls imposed, and runs experienced by banks elsewhere in Central and Eastern Europe. [31]

On July 16, Secretary of State Stimson conveyed to Hoover from Paris a French proposal for a Franco-British-American loan of $500 million to Germany secured by customs receipts. Hoover and Mills rejected the proposal (the Bank of England and the British Treasury also opposed it, they learned) and offered instead to the conference convened at London July 20–23 by British Prime Minister MacDonald a "standstill agreement" among banks holding German and Central European short-term obligations. Accepted by the London Conference, the proposal emerged as too little and too late. [32]

The European situation worsened in September 1931 with Great

Britain's abandonment of the gold standard and its devaluation of the pound, following on the heels of the formation of a new National government in August. Long-term and immediate considerations influenced the decision. The Bank of England had maintained the international gold standard through two major periods, 1872–1914 and again from 1924/25 through September 1931. During the first era, one of major economic expansion, England managed successfully as banker of the world, but the Bank of England's attempt to reassert management of the gold standard and its function as creditor of the underdeveloped nations in the second period was at best tenuous. World War I cut into London's creditor status because of heavy wartime borrowing, and by the end of the war England had become a short-term debtor nation. Her international financial position was further weakened by a general failure to attain a substantial postwar recovery, also by the tendency of England's financial institutions to underwrite internal industrial expansion and the deficits of Labor governments. In these circumstances, London banks could neither meet the demands for loans made by members of the sterling bloc, which ran heavy deficits in their balance of payments in the years 1928–1931, nor the needs of the depressed Latin American nations.

More immediate factors accounted for the abandonment of gold and the devaluation of the pound in September 1931. These included inadequate gold reserves and the shrinkage of international loan funds. Traditionally London bankers turned to Vienna, Paris, and Berlin to meet extraordinary demands for loans by debtor countries and the liquidation of sterling assets by foreigners. But these sources dried up by 1931. The crisis was further aggravated by the poor financial condition of the British government, usually attributed to heavy deficits incurred to underwrite social legislation and to high wage rates in England.[33]

Thus by the summer and fall of 1931 the Central and Eastern European banks had gone under and Great Britain, to avoid bankruptcy, opted out as banker of the world and devalued the pound. Debts and reparations hung in limbo. Tariff barriers, embargoes, currency restrictions, and a host of other devices heralded the efforts of nations to hoard their gold and preserve their solvency. Banks teetered on the brink and many, particularly in the United States, toppled over unable to meet the demands of the liquidity crisis. International economic warfare set in, ruthless and brutal in nature.

Perhaps the most succinct barometer of the intense economic nationalism that dominated the picture after September 1931 appeared in a set of summary figures formulated by W. Randolph Burgess of the Federal Reserve Bank of New York. In the determinative nine-month period, extending from September 1931 to July 1932, twenty-one nations either abandoned the gold standard or prohibited gold exports, with the United Kingdom leading the way. Twenty-eight countries, including Germany and Italy, instituted foreign exchange controls, and eleven, principally smaller nations, imposed moratoria on external governmental and/or commercial credit. Forty-four sovereignties, among them the United States, France, Great Britain, Canada, Germany, and Italy, utilized general tariff increases or specific tariff impositions as a further measure of self-preservation. Twenty-six utilized more novel methods of trade restriction such as import quotas and outright embargo of certain imports to protect currency and gold reserves as well as the domestic market for domestic producers. All in all, it added up to a world bent upon economic warfare.[34]

THE HOOVER–LAVAL CONVERSATIONS of October 1931 may be described as an epilogue to the still-born efforts at international economic cooperation in 1931, and as a prologue to the Geneva Disarmament Conference and the Lausanne Conference of 1932 as well as the World Monetary and Economic Conference convened at London in the summer of 1933. The Laval visit to Washington was suggested by James G. McDonald, chairman of the Foreign Policy Association, to the French Premier in Paris on September 18, 1931. McDonald urged that something should be done to resolve the differences between France and the United States, particularly on the question of disarmament. Probably the meeting came about, also, because Secretary of State Stimson returned from Europe with the conviction that "we can hope for Laval to give moderate French policy a new leadership." [35]

Hoover's papers, at the Presidential Library in Iowa, contain a memorandum of "Subjects for Laval Conversations" which is astonishing in its projected range. It broached seven subjects for discussion.

1. Reparations: Moratorium—what to do by or before July 1, 1932; German-American Mixed Claims; Revision of the Young Plan. . . .
2. War Debts: Capacity to pay; French final settlement with Germany and with U.S.
3. Finance: Franco-British relations; Gold standard, gold distribution; Silver—silver conference; Currency Conference; Cooperation of Central Banks.
4. Commercial Matters: General—tariff; Most-Favored Nation Treatment; Regional Agreements; European Union. . . .
5. Disarmament and Security: *1.* Definition of the French conception of security: is it (a) the perpetuation of the status quo, or (b) the tranquilization of Europe by removing causes of unrest. *2.* Revision of the Treaty of Versailles. *3.* Territorial questions arising from Treaty of Versailles. Polish boundaries, chiefly the Danzig corridor; to a lesser degree, Upper Silesia. *4.* France and her Allies: the Little Entente and Poland. *5.* Franco-German political relations: (a) the recent Laval visit to Berlin; (b) the new Franco-German Economic Committee; (c) the disparity in armaments between France and Germany; (d) the prohibition to Germany by the Treaty of Versailles of certain weapons.
6. France's desire for further assurance of security, chiefly from Great Britain and the U.S.
7. Implementing the Kellogg Pact. . . .[36]

A viable economic and financial position for the United States in the Laval talks was hammered out at an all-day meeting held at the offices of the Federal Reserve Bank of New York on October 19, 1931. In attendance were Undersecretary of the Treasury Ogden L. Mills, Assistant Secretary of State James G. Rogers, S. Parker Gilbert of J. P. Morgan & Co., Walter Stewart of Case Pomeroy,

Emanuel Goldenweiser of the Federal Reserve Board, Herbert Feis, State Department Economic Adviser, and intermittently Governor George Harrison of the Federal Reserve Bank of New York; Ralph [?] Crane, deputy governor of the FRB of New York; and Eugene Meyer, governor of the FRB. The cast, in short, included the nation's principal financial statesmen. Of the vast range of matters subject to international resolution, debts and reparations pressed as most immediate, disarmament and consequent reduction of governmental expenditures as of greatest long-run importance. The figure most often proposed in the day's discussion of debts/reparations relief approximated a reduction of 50 percent. Hoover followed this course in the Laval discussions, though no percentages appear in the record.

The knottiest problem Hoover and Laval faced, the Wall Street conferees conceded, involved procedures required for a frank airing of the necessity for reduction of intergovernmental obligations. Private agreements were one matter, since Hoover and Laval accepted downward revision as a practical necessity, but their constituencies opposed reduction and national legislatures echoed similar sentiments. Further, the United States traditionally rejected Europe's assertions since the war that debts and reparations were connected. A general conference on the two subjects seemed a political impossibility in view of that position. Yet, sooner or later, those assembled believed, the United States either would be drawn into such a conference or would be confronted by default.

By the end of the day the Wall Street conference arrived at a procedure which led to the Lausanne reparations reduction of 1932 and to the requests for debts reduction which descended upon our State Department as Hoover prepared to turn over his office to Roosevelt. Hoover was advised that Germany should take the initiative and request her creditors to reconsider the reparations settlement. Germany's creditors meantime should be reassured by a Franco-American statement to the effect that the United States would reconsider a revision of the debts settlements. This procedure, Herbert Feis reported, attracted Ogden Mills, S. Parker Gilbert, and Walter Stewart. A debt settlement, they believed, could be negotiated through a reconstituted debt funding commission.[37]

Thus emerged the strategy for European economic diplomacy vis-à-vis the United States from the autumn of 1931 through the London Economic Conference of 1933. The Lausanne Conference of 1932, wherein Germany's creditors agreed to reduce reparations by 90 percent in exchange for U.S. reduction of debts,[38] had its sanction in the Hoover–Laval conference. The French premier, before leaving Washington, informed the German ambassador to the United States, Herr Friedrich W. von Prittwitz und Gaffron, that Germany should request a commission of inquiry on reparations under the Young Plan provisions. "It is the President's idea," Lawrence Richey, secretary to Hoover, wrote to Ambassador Dawes, "that when this commission has made a report, and when the Allied Governments have determined what they are able to do in respect to Germany, that the American government can then consider what its course should be in respect to the debts." Hoover insisted to Laval that he unalterably opposed the calling of a general conference on debts and reparations because of the potential economic and political disturbance it would provoke. Rather, the United States, once reparations reductions took place, would deal by direct negotiation with its individual debtors. Hoover also stipulated that debts and reparations should not become part of an international monetary conference which the British favored.[39] Britain's Prime Minister MacDonald, then in the process of forming a new government, agreed with Hoover's views, including the desirability of excluding debts and reparations from the monetary conference.[40]

Herbert Hoover had the desire to become his own historian as well as his own memoirist. In addition to three untidy and inaccurate volumes of memoirs, he sometimes attempted in his papers to set the record straight for scholars. The result is unfortunate. In an effort possibly during the 1932–1933 interregnum to counter the suspicions of Moley and Roosevelt and the charges made on the floor of the Senate that he had made a commitment to Laval on debt reduction he addressed a memorandum to Secretary Stimson which he maintained should serve as an account of his conversations with Premier Laval. Though dated "October 1931?," the document refers to the Lausanne Conference of June 1932, which reduced reparations on the condition that the United States reduce the debts; also, to our debtor's default, which did not occur until November–December 1932. The Hoover memorandum contends that no commitments emerged during the October 1931 conference except the reexamination of capacity to pay.[41]

It must be conceded that in the strictest possible interpretation of the Hoover–Laval talks, Hoover did not guarantee debt reduction. But he did propose after all that Germany petition its creditors for reparations reduction, and, once accomplished, reconsideration of the debts. The implication was obvious. As any Midwestern senator would taunt on the Senate floor, reconsideration of the debts meant downward revision. This interpretation is confirmed by the Stimson Diary. Hoover, Mills, Stimson, and Laval were the principals on October 23, 1931:

> The President then changed the subject to reparations and debts. He brought forward the Mills suggestion of the other day of invoking a conference under the Young Plan to determine Germany's ability to pay reparations during the time of the depression; to be followed by a re-examination of the debts. Laval didn't dispute this. I think he was a little surprised at the President making it.

The following day Laval agreed that Germany required reparations relief during the depression, but expressed the wish that it be stated with caution in the joint communique. Otherwise there would be unfortunate results at home. Hoover conceded, in return, "that if Germany was helped in their reparations, we would have to help our debtors on debts."[42]

During the course of the discussions Laval made it clear that France would not consent to the complete abolition of reparations, since it would give German industry an unfair advantage over that of France, England, and the United States. "They have no debt. Their debt has been wiped out," he argued. "They could start in and beat us all. Then came up the suggestion of the President as to transferring the present reparation charge of the German Government over to German industry. He [Hoover] asked Laval whether that wouldn't be possible. This plan was . . . suggested by Garrard Winston. To the surprise of all of us we found that the French had been working exactly upon the same plan."

No agreement was achieved on such other matters as disarmament and the question of the Polish Corridor. The French offered concessions in exchange for a consultative pact with the United States. But political considerations prevented Hoover from entertaining the notion. [43]

HERBERT HOOVER focused his diplomatic energies in the closing months of 1931 on the problem of intergovernmental obligations. It made sense. Great Britain, in dire straits, seemed hardly prepared to negotiate on currency stabilization or a return to the gold standard or tariff reduction. [44] Resolution of the reparations/debts tangle seemed the first logical step toward a future conference on monetary and economic problems. Yet, as one views the Republican President's handling of the situation it seems timid at best, inept at worst, marked by ambivalence and vacillation.

For a moment, upon the conclusion of Pierre Laval's discussions with Hoover on October 25, 1931, it seemed that the two heads of government were on the brink of setting machinery in motion that might resolve the dilemma during the postponement year. Their terse communique, issued jointly, acknowledged that the moratorium year could be utilized to achieve an agreement covering the period of the business depression. "The initiative in this matter," they proposed, "should be taken at an early date by the European powers principally concerned within the framework of agreements existing prior to July 1, 1931."

Behind the stiff diplomatic language lay a clear strategy delineated by economic adviser Herbert Feis: "The President and the French Prime Minister appeared to have agreed (a) that Germany will need relief in regard to the reparations during the depression period; (b) that the procedure should be application by Germany for the convocation of the special advisory committee . . . of the Young Plan; (c) that if this committee reported an adjustment of the reparations burden to be advisable, . . . the President will recommend to Congress that it reduce the debts owed to us." [45]

The next step in the Hoover–Laval plan was undertaken at Paris at a series of private conferences held by Laval, following the Washington visit, and Bernard von Bülow. They agreed that Berlin would request the creation of an Advisory Committee (known as the Basle Committee) by the Bank for International Settlements in accordance with Young Plan procedure. Further, that this would really constitute the initial step towards a creditor-debtor conference on reparations. Yet, tensions quickly developed over what was to be finally achieved. Laval favored a two- or three-year extension of the moratorium, whereas Von Bülow and Brüning stipulated that political conditions in Germany mandated immediate reduction or cancellation. [46]

Brüning's seeming intransigence reflected an increasingly complex set of domestic economic and political problems. Ascetic, intelligent, highly regarded for his acumen in finance, the last leader of an ailing, divided Weimar, Brüning faced a collapse in agricultural prices and large-scale unemployment in 1930, then the financial collapse of 1931. Yielding to internal pressures, he asserted in early 1932, that his government planned to abandon the reparations settlements following the moratorium, despite a favorable trade balance. His tenuous political position was reflected, too, in his support of the *Reichswehr*'s military aspirations.

Germany's conservative Centrist Chancellor was a paradigm of the tragedy of Weimar's political leadership in his inability to collaborate with the Social Democrats and thereby to master the nuances of parliamentary government. His respect for order and the military, especially in the person of President von Hindenburg proved misplaced. And he failed in his appeal to German nationalist sentiments in the vain hope of outshouting the extremists.

Tragically, he fueled the very fires he sought to extinguish by pressing for a customs union with Austria in 1931, a prelude to *Anschluss*, a course he abandoned to the dismay of the National Socialists and their cohorts, and for the elimination of Germany's payment of tribute, as patriots categorized the reparations. Brüning's diplomacy simply heightened France's fear of the Reich and massaged the egos of Weimar's mortal enemies. When Hindenburg dumped him unceremoniously on May 30, 1932, on the issue of Prussian land reform, Franz von Papen and General Kurt von Schleicher, anxious to use one another and to use the Nazis for their own ends, were the beneficiaries.[47]

The haggling process had begun with politicians often willing privately to compromise, fearful of domestic political sentiment. Hopeful of accommodation with Germany, Pierre Laval felt compelled to save his own regime, one of many in France that came and went with the seasons, by delivering a stridently nationalist speech in the Chamber of Deputies on November 27, 1931. The French Premier won a vote of confidence by a margin of 45 thanks to the assertion that he would not consent to a revision of reparations unless war debts were reduced in equal measure. Anxious to avoid tensions with the German government beyond those that existed, Laval read key portions of the speech to Bernhard von Bülow several days before its delivery. Stunned, Germany's Staatssekretär, urged Laval to modify his position. The French leader countered that he, too, was under fire from both the Left and the Right and that his government would fall if it showed any willingness to compromise the Young Plan terms. Likely he had in mind the stunning upset suffered by the moderate French statesman Aristide Briand when Paul Doumer won the French presidential election of May 31, 1931. The vote by the French National Assembly was interpreted as a sign that the nation had tired of Briand's policy of conciliation. Indeed, it seemed to many Frenchmen that concessions simply bred more demands. Briand, in fact, resigned as foreign minister. The burden of reconciliation ultimately depended upon Hoover's willingness and ability to carry through with the policies he initiated.[48]

Hopeful that reparations would be reduced the following year, the President opened the question of debts reduction, the second phase of the plan he and Laval developed, with the Congress on December 10, 1931. While insistent upon the sanctity of the arrangements made by the World War Foreign Debts Commission in 1922, in which he participated as Commerce Secretary, he also observed that the fabric of intergovernmental debts "weighs heavily in the midst of depression." In language that was characteristically ponderous and cautious, the President requested ratification of the moratorium and re-creation of the War Debts Commission "with authority to examine such problems as may arise in connection with those debts during the present economic emergency and to report to the Congress its conclusions and recommendations." This timid statement did not include the more urgent tone Ogden Mills suggested to Hoover. For they were fully apprized of Great Britain's inability to return her currency to its former parity with the dollar or carry out the terms of her postwar debts agreement. Executive responsibility for enlightenment dissolved on the shoals of fear of public opinion.[49]

Congress gleefully took the lead in the matter. In the debate which ensued, leading to the Joint House–Senate Resolution of December 22, 1931, notice was served that debts would neither be canceled nor reduced in any circumstance. Demagoguery smothered any attempt at economic reasoning. "Let any nation default that desires to do so," Senator Hiram Johnson of California challenged, almost hopefully, for it would stand as a lesson to those who persuaded this nation to intervene in 1917. Republican stalwarts, fingers to the wind, joined their Progressive colleagues in a rare display of unanimity. Even Hoover intimate conservative Senator David A. Reed of Pennsylvania wondered if debts reduction was confected by the bankers and bond houses that made huge private loans to Europe in the 1920s. "We have canceled all we are going to cancel."[50]

British Prime Minister J. Ramsay MacDonald, a passionate believer in Anglo-American amity, sent a personal message to Stimson, a blunt warning of events to come. "Reports have been made that Congress, in ratifying the one year moratorium, may atempt to impose conditions precluding further remission on the debts." The result, he predicted, would be an impasse. "Since last summer the situation in Europe has so deteriorated (and is still deteriorating) that for a long time there can be no prospect of reparations. France, in the absence of reparations will refuse to pay her war debt annuities to us and it would not be possible for us to meet the charge for the American debt out of our own resources unsupported by receipts from France and Germany." While willing to allow the Hoover administration to argue the separation of debts and reparations for public consumption, actually, MacDonald claimed, they were connected. He expressed the hope that means would be found "which will enable us to avoid anything that might be represented as repudiation." The unmentionable word surfaced at last.[51]

The worst fears of the British and French governments materialized on December 17, 1931, when a joint resolution introduced into the House and Senate, approving the moratorium, warned:

> Sec. 5. It is hereby expressly declared to be against the policy of Congress that any of the indebtedness of foreign countries to the United States should be in any manner cancelled or reduced; and nothing in this joint resolution shall be construed as indicating a contrary policy, or as implying that favorable consideration will be given at any time to a change in the policy hereby declared.

Five days later the House and Senate, with Hoover's staunchest legislative supporters joining the nationalists, "rapped my knuckles," as he later put it in his memoirs, and passed the resolution.[52] Hoover hardened on the debts question in 1932, in fact reversing the understandings reached at his conference with Laval. Only in the 1932–1933 interregnum, following the election of Roosevelt, did the President summon the courage to ask the President-elect to join him in what he assayed as an enterprise in political suicide. It is understandable that Roosevelt refused to endanger his domestic program.

With Hoover's abdication of leadership in the securing of international economic cooperation on debts and reparations, Britain's J. Ramsay MacDonald stepped into the breach. Despite the handicap of a nationalist cabinet, MacDonald urged France toward Lausanne and the debts/reparations washout and the United States toward the London Monetary and Economic Conference of 1933. The first step in this long tortuous process was undertaken on December 21, 1931, when the British government proposed to Laval's administration that it assume the lead in restoration of the German financial situation. A wise creditor, the London government admonished Paris, "can always revise a settlement which has not worked out in practise," rather than bankrupt its debtor. "The British government desire above all to place emphasis upon the urgent need of a solution of the whole question of intergovernmental indebtedness." Left unstated was Great Britain's own dire economic position which foreign office and financial experts believed would benefit in the process. On December 23, the Basle Committee concluded that Germany could not meet the Young Plan payments for two years. Germany's creditors agreed to a conference at Lausanne on January 18, 1932, to resolve the situation. Actually, the Lausanne Conference was postponed until June.[53]

Two factors contributed to the delay. One was the desire by Germany, Great Britain, and France for U.S. participation. With the passage of the Joint House–Senate Resolution of December 22, 1931, however, Hoover and Stimson adopted a firm course announced by the Secretary of State to a bewildered and stunned parade of diplomats summoned to his office. The United States would not join in a general reparations conference. Only after reparations reduction would it take up the debts issue on a nation by nation basis with capacity to pay the determining factor. When the British ambassador, Sir Ronald Lindsay, protested on Christmas Eve in Stimson's office, "But this means that you cannot make any further step until the world has gone bankrupt," the dour, humorless State Department head retorted that U.S. public opinion was not easily budged on the issue.[54]

The situation was further complicated for MacDonald by Laval's and Brüning's timidity in the face of nationalist pressures. The French Premier was confronted by a general election in April 1932, and Brüning by Prussian elections in May. Fearful that his regime could not otherwise survive, also for President Hindenburg's tenure, Brüning capitulated to the Hitlerites and demanded the termination of the entire reparations system. Anxious for British cooperation in the matter, he pledged that the Reich's position would be stated at Lausanne in a fashion that would avoid wounding French feeings. Evidently Brüning brandished the Hitlerite "threat" as a means of exerting pressure. Yet, as U.S. Ambassador to Berlin Frederic M. Sackett observed, the threat was no less "real in that no German Government could stand if it formally agreed to continue reparations payments." [55]

For a time the French position remained equally uncompromising. The powerful Pierre E. Flandin, Minister of Finance in the Laval cabinet, warned ominously that German termination of reparations payments was tantamount to repudiation of the Versailles Treaty. "No Frenchman," he intoned, "could accept the unilateral denunciation of contracts fully signed; . . . such a step by destroying confidence would render the crisis in world credit insurmountable; and . . . the meeting of the Lausanne Conference would be useless." In Washington, still hopeful in January of U.S. participation in a broad economic settlement that would include reparations and debts, Ambassador Claudel claimed accurately that America would not escape the situation. Should reparations be terminated, he observed, France would refuse to meet her debts payment.[56]

As the January 18, 1932, deadline passed for the convening of the Lausanne Conference, it seemed that the entire business of intergovernmental obligations would simply fall into limbo along with other issues such as armaments levels. At one point Laval proposed a one-year extension of the moratorium under French-American sponsorship, considered and rejected at a White House meeting of Mills, Dawes, Stimson, and Hoover on January 17, 1932. The deadlock was broken by the firm conviction in British financial and political circles that recovery of world trade was at stake, a view reflected by Neville Chamberlain, Chancellor of the Exchequer, in the House of Commons. He asserted as the government's policy achievement of "a comprehensive permanent settlement," to be attained as quickly as possible, with "general cancellation of reparations and war debts as its aim." [57] After considerable pulling and hauling behind the scenes, the governments of France, Germany, the United Kingdom, Italy, Japan, and Belgium agreed to meet at Lausanne in June to reach an accord on what had become an unbearable economic legacy of the war.

The opening months of 1932 witnessed frantic negotiation as British and French treasury officials attempted to arrive at a common position on reparations and as Secretary Stimson sailed to Europe to prod the flagging Geneva Disarmament Conference. Tension grew as the American Secretary of State evolved his policy of nonrecognition of Japan's seizure of Manchuria (the Stimson Doctrine). It seemed, as Will Rogers quipped, that so many notes were sent between nations that they might run out of stationery. [58] Yet, the more statesmen exchanged views the less they accomplished. The Versailles agreements and the Great Depression had bred an unquenchable jingoism: reparations constituted tribute; the United States was Uncle Shylock; Frenchmen were frightened by Germany's population and industrial advantage; Germany coveted the Polish Corridor and Upper Silesia.

No firm leadership seemed in the offing. The pacifist-internationalist Prime Minister of Great Britain, J. Ramsay MacDonald, was actually the captive of a nationalist empire-oriented cabinet dominated by Chamberlain at the Exchequer, Sir John Simon as Foreign Secretary, and Walter Runciman as President of the Board of Trade. In Paris, the game of musical chairs resumed with Laval's ouster as Premier in February 1932 and his replacement by the tough André Tardieu, who gave way in June to the moderate Edouard Herriot. Brüning's days were also numbered and in May, abruptly, President Hindenburg replaced his political ally with the dapper, wily Franz von Papen, anxious to force the Nazis to assume a position of shared responsibility. In Japan, the militarists came to power and quickly extended their mainland gains to much of China north of the Great Wall. It seemed, as Raymond Sontag later depicted the scene, *A Broken World*,[59] a title borrowed aptly from Gabriel Marcel's play of 1933, *Le monde cassé*.

Statesmen, who placed their faith in cooperative endeavor as a means of avoidance of another war, despaired. Symbolically the ailing Sir Arthur Henderson, an internationalist replaced by the hard-boiled Sir John Simon as British Foreign Secretary, presided at Geneva on February 2, 1932, at the opening of the World Disarmament Conference. This gathering of the nations had been taking shape since 1925 when the League of Nations Council invited nineteen sovereignties, including the United States, to participate in a Preparatory Commission. As one historian observed, "it had been planned too long . . . and the statesmen of the world would have abandoned it if they dared."

The Geneva Disarmament Conference foundered, then collapsed, because of German insistence on the right to rearm as part of a general release from the Versailles restrictions and British and U.S. refusal to afford France guarantees against a rearmed Reich. In the wake of President Hoover's insistence that land weapons on the European continent did not concern the United States, Stimson's personal diplomacy at Geneva in April and May proved futile. The talks formally collapsed in October 1933, when Adolf Hitler, now Germany's Chancellor, took his nation out of the League and its Disarmament Conference.[60]

The first stage of Herbert Hoover's attack on the Great Depression terminated in the winter of 1931–1932. Although he attributed the coming and deepening of the debacle largely to international conditions, he proved incapable of bringing them under control. Instead of determined initiatives to remove the economic and financial causes of the steadily deteriorating world situation, he evidently failed to mobilize the enormous resources of the postwar United States and to assume its responsibilities in the modern world. His leadership in foreign affairs lacked the vigor and realistic grasp conditions called for.

5

"A Pleasant Man Who . . . Would Very Much Like To Be President"

THE OPENING WEEKS of a convention-campaign year are critical for a leading contender, for his flanks are bound to be tested. All the more so in 1932 in the contest for the Democratic nomination in the light of Herbert Hoover's mounting unpopularity and the intensity of the depression. From the outset, Franklin D. Roosevelt was conceded a delegate majority at the party convention. But the requirement of a two-thirds vote for the grand prize had derailed more than one front-line hopeful in the past. Few political mistakes could be tolerated.

Further complicating the picture was the raising of a long latent issue, pressed not coincidentally by the conservative internationalists. The bearer of a valued political name, well liked, FDR had never been taken too seriously by many who knew him casually in the Wilson years. During his governorship he had avoided taking Tammany head on. Wherever Democrats gathered and in their correspondence in the winter of 1931–1932, an undercurrent of doubt surfaced. A consensus seemed to be shaping to the effect that the Hyde Park squire was too intellectually shallow, a "boy scout," as Bernard Baruch claimed or, as George Creel put it, "a gay, volatile Prince Charming," who was not up to the demands of a depression presidency.[1] Most devastating were the widely read and respected columns of Walter Lippmann which offered a view best summarized as the "squire thesis" and an alternative candidate whose profile more nearly fitted the predilections of the conservative internationalists.

The Lippmann indictment extended over a period of months, culminating in open endorsement of Newton D. Baker as the party's best choice for the presidency. It contained several basic elements. The pundit insisted on Roosevelt's artifice as a politician, an argument not lacking in merit, since he was gifted in the art of politics. "Sooner or later," he proposed perhaps wishfully, "some of Governor Roosevelt's supporters are going to feel badly let down. For it is impossible that he can continue to be such different things to such different men." The squire, the columnist intoned, had mastered the art of carrying water on both shoulders. "Every newspaperman knows the whole bag of tricks by heart. He knows too that the practical politician supplements these two-faced platitudes by what are called private assurances, in which he tells his different supporters what he knows they would like to hear. Then, when they read the balanced antithesis each believes the half that he has been reassured about privately and dismisses the rest as not significant."

The second part of the Lippmann analysis bore down on a presumed lack of character and determination. Roosevelt was characterized as highly impressionable, lacking a firm grasp of public affairs or any clear convictions. Then, the famous indictment: "Franklin D. Roosevelt is an amiable man with many philanthropic impulses, but he is not the dangerous enemy of anything." And, finally, the contention that the squire's intellectual capacities were so limited as to disqualify him for the presidency. "Franklin D. Roosevelt is no crusader. He is no tribune of the people. He is no enemy of entrenched privilege. He is a pleasant man who, without any important qualifications for the office, would very much like to be President." [2]

The tendency to cast Roosevelt in a superficial mold, a Democratic Harding as it were, seemed ended in the Age of Roosevelt and in the early stages of analysis by historians. Whether regarded as a liberal innovator by his admirers or as a menace to free institutions by conservative critics, few claimed that he offered less than dynamic leadership and substantial alteration of American life in the political and economic spheres, later in his diplomacy. Among liberals debate focused usually on the question of the "first" New Deal's liberalism versus the "second" New Deal's partial reversion to conservative principles or the reverse.

Yet, increasingly, in recent years, a younger generation of historians has exhumed the "squire thesis," depicting Roosevelt as ambivalent and vague in his economic choices and understanding. The opinion is offered that he was at times a captive of his academic advisers, at times capricious as he played them off against one another as opposed to serious inquiry into their viewpoints, always superficial in his utterances and perception of the basics. This reversion to the Lippmann thesis needs to be tested in the context of Roosevelt's response to the challenge of the depression.[3]

THE OPENING SALVO of the 1932 campaign for the Democratic nomination was a simplistic statement by William Randolph Hearst in a radio broadcast on New Year's Day. The lord of San Simeon, with a finger on the pulse of middle America, insisted on no entangling American commitments in Europe's affairs. The nomination of Woodrow Wilson in 1912, he declared a mistake. Wilson proved an "unstable thinker and unreliable performer" who had led the Democratic party to a catastrophe because of his advocacy of U.S. membership in the League of Nations and the World Court. Following Wilson's presidency, the party had gone down to three disastrous defeats, led by candidates who supported the League. Hearst rejected Franklin D. Roosevelt, Newton D. Baker, Albert C. Ritchie, and Alfred E. Smith as internationalists, like Hoover, fatuous followers of Wilson's "visionary policies of intermeddling in Europe's conflicts and complications." The newspaper czar and cattle rancher endorsed instead John Nance Garner of Texas, Speaker of the House of Representatives, as a worthy successor to

Speaker Champ Clark of Missouri, Hearst's choice over Wilson in 1912.[4] Hearst by no means confined himself to the League and the World Court. He also damned internationalists in general and the international bankers in particular. It was a clarion call from America west of the Alleghenies against Wall Street's economic and political connections with Europe.

The initial response was made by Newton D. Baker. The principal obstacle to his nomination in 1932, even more than his advocacy of the open shop in the twenties and his association with the power interests, was his identification with the League of Nations. Every prominent Democrat of that period recalled vividly his brilliantly moving address advocating League membership before the 1924 Democratic Convention, which seemed bent upon equivocation. The platform committee's majority report dodged the issue, yet wanted to avoid offense to the party's Wilsonian wing by advocacy of a national referendum on the subject. Wilson's former Secretary of War, speaking from rough notes, delivered an attack worthy of Bryan's "Cross of Gold" speech.

Baker swore an obligation to the dead American soldiers, whom he had sent to the battlefields in Europe. It was an emotional statement, for after all Baker was a pacifist recruited by Wilson to service. "In season and out, by day and by night," he swore to Wilson and America's dead soldiers, "in church, in political meeting, in the marketplace," he would "lift up his voice always and ever until their sacrifices are perfected." Wilson looked down on him, admonishing him "Save mankind! Do America's duty!" To no avail, for the Democratic party no longer regarded Wilson as an asset and wanted to avoid the Versailles agreements as one would the plague.

Baker, a man of modest physical stature, was regarded highly by his contemporaries as possessing courage and integrity, and deservedly so. He continued his pursuit of Wilson's ideals in the twenties, despite the temper of the times, through personal addresses, the League of Nations Association, and the Woodrow Wilson Foundation. It can be argued, for he became one of Wilson's few confidants in the period of his service as Secretary of War, that Baker was Wilson's heir apparent.[5] As late as November 18, 1931, Baker urged on New York attorney Frederic R. Coudert even greater activism by League supporters. But in January 1932, following the Hearst broadside, he compromised his position after weeks of what must have been an agonizing reassessment of the situation.[6]

The shift on the League issue reflected the dictates of political availability. As his backers in the Smith camp explained, they did not insist upon Baker's abandonment of his fundamental beliefs as an internationalist, only his pro-League militancy. Opposition to U.S. membership was so strong in 1932 as to make the question politically untenable. The issue needed to be put off for a few years. Baker's principal adviser, Ralph Hayes, concurred.

Baker modified his stand on the League of Nations as he boarded ship for a Mexican vacation on January 26, 1932, in a perfect political straddle. The imperious Belle Moskowitz expressed approbation, and the Smith forces could now proceed with the basic strategy agreed upon in 1931. Smith threw his hat into the ring on February 8, 1932, in an effort to garner the delegates of the urban-industrial states of the Northeast and the conservative Ohioan would serve as the coalition's dark horse.[7]

When asked by newspapermen whether the question of League membership would come before the Democratic convention again in 1932, Baker replied: "I am not in favor of a plank in the Democratic national platform urging our joining the League. I think it would be a great mistake to make a partisan issue of the matter." He believed in the inevitability of U.S. entry, but only after the majority of the American people "have had a chance to see the League in action, and to study its action enough to be fully satisfied as to the wisdom of such a course."

Although unwilling to make any further statements on the question, privately Baker maintained his integrity with the old Wilsonian internationalists. The essence of the matter, he explained to his old friend, former Supreme Court Justice John H. Clarke, came down to Roosevelt's inability to provide leadership in international affairs. The League, he argued, was not a practical political question. "We ought to cooperate with the League," he explained, for "Europe is a powder magazine, and the consequences of another war over there would be indescribable." Immediate entrance, however, was a practical impossibility. Only when the issue became a nonpartisan one could the Democratic party, as the normal minority party, afford the luxury of League of Nations endorsement.[8]

Concentration on the question of League membership, Baker urged upon disappointed admirers was to lose perspective, and fundamentally he was correct. He remained an internationalist and he maintained an internationalist approach toward the problems of Europe, political and financial, and on the Manchurian question as well.

> As I see it [Baker wrote Byron R. Newton, an intimate of Wilson's, in the 1932 campaign] the policies of the Republican party from 1921 until now have aimed at political and economic isolation in a world in which such isolation is almost impossible and full of peril where possible. It does not seem to me that any real progress forward can be made until an entirely different theory of our country's relations to the rest of the world is adopted. This theory I do not believe the Republican party can adopt. Its commitments to the opposite philosophy are so deep that any departure from it would be incredibly difficult. The Democratic party, on the other hand, has at least a tradition of another kind, and while it is true that a good many of our so-called Democrats in the House and Senate have not behaved with any conscious adherence to the great tradition, many of them have.[9]

The genuine issue of the early thirties was not League membership, which a majority of Americans either rejected or cared little about, but rather the internationalist approach toward the depression as opposed to stress by reformers on domestic priorities. Baker's appraisal of the course that should be pursued harmonized with the views of Herbert Hoover, Cordell Hull, Russell Leffingwell of J. P. Morgan & Co., Henry Stimson, Herbert Feis, and Norman Davis. The internationalist group had as its ends an enduring peace and improvement of economic conditions through international cooperation. Whether the stress lay in Hoover's aspirations for disarmament with its lessening of tensions and concomitant budgetary reductions, in the President's willingness to cooperate with Britain's Prime Minister MacDonald in setting in motion the machinery for the World Monetary and Economic Conference, or Hull's advocacy of reciprocal tariff agreements, or the international bankers' desire to shed the millstone of Allied debts and German reparations, the approach and aims remained the same: solution of worldwide economic problems and diplomatic tensions through international arrangements arrived at with U.S. participation. Little heed was accorded to domestic reform or to the necessity for direct intervention in the economy. Conflict arose when the realization emerged that domestic priorities, meaning reform and recovery, could not be secured without temporary insulation from the world marketplace.[10]

The press correctly interpreted the Baker statement on the League as an avowal of candidacy. Mark Sullivan's observation was in fact precisely accurate, reflecting his own intimacy with both Hayes and Baker. The League statement, he wrote "is generally interpreted as meaning that he is willing to be drafted. . . . He will take it if it is thrust upon him, but he will not seek it." [11] The ball was now in Roosevelt's court. Baker could now wait in the wings for the expected blunders.

Roosevelt's concern, on the heels of the Ohioan's January 26 statement, was expressed to Robert Woolley, his principal contact with the old Wilsonians. "Let me know," the governor pressed, "what people in Washington say about Newton Baker coming out against our entry into the League. He has, of course, said the right thing, but I wonder if a lot of people will not regard it as going back on his previous declarations." Woolley, with customary condor, hardly offered reassurance. After conferring with several of Baker's supporters and with the Secretary of the League of Nations Association, Woolley concluded that Baker's statement on the League had their endorsement and that his political position had been strengthened. Again Woolley warned Roosevelt: "Let us not hold this Baker movement cheap." He stressed the probability that Smith did not regard seriously his own chances for the nomination, as well as the widely held conviction "that he can prevent your nomination." [12]

AT ALBANY, in a speech before the New York State Grange on February 2, 1932, Roosevelt attempted to achieve four major goals: to tell Hull that he was an internationalist, to convince Hearst that he was a nationalist, to head off Baker's candidacy and the Smith–Baker coalition, and to give the impression that he had a viable farm program, capable of raising domestic farm prices. Howe and House, authors of the speech, couldn't pull it off. The Grange address did not successfully enunciate a practical foreign policy or a workable agricultural program. This was its principal intellectual failure.

In his exchange with Baker, Roosevelt shared all of the disadvantages and none of the advantages of a front-runner. Whereas Baker genuinely would serve as the party's nominee only if drafted, primarily because of the heart attack he had suffered four years earlier, Roosevelt desperately needed a statement which could hold together the motley assortment of troops he required for a two-thirds vote. He needed to retain the support of the internationalists who may not have commanded a large delegate strength, but who were a powerful force in the party. He wanted to shed his own image as a League advocate, inherited from the 1920 presidential campaign. Yet, at the same time he needed to enlist the nationalists such as Hearst, Senators Burton K. Wheeler and C. C. Dill, and eventually even Republican Hiram Johnson of California.

The attempt at Albany to frame a statement satisfactory to both the internationalists and the nationalists, to cut the wind from Baker's sails, and at the same time to propose a cure for the agricultural depression did not merit the colorful and charitable metaphor that Roosevelt succeeded in wafering an anti-League statement "between two more palatable internationalist themes." [13] Fundamentally a nationalist statement, chock-full of dubious economic propositions, it can be viewed as a portent of his two bombshell messages sent to the London Economic Conference eighteen months later. Hiram Johnson felt vindicated, especially when Roosevelt repeated the performance some weeks later for his benefit. [14] There was no wafer for the internationalists and they choked on the diet.

The initial portion of the Albany address, intended for the farmers and the Hulls of the party, urged the restoration of American agriculture through barter and reciprocal trade agreements. [15] The nations of Europe, Latin America, and Asia, Roosevelt explained, refrained from making purchases here of commodities and manufactures for the lack of currency and gold. High tariffs, especially Smoot-Hawley, exacerbated the situation. The analysis was an accurate one. But there was little likelihood that the major importers of our agricultural commodities could absorb our surplus through barter agreements. Great Britain and the Commonwealth, our largest customers, had already set in motion an imperial preference system favoring Canada's and Australia's huge agricultural output. Continental European nations were bent on autarchy, and the nations of Latin America and the Far East lacked the gold or hard currencies to purchase our farm goods.

Barter might have made a small dent in our huge agricultural surplus. But the problem could not be resolved in this fashion in 1932. American labor and industry could hardly be expected to watch idly a sharp rise in importations of European manufactures. The Congress historically had been the arena of protectionist pressures and surely could not move toward freer trade in 1932. The handwriting was on the wall as early as 1930 when congressional Democrats, despite a low tariff tradition, mustered only perfunctory opposition to Smoot-Hawley. [16]

Firm insistence on repayment of the debts owed by our wartime Allies in the closing portion of the Grange speech, in any event, closed the door to the very sort of quid pro quo arrangements suggested in the initial portion of the address. France and Great Britain believed they were in no position financially to absorb our surplus. Yet, to our major debtors, Roosevelt admonished that the war debts remained national debts of honor, which no respectable nation could cancel or repudiate. Roosevelt danced to Hearst's tune as he delivered a statement written by Colonel House:

> Europe owes us. We do not owe her. Therefore we should call a meeting of our debtors here and not in Europe and demand an understanding. If it were considered advisable in the present condition of world finance to postpone the payments of debts for a while, we should nevertheless insist upon an accord as to when payments should begin and in what amount.

Roosevelt's declaration on the League came across as unequivocally nationalist as the debts statement. The League of Nations, he contended, scarcely resembled the organization contemplated by Woodrow Wilson. Rather it had become "a mere meeting place for the political discussions of strictly European political national difficulties. In these the United States should have no part."

> The fact remains that we did not join the League. The League has not developed through these years along the course contemplated by its founder, nor have the principal members shown a disposition to divert the huge sums spent on armament into the channels of legitimate trade, balanced budgets and payment of obligations. American participation in the League would not serve the highest purpose of the prevention of war and a settlement of international difficulties in accordance with fundamental ideals. Because of these facts, therefore, I do not favor American participation.

The statement was neither accurate, nor economically sophisticated, nor politically productive. We were indeed considerably involved in League agencies and agreements and unofficially the United States had representation at Geneva. The speech yielded no farm program worthy of serious discussion. And William Randolph Hearst turned to John Nance Garner as his choice. Yet, it proved significant in two respects. It forecast FDR's willingness to abandon his Wilsonian instincts if driven by economic necessity or political expediency. And the brouhaha raised by the old Wilsonians in the party, who sensed the nominee's willingness to cater to the nationalist trend of the times, dictated a new arrangement at Albany. The Howe–House team would not do in the contemporary climate. Satisfactory at best as a political team, they were inept at coping with the great depression. Howe's tendency to have Franklin appear to be all things to all men, to walk a tightrope to Chicago, no longer sufficed.

Most important, the Grange speech represented a perceptible shift from Roosevelt's traditional image as a Wilsonian. Nearly a dozen years earlier, in the 1920 campaign, it needs to be recalled, he had championed Wilson's League of Nations when he campaigned with newspaper publisher James Cox on the Democratic ticket. Wisely or not, Cox and Roosevelt allowed the League of Nations to become the dominating theme in their effort. Following the defeat by Harding and Coolidge, Roosevelt remained committed to League membership, but accepted the conditions of the reservationists who would accede to U.S. membership only if we were not bound by League actions. This is illustrated with Roosevelt's proposal made in 1923 for a Society of Nations along reservationist lines. On debts and reparations, however, Roosevelt sided with those nationalists who opposed reduction.[17]

Roosevelt as active politician recovered from his bout with polio, had no penchant for lost causes. The Hyde Park squire knew when to equivocate, lacking the intellectual's gift for consistency and political suicide. By 1928, he revealed a shift on the issue of American involvement in world organizations. In an important piece written for the journal *Foreign Affairs* (Ogden Mills presented the Republican side), entitled "Our Foreign Policy: A Democratic View," Roosevelt retreated on the question of League membership and hedged on the debts with a metaphor. The article had an internationalist flavor, urging as it did sympathetic approval of the League of Nations and "definite official help." But the majority of Americans declined to join the League or the World Court earlier and were still opposed. We could cooperate with the League without entering into European politics, but agitation of the question of our membership was pointless.

"So too with the World Court," Roosevelt continued, whatever that meant. On the advice of Norman Davis, a Democratic diplomat in the service of Republican presidents in the twenties, he took a more lenient position on repayment of the war debts than he had earlier or would later. It assumed the form of a metaphor. "We wanted to eat our cake and have it, too," he observed, by demanding repayment while raising our tariffs to exorbitant and discriminatory levels. High tariffs, he analyzed correctly, only served to make it doubly difficult to repay the debts. But what the Democrats should do about tariffs, or the debts, or the World Court remained not clear.[18]

Domestic requirements were foremost in his mind, not Wilsonian internationalist aspirations, at least in 1932 and during the early years of his presidency. This was especially true in the depression years when his economic diplomacy reflected the nation's fundamental requirement for recovery. Yet, he always kept a door open to the internationalist wing of the party. Particularly important was his association since Wilson's days with Norman Davis and, beginning with his presidential campaign, a growing contact with Cordell Hull. Frustrating as it may have been to the Brains Trust, Roosevelt kept his options open.

Norman Davis' memoranda, which constituted the background Roosevelt required for his article, initiated a line of argument, internationalist in persuasion, which he pursued relentlessly in the pre-election period and in the presidential years prior to our involvement in World War II. In the shaping of the New Deal, then in its early years, Roosevelt pursued a course marked by intranationalism (the accordance of priority to domestic recovery) and an independent role for the United States in world affairs.[19] It is a tribute to sheer persistence that Davis served Hoover in 1932, when his views were abandoned, and later Roosevelt when he and Hull would frequently find that the rug had been pulled out from under them.

When the depression engulfed the United States and then Western Europe, Davis urged freer trade through tariff reductions as the surest cure. The world, he wrote Roosevelt following the resounding gubernatorial victory of 1930, when the New Yorker began to look more and more like the party's next presidential nominee, was a single economic unit. Yet, separate political units "have increased and have adopted fiscal [and tariff] policies attempting to make separate economic units, which it is impossible to do, and by strangling world trade they have brought distress upon themselves." [20]

Davis' convictions echoed those of one of the Senate's most powerful and outspoken Southern Democrats, Cordell Hull of Tennessee. For Hull the quintessential issue of his time was reduction of tariff barriers as a guarantee of world peace and prosperity. He attributed the decline in farm income and raw materials prices, the high unemployment and the maladjustment of credit, in short the economic collapse of 1929–1932, to the unprecedented high tariffs of the 1920s, with Smoot-Hawley as the capstone. Because of John J. Raskob's high-tariff convictions Hull fought the party's National Chairman with the tenacity of a religious crusader. He wanted, he stated in a press release, "a return to first principles—a spiritual change." And he damned those who preached the doctrines of "industrialism," "economic nationalism," "economic imperialism," and "economic self-determination." Smoot-Hawley had induced an international rush to self-containment, to "tariffs mountains high" and to the scourge of "rabid, selfish, and blind nationalism." [21]

Norman Davis and Cordell Hull were part of an internationalist group, unaffiliated except in their common condemnation of economic nationalism and their mutual fear of renewed warfare. Motivation, stress on particular issues, party affiliation, and general political philosophy varied, but in common they viewed the huge surpluses and unemployment, the depressed agriculture and industry, the banking deterioration, the credit collapse—in general the economic stagnation of the depression—as rooted in an excess of nationalism. Russell Leffingwell, a Democrat and a J. P. Morgan

& Co. partner, like Hull endorsed tariff reduction and elimination of export subsidies. But in Leffingwell's spectrum of affairs, international banking, the debts and indemnities, a legacy of World War I, most damaged prospects for international recovery. "I agree with you fully," Leffingwell wrote Hull, "that tariffs, exchange controls, quotas and embargoes must be lowered. . . . [But] war debts . . . forced the rest of the world to erect these trade barriers." [22]

Franklin D. Roosevelt gave Cordell Hull every reason to believe, prior to the Albany address, that he concurred with the internationalists' views on the necessity for lower tariffs and cooperation with other nations. Yet, despite Louis Howe's blandishments and their joining of forces in fighting Raskob's efforts to saddle the party with his wet, high tariff stand, the Senator from Tennessee scrupulously avoided open endorsement of Roosevelt as nominee as the year 1932 opened. The reason was simple enough. In the fight Hull waged with Raskob, he depended less on Howe and Roosevelt than their biographers later inferred, for they had little power in the party structure. (Hull relied principally, he recalled, on Virginia's Harry Byrd, Senator John S. Cohen of Georgia, Senator Claude Swanson of Virginia, and the powerful Senator Joseph T. Robinson of Arkansas.) When 1932 opened, Hull could afford to reserve judgment on a candidate. [23]

Was Roosevelt, in fact, a nationalist or an internationalist? Hull's reluctance was more than matched by Hearst's impatience. In an open letter to E. D. Coblentz, editor of the *New York American,* Hearst demanded to know the answer. Farley's private assurances would not do. "If Mr. Roosevelt has any statement to make about his not now being an internationalist," Hearst snorted, "he should make it to the public publicly and not to me privately." He reminded the governor of his numerous public utterances "that he *was* an internationalist and *was* in favor of our country joining the League of Nations, even at the sacrifice of some portion of our nation's sovereignty. . . . He [Roosevelt] should make his declaration publicly that he has changed his mind and that he is *now* in favor of keeping the national independence, which our forefathers won for us; that he is *now* in favor of *not* joining the League, or the League Court." [24]

There is no evidence to support the view that Hearst was mollified by the Albany statement. He remained firm in his endorsement of Garner through the pre-Convention months and did not engineer the switch by the Garner forces to Roosevelt during the crucial fourth ballot. In other words, the Grange speech proved worthless as a humbling before the lord of San Simeon. It did forecast Roosevelt's willingness to move toward a nationalist economic diplomacy, and correctly in these terms the old Wilsonians condemned it and began a serious consideration of Baker's candidacy.

Some of the rage of the old Wilsonians was funneled through House, who probably hastily added a note on the speech draft denying a decisive role in formulating its content.[25] And privately, with Hull providing the leadership, others of the internationalist group initiated discussion of Baker as an alternative.[26] "If F.R. flinches on the World Court he is through," House wrote Robert Woolley. In more guarded terms the Colonel delivered a veiled threat to Farley on behalf of the internationalists. Roosevelt's Albany speech had created a panic among Wilson's followers. "Many of them have written, telephoned, and told me in person that if he takes the same position on the World Court that they cannot support him. This comes from some of his warmest and most influential friends." [27]

Woolley, never hesitant in his relations with Roosevelt, waited ten days for his temper to cool, then wrote the governor that his disavowal of the League had sickened him, following as it did so closely on the heels of Hearst's open letter to the editor of the *New York American*. He had conferred with other Roosevelt supporters, including Hull, Daniel Roper, Huston Thompson, and W. D. Jamieson.

> We are all still ardent worshippers at the Shrine of Woodrow Wilson. We hold the League of Nations to be a lofty concept. We be-

lieve it is today, in all of its essential features, as Woodrow Wilson
founded it and that it is carrying on. We hold that for falling short of
accomplishing its high purpose America is tragically to blame. We
believe it to be to the best interests of the League of Nations not to
inject it into partisan politics again, especially in the approaching
presidential campaign. We had cherished the belief, remembering
your splendid advocacy of the League as late as 1928, that you vi-
sioned its destiny and felt toward it as we did. But you saw fit, following close upon a public warning from Hearst, to hold it up to ridicule. You wrought a mighty wreck in the hearts of millions of men
and women to whom the League of Nations is a holy thing.

Woolley perceived Roosevelt's statement on the tariff as a meaningless generality. If he took the same position on the World Court
as he had on the League, Roosevelt would risk repudiation by the
old Wilsonians. "God knows it is our desire to continue to support
you to the end that the Democratic party may again return to
power in the nation. Will you give us the chance?" [28]

The governor's reply assured Woolley of his loyalty to the ideals
of Woodrow Wilson, but argued the necessity for finding new
means of attaining them. "Ideals do not change, but methods do
change with every generation and world circumstance. . . . Here
is the difference between me and some of my faint-hearted friends.
I am looking for the best modern vehicle to reach the goal of an
ideal while they insist on a vehicle which was brand new and in
good running order twelve years ago. Think this over! And for
heaven's sake have a little faith!" A careful reading of Roosevelt's
letter to Woolley reveals that despite his desire to appease the internationalists his position on the League would not change. The
point was made clear later that year when William E. Dodd was
asked not to infer that Roosevelt "feels one way and speaks another" on the League of Nations. "I hope that in your articles,"
Daniel C. Roper advised after consultation with Howe, "you may
be able to avoid this impression." [29]

Feelings ran strong among the followers of Wilson. Mary W.
(Mollie) Dewson, who headed the Democratic Party's Women's
Division, reported to Louis Howe that deep depression followed

the governor's stand on the League. Josephus Daniels complained to Hull not only of Roosevelt's League stand but of his subsequent speech at Buffalo which contained a reaffirmation of his 1930 position on repeal of Prohibition and a return of the question of regulation of alcoholic beverages to the states. "I have said nothing," Daniels confided to his son, Jonathan, "because I have hardly known which way to turn. We cannot win dry and we cannot win wet and we ought not to win by abandoning our belief that international agreements are the only road to peace. I did not like Baker's statement, though it was much wiser than Roosevelt's. We seem to be in a very disturbed situation." Thomas J. Walsh of Montana expressed the view that Roosevelt's chances for the nomination had been damaged more by his speeches on the League and Prohibition than by Smith's announcement of his candidacy.[30]

On the surface, Hull's open endorsement of Roosevelt in February and his letter to Josephus Daniels later that month affirming that support apparently ended the old Wilsonian flap about the Grange speech. Hull informed Daniels, after several gatherings at his Senate office of powerful Washington Democrats, that he felt compelled to choose between Roosevelt and the abandonment of the party's historic free trade position under the aegis of the Smith–Du Pont–Raskob coalition. The latter group, he claimed, differed from Hoover's views only on the prohibition question. Should it manage to destroy the Roosevelt candidacy, it would run roughshod over the assorted "favorite son" candidacies, write its own platform, and choose its candidate. This, Hull explained to Daniels, determined his support of Roosevelt. Control by the Smith–Raskob group of the convention, he predicted, would culminate in the dissolution of the Democratic party after 1932.[31]

One wonders why Hull did not indicate to Daniels his private willingness to consider Baker as an alternative to Roosevelt. We can guess that Daniels' open hostility to the private power interests and his displeasure, related to Hull and others, with Baker's willingness to represent them in major cases, explains Hull's reluctance to broach the matter. For there is evidence that Hull, Wool-

ley, and others of the internationalist group choked on the soothing
syrup administered by Howe and Roosevelt following the Albany
declaration of a nationalist diplomacy.

In early March 1932, Louis Brownlow, a Baker supporter, met
with various members of the old Wilsonian coalition in Washington,
among them Daniel C. Roper and Robert Woolley. Woolley
showed him the angry letter he had sent Roosevelt in mid-
February on the League and the war debts. From the conversation,
Brownlow reported to Ralph Hayes, Baker's campaign manager,
"I got the distinct feeling . . . that while they were still on
the Roosevelt bandwagon they were distinctly uncomfortable in
their seats. It seemed to me that the matter of advancing Senator
Hull for chairman of the Committee on Resolutions might be a
most useful means of keeping in contact with this important group
within the Roosevelt ranks." Brownlow gained the impression that
they, and others of their group, would be happier if the convention
resulted in the nomination of Baker. From other sources as well,
Hayes and Baker learned by April that Hull, less than a die-hard
Roosevelt supporter, would be just as comfortable with Baker as
the party's nominee.[32] Baker incidentally followed up Brownlow's
suggestion that he initiate a collaborative effort with Hull in the
drafting of the party's platform.

By late February, Roosevelt found himself confronted with the
internationalists's demand that one of their own assume the political management of his campaign. This he could not do. But he
reached the conclusion, as a result of his initial exchange with
Baker, that the Albany group had outlived its usefulness. House
and Howe were shunted aside as his principal advisers on political
tactics and meeting the issues of the depression. Roosevelt undertook personal management of his political destiny and created what
he joyfully dubbed initially his "privy council" (the backyard variety as opposed to that enjoyed by the Crown), later the Brains
Trust, for the formulation of a coherent set of policies on the economic front at home.

"Howe," House wrote Woolley in late February, "was now

steering the wheel," and to others not infrequently in the course of the campaign year he lamented his diminished access to Roosevelt's ear. Howe, in turn, complained that the governor was increasingly inclined to act on his own.[33] Was it a ploy designed to shunt aside the aging puppeteer? In part. Certainly the Howe–House collaboration ended, and from the evidence, it seems that most major tactical decisions, beginning in March 1932, were made by Roosevelt alone. The following key maneuvers are illustrative.

There is no evidence that Howe, House, or Farley were consulted in the formation of the Brains Trust and there is concrete evidence that the deliberations of the Brains Trust and the shaping of the New Deal never fell in their province. In these deliberations Howe served only as someone who had been around Roosevelt for a long time, a crochety member of the family who needed to be placated on occasion. There is no evidence, further, that in the key political decision to shift support from Jouett Shouse to Thomas J. Walsh of Montana as permanent chairman of the Democratic National Convention that anyone but Roosevelt functioned as the prime mover. His agent in this risky but vital maneuver to secure the nomination was the sophisticated but relatively little known Robert Jackson of New Hampshire. Then again, in the vital matter of the Smith–Baker coalition and the Baker candidacy, there is no evidence that Roosevelt discussed with either Farley or Howe his decision, reached following the Democratic Convention's third ballot, to consider giving his support to Newton D. Baker in order to break a developing deadlock.

IN THIS CONTEXT, the Albany Grange address and the repercussions which ensued, Samuel Rosenman's explanation of the origins of the Brains Trust seems more valid than Raymond Moley's. It was natural, Moley contended, for Roosevelt to assemble, beginning in March 1932, a group of experts on the subjects that would need to be discussed in the ensuing campaign for the presidency, since it had been the governor's custom to rely on the talents of academicians for the resolution of the state's problems.[34] But it was one thing, as Rosenman explained, to entrust the solutions of a state's technical problems such as agriculture or waterpower development, and distinctly another to trust university faculty, a notoriously impractical lot, with the formulation of ideas needed to win an election.

On a March evening in 1932 Samuel I. Rosenman, for four years the governor's legal counsel and close adviser on state problems, suggested to Roosevelt the gathering of a group of academic experts to advise on national issues. Academics talked too much on the outside, Roosevelt countered. There was silence for a time. Rosenman suspected that the governor's mind turned to pressing speech commitments on national issues. "Well," the squire decided, "we'll just have to take our chances on that." [35]

Left unstated were the inadequacies of the Howe–House team, also Rosenman's own lack of mastery of the complexities of the depression and his expectation of securing an appointment to the New York State Supreme Court. Thus it was that Franklin D. Roosevelt turned to Raymond Moley who, with a group from Columbia University, shaped in 1932 the broad economic outline of the modern era.

6

The Brains Trust 1:
Moley and Politics

To meet this danger of radicalism by reaction is to invite disaster. Reaction is no barrier to the radical.

—RAYMOND MOLEY *

THE NEW DEAL emerged as the creation of the Brains Trust, shaped in 1932 by Raymond Moley, Rexford G. Tugwell, and Adolf A. Berle Jr., in collaboration with Franklin D. Roosevelt. Its domestic policies and early diplomacy took form between March 1932, when Raymond Moley replaced Edward M. House as Roosevelt's major adviser, and March 1933, when Roosevelt delivered his first inaugural address. During the course of that twelve-month period, despite the host of personalities in the Roosevelt political and intellectual entourage, the Roosevelt–Moley relationship proved decisive for the nation's future.

There were no two New Deals, distinct periods of domestic reform, sharply demarcated in intellectual leadership and economic approach, as suggested by Arthur Schlesinger Jr. in *The Age of Roosevelt*. The belief that there was a "first" and a "second" New Deal, that a sharp shift took place in the domestic policies of the Roosevelt administration, rests on the assumption that the idea of an organic economy conceived of by the original Brains Trust at Columbia University, and especially by Rexford Guy Tugwell, was

* Memorandum, May 19, 1932, Moley Papers.

superseded in the mid-1930s by the economic ideas of the "Happy Hot Dog" school, the Harvard Law School protégés of Brandeis and Frankfurter. Schlesinger had in mind especially Thomas G. Corcoran and Benjamin Cohen, who opposed the notion of acceptance and regulation of the huge corporate and financial aggregates. "By 1935," Schlesinger points out, "Moley, Johnson, Richberg, and Berle had left Washington. Tugwell remained, but he was shunted off to a siding; in 1937 he left too." The departure of the original Brains Trust from the charmed circle suggested to Schlesinger the abandonment of the partnership thesis, of "the original and probing ideas of Berle, Means, and Tugwell," and the substitution of the "free-market clichés of Brandeis and Frankfurter."

Schlesinger assumed that this change in advisers meant a deep and profound shift in direction, since the laws drafted by the original Columbia group were demolished by the Supreme Court "because of loose draftmanship and emotional advocacy. The laws drawn by the Second New Deal were masterpieces of the lawyer's art; and they survived." The main thrust of the "first" New Deal, which accepted the concentration of economic power as a main trend of American history and sought to balance it with central planning, was, according to Schlesinger, an attempt "to reshape American institutions according to the philosophy of an organic economy and a coordinated society." The Frankfurter–Brandeis school, on the other hand, attempted the restoration of a "competitive society within the framework of strict social ground rules."

No brief summation can do the two New Deals hypothesis sufficient justice, for it has played a major role in the literature of the Age of Roosevelt from the very outset. It relies on the Supreme Court's rejection of some of the key legislation of the "first" New Deal, on Roosevelt's subsequent struggle with the Court in his effort to avoid judicial strangulation of social and economic change, on the shifting political alignments of 1936, and on the presumed threat from the "Left" represented by Huey Long, Dr. Francis E. Townsend, and Father Charles E. Coughlin. Also there developed a growing acceptance of the idea of governmental spending as a means of securing economic survival.[1] Suffice it to say that the two New Deals thesis had been suggested by Raymond Moley in 1939 in his memoir, *After Seven Years*, as an explanation of his departure from the Roosevelt circle (Moley stressed the shift to a more urban, class-oriented political appeal and to welfare legislation), and then it appeared in Basil Rauch's *The History of the New Deal*, published in 1944, before the papers of Franklin D. Roosevelt were opened to scholarly investigation. Schlesinger's seemingly indefatigable research and brilliant, articulate, almost captivating style, gave this hypothesis its highest scholarly and literary expression. The massive legislative accomplishment of the Roosevelt administration had finally, it appeared, surrendered to intelligibility.

At issue, Otis L. Graham observed in a summary article on the New Deal historiography, was whether Basil Rauch concluded correctly that the "second" New Deal represented a progressive shift leftward or whether Schlesinger validated his view that the neo-Brandeisians had fostered a retreat to nineteenth-century virtues. Was the "first" New Deal of Moley, Berle, and Tugwell truly progressive in its acceptance of business-government partnership and centralization, as they proposed and as Richard Hofstadter agreed, or conservative because of its rapprochement with the business community, as Basil Rauch suggested? Graham, it seems, never thought to challenge the existence of "separate New Deals" and "their distinct and in many ways irreconcilable answers to the crisis of the Thirties." "The wind," he simply concluded, seemed to be blowing "against the Second New Deal," an echo of the Schlesinger view.

Although the two New Deals thesis does not seem to structure the most widely regarded single-volume treatment of the period, William E. Leuchtenburg's *Franklin D. Roosevelt and the New Deal*, it offered only an equivocal challenge. At one point Leuchtenburg observed that both the planners and Brandeisians offered useful insights into the dilemmas of the 1930s and that the two schools exaggerated the extent of the 1935–36 drift. Then, however, Leuchtenburg concluded with Schlesinger that the Brandeisians chafed in the Hundred Days while the advocates of NRA dominated the Washington scene. With Brandeis sitting in judgment, the Supreme Court wielded the death blow. Roosevelt turned to Frankfurter who "insisted that the attempt at business-government cooperation had failed, and urged Roosevelt to declare war on business. Once the President understood that business was the enemy, he would be free to undertake the Brandeisian program to cut the giants down to size: by dwarfing the power of holding companies, by launching anti-trust suits, and by taxing large corporations more stiffly than small business."

The contents of the recently opened papers of Moley and Frankfurter, and Frankfurter's recollection that the Schlesinger hypothesis was faulty, dictate a reexamination of the approach, perhaps its modification, even its abandonment. Much factual data supports the division of the early years of the New Deal into two distinctive periods, but it is, conceivably, an oversimplification of issues and an exaggeration of personality differences, perhaps to the point of melodrama. Schlesinger's greatest gift is a felicitous style; he has produced deeply etched portraits which no historian has been able to emulate. *The Age of Roosevelt* is superb literature; but is it great history? For despite Brandeis' fulminations on the "curse of bigness," which can be amply documented, Moley was a frequent visitor in the period of the so-called "first" New Deal and there is no evidence in the Frankfurter–Brandeis–Moley correspondence in the period 1932–35 of the sort of ideological conflict one would have anticipated. On the contrary, they emerge as collaborators rather than as antagonists. The essential difference between Moley and Frankfurter, admittedly of considerable importance, but one which engendered no bitterness in their collaboration, was in their approach toward foreign policy as Moley shifted late in 1932 to an extremely nationalist position.

The most trenchant challenge to the prevailing view of distinct time periods dividing the domestic New Deal has been offered, thus far, by one of the principals, Felix Frankfurter. At a White

House visit in 1963 with Arthur Schlesinger Jr. and President John F. Kennedy, shortly before the latter's death, Frankfurter was strangely evasive when the chitchat got around to *The Age of Roosevelt*, most especially the third volume on *The Politics of Upheaval*. Evasiveness, as Schlesinger knew, was scarcely a Frankfurter attribute. In short order, Frankfurter explained himself in a letter to the historian:

> After leaving the White House on Monday . . . I reflected on the inadequacies of the answer I made to his [President Kennedy's] question as to why I disagreed with your view on the Roosevelt administration in the 30's, and more particularly that there were two New Deals. I did not tell him my basic reason for disagreement. It is that from your several references to your private interviews with Thomas G. Corcoran I gathered they had a considerable influence on the interpretation you gave in your book about the two New Deals, for Tommy is a very persuasive raconteur. . . .
>
> There are a few more things to be said. I must reject your assumption that there was a real clash of views between Moley–Tugwell and F. F.–Brandeis. This assumes that the respective parties had coherent and systematic views on some of the problems that are involved in Roosevelt's policies.
>
> You are also wrong in assuming that I saw completely eye to eye with Brandeis on socio-economic matters, any more than it is true that I was an echo of his outlook on the law, particularly constitutional law.[2]

The shape of the New Deal was determined in the year extending from March 1932 to March 1933, with profound implications for U.S. diplomacy. It was in the Hundred Days, under Moley's guidance, and in the legislative surge of 1935, with his collaboration, that much of the New Deal was legislated. Even the Wagner Act (1935), though unsupported by the administration as it wended its way through the Congress, the Social Security Act (1935), and the Fair Labor Standards Act (1937) fall well within the conceptual frame developed by the Brains Trust in 1932. The demise of the Brains Trust as a functioning mechanism in March 1933 becomes quite comprehensible in this light. Intellectually, it had spent itself in Roosevelt's cause. Subsequently Moley negotiated principally with legislators, rather than Berle and Tugwell, for congressional support was needed to enact into law the broad concepts involved.

The critical point is that both Roosevelt and Moley are central to an understanding of the New Deal. Moley proposed in 1932 that the Democratic party shift its base to the lower classes and its philosophic orientation to a liberal position more worthy of twentieth-century needs and problems. This constituted, in fact, the original context of the "new deal" phrase in the Moley memorandum of May 19, 1932. The memorandum limned also, based on discussions with Berle, Tugwell, and James Bonbright of Columbia, Paul Mazur of Lehman Brothers, as well as others, most of the economic innovations introduced by Roosevelt as President in the period 1933 through 1937.[3] Yet, curiously, the historians of the New Deal give Moley scant attention until his break with Roosevelt in 1936. Neither Moley, the leading architect of the New Deal other than Roosevelt, nor the Moley papers, the principal source on the shaping of the New Deal, has been given much consideration in the huge literature on the subject. This odd procedure has a history of its own.

Evaluation of Raymond Moley's role in the shaping of the New Deal has been warped by several circumstances, some of his own making and some a reflection of memoirists' and historians' attitudes toward him. He won scant popularity with many of his Washington colleagues in 1933, particularly in the State Department, when he took office as Assistant Secretary under Cordell Hull. "Cookie pushers," he dismissed them, and he regarded them as potential saboteurs, considering their internationalist orientation, of the New Deal's domestic priorities.[4] He fared badly with the memoirists who originally had little affection for him and his brusque ways and subsequently regarded him as a traitor for his abandonment and opposition to the very cause he created and nurtured. More important he gained minimal notice from the liberal consensus historians who recreated the Roosevelt era at a time

when Moley openly supported in *Newsweek* the powerful Taft–
Bricker wing of the Republican party. Remarkably neither Schlesinger nor William E. Leuchtenburg, who passed definitive judgments on the Roosevelt era, made use of the Moley papers, the
richest source on the origins of the New Deal.[5]

Moley's own later disenchantment with Roosevelt and his growing attachment to conservative business interests and the Republican party's conservative majority, added another dimension to the
New Deal's misshapen historiography. He keenly desired a more
accurate appraisal of his personal relationship with Roosevelt and of
his role at the London Economic Conference vis-à-vis Cordell
Hull, who charged him with perfidy. Yet, he also wanted, when
the time had come to set down the record, to be dissociated with
much of the New Deal's theology. Liberal—even radical in his convictions for the time—and internationalist in his views early in
1932, he stressed in his recollections mainly the conservative facets
of his contribution and a nonexistent consistency of thought. Consciously, in all likelihood, he allowed the historical void to be filled
by Rexford G. Tugwell. And historians have more than obliged.
There seemed a certain ideological purity about Tugwell, which
appealed to academicians rather than politicians, and Moley instead stressed in later years a continuity with Herbert Hoover and
Ogden L. Mills, whereas actually there occurred a sharp departure.

Several sets of needs were thus serviced: Moley's wish to explain
his break with Roosevelt in 1936 in terms other than his own shifting convictions; and Arthur Schlesinger's lament for the end of
planning in our economy, as if overhead management had really
existed in the period of the "first" New Deal. A planned economy
did not emerge in the period 1933–1935 in the normative sense of
the term. Elements of planning were introduced in delimited areas
and the economy can be appraised as organic only in so far as it is
discernible as a web of interrelated parts. It served, furthermore,
the requirements of a successor generation of more radical historians. They imagined the 1932 campaign, the 1932–1933 interreg-

num, and the Hundred Days of early 1933 as a lost moment in American history because, in the words of one of them, Barton Bernstein, "Marxism or even . . . native American radicalisms that offered structural critiques and structural solutions" might have been introduced. Yet, strangely, they never considered the proposals Moley made in 1932, nor do the revisionists trifle with any of the realities of American political life. It is as if the history of the New Deal era has become something of a shell game.[6]

There is another complicating factor in the evaluation of the Moley–Roosevelt relationship and of Moley's role in the molding of New Deal policies, much less significant today but vital a decade or two ago when the definitive treatments were written. Many an old colleague at Columbia, possibly because of personal pique, while willing to concede Moley's gift as a literary craftsman, stood equally convinced that intellectually he proved "a mediocre man who had made no mark in the academic world by original contribution to thought." While aware of these views, widely held in the academic community, given credence in *The Age of Roosevelt*, Moley never saw fit to challenge them.[7] The myth persists for, as late as 1971, at a session of the Organization of American Historians, Moley remained a conservative critic of the New Deal rather than its progenitor.[8] Moley's intellectual caliber and political viewpoint in 1932 are ultimately of major consequence to the history of that era. To the extent that his role in the shaping of the New Deal has been minimized, he remained content. But the result has been to distort the New Deal. And our understanding of it and American history, as a consequence, suffers.

There were no two New Deals. Moley was not a conservative in 1932. Roosevelt was not the vacuous fuzzy-minded squire described by Paul Conkin in his summary essay on the Hyde Park aristocrat and his era. The decision to adopt a new orientation for the Democracy toward the lower classes originated with Moley's recommendation and Roosevelt's political needs in 1932, not in 1936. Relief and public works, the concept of the social minima (including social security and unemployment insurance), a willingness to create an emergency (unbalanced) budget for purposes of relief and recovery—these and other proposals originated in the Moley–Roosevelt collaboration of 1932.

In his summary view of Roosevelt and the New Deal era, Conkin also surmised that "The main harvest of New Deal scholarship is at hand." The synthesis seemingly was arrived at. Just the contrary is true, for the New Deal historiography is fettered with an incredible mythology. The time has come to reopen the ledger, not to close it.[9]

RAYMOND MOLEY'S HOSTILITY toward the international bankers and the "fat cat" Republicans of Wall Street, and his sympathy for the little man of rural and small-town America derived from his Ohio background. His desire for regulation of large corporate and financial aggregates in the public interest and for "social justice" legislation, nourished in the Populist/Progressive tradition, shaped his thinking as a young man.

Born in Berea, Ohio, in 1886, he grew up, attended school, and then taught in the tiny community of Olmsted Falls. Following in his grandfather Hypolite Moley's Democratic footsteps, he became early in his youth a passionate admirer of William Jennings Bryan and subsequently of Cleveland's Progressive Mayor Tom L. Johnson. The Ohioan's early political convictions were set down when he was a freshman at Baldwin University, which he entered in 1902. In an explanation of "Why I Am A Democrat," he focused on his family's sympathies for the party of Jefferson and Jackson and his own admiration of Tom L. Johnson as the embodiment of the party's legacy. Mark Hanna, symbol of Republicanism in Ohio, would be tempted to work for selfish industrial interests. He preferred Johnson, "a true friend of the people," to the control of huge railroad corporations. "The principles which he upholds are such as will appeal more directly to the working classes than those opposed to them."

Tom L. Johnson's impact was deeply felt by a generation of

reform-minded Clevelanders. The immediate issue crystallized in the form of a cheaper street railway fare, the broader one a struggle against the privileges of monopoly "made possible," Johnson explained, "by the exemption from taxation of land values." Johnson's thinking had been triggered by the reformist writings of Henry George and he sought out an issue, street railway fares, that could be grasped by the common man. Johnson apprised his cause as "the first great struggle of the masses in our country against the privileged classes." In his young manhood, Moley joined the struggle.[10]

Moley became a disciple of Henry George, Johnson's hero. Decades later, Moley recalled that "In those days Cleveland was alive with Georgism, and my copy of *Progress and Poverty* is dated when I was sixteen years old." George's impact transcended the customary emphasis on his scheme for land taxation. As Moley recollected, "The subjects George considered in his many speeches and his writings touched almost all of the corrective influences which were the result of the Progressive movement. The restriction of monopoly, more democratic political machinery, municipal reform, the elimination of privilege in railroads, the regulation of public utilities, and the improvement of labor laws and working conditions— all were in one way or another accelerated by George." [11]

In 1909, while teaching at Olmsted Falls and studying law, Moley discovered that he suffered from tuberculosis, which required two years' recuperation in New Mexico and then Denver, Colorado. He utilized the time to read widely in the classics and to take some graduate courses in economics and political science at the University of Denver. Following his return to Olmsted Falls, in 1911, he shifted his professional studies from law to political science and took a master's degree at Oberlin College. There followed two years of teaching at West High School in Cleveland, the feeling that he had reached an intellectual dead end, and enrollment consequently for the Ph.D. at Columbia University in New York.

At Columbia, in 1914, the young political scientist's imagination became fired by the charismatic Charles A. Beard. The maverick scholar, Moley reminisced, proved "the most powerful influence on me so far as my education in politics and government were concerned. . . . There was a great deal of discussion in the faculty and in the public press about Beard's famous book, *An Economic Interpretation of the Constitution of the United States* [1913] and then his *Economic Origins of Jeffersonian Democracy* [1915]. Beard was a teacher of such power and magnetic personality that his students were swept along by his views. In these days it would be called progressivism, although there was a tinge of sympathy in Beard for socialism." [12] Moley had his own socialist twinges, believing for a brief time that perhaps it served as the only answer to the evils of big business and the manipulations of Wall Street in American society. He moderated his own views, he recalled in later years, "not because of its economic implications but because of its atheism." [13]

In the fall of 1916, at age thirty, the Ohioan received an appointment as instructor in political science at Western Reserve University and three years later as an associate professor at the University of Minnesota. He rejected the Minnesota appointment to serve instead as director of the Cleveland Foundation. The basis for the choice is insightful and explains his later desire to serve in Roosevelt's cause in 1932. For he rejected the role of academic theoretician and preferred whenever possible direct contact with the political mechanisms of our society. Nor did he believe in independence in politics. He preferred the role of activist and became an admirer of Woodrow Wilson's assumption of a major role in national politics following a successful career as academic analyst of those institutions that stood at the heart of American political life. In 1912, Moley wrote to newspapers in Wilson's behalf and in 1916 actively campaigned for his reelection. Moley himself had served as a village clerk at 21, superintendent of schools and then as mayor of the tiny community of Olmsted Falls. The appointment as director of the Cleveland Foundation in 1919 suited his rejection of a cloistered academic career.

The Cleveland Foundation, a marriage between the city's reform and business elements, represented the culmination of business-sponsored civic reform in the progressive era. It was the brainchild of Frederick H. Goff, a conservative attorney, once associated with the Rockefellers, who came to head the powerful, conservative Cleveland Trust Company. It served as a powerful force for civic improvement, with a majority of its membership appointed by public officials; also as the nation's first community trust, a funnel for the direction of local philanthropy into community-approved projects judged to be of substantial worth. Its real underpinning derived from the faith of that generation that remedy could be found at the local level for the community's problems through research, collection of data, analysis and application of scientific findings. Business techniques were wedded to the social sciences and directed at the problems of the city, often with seeming success. It was a paradigm of the 1920s.[14]

While the work of the Cleveland Foundation varied, sponsorship of a survey of the administration of criminal justice served as the vehicle for the next stage in Moley's career. In his capacity as director he secured the collaboration of Dean Roscoe Pound and Professor Felix Frankfurter of the Harvard Law School and the resulting Cleveland Crime Survey attracted nationwide attention. It served as a model for other cities and states for a decade. Moley's appointment to an associate professorship at Barnard College of Columbia University in 1923 afforded the opportunity to direct a series of similar city and state surveys in which he functioned as research director. Two books published at the end of the twenties summarized his views on police, prosecution, and the courts and established a national reputation in the field: *Politics and Criminal Prosecution* (1928) and *Our Criminal Courts* (1930).[15]

Moley was appointed research director of the New York State Crime Commission in 1927, at about the same time that Roosevelt arranged a position for Howe as assistant to the chairman of the National Crime Commission. The faithful Howe needed the $400 a month, for at the time Roosevelt could not afford to maintain his adviser. Neither Howe nor Roosevelt knew much about the subject other than what they read in the newspapers, but it appeared worthwhile and the former newspaperman could surely gather some statistics, issue reports, and sustain himself and his family. Howe secured Moley's assistance and in return "Louis" spoke on practical politics before Moley's classes at Barnard College.

Moley's initial contact with Roosevelt came in connection with the 1928 gubernatorial campaign. Howe summoned Moley from Chicago, where he was laying the groundwork, as research director, of the Illinois crime survey. At his campaign headquarters in the old General Motors Building Roosevelt explained that he wanted to institute some reforms in the administration of justice in New York. Would Moley write a speech on the subject? On the law's delay, the congestion in the courts, the need for prison reform? In the address, delivered in the Bronx on October 28, 1928, Roosevelt suggested, also, the establishment of a fact-finding commission to examine the causes of delay in the courts. As a quid pro quo, Moley informed Howe, he desired an appointment as one of the lay members of the commission, but because of difficulties with a recalcitrant Republican legislature, Roosevelt was unable to secure a state commission on the administration of justice until 1931.[16]

It was a trying period in Moley's career. Bored with the repetition of his work, in his early forties, he believed he had reached an academic plateau. His work of a decade in the administration of justice, while rewarding, no longer seemed adequate as an intellectual challenge. He wanted once again an active role in practical politics. Like so many academics of that time, he was shorn with the rest of the sheep in the stock market debacle, which few realized heralded what was to be a decade of depression. And he began to worry about a recurrence of tuberculosis. His physician advised loss of weight and more work, but there appeared to be no new fields to conquer.

At that time, in 1929, Samuel May, of the University of California at Berkeley, offered the Columbia professor of public law the opportunity to establish new courses in the field of his specialization in the department of Public Administration. Moley grasped at the opportunity for a change of scenery and took a semester's sabbatical leave from Columbia beginning in September 1930. Two months after his arrival at Berkeley an invitation was tendered to join an investigation of New York City's magistrates' courts and their enforcement of the criminal law. Conducted by Judge Samuel Seabury under the auspices of the Appellate Division of the New York State Supreme Court, it developed as the first of the great Seabury investigations of that era.[17]

Once active in the magistrates' investigation (Moley served also on the New York State Parole Commission and participated in the second Seabury investigation, this time of the New York District Attorney's office), Moley reminded Louis Howe of his desire to be appointed to the Commission on the Administration of Justice, authorized by the state legislature in the summer of 1931. Roosevelt obliged and Moley served as the Commission's research director. Convinced by this time that Roosevelt was destined to be the party's nominee for the presidency, Moley cherished an active role in the 1932 campaign. The opportunity soon presented itself to make his wish known directly to the governor.

In December 1931, the Columbia professor prepared a memorandum on the work of the Commission on the Administration of Justice for the governor's use in his annual message to the legislature. "I am delighted with your letter," Roosevelt replied, "and also with the memorandum and they fully justify my insistence last July that you be charged with this great task." Included was an invitation to luncheon. "I want to see you some day soon . . . any time after January 6th." At the Albany luncheon on January 8, Moley remembered, there occurred some discussion of political matters and he offered his services in the forthcoming campaign. There seemed a nodding approval. "He would be glad to call on me, he answered." [18]

As a result of the third Seabury investigation, this time of the government of the city of New York (Moley did not participate because of a growing conviction that Seabury had his own ambitions for the presidency and wanted to embarrass Roosevelt with evidence of bold corruption by Tammany), Roosevelt decided to remove Sheriff Thomas M. ("tin box") Farley. In a reversal of the normal rule of jurisprudence which placed the burden of proof on the state, Roosevelt insisted that a public official be required to account for major sources of income obtained while in office. When Farley failed to oblige to his satisfaction, Roosevelt summoned Moley, who wrote the removal statement. Almost immediately, Moley recalled, "the political activities started." [19] The Moley–Roosevelt collaboration was inaugurated.

The conflicting views of Moley and Samuel I. Rosenman on the details of the origins of the Brains Trust are of small moment to the New Deal historian. In any event they involve only pride of authorship and are easily reconciled. Their recollections—Moley's suggestion to Roosevelt of his willingness to serve in the presidential campaign and Rosenman's proposal that the governor seek academic expertise in resolving the depression crisis—dovetail with the collapse of the Howe–House collaboration in the early months of 1932. House's views proved antediluvian and Howe gaged the nation's condition essentially from the perspective of the stock market pages of his daily tabloid. Surely Roosevelt and Rosenman understood that the Albany entourage lacked the sort of expertise required for the solution of the crisis of 1932.

As in the instance of so many key decisions arrived at by Franklin D. Roosevelt, there is scant direct evidence, other than Rosenman's appraisal of the needs of the 1932 campaign and of the absence of anyone in the Albany entourage who fitted these needs, of what motivated Roosevelt to forge a political collaboration with Moley. The venture emerged with no fanfare. Certain of Moley's attributes, we may surmise, must have been appealing in the light of Roosevelt's requirements. Moley's direction of the Cleveland Foundation and of numerous inquiries into the administration of justice in the previous decade surely demonstrated an ability to harness men and ideas as well as a talent for rendering complex notions into acceptable prose. Unlike the preponderance of academics, Moley could write for public consumption. Also, in personality Moley proved sparing of words, businesslike, and practical.

Interestingly the record suggests no evidence of an awareness by Roosevelt of Moley's convictions on major issues. This sort of thing seldom troubled Roosevelt even as President. Yet, it is equally evident that the "Forgotten Man" speech, their initial major collaboration, reflected the progressive convictions of both men. The flamboyant, gossipy squire of Hyde Park and the taciturn, no-nonsense professor of public law at Columbia University, never really part of the Roosevelt social circle, launched a political and intellectual relationship which left its mark on the American experience for a generation.

THE AMBIANCE of the New Deal, suggested in April 1932, in the "Forgotten Man" address and in the speech at St. Paul, Minnesota, reflects exclusively the work of Roosevelt and Moley. Nearly a year later the first inaugural address, another Roosevelt–Moley collaboration, spelled out the conclusions they reached after à year of discussion, campaigning, and examination of the causes of the depression and the remedies they judged available. These three speeches, their most important, created the tone of the New Deal. Moley's memorandum of May 19, 1932, more specific in its consideration of political and economic alternatives and solutions, anticipated much of its future content.

In March 1932, Roosevelt received an invitation from Jouett Shouse to deliver a radio broadcast on the Lucky Strike Hour, one of a series of brief talks by Republican and Democratic politicians sponsored by the American Tobacco Company. The governor of New York was assigned the evening of April 7, and relegated the task to Moley. Their initial collaboration in the political arena drew a sensational response.[20]

The "Forgotten Man" address, liberal and humane, proclaimed

for the national government a set of responsibilities that it had not yet assumed. Roosevelt announced his ambition to elevate the lower classes from the poverty imposed by the depression. Stress was placed on the nation's rural poor, the millions of small-scale farmers who had suffered loss of income and their farms and were submerged by the agricultural depression, which for them had begun in 1921. It reflected Roosevelt's and Moley's conviction that the root cause of the Great Depression lay in the collapse of agricultural income and purchasing power which had antedated by nearly a decade the Wall Street collapse. Nearly 50 percent of the nation's population resided either on farms or in small towns dependent upon farming. Industrial workers suffered, in turn, because they "cannot sell industrial products to the farming half of the Nation. . . . No Nation can endure half bankrupt. Main Street, Broadway, the mills, the mines will close if half the buyers are broke. I cannot escape the conclusion," Roosevelt drove the point home, "that one of the essential points of a national program of restoration must be to restore purchasing power to the farming half of the country. Without this the wheels of railroads and of factories will not turn."

But the focus on the "Forgotten Man" speech simply as a pro-agrarian statement is too narrow. It had broader implications. Roosevelt thrust at Herbert Hoover's emphasis on attainment of recovery through the Reconstruction Finance Corporation as elitist, its reliance being too exclusively on business recovery and banking solvency. A trickle-down approach toward recovery seemed economically insufficient. Recovery, Roosevelt argued, needed to come as well through the nation's lower classes:

> It is said that Napoleon lost the battle of Waterloo because he forgot his infantry—he staked too much upon the more spectacular but less substantial cavalry. The present administration in Washington provides a close parallel. It has either forgotten or does not want to remember the infantry of our economic army.
>
> These unhappy times call for the building of plans that rest upon the forgotten, the unorganized but the indispensable units of eco-

nomic power, for plans like those of 1917 that build from the bottom up and not from the top down, that put their faith once more in the forgotten man at the bottom of the economic pyramid.

Roosevelt and Moley did not reject the concept of spending for urban relief and large-scale public works projects, as Alfred E. Smith charged and Moley later suggested in his recollections in more conservative years; rather they never viewed the relief/public-works approach as fundamentally curative. They preferred instead more basic remedies. "People suggest [an allusion to Smith, already an announced candidate] that a huge expenditure of public funds by the Federal Government and by State and local governments will completely solve the unemployment problem." This Roosevelt denied. Public works constituted a palliative, not a cure. "A real economic cure must go to the killing of the bacteria in the system rather than to the treatment of external symptoms."

Roosevelt promised relief to the farmer or homeowner threatened by foreclosure as another indication of a desire to build, as he put it, "from the bottom up." He laced into the Smoot-Hawley Tariff and the strangulation of world trade in an appeal to the internationalist wing of the party and to the large segment of rural America which put its hopes in dumping our surplus on the world market.[21] But the main argument of this brief radio talk, as the *New York Herald-Tribune* surmised the next day in its headline, was that it had made "aid to the masses [the] issue." Ten days later, at St. Paul, Minnesota, Roosevelt took another step away from the American past as he asserted his intention to eliminate the vicissitudes of economic life that remained the legacy of the age of laissez faire.

Liberals waxed enthusiastic as they sensed a profound change. Herman Oliphant of the Johns Hopkins Law School observed that the governor had cut through to the consciousness of the mass of popular thought in this country like a white-hot flame and he pleaded with Moley that the new spirit be maintained. The depression would pass. "The great question is whether . . . [it] will be . . . used as the excuse for tearing down the few humanitarian attitudes and measures we have so slowly and painfully built up since [Theodore] Roosevelt, and Wilson, in turn, thought of the 'forgotten man' and taught a growing circle to remember him." [22]

Moley seemed no less enthusiastic about Roosevelt and the possibilities offered by the collaboration he had so much desired. In a letter to his sister Nell he rendered a candid and fresh portrait of Roosevelt, unfettered by his later reservations about having ushered in a political behemoth. He toiled in those days as a passionate defender of Roosevelt, sneered at in Columbia's faculty gathering-spots as a pseudo-Progressive. Moley quarreled in fact with Allan Nevins, stalking out of his home as a result, and labored with difficulty in an effort to convince Adolf A. Berle Jr. to join the Roosevelt advisory group. Berle preferred the Baker candidacy. When Moley's sister queried him concerning Roosevelt's sincerity on the issue of the "Forgotten Man," he provided a detailed impression which remains as one of our finest contemporary portraits.

Roosevelt, Moley believed, would remain inured to the attacks of the country's conservative press, which regarded the speech as demagogic. In his personality, the governor could be stubborn, resourceful, and relentless in pursuit of a goal. He loved the banter and pleasantries of politics and used much of teatime for the purpose of relief, "a rite which he follows but which is quite strange to my Ohio sensibility."

> The man's energy and vitality are astonishing. I've been amazed with his interest in things. It skips and bounces through seemingly intricate subjects and maybe it is my academic training that makes me feel that no one could possibly learn much in such a hit or miss fashion. I don't find that he has read much about economic subjects. What he gets is from talking to people and when he stores away the net of conversation he never knows what part of what he has kept is what he said himself or what his visitor said. There is a lot of autointoxication of the intelligence that we shall have to watch. . . .

Moley appeared impressed—even frightened—by Roosevelt's receptivity to ideas, but on balance believed that his freedom from dogmatism constituted a virtue as opposed to Hoover's tendency to cling to the past. As for the radio address, Moley explained, Roosevelt wanted to reach the underdog and "I scraped from my memory an old phrase, 'The Forgotten Man,' which has haunted me for years." [23]

Party conservatives took a jaundiced view of the initial Roosevelt–Moley collaboration. Cordell Hull, terribly disturbed "over the radical tendency displayed in the Governor's radio talk" and fearful of what might be said at St. Paul, planned a trip to New York to head off "another Bryan campaign of 1896." Rumors circulated, also, that the powerful Times Council, the principal editorial writers of that newspaper, which until then privately favored a Roosevelt candidacy, had second thoughts because of the governor's recent radical tendencies. [24]

The most vigorous and sensational criticism of the "Forgotten Man" speech took shape as a blistering attack leveled by Alfred E. Smith on April 13, 1932, at the party's annual Jefferson Day dinner in Washington, D.C. Appropriately, most of the luminaries in attendance represented the party's self-styled Jeffersonian wing, including Newton D. Baker, Harry F. Byrd, John W. Davis, and James Cox. Flushed with anger, Smith charged Roosevelt with attempted deception and the stirring up of class against class, the poor against the rich, at a time when millions were hungry. "I protest," the Happy Warrior fumed, "against the endeavor to delude the poor people of this country to their ruin by trying to make them believe that they can get employment before the people who would ordinarily employ them are also again restored to conditions of normal prosperity. . . . I will take off my coat," he challenged, "and fight to the end any candidate who persists in any demagogic appeal to the masses of the working people of the country to destroy themselves."

The accusation of demagoguery is a fascinating one, for it is Smith's position that seems deceptive in retrospect. Presumably a spokesman for the urban masses, his support derived from wealthy reactionaries who opposed interventionism at the federal level. Smith's advocacy of a large-scale public works program of $5 billion amounted to an illusion. He had nothing radical in mind. His proposed sale of bonds in small denominations to the public to finance works projects ruled out direct federal spending. It could not be realized in the depression and subscriptions would have drained smaller banks of their cash reserves. Moreover, the issuance of such bonds, tied to self-liquidating public works, meant that by every estimate only about $1 billion could be found. No spender, Smith bitterly attacked the Democratic Chairman of the House Ways and Means Committee (Robert L. Doughton of North Carolina) for his advocacy of greater federal appropriations and his opposition to heavier taxation.[25]

The sum of Smith's views may be found in a brief statement made before a business group at the Fifth Avenue Hotel in New York City only two days earlier. "We will grow out of the business depression naturally." His position in economic questions in many respects resembled Hoover's, and echoed Bernard Baruch's famous aphorism that business, much as it had done in the 1893–1898 depression, would need to go through the wringer.[26]

The Smith–Roosevelt exchange drew national attention and revealed publicly the split between the party's conservative and liberal wings. Nothing could better illustrate the traditionalist views of the party leadership than the gamut of addresses delivered at the Jefferson Day dinner. Despite pressures by progressives and Eastern urban liberals in the Congress for passage of relief measures, the party's principal spokesmen excoriated Hoover for fiscal profligacy and offered nothing in the way of a remedial program beyond retrenchment.[27]

As Roosevelt and Moley prepared for the St. Paul address, the party's alternatives and their own clarified. They could retreat from the radical implications of the "Forgotten Man" speech or they could pursue a new set of objectives for the national government. It has become axiomatic among New Deal historians, that with the assistance of "cagey advisers and speech writers [who] usually neutralized his political liabilities," the deeper economic issues were glossed over by "moral rhetoric."[28] The conclusion that Roosevelt

marked time during the 1932 campaign and that the legislation of
the Hundred Days bore the mark of improvisation is incorrect.
There is too much evidence to the contrary to allow this to stand as
the verdict of history.

INITIALLY MOLEY planned a direct assault on Smith as a reactionary and prepared, with Roosevelt, a broad statement of the
"ten articles of my faith," an unfortunate phrase which they abandoned. Prudence dictated a compromise at St. Paul, Minnesota, on
April 18, 1932. Two factors were involved: fear of alienation of the
party's conservative and internationalist wings, and the need for
further evaluation of long-range proposals. Yet the St. Paul speech
marked the next step toward the enunciation of the New Deal program.[29]

Edward M. House, Cordell Hull, and Louis Howe, powerful
members of the Roosevelt circle, urged caution. "I am clear on one
thing," House admonished, "and that is that you should strike a
conservative note in your St. Paul speech." Otherwise the New
York governor risked defection of the old Wilsonians and the
party's business elements. House invoked visits made to him by
Gordon Auchincloss, Frank Polk, and Robert Field of New York as
well as his correspondence with Daniel Roper, Cordell Hull, and
Robert Woolley. Roosevelt's speech should strike the note that
"This is no time to drain the Treasury" and again "This is no time
to experiment with financial nostrums." Above all, House wanted
abandonment of the radio statement which he regarded as a mis-
taken commitment to the lower classes. Instead, he urged on the
candidate "My suggestion to Gov. Roosevelt for his speech at St.
Paul, April 18, 1932":

> To those who have followed my public career it is not necessary to
> assure them of the general direction of my thought and purposes.
> . . . In the future as in the past I shall devote my energies toward
> promoting the general welfare. I shall not favor the rich as such, nor

shall I favor the poor as such, for to do so would be helpful to neither.

What this country needs, what humanity in general needs is equality of opportunity for all and special privilege for none.[30]

Louis Howe was equally concerned and preached caution to Moley. "The Minnesota people are just as anxious as our Eastern friends that the Governor's speech should not be treated as radical." Democrats feared, Howe warned, the selection of a radical candidate who "could not command the support of the more mildly progressive East." Howe invoked the authority of no less a Midwestern radical spokesman than Senator Burton K. Wheeler of Montana: "He suggests an enlargement of the tariff [issue]; the avoidance of new issues . . . at this time; an explanation that in calling attention to the necessity of doing something for the foundation [the "Forgotten Man"], he did not mean to criticize any proper efforts to repair the roof."

Howe's advice could not be dismissed lightly. He had devoted most of his adult life to the single purpose of securing Roosevelt's nomination and election to the presidency. Moley was instructed to avoid mention of the La Follettes "or any of that group" and radical statements on behalf of "the little fellow." "We should not advocate a soviet plan of abolishing marshalls, but merely to keep the path of promotion of high privates always open." On the issue of public power Howe desired emphasis on private distribution "if a really fair arrangement could be made with private enterprise." [31]

For Roosevelt the choice was clear cut: reversion to the economic clichés of his Harvard and Groton training and to the conservatism of the Howe–House period of advisement, or continued exploration and exposition with Moley and now Rexford Tugwell who joined the Brains Trust of a wider and newer range of ideas on the causes and remedies of the depression. The St. Paul speech represented a clear choice, and there was nothing fuzzy in either the decision or the rhetoric. While it reflected Moley's felicity for style and attention-getting phraseology, it represented Roosevelt's determination that "I certainly tried to keep my temper and at the same time I took back nothing!" Phrased in historic terms, it represented a commitment to national economic planning. Roosevelt not only refused to eat crow on the stand he took in the "Forgotten Man" speech, he went beyond it.[32] He rejected the "class control" represented in the Hamiltonian tradition and by the Hoover administration and proposed instead the planning of our economic life by "a true concert of interests."

St. Paul marked Raymond Moley's initiation into the political nightmare of speechwriting under pressure. He had gone to Cleveland for a rest with his family only to be summoned to meet Roosevelt's train at Detroit. Apparently the governor was less than satisfied with Moley's original text.[33] Together, on the train, they labored over revised drafts. They wanted to bring together "the scattered farmers, workers, [and] businessmen into a participation in national affairs" through the mechanism of the Democratic party, "the instrument of a true concert of interests." And Moley added at the very last moment, "If that be treason make the most of it."

At the Lowry Hotel in St. Paul the work continued. Moley drafted the most memorable passage of the speech:

> I am not speaking of an economic life completely planned and regimented. I am speaking of the necessity, however, in those imperative interferences with the economic life of the Nation that there be a real community of interest, not only among the sections of this great country, but among its economic units and the various groups in these units; that there be a common participation in the work of remedial figures, planned on the basis of a shared common life, the low as well as the high. In much of our present plans there is too much disposition to mistake the part for the whole, the head for the body, the captain for the company, the general for the army. I plead not for class control but for a true concert of interests.[34]

St. Paul was the opportune locale for a statement as well on the question that liberal progressives of that generation saw as the most vital issue of their own time—prevention of the transfer of publicly owned power resources in the public domain to private ownership for development and exploitation. As Roosevelt and Moley prepared for the St. Paul address, the collapse of the Insull utilities empire made that issue topical and relevant to the occasion, for the pyramid of holding companies and its watered capital stock which guaranteed huge profits for a few had also meant steep rates on electrical consumption for the many. No less a critic of Roosevelt's presumed superficiality on the hard economic issues of his time, Walter Lippmann, sensed the significance of the New York governor's grasp of what needed to be done.

> What he said [Lippmann wrote] about the electrical utilities had four main points: the first was that the ownership of public sites should not be alienated from public possession; the second was that the effective way to insure public rates is to have governmental authority empowered and ready to undertake the transmission and distribution of power if the function cannot be performed on satisfactory terms by private initiative; the third was that utilities doing an interstate business should be subjected to Federal control; the fourth was that the development of the holding companies to an inconceivable degree of complexity and of capital inflation has made it necessary to bring these institutions under national control.[35]

Finally, at St. Paul, Roosevelt challenged the efficacy of so-called scientific determination of tariff schedules. He insisted instead on "bi-lateral or group international agreements" to stimulate trade, in effect, barter arrangements.[36] As yet, neither Moley nor Roosevelt saw a connection between their desire to elevate domestic farm prices to an artificially high level and the need, as a result, to restrict the impact of prices set in world trade on the domestic economy.

By April 1932, Roosevelt and Moley were moving in new directions. As they labored over the St. Paul address they rejected the demands of Howe, House, and Hull for the enunciation of a conservative program, and decided instead that the first requirement was to have a rounded program as their best defense against Smith and the party conservatives. "The ten articles of my faith," including federal regulation of waterpower resources and electrical utilities, the tariff, farm relief, recognition of Russia, participation in in-

ternational arrangements, Prohibition repeal, and the creation of
an Economic Council, were only partially developed at St. Paul.[37]
Moley required more time. The resulting memorandum of May 19,
1932, became the single most important document of the New
Deal era.

THE MOLEY MEMORANDUM broached most of the ideas that constitute the domestic New Deal of the years 1933 through 1937. As
such it refutes the two New Deals hypothesis. In that document
Moley proposed a rearrangement of business-government relationships; a political-economic reorientation of the Democratic
party toward more liberal and humane purposes and a lower-class
constituency; the institution of large-scale public works and of welfare measures and of a separate emergency budget to finance such
measures; taxation of undistributed surplus corporate income and
heavier taxation of the wealthy as a means of redistributing income;
regulation of utilities holding companies (broached at St. Paul);
banking and securities exchange reforms; and recognition of the Soviet Union as a stimulus to U.S. commerce and industry. There
was no need for Moley and Frankfurter to quarrel, and they never
did.

The Moley memorandum opened with a proposal for the realign-
ment of political parties. Moley as political scientist favored the
clearly demarcated liberal and conservative groupings of the British
party system as opposed to the Tweedle-dee and Tweedle-dum nature of our own parties. The Republican party, he argued, was a
bastion of Toryism and reaction. The Democrats should pose a
clear alternative as exponents of liberal thought and planned action. Moreover, to meet the danger of radicalism by reaction, as
Hoover had done, courted disaster. "It is a challenge and a provo-
cation. It is not the pledge of a new deal; it is the reminder of
broken promises. Its unctuous reassurances of prosperity around
the corner are not oil poured on troubled waters; they are oil
poured on fire." [38]

Constant references in the "Forgotten Man" speech, the memoranda and drafts of the St. Paul address, and again in the Moley memorandum of May 19, 1932, to the nation's "economic infantry" cannot be dismissed as a cliché. As Al Smith had discerned, Roosevelt was determined to shift the party's orientation to the laboring class, the farmer, and the small businessman. Moley rejected the notion of the desirability of two Tory parties.

> There are two ways of viewing the government's duty in matters dealing with economic life. The first sees to it that a favored few are helped and that some of their prosperity will leak through to labor, to the farmer, and to the small businessman. This is the main theory of the Republican Party. It was the theory of the Federalists against whom Jefferson led his victorious party. And it is, I assert, the theory of some of those Democrats [Smith] who are ready to call those who do not agree with it "demagogues."
>
> This theory, wrong though it may be, is one way of interpreting our duty. It belongs to the party of reaction, of Toryism, and now the party of ruined prosperity. But it is not and never should be, the theory of the Democratic Party. There is no room in this country for two reactionary parties.

The American people, Moley suggested to Roosevelt, desired a genuine alternative in 1932, "not a choice between two names for the same reactionary doctrine. The alternative should be a party of liberal thought, of planned action, of enlightened international outlook, of . . . democratic principles." He predicted two distinct contests. One between liberal supporters of Roosevelt as opposed to proponents of a party modeled on Hoover's views with either Newton Baker or Owen Young as the conservatives' choice. This, he believed, would be the final outcome of the Smith opposition. Then, a contest between conservatives and liberals in the presidential campaign.[39] It needs to be added, in retrospect, that the Hoover–Mills–Smith anti-statist views mirrored the opinion of a majority of the nation's economic, political, and intellectual communities.

Moley developed his economic and diplomatic proposals principally in consultation with Rexford G. Tugwell and Adolf A. Berle

Jr., who rounded out the Roosevelt privy council, and to a lesser extent sought the advice of Columbia's James C. Bonbright and Wall Street's Paul Mazur. He produced an elaborate set of proposals, often rough and tentative, intended as the nucleus of the 1932 campaign and the presidential program after election and the inauguration. An examination of these proposals shatters the traditional view that the New Deal was a political improvisation.

The Columbia University professor of public law dealt first with corporate surpluses, one feature of the unhealthy prosperity of the twenties. Extraordinary gains in efficiency and industrial productivity, made possible by the use of machinery, power, improved materials, and processes, facilitated a nearly 50 percent increase in labor productivity. Instead of provision for higher dividends and wages paid to labor, the benefits of increased productivity were funneled into retained corporate profits that proved sterile and unproductive. All too often these profits made their way into foreign loans, improved equipment for even greater productivity, which could not be consumed at prevailing wage rates, and into the call money market for investment or speculation in securities. Underconsumption and speculation with excess profits could be remedied by the "forcing [of] undistributed surplus into the general market for capital."

> . . . We should carefully consider a modification of taxes on corporate income, aimed at discouraging undue accumulation of corporate resources, and stimulating distribution of such reserves to the millions of small investors who are their rightful owners. . . . Such a tax program would tend to restore the balance between production and consumption; and would liberate a tremendous amount of purchasing power.[40]

When Roosevelt proposed a tax on corporate surpluses three years later, as part of a package involving heavy corporation, income, and inheritance taxes, Moley protested. He and Roosevelt rejected the proposal in 1932 on the advice of Adolf Berle, he claimed. But Rexford Tugwell contradicted that recollection and remembered a more favorable climate for the proposal in the

Brains Trust's discussions. "I thought it a very good idea because it would allow capital to be distributed according to the public need, not according to corporate estimates of their fancied need to save for a rainy day or to enlarge their capacities beyond need. At that time there were many concerns operating at less than half their capacity." Neither he nor Berle opposed the scheme, Tugwell wrote, revived by Roosevelt in 1935. The only reconciliation of these disparate recollections is the likelihood that Moley, grown more conservative, shifted his views on the subject.[41] For there are other elements of the May 19 memorandum that scarcely reflected Moley's views in the mid-thirties when he broke with Roosevelt and the New Deal and in 1939 when he wrote *After Seven Years*.

The general collapse of security values and the malfunctioning of securities markets suggested to Moley the need for divorcement of investment banking from commercial banking and the treatment of investment banking as a public utility requiring federal and state regulation. Also, he wanted federal encouragement of stricter state laws of incorporation to attain more stringent regulation of large corporations and their practices. And he recommended federal enforcement of publicity of accounts of corporations doing an interstate business and oversight by the states of speculative activities on securities exchanges. The nation's railroads, already a problem industry, and even more closely linked to the economy in 1932 than they are today, were the subject of two recommendations: encouragement of consolidation, and utilization of the Reconstruction Finance Corporation to stave off further bankruptcies.

Public power, a vital issue intrinsically and politically for Roosevelt, presumably had been dealt with at St. Paul. Moley remained content with that position. But the approach would be expanded at Portland during the campaign and finally by Roosevelt's broadening of the concept into development of a valley resource program, human as well as ecological, on the eve of his inauguration as President.

Amelioration of the plight of the agrarian community appeared crucial to the nation's economic revival and to the party's political chances. Restoration of purchasing power stood at the heart of the matter, but the means of its attainment seemed elusive. Hence the recruitment of Rexford Tugwell to the Roosevelt advisory group. The economist drew the assignment of conceptualizing a viable farm program, one which would translate the instincts offered in the "Forgotten Man" address into workable mechanisms.

The May 19 memorandum contained the very internal contradictions on spending and relief which characterized the Roosevelt campaign and presidency. Moley's suggestions for relief, spending for public works and slum clearance, and for the construction of new housing could scarcely be sustained by a budget normal for those times. Yet unbalanced budgets were no more acceptable in the academic community than among businessmen and financiers. Keynesian economics remained to be fully developed or even understood. As yet, there existed no economic rationale for deficit spending. Unbalanced governmental budgets were equated with the irresponsibility of populism and the German debacle of the early twenties. Conversely, confidence in government, which needed to be restored, rested on its ability to meet its budgetary obligations. Nor could one discern a market at the time for huge flotations of securities. Moley and Roosevelt could be included among the believers in the traditional gospel, and Hoover appeared vulnerable on the issue of excessive spending. Yet, the relief issue pressed for resourceful action especially among Eastern Democratic liberals and midwestern Republican Progressives in the Congress.

At the outset, Moley urged the assumption of direct responsibility for relief by the federal government, a view rejected by Hoover in his contest with the Congress. He was aware of two figures commonly mentioned as feasible for relief and public works. Al Smith had put forward a proposal for $5 billion in public works expenditures to be financed by the public sale of bonds in small denominations, as in wartime. President Hoover, in his conflict with urban liberals and Senate progressives, who favored greater expenditures for relief and public works, clung desperately to about $1 billion as a reasonable estimate when he conferred with the Senate's minority leader, Joseph T. Robinson of Arkansas. Robinson favored $2.3 billion, in effect, a compromise. Even the Senate's foremost proponent of public works measures, Robert F. Wagner of New York, also an advocate of the $2 billion figure, like Smith and Robinson, suggested financing through the sale of long-term government bonds. As Wagner's biographer put it, "the era of Lord Keynes had not yet arrived." [42]

Moley proposed to Roosevelt a relief/public-works package of some $2.5 billion. It included federal relief of $500 million for the winter of 1932–1933 "to the end that so far as the federal government is able to prevent it, no one will starve." Second, it embraced the implementation of the $1 billion in public works proposals contemplated by the Hoover administration as a permanent improvement. These were usually large-scale self-liquidating projects, such as bridges and tunnels, which focused on urban centers. Moley also desired an employment program directed at smaller communities and the nation's rural poor. It involved a $500 million expenditure, this sum to be raised through the device of a federal bond issue to be exchanged for the bonds of states, counties, and municipalities. The proceeds would be used for expenditures on rural roads, schools, and recreational facilities. Finally, Moley also proposed creation of an emergency housing corporation, which would provide subsidies for housing amounting to some $500 million.

Although he considered some use of bond issues and heavier taxation of private wealth through income and estate taxation and corporate levies, unlike Smith and the Senate progressives, Moley concluded that "it was absurd to bal[ance] budget if all must be paid out of *taxes*." He anticipated a relief program that would last for three years. "Ordinary outlays should be balanced." But "unusual relief" expenditures required a segregated, emergency budget.[43] These contradictions, the desire for a balanced budget, and the advocacy of measures, especially in connection with relief and public works, which required a violation of budget balancing as a principle, were a hallmark of the 1932 campaign and of the peacetime administration of Roosevelt.

One of the foremost problems of American economic life which had emerged in the decade of the 1920s was the concentration of control of finance and industry in a relatively few hands. The Brains Trust adopted as their Old Testament Charles R. Van Hise's *Concentration and Control: A Solution of the Trust Problem in the United States*, published in 1912, with its acceptance of corporate bigness. "Concentration and cooperation in industry in order to secure efficiency are a world-wide movement. The United States," Van Hise argued, "cannot resist it. If we isolate ourselves and insist upon the subdivision of industry below the highest economic efficiency and do not allow cooperation, we shall be defeated in the world's markets." And just as cooperation of capital should be allowed, Van Hise concluded, "so cooperation of laborers should be permitted." The answer to unrestricted competition which wasted the nation's natural resources, Van Hise believed, could be found in general codes of fair business practice and in the Wisconsin idea of regulation by administrative commissions.[44]

Van Hise's work proved prescient as Adolf Berle and Gardiner C. Means demonstrated in *The Modern Corporation and Private Property*, published in 1932. Nearly 50 percent of American industry (one-half of non-banking corporate wealth) was owned by some 200 corporations on January 1, 1930. Some 2,000 men were in effective control of these industries, which represented 22 percent of our national wealth and 38 percent of business wealth. Yet, they were devoid of responsibility either to their stockholders or to society at large. "They have a moral responsibility but there is not sufficient legal machinery to enforce the moral implications of their position." [45]

The Moley memorandum accepted the structural analysis offered in the findings of Van Hise and Berle and suggested as a solution expansion of the role of the central government in the economic life of the nation. Presumed Marxist alternatives, suggested by a later generation of historians, did not exist as a reality. The range of deliberation in 1932 was delimited by Roosevelt's and Moley's rejection of the extremes of laissez faire, which they associated with Hoover, and a totally planned economy. As Moley noted in the May memorandum, it seemed most desirable to pursue "Not a planned life—such a regimented way of life is abhorrent to . . . American . . . individualism—but a planned govt. participation." In its broadest sense this was the sum of the 1932 campaign and the New Deal.

In the May 19 memorandum Moley made frequent reference to "planning" in the form of an Economic Council. It was the brainchild of Rexford Tugwell and conceivably the origin of the later National Emergency Council (1933–1936) and the postwar Council of Economic Advisers. "Such a council," Moley believed, "attached to the Executive and operating under his direction could provide . . . advice and information . . . in the direction of real leadership in economic affairs." Moley's concept and that of Roosevelt presumably of "reasoned planning and expert persuasion" was the inception of the interventionist state. It was not intended, however, to herald, in a more structured sense, a planned economy.[46]

Overall, the head of the Brains Trust urged upon Roosevelt a rejection of the sort of thinking that had dominated the nation's economic theology since the Civil War, particularly the notion that our economic system need be dominated by immutable laws. "What do people want more than anything else?" Moley asked rhetorically. His reply:

> To my mind two things, first work, with all the moral and spiritual values that go with it. Idleness is stagnation. Stagnation is disintegration. And disintegration is death.
>
> Second they want a reasonable measure of security for themselves and for those who depend upon them. . . .
>
> It is all very well for those who speak for the present administration to speak of economic laws. But men starve while economic laws work out. And it is a fair question as to whether economic laws exist which cannot be controlled by the laws of men.

This was the distinguishing feature of the outlook of Roosevelt and the Brains Trust as opposed to their predecessors in government. Convinced that the nation's economic system "is a human thing built by human beings," they believed that "it can be controlled by human beings and for the general good."

THROUGH MUCH of 1932, at least until the campaign, Moley saw no contradictions between the domestic objectives of Roosevelt and the Brains Trust and the apparent need for international diplomatic and economic cooperation. Although Moley's commitments and instincts focused on domestic politics, he was nevertheless in his academic pursuits an Anglophile, an admirer of English legal and political institutions. On international economic questions his opinions seemed usually swayed by Columbia's economists, especially the venerable Edwin R. A. Seligman. In 1927, for instance, Moley commended Seligman for his draft of an academic round-robin addressed to the Secretary of the Treasury, Andrew Mellon, advocating the cancellation of intergovernmental debts. "It cuts through the mass of sophistry that the Administration has built up around its position. . . . We all owe you a deep debt of gratitude for defending our problem so effectively." Although Moley became convinced in later years that Seligman's position on debts cancellation reflected his connections with "the international banking firm which bears his name," Moley inclined in his Columbia years toward internationalism in economic matters. The May 19 memorandum recommended an internationalist position, a reversal of the tone created by the Albany (Grange) address in February.[47]

Echoing the sentiments of the Republican maverick, Senator William E. Borah of Idaho, Moley proposed cancellation of the wartime debts owed the United States by its former Allies in exchange for a quid pro quo in the form of substantial reduction of German reparations. But these issues, he believed, embraced only part of a larger set of questions. They included disarmament, the tariff, and agricultural surpluses which seemed "interrelated to such an extent that they constitute a single problem of international concern necessarily subject to simultaneous negotiation." They

could not be settled on an individual basis, Moley believed, but
required adjustment at an international conference with U.S. participation.

Moley's position on the tariff also followed the liberal internationalist view. He suggested that Roosevelt be guided by the principles laid down at St. Paul, namely, that reciprocal tariff arrangements be made through the device of "bi-lateral or group
international agreements to effectuate their exchange." Later, in
the course of the 1932 campaign Roosevelt and Moley learned to
hedge on the tariff issue. As yet they did not see the contradiction
between reduced tariffs and artificially stimulated wages and
prices. In time, they would learn their economic lessons from Tugwell, Berle, and hard realities.

Moley also recommended recognition of the Soviet Union despite the existence of some pressures to the contrary. This, he insisted, appeared the only realistic position the United States could
take. He had the following conditions in mind:

> (a) Russia shall, by specific treaty, agree that propaganda will not
> be carried on in the country by official agents and the government of
> Russia shall prevent to the limit of its power any propaganda by
> private Russian agents. . . . (b) some proper disposition of the con-
> flicting claims between the United States and Russia, not only as to
> the debts of the Russian government, but certain private obligations
> should be made. (c) In any negotiations the old shibboleths as to
> whether Russia is a democratic government or not . . . should not
> weigh in the discussion. . . . We should apply to Russia at this time
> the policy of recognizing a de facto government, without attempting
> to force it into the form of our conception of what a government
> should be.[48]

In time, Moley abandoned the internationalist persuasion and
became the most determined advocate of economic nationalism in
the Roosevelt entourage. The shift, however, was gradual, an out-
growth of his many exchanges with Tugwell, Berle, and leading
Senate Democrats, especially Key Pittman, Thomas J. Walsh, and
James Byrnes. The Brains Trust concluded by October that economic recovery dictated a period of insulation from international
economic tides. Senate Democrats, he came to learn, regarded

Cordell Hull's views worthy of Pollyanna. "I not only saw the light," Moley quipped in later years, "but I felt the heat." [49]

The May memorandum hinted at Moley's later reversal of his position on the debts and the broader requirements of international cooperation by the United States on economic issues. "What is the depression?" Moley scrawled on a lined yellow legal sheet, his favored medium for random ideas worth considering for future reference. The answers, he surmised, appeared essentially domestic. "Foreign trade only 1/10 of the problem." By October, the shift was complete. He came to the conclusion that "The problem [is] starvation amid plenty" and that "The solution [is] to get control of the two ends of the equation—but you can't if one end is abroad." To distinguish his position from that of the bitter-end isolationists, he coopted the term "intranationalism," with its focus on internal priorities. The Ottawa Agreements, intended to make Great Britain and the Commonwealth independent of vanished markets, seemed to make such a policy essential. [50]

The Moley memorandum of May 19, 1932, should inter several of the most persistent misconceptions of the New Deal historiography. The categorization of Moley as fundamentally a writer of catchphrases for Roosevelt simply breaks down under the weight of that document. Moley's own assertion of a consistency of thought on the issues he and Roosevelt faced also collapses in the process. Even more important, it simply cannot be argued that the 1932 campaign was a vacuous affair and the New Deal an improvisation. The New Deal was framed in 1932.

The Moley memorandum remained subject to revision and additions. In its approach toward our economic diplomacy it would be reversed by Moley and Roosevelt in the campaign and the 1932–1933 interregnum. But, in spite of its limitations, it never merited the burial to which it became subjected by the consensus historians in their reconstruction of that era. For in its recommendations, its approach, even its inconsistencies, it projected the main thrust of the political and economic policies of Franklin D. Roosevelt and the New Deal.

7

The Brains Trust 2:
Tugwell and Agriculture

The ephemeral prosperity of the postwar years has ended in disillusion. We were so sure of the rightness and permanence of our business system then that the shock of depression has awakened us really for the first time to the consideration of alternatives.

The pursuit, by each individual business of its own aims, has led us directly into a situation in which none of these aims can be achieved because none of them fit into others. And we have before us, in Russia, an illustration we cannot escape, of purposes fitted into a master plan, each part serving the whole. That Russia is far behind us in productive development does not blind us to the far more rapid rate of advance she has succeeded in establishing by the elimination of frictions. . . .

We shall all of us find, when serious study begins to replace enthusiasm, that something is called for which Americans have never taken too kindly. There will need to be a discipline, a sacrifice of one to many, a merging of interests which will require deep changes in our way of doing things. There will have to be controls—of production, of prices, of the uses of property— and when controls are used some of us will find our privileges curtailed. The Russians have been sustained by an almost religious faith, which has made discipline a kind of joyous sacrifice for a great cause. Our commitment, if we make one, will need to be of a similar sort.

—REXFORD G. TUGWELL *

ON A BLUSTERY MARCH MORNING in 1932, Rexford Guy Tugwell remembered, he encountered Raymond Moley on Morningside Heights. Though colleagues at Columbia University and neighbors on Claremont Avenue, where much of the faculty re-

* To J. R. Brackett (Associated Press), April 11, 1931. Tugwell Papers.

sided, their acquaintance was casual. The two men, relatively young, in their forties, each academically ambitious and established in his discipline, had followed disparate paths. Moley, professor of public law, spent a decade as a specialist in the administration of justice in various states and in the city of New York. He liked to think of himself as a practical, hard-nosed student of American politics. Tugwell, professor of economics, an advocate of experimental economics, and a theoretician, confessed to "badly repressed hopes, a certain yearning for re-creation." Together, in 1932 and the early months of 1933, they forged much of what became known as the New Deal, in spite of their mutually acknowledged differences of opinion. In later years, in their recollections of these creative months, they dwelt as much on their frustrations, perhaps even more so, than on what they had accomplished.

Evidently, the young economist surmised, Moley had something more concrete on his mind than the casual banter in which they engaged. Aware that the political scientist had become an adviser to the governor of New York, who recently conceded his presidential aspirations, he anticipated some concrete proposal. Perhaps, Tugwell sensed, the bitter March wind or the shrill cries of the children playing nearby—he could not be certain—caused his colleague to hesitate. Shortly thereafter, at any rate, at his office, Moley broached the issue.

One can only speculate on what coursed through Moley's mind. Reticence, a tendency toward calculation rather than impulse, in manner and speech, were characteristic. A week earlier, at Albany, Roosevelt, Moley, and Samuel I. Rosenman reached agreement on a series of subjects which required detailed and imaginative exploration for future speeches on the causes and remedies of the depression. Agriculture gained primacy because of the assumption that its depressed condition for a decade had unsettled other sectors of the economy. Moley received the assignment to recruit advisers for the campaign among his colleagues at Columbia University.

Tugwell, Moley knew, had studied agricultural problems in the

United States and the Soviet Union in the previous decade and had presented a memorandum on the subject to Alfred E. Smith's advisers in the 1928 campaign. Moley gaged Tugwell as politically naive, possessing, as he put it later, "exceedingly liberal tendencies" and "a turn for philosophical economics." He believed Adolf A. Berle, recruited to the Brains Trust a few weeks later, could be regarded as "much more practical." Moley suspected that Tugwell could be enlisted in Roosevelt's camp because of a deeply felt conviction that the nation's economic condition required basic changes and his openly expressed hostility toward the Hoover policies, but these remained private observations, not reservations. At his Barnard College office Moley invited the youthful-looking economist to participate in a ritual passed subsequently only by Berle of the Columbia Law faculty.

Would he be willing, Moley inquired, to be screened for service as an adviser to Franklin D. Roosevelt in the developing presidential campaign? Although a trifle miffed by the procedure, Tugwell, deeply distressed by the depression and the ineptitude of the Hoover administration in meeting its challenge, agreed to an interrogation by Moley, Rosenman, and Basil (Doc) O'Connor, Roosevelt's law partner at the Metropolitan Club at 26th Street and Madison Avenue.*

The more Tugwell bared his views, the more he fascinated his listeners. "He was," Moley later observed, "a first rate economist who had pushed on beyond the frontiers of stiff classicism, and his original and speculative turn of mind made him an enormously exhilarating companion. Rex was like a cocktail: his conversation picked you up and made your brain race along." Tugwell introduced his concept of a concert of interests. "I thought that the business community were being poor sports about it—they weren't allowing the farmers to get in on the prosperity and finally the situation had reached the point where they were suffering for their own selfishness." When Tugwell departed, having elaborated his thinking on the depression, O'Connor turned to Moley and re-

* Rosenman placed it at his home.

marked with awe, "He's a pretty profound fellow, isn't he." Rosenman concurred. A few days later, Tugwell and Moley made what would become a familiar journey up the Hudson Valley on the New York Central Railroad to confer with Roosevelt at Albany. Thus, Rexford Guy Tugwell, who emerged subsequently as the New Deal's *enfant terrible*, enlisted in the governor's academic coterie.[1]

Tugwell retained his role as catalyst and advocate of drastic change in the chronicling of the New Deal. He later argued that Roosevelt refused to follow the hard road toward collectivism and that consequently he scarcely pursued a course other than that already charted by Herbert Hoover.[2] But he never explained to a later generation that much of what he actually proposed to Roosevelt became a part of the New Deal program. This is not because of evasiveness, but rather because Tugwell proved unable to recall the details of events, memoranda, and proposals in 1932, and New Deal historians have neglected to reconstruct in specific terms what he advocated.[3] Tugwell's dual role as participant and historian of the New Deal, like Moley's, presents a challenge to the historian. Perhaps the solution lies in beginning again at the beginning.

The Columbia economist's role in shaping Roosevelt's determinations in 1932 proved more substantial than he later conceded in his memoir, *The Brains Trust*, or than Moley suggested by relegating Tugwell's influence to the profferment of agricultural advice.[4] A critic of our society, Tugwell affected the decisions reached on most issues in 1932 and proved as determinative as any adviser. But in one vital area, it needs to be conceded, in the creation of a National Economic Council, Tugwell lost the issue to Adolf A. Berle's economic advice and the political requirements of the campaign. Equilibrium emerged as a priority, as well as the achievement of a better social and economic balance, in the "concert of interests" speech at St. Paul and in the Moley memorandum of May 19. The temporarily entertained notion of a totally managed economy, however, with its potential for corporativism was ultimately rejected by Roosevelt. In that critical sense, there existed only one New Deal, not two. And the decision was reached in 1932.

The restoration of agriculture's purchasing power, accorded economic priority by Roosevelt and the Brains Trust, coincided with the party's political needs. Farmers of the Midwest, traditionally Republican, experienced economic ruin. The harmony of economic goals and the party's interests contained political and economic appeal. Able to win over Roosevelt and Moley to acceptance of the need for planning in agriculture—farmers remained, in fact, far from sold on the idea—Tugwell insisted in July on the next logical step, a planned industrial economy. It seemed to him the pattern and the logic of the times. Great Britain moved away from laissez faire and toward a managed economy even before World War I; Italy moved toward the corporative state in the middle and late 1920s; and the Soviet Union made the transition in that decade from the mixed economy associated with the New Economic Policy to the dominance of the planners.

Historians in recent years, as the academic world has shifted toward a more critical analysis of the New Deal and Roosevelt's leadership, assume that Tugwell must have been right and Roosevelt wrong, or at the very least, in a regression to Walter Lippmann's unfavorable estimate of Roosevelt's intellectual grasp of larger issues, that the fuzzy-minded squire could not comprehend Tugwell's frame of reference.[5] On the contrary, the possibility needs to be explored that Roosevelt, Berle, and Moley comprehended Tugwell's bend of mind. They rejected the proposal for the elimination of a profit-oriented privately owned industry and opted for an organic evolution of an economic constitutional order.

Although one can only speculate on what might have developed, Tugwell's proposals, it seems, if fully executed, could have projected an essentially conservative society to the corporative state. In the last analysis, Moley and Berle accepted planning where they believed it requisite for recovery, but not for the sake of planning. This is where they differed with Tugwell. "I could see," Moley recalled, "that the farm sector needed somebody to plan for everybody—but I never conceived of planning in industry. It seemed to run against the whole pattern of life." [6] Berle preferred an evolutionary approach. "Adolf and I were usually on the same side,"

Tugwell asserted in his memoir of that year.[7] On the contrary, Berle reversed Roosevelt's decision, reached in May with Moley, to institute the first stage of a managed economy. In the drafting of the Commonwealth Club speech, interestingly labeled at the time as an address on "Individualism," Berle suggested federal intervention in the economy when called for, but not the stringent overhead management envisaged by Tugwell.

Historians will never agree on what course Franklin D. Roosevelt should have followed in 1932 when the New Deal was conceived. In an earlier era, some conservative academicians perceived the Roosevelt leadership as a threat to free institutions and traditional values in American society.[8] Later, radical critics of the New Deal faulted his lack of willingness to think and act outside of a political context, and framed Roosevelt's options in terms suited to the economic and social issues and concepts of their own times. Keynesians would have preferred more imaginative fiscal management, despite the fact that Keynes had no followers of prominence in the United States. In a strange and curious way, many academicians in their assessment of Roosevelt, regardless of their views, have refused to abandon the mystique that is the oldest myth of all, namely, that Franklin D. Roosevelt functioned in a vacuum and could have done very nearly what he wished. Plainly stated, many of the retrospective alternatives posed in the recent literature of the New Deal emerged in a later generation and have little reference to the economic challenges and traditional attitudes Roosevelt and the Brains Trust confronted in 1932.

THE AGRICULTURAL DEPRESSION had gnawed away at the nation's economic vitals for a decade, since 1921. Heavy wartime demand had stimulated substantial borrowing for the purpose of investment in land and equipment. But with the conclusion of World War I, the European market, for decades a major outlet for the farmers' product, dried up. Edwin G. Nourse, then associated with the Institute of Economics, suggested as early as 1923 that European nations, transformed from creditor to debtor status vis-à-vis the United States, could no longer serve as a satisfactory market for our agricultural surplus. "Agricultural exports," he warned, "may be expected to drop still further in 1924 and thereafter." [9] Expansion of production of basic commodities on a worldwide basis in the twenties produced a glut and resulted in inadequate prices in the international marketplace. Yet millions of small producers in the United States, often working marginal land, found themselves unable to emulate the practices of large corporations which introduced efficiencies and curtailed production when demand faltered.

Economists sensed the fundamental qualities of the issue. Proposals emerged along the lines of land-use planning, greater efficiency in production, and conversion of marginal and submarginal land to better purposes than the inefficient production of surplus basic commodities. The marginal cultivator, moreover, posed a social dilemma. Edwin R. A. Seligman, the prestigious Columbia economist, in an analysis made for the Smith campaign of 1928, raised the specter of a permanently inferior agriculture in relation to industry "which may bring with it the replacement of the American farmer by a low-standard cultivator." [10] The nation's farmers, M. L. Wilson warned, with only slight exaggeration in 1932, faced the shadow of peasantry.

Some of the nation's industrialists, even before the depression, foresaw the overall implications of an impoverished agriculture. A report published in 1926 emphasized that the continued economic imbalance between agriculture and other branches of the nation's economy could ultimately affect the nation's broader economic outlook, its security, and its way of life. Sponsors of the study included Alexander Legge of International Harvester, Edward A. Rumely of the Vitamin Corporation of New York, and Owen D. Young, chairman of the General Electric Company. [11]

The solution offered by Franklin D. Roosevelt in 1932 at Topeka, Kansas, the matching of production with demand, could have evolved in the 1920s. Rexford G. Tugwell and Henry A. Wallace, both Republicans, explored the possibility of acreage allotment for farmers based on estimates of domestic needs, but the idea of government intervention offended a generation nurtured on the philosophy of Herbert Spencer. As Secretary of Commerce, than as President, Herbert Hoover epitomized the prevailing view of self-help and voluntarism in a decade of lackluster political leadership. The possibility of economic and social disequilibrium did not propel conservative Republican administrations into acceptance of direct federal intervention. They favored indirect mechanisms such as the tariff, encouragement of cooperatives, and the enlargement of credit.

"We have known no more negative era in our history," Henry Steele Commager and Richard B. Morris lamented in their condemnation of "responsibilities evaded and . . . opportunities missed." [12] Valiant efforts to rehabilitate that decade and its leaders in historical esteem seem to have yielded meager results. This is hardly surprising for as one reads the correspondence of men of social conscience of that era, George W. Norris of Nebraska, Felix Frankfurter of the Harvard Law School, and Harold Ickes, there comes through a deeply felt frustration with the unwillingness of those in power to accept a reasonable enlargement of the responsibility of government in the face of needed change. The positive state and the requirement of massive federal intervention to correct the imbalance between agriculture and industry, first apparent in the early 1920s, waited for the calamity of the Great Depression and the challenge to previous orthodoxy offered by Franklin D. Roosevelt and the Brains Trust.

The threat of economic ruin in the early 1930s opened the farm community and its leadership to a reluctant acknowledgment of the need for federal planning in agriculture. Agrarian intellectuals pressed even harder than before for acceptance of the notion of federally administered production controls, an idea accepted by Roosevelt and the Brains Trust in the form of domestic allotment. But they did not know how to make it work. Desirous of injecting a quick boost to farmers' income, Roosevelt's advisers knew of no satisfactory mechanism to accomplish that end in a rational way. They toyed with McNary-Haugenism (the equalization fee) as a possibility. They were battered by the inflationists who, in more sophisticated academic terms than those used by cheap money advocates, plumped for fiscal measures as a depression panacea. But the Brains Trust wanted more fundamental reforms and a farm program that would begin to broach basic long-range problems.[13]

By May 1932, based on suggestions by Rexford G. Tugwell, Adolf A. Berle, and Henry Morgenthau Jr., the head of the Brains Trust came to certain fundamental conclusions. For the long haul Moley and Tugwell agreed on the need for "a planned government participation" in the nation's economic life and for long-range planning in agriculture. They also concluded, based on a memorandum submitted by Tugwell (Moley's handwritten notation refers to the Tugwell memorandum), that planned government participation does not mean "a planned economic life—such a regimented way of life is abhorrent to the American [?] to individualism." Adolf Berle's proposal for a federal survey of every acre of land in the United States for appropriate use seemed eminently desirable. Marginal land could be converted to the production of trees—a throwback to Roosevelt's experience in New York State. At the same time, Berle urged, a million men could be given temporary employment by the federal government in reforestation work, farmers could be removed from unproductive land, and the government could buy up foreclosed mortgages and in other instances refinance mortgages by issuance of its own bonds. The immediate and therefore most difficult problem was the restoration of the farmers' purchasing power, Tugwell's assignment.

Although keenly aware of the many and complex causes of the depression, the Brains Trust and Roosevelt accepted Tugwell's proposition that the nation's vast industrial machinery became immobilized largely because farmers could not afford to buy its output. Based on an index of 100 in 1914, Tugwell calculated, farm prices were at 65 in January 1932, as opposed to 99 for wholesale prices of all commodities in the United States. Farmers, it must be remembered, still constituted about one-third of the population. To pay his debts, the farmer needed to produce four times as much as he had before World War I. Taxes required three times prewar farm production and the necessities of life twice the output of an earlier era. The disparity between farm income and the prices of goods purchased by the farmer required remediation. Or, as Tugwell put it, "the two lines of the graph must be brought together." [14]

Tugwell was well equipped for the task. Rooted in rural upstate New York, where he was born in Sinclairsville in 1891 (his father became a successful orchard farmer and canner of fruit and vegetables), Tugwell grew up at Wilson, north of Buffalo, on Lake Ontario. The key to his father's modest success, Tugwell explained to Seligman as both labored on an agricultural program for John J. Raskob and Alfred E. Smith in 1928, was acreage limitation. "My father is a canner and I know his practice in caring [?] for surpluses. He contracts in winter for *acreage*, not for tons; when goods are in cans or in warehouse they can be held. Time ceases to press. And since given acreage averages out, in any 5 year period, a certain yield, he can arrange his marketing to suit. This seems to be one key. The other I got from War Industries Board practice: Priorities in shipping and warehousing for the produce of approved acreage." [15]

As an economist, Tugwell's deep "philosophic values, as well as his highly developed esthetic sense, drove him to a dream of order and symmetry," and thereby toward social and economic planning. He received his academic training at the University of Pennsylvania, taught there and at the University of Washington. In 1920 he moved to Columbia University to teach a new course in contemporary civilization, and a decade later he became a professor of economics. The principal formative influences on his thinking were Scott Nearing, who taught at Pennsylvania in Tugwell's student years, John A. Hobson's underconsumptionist views, and the work of Simon Patten. Patten proved a particularly influential mentor and *The Theory of Prosperity* pointed Tugwell toward experimentalism which stressed "the power of creative intelligence" as opposed to "received dogma." [16] Tugwell synthesized his views for New York University's Willard E. Atkins in 1931:

> My attitude is perhaps not entirely institutional. Ways of thinking and of behavior which you define as institutions seem to me to need acute and imaginative description. The old economics actually prevented us from seeing them as they are. But to me even these are only a sort of springboard into a new economy which creative thought can project and bring into being. I have called this experimental economics to emphasize the creative notion of manipulating in thought, perhaps even in practice, those mechanisms of controlled change, which we must work with. Institutional economics seems to me only to state conditions, to describe the materials with which we must deal. It does not go far enough to provide means of improvement—unless you widen the definition to include the influence of experimental thought. Perhaps you do. I think Veblen did not. To him institutions were the manifestation of a variety of activity experiences and his essential method was to describe these and to define their rooting even in primitive life.
>
> You see I think of myself as deriving from Patten rather than from Veblen. Still I can't help feeling that your kind of book and anything I may do have, at this juncture, a common purpose. To clear away the rubbish of elements, factors, equilibria; to break down the one-thing-at-a-time method; and to substitute for these a growingly realistic analysis of men's tragic and beautiful experiences with the materials of economic life. That is, of course, further, really, than we shall go in our time. But I confess to badly repressed hopes, a certain yearning for re-creation. To me it seems so entirely evident that the experience of work and of consuming could be made at least better— whatever one's tests may be—that I cling to my pleading for experimentalism perhaps beyond all reason. [17]

Tugwell's earliest work as an economist dealt with the problem of milk distribution and the need for the regulation of business for the consumer's benefit. [18] It stemmed from his experience as a graduate student when he served as an investigator for the governor's Tri-State Milk Commission (Pennsylvania, Delaware, and Maryland) and as a researcher for Gifford Pinchot's Rural Progress Association. His conclusion that milk distribution should be regarded as a public utility, in part because of consumers' ignorance of marketing conditions, led to the writing of his doctoral dissertation on *The Economic Basis of Public Interest* (1922). It articulated a broadened concept of government police powers for the purpose of business (price) regulation. He pressed, as he would later, for lowered prices rather than higher wages as a stimulus for consumption, for the acceptance of business bigness, and for the need to regulate in the marketplace on behalf of the consumer.[19]

Through much of the "new economic era" the young economist challenged the orthodox assumptions of the vast majority of his colleagues and the Harding and Coolidge administrations. Increasingly, especially after a visit to the Soviet Union in 1927 in the company of Paul Douglas, Stuart Chase, and a group of American trade unionists, he moved from regulation toward national economic planning. Tugwell accompanied the group as an agricultural expert and described in his *Soviet Russia in the Second Decade* a "renaissance" in Russian agriculture. Evidently the Columbia economist came away from the Soviet visit with the conviction that the Russian experiment in national planning needed to be studied for its applicability to the American system.[20] Peacetime planning in the Soviet Union, under Gosplan (National Planning Commission) offered to dissident economists and even some businessmen, politicians, and agrarians, disturbed by the economic eccentricities of the postwar decade, possible alternatives to laissez faire.[21] It needs to be suggested, further, that Tugwell did not discover planning in the Soviet Union; rather the Soviet trip, usually regarded as a turning point in his thought, served as a confirmation and crystallization of conclusions previously arrived at.

In an essay published in 1924, Tugwell suggested that the rapid tempo of social and economic change which dominated Western society from the onset of the industrial era, had slowed down and might well yield "to nature's pressure for adjustment and equilibrium." He predicted the likelihood of a static economy and of surplus production and productive capacity. The time had come, Tugwell believed in 1924, for the substitution of experimental economics, based on man's creative intelligence, for the economic thought of the previous century, dominated by Adam Smith and Herbert Spencer and rooted in so-called natural or physical laws. The economic laws of the laissez faire era were passive, mechanistic formulations used to justify economic and social preconceptions and had no real purpose in the third decade of the twentieth century. Experimentalism, he believed, based on scientific inquiry, research, and the gathering and analysis of data, could be made to embrace not only the discipline of economics but the study of human behavior as well. In the process, Tugwell wanted the introduction of ethical considerations into economics. As an example of this newer approach, he questioned the profit motive, long accepted as axiomatic, as a genuine inducement toward economic enterprise and he proposed consideration of alternatives.[22]

Shortly before the journey to the Soviet Union, in a letter to *The New Republic*, Tugwell confirmed John Maynard Keynes's view that "the ground has long been cut from under laissez faire." A whole school of young economists, he claimed, believed in experimentalism, in intelligent control "not from dogmatic principles but toward favorable results." This had been accomplished in wartime in the capitalist nations as they organized their consumption and production. "America's War-Time Socialism," the radical economist argued in *The Nation*, in reality the management of our economy by the War Industries Board under Bernard Baruch, suggested a satisfactory balance between cooperation and the need for individuality. In the "fierce new heat of nationalistic vision" businessmen staffed government, the Sherman Act was abandoned, and cooperation replaced competition. Technical information was exchanged, production, prices, wages, and consumption controlled, and the economy thrived.

Following the Great War, in Tugwell's view, the United States regressed to earlier forms of competition and an abandonment of needed price regulation. Income, he cautioned, scarcely kept pace with productivity and in time buying would slow up. "Warehouses," he predicted, "will suddenly be discovered to be

dangerously full of things." And it would be realized that prices
were too high and goods too plentiful. "Something has to be done,"
the economist warned. "We are at the crisis." Industry had come
of age "but society struggles ineffectually with the discipline of industry. . . . There is a distinct lack of maturity in our social sense
of order and symmetry."

The voluntary socialism of wartime had given way, according to
this analysis of our economic condition, to Calvin Coolidge's determination to accomplish a reversion to the free play of competition.
The postwar lassitude, regression to the dogma of laissez faire and
antitrust prosecutions, ran completely against the currents of the
era. At a time when most economists extolled the "new economic
era," Tugwell probed and questioned the accepted way of doing
business. Real income scarcely matched productivity. Moreover,
the new currents of the time—research, standardization, serializa-
tion, mechanization, personnel administration—flew in the face of
the haphazard, unregulated competition and the casual economic
attitudes encouraged by the Coolidge administration.[23]

It can be argued that Tugwell exaggerated somewhat the degree
of competition that existed. The Webb-Pomerene Act of 1918 permitted export associations to ignore the limitations of the Sherman
Act in overseas trade, largely as a response to the competition of
European cartels. In some instances these associations joined the
cartels in the division of markets and in price-fixing arrangements.
Within the United States, cooperative practices initiated and encouraged in wartime, flourished under the trade associations
operating under the aegis of Herbert Hoover's Commerce Department. Information was exchanged on prices, methods of production, employee relations, and general business techniques.[24] The
pattern of much of American industry in the 1920s was one of
oligopoly and of price maintenance. Competition frequently took
the form of advertising or promise of services. Superficially Tugwell's views echoed Hoover's attainments at Commerce in pressing
the nation's economy toward associative activity. But, critically,
Tugwell urged the substitution of public for private control.

Tugwell's trip to the Soviet Union in the summer of 1927 broadened the dimension of his arguments. When he returned he addressed the students of the Robert Brookings Graduate School and the Department of Philosophy at Columbia University. Evidently, he had found guidelines for the United States in the economic changes introduced by the Soviet Union as that nation moved into the industrial stage. Tugwell appealed for an end to what he referred to as purely literary (ideological) abstractions concerning capitalism, communism or socialism, and fascism. As he put it, the "literary theories" of communism or capitalism often stood at variance with economic practice. Thus Lenin introduced capitalist measures under the New Economic Policy and the famous dinners hosted by Judge Gary of United States Steel were designed to eliminate price competition. Similarly, "Communism in Russia and Fascism in Italy have numerous common characteristics in spite of the wide difference in ultimate objectives. And Italian Fascism, like Russian Bolshevism, is to be understood rather by what it does than what its apologists say what it is." Quoting John Maynard Keynes's recent *Communism and Laissez faire* (1926), he observed that if "communism is a religion, capitalism is a fetish." [25]

Central to Tugwell's argument was his belief that, despite a revolutionary ideology, the Russian economy followed experimentalism and practices worthy of closer study in the United States. Russia, he explained, organized its economy in order to attain industrialization and self-sufficiency, yet also successfully involved its laboring force in the attainment of national goals. The gathering of facts and planning had been assigned to the Council of Labor and Defense and its right arm, Gosplan. Gosplan set as a long-range objective a better balance between agriculture and industry. In the process the locus of control shifted from the business classes to engineers and the civil service. "It will pay to watch them. For . . . they are achieving that balance of industrial functions for which the orthodox economists have always longed and which they have waited so patiently to see developing from free competition and voluntary activity."

Although both economic systems aimed at a balanced economy, the Soviet system, according to Tugwell, seemed more likely than ours to attain that balance. America's greater prosperity, he attributed to an earlier start. The Russian effort at a balanced economic system through socialized control, directed by centralized agencies, would in the long run more likely produce necessities and even luxuries for all than our own competitive system. Excluding ideological prejudices, he asked: "How shall we settle our irrepressible agricultural problem except by some such series of devices as the Soviets use?" [26]

Although his favorable reaction to Soviet developments in the mid-1920s moved Tugwell in new directions, it needs to be stressed that planning had taken hold almost everywhere in the industrial world outside of the United States. Beginning in the late nineteenth and early twentieth centuries, Great Britain without reference to Marxism, moved away from laissez faire toward "planned prices, planned manpower, planned investments, planned allocation of materials—and the redistribution of incomes that has taken place through steeply graduated taxation." Despite the pursuit of Edwardian prosperity and the gold standard in the 1920s, British governments, often hostile to socialism, under the pressure of social malaise and economic discontent as well as a powerful organized laboring class, seemed unable to reverse the collectivist trend. [27] Bismarck's backing of national railroads and health insurance in Germany, as well as the growingly dominant role of powerful industrialists also reflected prevailing economic and social trends in Europe.

In Italy, the laissez faire policies of the years 1922–1925 gave way in 1925–26 to the syndicalist state with workers and employers organized into twelve national syndicates. Business and government entered into a formal partnership under Fascism. The relationship that developed, in the opinion of one recent observer, represented an institutionalization of patterns followed by Western democracies in more disguised forms. "The difference was more in form than in substance with the Fascists shouting what the others, perhaps more wisely, preferred to whisper." [28] While probably generally true of Europe, the United States remained an exception.

The year following Tugwell's return from the Soviet Union, Lindsay Rogers, a senior member of the Columbia faculty and a Smith adviser, asked the economist to submit a memorandum on the agricultural problem for possible use in the 1928 presidential campaign. Tugwell's proposal, mild medicine by his own standards, reflected the broader views he formulated on the need for economic balance or equilibrium, planning, and central economic management. The attainment of a better balance between the product of agriculture and market demand, between farm and industrial income, and the need for a central agency to control agricultural production formed the basis of his Advance Ratio Plan for agriculture. Tugwell also suggested adoption of the parity concept that later became a vital element of the New Deal's agricultural program. "My idea," he recalled years later, "was that by knowing the number of acres and the average amount of production per acre and the amount of consumption in the United States, you could adjust the production to the consumption . . . a year ahead. You could guarantee farmers a price which was based on a ratio with an index of industrial prices." A government board would serve as a marketing agent for farmers, contract for acreage, buy the farmer's product at a predetermined ratio price (later known as parity), determine domestic market requirements, and create a fund to sustain possible financial losses. [29]

Alfred E. Smith's advisers rejected the scheme. Perhaps, as Tugwell later surmised, the principals who guided Smith's campaign preferred a purely political appeal for the farm vote as opposed to a genuine solution for the farmers' economic dilemma of overproduction and a substandard income. Following his nomination at Houston in 1928, Smith chose McNary-Haugenism favored by George Peek and others of more orthodox viewpoint. It would not disturb Republicans and Eastern conservatives if Smith proposed the dumping of our surplus abroad, Smith's advisers concluded. They simply would not accept the idea of a domestic solution which required economic controls.

Tugwell attempted to convince Belle Moskowitz. When she objected to the Advance Ratio Plan for agriculture on the ground that food prices would rise for consumers, the Columbia economist countered that increased farm income would lead to benefits for industry and labor through increased consumption of their output. To no avail.[30] Later, when Tugwell joined the Brains Trust, he convinced Roosevelt and Moley of the logic of his argument, presented as the "concert of interests," meaning the interdependence of classes and of segments of the economy. It resulted in Roosevelt's stress on agricultural recovery as meriting priority.

TUGWELL VIEWED the nation's tottering economic structure and Herbert Hoover's leadership in the depression with dismay. In later years he pictured Hoover and Roosevelt virtually as birds of a feather, nurtured in outmoded Progressive preconceptions no longer valid in the crisis situation they faced as President. The Brains Truster's attitude toward Hoover had become virtually benign, toward Roosevelt one of frustration for lost opportunities. In correspondence with Raymond Moley in their twilight years, both credited Herbert Hoover with the invention of "most of the devices we used."[31] Nothing could be further from the facts of the situation.

Tugwell's appraisal of the Hoover administration in 1932, if somewhat vitriolic, offers greater insight than his later efforts to force Hoover and Roosevelt into the same mold. For he presented the tempting thesis, which may never be documented, that when Hoover finally reacted to the depression in the form of the moratorium on intergovernmental obligations, it stemmed from fear of impending (Bolshevik) revolution in Germany and of an internal threat to capitalism in the United States. *Mr. Hoover's Economic Policy*, a brief, hostile evaluation of the native Iowan's shortcomings as a national leader in crisis, stressed the President's willingness to support financial institutions at the apex of the economic structure as opposed to his refusal to minister to the needs of the lower classes. A loss of $12 billion in wages, Tugwell charged, was compensated for by less than $800 million in relief, 25 percent of that from private sources. Hoover's support through the Reconstruction Finance Corporation of inflated business values of the 1920s and his attack on the European dole (aid to the lower classes) seemed the opposite of what the situation demanded.

Hoover's dogma, Tugwell claimed, rested basically on an outmoded belief in individualism, competition, and in the nation's business system. He feared above all the notions of economic planning and government in business. "He is alert," Tugwell charged, "to any threat from competing ideas and especially wary of those whose source is Russia." Planning particularly, in Hoover's view, was an "infection" from the Soviet Union. He seemed unable to accept fundamental revision of our institutions, crippled by fear of a bureaucratic superstate.[32]

Tugwell rejected John Maynard Keynes's approach and generally the ideas of the monetarists who regarded government spending and inflation of values as the way out of the abyss. He concluded that no degree of currency manipulation or artificial manipulation of values could redress the profound economic dislocations which erupted in the decade of the 1920s. Devices such as the Reconstruction Finance Corporation and in general proposals of the monetarists would only shore up the excesses of the previous decade. In language reminiscent of Bernard Baruch's conservative intonations, Tugwell argued that "values had to retreat until goods could issue from the industrial process priced so that their purchase was possible with the available funds of consumers. This called for a policy of deflation: of capital values, of securities, of retail prices, of industrial excrescences such as advertising and huge [financial] reserves."[33] An exchange of views between Tugwell and the liberal Republican, Frank O. Lowden, former governor of Illinois, is instructive.

Lowden had been reading Keynes's "Treatise on Money," he

wrote Tugwell, a former adviser on agricultural problems, in the autumn of 1931, and had heard a series of lectures delivered by Keynes at the University of Chicago. He inquired if the Columbia economist had taken a position on the matter, particularly in view of farm belt pressures for inflationary measures. Tugwell replied that inflation offered no cure. "We cannot perpetuate a rising price level. . . . Stronger and stronger injections of currency would be necessary to keep the rise going and eventually demoralization would result." Instead he preferred a managed economy.

> But I think it ought to be managed to achieve stability of prices not as an instrument for favoring one or another group in the community. If we want to do that . . . there are more direct and efficient ways of doing it than by using the currency. The way to cure a disease is first to discover its causes and then to treat them. Temporary relief from symptoms is a poor aim for medicine. But it is a poor aim for economists, too. The trouble with agriculture today certainly did not arise out of currency disturbances. Consequently I find it difficult to believe that efforts expended in this direction will be of much benefit though they may alleviate symptoms.

Lowden disagreed. While willing to concede the necessity for fundamental economic remedies, he insisted that in the management of the nation's currency, prices had fallen too low. Some degree of price recovery seemed necessary "before we seek the stabilization which we all regard desirable." [34] By late 1932, Tugwell found his way toward Lowden's point of view which stressed price recovery, a better relationship among restored prices, and restoration of frozen credit. Basically, however, he remained a deflationist in his opposition to cheap money schemes which, he believed, literally papered over the excrescences of the 1920s.

Instructive, also, is an exchange between Tugwell and an old acquaintance, Walter H. Edson of the Chautauqua County Bank of Jamestown, New York. Edson asked for Tugwell's reaction to a paper read by Robert H. Jackson, then a Jamestown attorney, later a Justice of the United States Supreme Court. Jackson suggested the incompatibility of planning and capitalism, that a general economic program involving planning could be carried out only under "an autocratic communist system." Edson sought from Tugwell confirmation of his own position that planning and capitalism could coexist and that controls could be grafted onto the "progressive kind of capitalism developed in the United States." Tugwell rejected Edson's view. Basically, he replied, he agreed with Jackson. For additional insight into his own position on the nation's economic system and what needed to be accomplished he referred Edson to a paper he had recently delivered before the American Economic Association, in December 1931 on "The Principles of Planning and Laissez Faire." [35]

Absolutely essential, Tugwell believed, were "fundamental changes of attitude, new disciplines, revised legal structures, unaccustomed limitations on activity . . . if we are to plan. This amounts . . . to the abandonment, finally, of laissez faire. It amounts, practically, to the abolition of 'business.' This is what planning calls for." He rejected an outmoded faith in the profit motive. Labor, he felt, had no stake in corporate earnings, and with the increasing separation of ownership and control, demonstrated in Gardiner Means's work, he doubted that even management had much profit incentive. Moreover, profits had all too often led to economic instability by their accumulation as surplus reserves or because of their use in the creation of industrial overcapacity, in money market operations, and for the purchase of securities in other corporations and industries. Soviet institutions, he maintained, had not collapsed despite the absence of the profit motive, and in Western society the profit system merely stood as a hindrance to the advancement of planning.

Other factors also pointed to the substitution of planning for laissez faire. For instance, the new technology of work elimination (Taylorism) required coordination and control. Otherwise another economic disaster would follow. And planning, he argued, required social control of economic activity. He viewed as inadequate the creation of a central group of economic experts charged with planning, existing as an advisory body, proposed by some

businessmen, among them General Electric's Gerard Swope and
Henry I. Harriman, president of the Chamber of Commerce. It
could not stem speculation in the form of profit-making. Planned
production and planned consumption required the social control of
profits. A purely advisory National Executive Council, Tugwell
believed, "might guess but could not plan; and the difference between guessing and planning is the difference between laissez faire
and social control."

By social control Tugwell meant federal planning for every industry and every facet of the economy as well as abandonment of
the distinction between private and public employment. Ultimately "business will logically be required to disappear. This is not
an overstatement for the sake of emphasis; it is literally meant."
Tugwell explained why this would occur:

> The essence of business is its free venture for profits in an unregu-
> lated economy. Planning implies guidance of capital uses; this would
> limit entrance into or expansion of operations. Planning also implies
> adjustment of production to consumption; and there is no way of ac-
> complishing this except through control of prices and profit margins.
> . . . To take away from business its freedom of venture and of expan-
> sion, and to limit the profits it may acquire, is to destroy it as busi-
> ness to make of it something else. That something else has no name.

The substitution of a "kind of civil service loyalty" for the nation's laissez faire profit-oriented economy, Tugwell conceded,
required a step by step process. He had seen the future in Russia,
the economist argued, and could not envision a planned society
within our present constitutional and statutory framework. Yet it
was not a revolution he wanted, but rather radical change.

> Perhaps our statesmen will give way or be more or less gently re-
> moved from duty; perhaps our constitutions and statutes will be
> revised; perhaps our vested interests will submit to control without
> too violent resistance. It is difficult to believe that any of these will
> happen; it seems just as incredible that we may have a revolution.
> Yet the new kind of economic machinery we have in prospect cannot
> function in our present economy. The contemporary situation is one
> in which all the choices are hard; yet one of them has to be made.[36]

These rather vague and visionary views were reiterated in concrete terms for the public at large through the Associated Press, on the radio, and before an audience at Columbia Teachers College in April 1932. In the Associated Press statement and his radio address Tugwell stressed the need for abandonment of the American business system in favor of Soviet-style planning and cooperation in agriculture and industry (see chapter's opening quote). The views expressed at Teachers College seemed more guarded and within the framework of the existing system, perhaps because of his recent recruitment into the Roosevelt circle. He advocated:

1. Strenuous opposition to the reduction of levels of wages.
2. Equally strenuous measures to force down retail prices until they matched the decline in wholesale prices.
3. Organized federal relief: a vast expansion of public works coupled with outdoor relief on a family basis.
4. The securing of funds to meet the expense involved by drastic income and inheritance taxes, avoiding sales taxes, which only tend to raise prices and further restrict buying.
5. The avoidance of budgetary deficits and monetary inflation.
6. The taking over by the government of any necessary enterprises which refuse to function when their profits are absorbed by taxation. [37]

Tugwell lamented in *The Brains Trust* that his construct was aborted before the New Deal began. But he failed to recall, as he reconstructed the events of 1932, that the ideas he presented to Roosevelt were framed in terms eminently more in keeping with what can be regarded as politically viable. There is no evidence that his most radical thoughts surfaced in the Roosevelt circle. Much of what he did propose proved acceptable. His quest for a planned economy unfolded in three stages: initially, at Oglethorpe University, in May, when Roosevelt offered the notion of central planning where it seemed necessary; then, at Chicago, in late June, when Roosevelt endorsed the concept of a planned agriculture, formulated by Tugwell, M. L. Wilson, and Henry A. Wallace; and finally, in August, when Roosevelt and Berle appraised Tugwell's ideas for a planned industrial order as premature. The Roosevelt group felt unprepared to follow the path toward a totally planned economy. It seemed too complex a subject for consideration in the heat of a presidential campaign. Industry seemed capable of planning for itself under federal oversight.

The first act in this drama occurred on May 22, 1932, when Roosevelt made a commencement address as he accepted an honorary Doctor of Laws degree at Oglethorpe University in his adopted Georgia. The speech originated with Ernest Lindley, the Albany correspondent of the *New York Herald-Tribune*. Lindley wrote a campaign biography of the governor in 1932 and rapidly became an intimate of the Brains Trust. He sympathized with their views and, accepting a challenge offered by Roosevelt, drafted a statement incorporating the rhetoric of planning and the planner's critique of the excesses of the competitive system.

At Oglethorpe University Roosevelt criticized our haphazard and wasteful industrial development, with its duplication of facilities, large-scale industrial and commercial failures, and squandering of natural reserves. Much of this waste he attributed to our society's individualistic values and, he argued, could be avoided by social planning. He excoriated the domination of our society in the 1920s by a small group of speculators in securities and money-lenders. He presented as the paradox of the depression the existence of a huge productive capacity that lay stagnant.

In his peroration the New York governor used language that appealed later on not only to Tugwell but also to a generation of liberal historians who believed they, too, were social experimenters. Roosevelt demanded "bold, persistent experimentation" and social planning. But when one reads the speech in its entirety its main line of argument shows its basic continuity with the "Forgotten Man" and St. Paul addresses and their emphasis on redistribution of income away from "speculative capital" and toward the laboring man and the farmer.

Nothing in the Oglethorpe address signaled the end of capitalism or the American business system. A cutting attack on the excesses of that era, it proposed the infusion of planning into the nation's economic fabric. Roosevelt rejected the notion that the working of the business cycle could be relied on to bring about recovery; he portrayed ours as a mature economy; and he defined as the nation's central problem "not an insufficiency of capital [but] . . . an insufficient distribution of buying power coupled with an oversufficient speculation in production. While wages rose in many of our industries, they did not as a whole rise proportionately to the reward of capital, and at the same time the purchasing power of other great groups of our population was permitted to shrink." [38] In later years Tugwell argued that the Oglethorpe University address ran completely out of character with Roosevelt's 1932 campaign. [39] Actually it did not. Planning for the sake of planning seemed less a real issue in the Roosevelt circle, as the nomination and the campaign approached, than the need for a viable agricultural program. This assignment, given to Tugwell, led him to Chicago on the eve of the Democratic Convention and to his recruitment of M. L. Wilson and Henry A. Wallace into the Roosevelt camp.

IN HIS CORRESPONDENCE with Edwin R. A. Seligman on agricultural relief in 1928, Tugwell insisted that any program providing for disposal of crop surpluses after they had arisen would not work. "Limitation, I feel, is the only honest approach. . . . This is the method of other businesses." The principal obstacles to crop limitation, he attributed to political rather than economic factors. The state of knowledge could easily provide remedy for the farm crisis. But influential agrarian economists, among them Lewis C. Gray, Henry C. Taylor, and George F. Warren, basically conservative, feared government interference in the farmers' way of life. [40]

Within a few years the picture altered. Under the Hoover administration the Federal Farm Board, with a fund of $500 million at its disposal for entry through cooperative associations into the agricultural marketplace, could not stem plummeting prices for agricultural products. Soon it turned to attempts to induce farmers voluntarily to curtail production. Again it met no success. By 1932, as a result, political obstacles to radical measures lessened as huge purchases in the marketplace and voluntarism, fostered by agricultural conservatives in the Hoover administration, proved a failure. Acreage control, advanced as a solution by William J. Spillman, Henry A. Wallace, M. L. Wilson, and Rexford Tugwell in the 1920s, received serious consideration for the first time as the agricultural depression reached catastrophic proportions in 1931–32 and as it appeared imminent that Herbert Hoover's days were numbered.

Yet, serious hurdles remained. Farmers and farm organizations feared any program that threatened a huge federal bureaucracy, and until 1932 there seemed no way to dissociate domestic allotment from the need for a sizable enforcement apparatus to oversee acreage restrictions. Also, while some radical groups focused on cheap money schemes, the huge and powerful farm organizations remained wedded to the proposals of the 1920s—McNary-Haugenism and export debenture—programs that had little chance for passage in Congress with increasing acknowledgment that the world marketplace had evaporated as a dumping ground for our surplus. More sophisticated analysts of American agriculture, such as Chester C. Davis and M. L. Wilson, regarded the leadership of the established farm organizations as hopelessly reactionary and inept in pursuit of agrarian interests. [41]

An acreage restriction program faced other impediments, legal and mechanical in nature. As Tugwell conceded to Seligman in 1928, "I haven't any set plan for limitation. Any interference, any departure from voluntarism, would run head-on into constitutional difficulties." Two schools of thought existed on the critical question of redistribution of income through a processing tax. Legal conservatives predicted that the Supreme Court would not tolerate "any plan involving the taking of the property of one person or class of persons by taxation or otherwise and giving it directly to another person or class of persons." The other school, relying on the broad doctrine of "national public interest" stressed by Alexander Hamilton and John Marshall, contended that "the Constitution does not prohibit the taking of A's property through taxes for the benefit of

Hoover's Inauguration, March 1929
Chief Justice William Howard Taft administers the oath. Outgoing President Calvin Coolidge looks on at right.

TWO INAUGURATIONS

Roosevelt's Inauguration, March 1933
Chief Justice Charles Evans Hughes administers the oath. Outgoing President Herbert Hoover looks on at right.

Bonus Marchers, Johnstown, Pa., 1931

More than 20,000 veterans, most of them unemployed and in serious financial straits, made their way to Washington D.C., demanding the passage of a bill providing for the immediate payment of their World War I bonus.

THE GREAT DEPRESSION

A Typical "Hooverville," New York City, February 1932

Thousands of destitute people, unable to pay rent, constructed shantytowns around city dumps or wherever unused land could be found.

"Hunger Line," New York City, February 1932

THE GREAT DEPRESSION

Jobless in Detroit, 1932

When banks failed and business could no longer provide jobs, the old view that poverty
was caused by shiftlessness slowly changed. One out of four people was jobless in 1932.

Roosevelt and Louis Howe

Roosevelt and Colonel Edward M. House

Roosevelt with Al Smith

Samuel I. Rosenman (left) with Roosevelt and Lieutenant Governor Herbert Lehman

Raymond Moley and Roosevelt

Rexford Tugwell

THE BRAINS TRUST

Adolf Berle Jr. and Charles Taussig

INS AND THE NEW YORK PUBLIC LIBRARY

A Man Who Might Have Been President
Conservative Democrats sought to check the Roosevelt nomination and proffered the candidacy of Woodrow Wilson's Secretary of War, Newton D. Baker. Had the convention gone to a fifth ballot, he might have won the nomination.

Demonstration for Al Smith, Democratic National Convention, 1932

Hoover Signs Autographs En Route to His Native Iowa

Roosevelt and the Vice-Presidential Candidate, John N. Garner

THE CAMPAIGN, 1932

Election-Year Reunion

Al Smith, who led the "stop Roosevelt" coalition at the Democratic Convention in July, shakes hands and pledges his full support at the New York State Democratic Convention in October. With the happy gentlemen are Norman E. Mack (left), who had placed Roosevelt's name in nomination, and James A. Farley.

An Unusual Study of President Herbert Hoover

A Ride from the White House to the Capitol
A glum Hoover avoids Roosevelt's attempts to make conversation.

THE INAUGURATION, 1932

Roosevelt in Triumph
At the top of the Capitol steps are Mrs. Hoover, Hoover, Garner, Eleanor Roosevelt, and
Charles Evans Hughes. Among familiar faces at the foot of the steps are those of Bernard
Baruch, Al Smith, Louis Howe, James Farley, and Adolf Berle. This caricature, by Covar-
Rubiss, appeared in *Vanity Fair*.

B," provided it served a public purpose or the general welfare. In most instances, liberals held, "the legislative conclusion, while not final, is controlling if there exists any substantial facts to support it." [42] Conservatives maintained, also, that production controls for agricultural products, unless completely voluntary in nature, would violate the Sherman Anti-Trust Act "regardless of the reasonableness of the reduction that might be involved." [43]

In May and June 1932, Roosevelt and Moley pressed Tugwell for mechanisms that would redistribute income to the farmer. They expressed no concern for legal objections voiced in conservative quarters and echoed by Hoover's Federal Farm Board. They wanted devices to restrict production and redistribute· income which would meet the test of political acceptability in the farm belt. In the meantime, Roosevelt kept his options open in the direction of the monetarist school, centered at Cornell University and basically dependent upon Henry Morgenthau Jr. for access to the governor. Tugwell looked upon the Babcock–Meyers–Warren cluster, which favored manipulation of the gold content of the dollar as a depression cure, with absolute horror, and he regarded the Morgenthau–Cornell group as a collection of economic Neanderthals:

> What we had to do was bring farm prices into some kind of better relationship with industrial prices. Their idea of doing that was inflation. That is to say they wanted to raise all prices. My view of that, and Berle's too, was that if you raised all prices you didn't do anything toward mitigating the disparities which existed. So I was what you might call a "sound money" man. Although I always had credit for having had something to do with the inflationary policies, I never agreed with them.
>
> There was quite a separation between those of us who believed in the correction disparities in the price structure and those who believed in simple "inflation." [44]

Tugwell discovered the mechanisms he lacked to secure acreage limitation and correction of price disparities at the second conference on agricultural policy and planning held at the University of Chicago, June 23–25, 1932, on the eve of the Democratic Conven-

tion. Officially the meeting convened under the auspices of the
Giannini Foundation for Agricultural Economics. In reality its principal motive force was the head of the Department of Agricultural
Economics at the Montana State College at Bozeman, M. L. Wilson. Deservedly he is regarded as the "apostle of the domestic
allotment."

Wilson, like Tugwell and George Soule of the *New Republic*,
favored the application of planning to agriculture. Through Soule
and Edward D. Duddy of the University of Chicago, Wilson attempted to induce Tugwell to attend the June conference. Tugwell
hesitated initially, promising in mid-May "to be present if it is at all
possible." [45] But vital information came to Tugwell's attention in
June and hesitation changed to enthusiasm. For one thing, a second more urgent note from Duddy indicated that Tugwell was
needed at a planning roundtable to replace the ailing John R. Commons of the University of Wisconsin. More important, Tugwell
learned that Wilson and Henry A. Wallace planned to attend. The
editor of *Wallace's Farmer*, an influential force in the shaping of
farm belt opinion, and Wilson, Tugwell learned from the economist Beardsley Ruml, had discovered the devices needed to make
domestic allotment workable. When he explained to Moley and
Roosevelt that Wilson had developed self-enforcement procedures
as well as a means of raising prices, the governor was elated. "That
. . . would be a real miracle. We ought to find out if it [is] really
feasible." [46] At Chicago, Tugwell met Wilson and Wallace for the
first time.

M. L. Wilson, modest farmer-professor, remains somewhat ob-
scure as a figure in an accounting of that era except to agrarian specialists. Apparently he wanted it that way, for the whole pattern of
his career seems to have been the expression of his thoughts
through others and avoidance of the limelight. Yet he is important
in two major respects: first, his utilization of concepts derived from
institutional economists and industrial planners for the benefit of
agriculture and, second, his realization that a successful agricultural
program required acknowledgment of economic nationalism and

of the disappearance of the international marketplace for our farm surplus. Politically he inclined toward the Republican party, but in 1932 he cannily observed that his future and that of the farmer rested in the hands of Roosevelt and his professor-advisers, as he called them. As Tugwell learned in Chicago, Wilson not only had the mechanisms, but a domestic allotment bill ready for the Congress, the Norbeck-Rainey bill, introduced on June 29, 1932. [47]

A shrewd tactician, Wilson had little hope for domestic allotment proposals in the 72d Congress. The Hoover record as Secretary of Commerce made it perfectly clear that he would veto such a measure in the remote event it could secure passage. Rather Wilson hoped that the Norbeck-Rainey bill (later the Hope bill) would serve an educational purpose and nudge McNary-Haugenism aside when the Congress and presidency came under new leadership in 1933. In 1932, undaunted, Wilson badgered Federal Farm Board officials and members of the Hoover administration, including Walter Newton, his secretary, and Secretary of Agriculture Arthur M. Hyde in a vain effort at their conversion. He bombarded farm organization leaders, testified before congressional committees, lobbied with farm bloc politicians in the Congress, organized conferences, sat on the Social Science Research Council, enlisted business support as best he could, maintained a huge correspondence with farmers and economists, and shuttled frequently between Bozeman, Chicago, Washington, and New York in his quest for money, ideas, supporters, and votes for his cause. In the closing days of June and in the months of July and August he succeeded also in recruiting Tugwell, then Roosevelt and Moley, to his cause. [48]

The consequences of domestic allotment proved far reaching. By August, the adoption of planning for agriculture gave Tugwell hope that he could induce Roosevelt to impose planning on industry. Before the 1932 campaign ended, Tugwell, and subsequently Moley, realized that it required abandonment of the route of economic cooperation with Europe, enunciated in the May 19 memorandum. By November, Tugwell and Moley formulated a set of concepts they dubbed "intranationalism." Their conflict with Cordell Hull, which raged during the campaign and continued through the interregnum and into the era of the Hundred Days and the London Conference, was rooted in the requirement for a self-contained economy and an artificial internal price structure. These originated as essential elements of Wilson's domestic allotment scheme. [49]

Like Tugwell, Wilson's roots were agrarian, and his economic thinking geared both to long- and short-range solutions for the nation's agricultural dilemma. Born and raised on an Iowa family farm, Wilson attended the Iowa State College at Ames, where he took a degree in agriculture, then attempted tenant farming in northeastern Nebraska and homesteading in Montana. Beginning in 1919, for four years, he attended graduate schools at Chicago, Cornell, and Wisconsin, receiving the M.A. in agrarian economics from Wisconsin.

Following his appointment at Montana, Wilson's energies focused on attempts at the application of scientific and business knowledge to agriculture. With the financial backing of John D. Rockefeller, he gave much of his energy to the Fairway Farms Corporation experiment. It aimed at a proper balance in terms of size, technology, investment, and machinery, one that would assure the profitability of small-scale family farming. At heart a decentralist, he aimed, also, at lowering the cost of wheat production in the dry regions of the nation and at the abandonment of marginal and submarginal lands. [50]

He initially learned of domestic allotment during his service in the Department of Agriculture's Bureau of Economics in the midtwenties. A respected senior colleague, William J. Spillman, in discussions with Wilson argued that the equalization fee and export debenture schemes, favored by farm bloc politicians, would be unworkable under current world market conditions. "Eventually," Wilson later recalled his colleague's argument, "we would be forced to think of the domestic consumption of our export commodities." Spillman presented his views in a little book favoring domestic allotment, *Balancing the Farm Output* (1927). No one, including Wilson, demonstrated any interest. The idea of acreage allotment and reliance on an internal market had not yet reached its time.[51]

Quite independently of Spillman's work, evidently, a year or so later, Beardsley Ruml, an economist who headed the Laura Spellman Rockefeller memorial, proposed to John D. Black of Harvard a book subsequently published as *Agricultural Reform in the United States* (1929). Ruml suggested a discussion of domestic allotment, which Black presented in his tenth chapter. Black described two versions of the domestic allotment idea, that originally formulated by Spillman and a later variation, the "transferable rights" plan. Under this later proposal farmers would be given allotments based on their production of a commodity over a period of time as well as on calculation of anticipated requirements of the domestic market. Farmers who took part in the plan could then sell transferable rights to processors, with their value equal to the tariff duty on the product. As Black conceded, the real cost of transferable rights would be passed on to the consumer in the form of higher domestic prices, but this was characteristic of any effective tariff. The major pitfall of the scheme, he conceded, would be the possibility of cheating by farmers who might produce more than their allotment and by millers tempted to buy "black market" wheat. But it offered the promise of curtailment of production in the face of a vanishing world market for this nation's farm surplus.[52]

It is generally accepted that M. L. Wilson's conversion to domestic allotment followed his reading of Black's work in 1930. "This is in my judgment," Wilson wrote, "the outstanding book of the times."[53] Yet Wilson began as a reluctant apostle in 1930 and much of 1931, largely because of his faith in more fundamental reform of agriculture through elimination of marginal land and producers and in adoption by remaining producers of scientific and business applications. As he explained to Frederick E. Murphy, publisher of the *Minneapolis Tribune* in July 1931, "I have no faith in legislative panacea in the way of price fixing or artificial control but I do believe that there are great possibilities in the development of an agricultural policy of better agricultural planning of retreat from sub-marginal lands, etc." The collapse of the wheat market, and a growing awareness of the applicability of planning in business to agriculture's need to curtail its output, led to Wilson's concentration on domestic allotment beginning in the latter months of 1931 and early 1932.[54]

Wilson, like Tugwell, favored the approach of institutional economics, but of a more conservative variety. John R. Commons of the University of Wisconsin, the pioneer labor historian, had been his mentor. Commons wished for the application of scientific knowledge to social problems in shaping governmental action. But, as Richard Kirkendall explains in his study of social scientists and agrarian politics of that era, "Commons did not believe that scientists should manage society; he simply believed that they should be one of the influential groups. They needed to cooperate with 'practical' men drawn from business and labor organizations and the like, for the experts could contribute indispensable technical knowledge while other groups could supply essential suggestions drawn from practical experience. Each group had its contributions to make, each its shortcomings." [55]

In his organization of study-action groups of scholars, farm leaders, and businessmen to develop ideas, formulate programs, and then press for their enactment, Wilson applied the techniques first developed by Commons in Wisconsin politics.[56] If Wilson's approach toward domestic allotment took on facets of Tugwell's experimentalism and clearly involved planning for agriculture, as it did, it appears to have been more restrictive in its definition of the role of the planner and the uses of planning. This was ultimately Roosevelt's approach toward the issue.

Whereas Tugwell stressed overhead planning and the domination of the economy by a small group of professional planners, "civil servants" he called them, Wilson carefully stressed repeatedly that the domestic allotment program emulated planning techniques advocated and used by forward-looking businessmen. He became particularly impressed with "principles suggested for business by the Swope plan [proposed by Gerard Swope of General Electric] and the United States Chamber of Commerce plan for Continuity and Stability in Business," the creation of Henry I. Harriman. Wilson admired business's ability to maintain prices, match production to demand, and eliminate unprofitable operations. While open minded, Wilson wrote in 1932, on what might emerge from the depression "with reference to national planning and greater stability and control of commodities," he insisted that planning *"has to be voluntary and by groups and I would not want to see it take any socialistic forms"* (Wilson's emphasis). In his correspondence, and later increasingly for public consumption, he stressed the word "voluntary" in association with the domestic allotment program, particularly its dependence on the farmers' vote and participation in the enforcement of acreage controls.[57] His views were summarized in November 1932 for Clarence Poe, editor of *The Progressive Farmer and Southern Ruralist*. Society, Wilson believed, had become "too complicated for laissez faire." He went on:

> If we could agree on this I would follow by saying that the humanitarian approach now is in the direction of economic planning and that changes in agricultural technology must be faced by agricultural and industrial planning. If you will accept this I will go as far as anybody in trying to develop thru the planning route in a manner which will keep us in democracy and not state socialism, an urban rural balance such that the standard of living can be greatly raised and the impact of the machine will lead towards higher standards of living throughout rather than unemployment, hunger, and suffering.[58]

Wilson conceded freely his reliance on Henry I. Harriman, president of the National Chamber of Commerce and a New England utilities magnate, for applications of successful business practices to agriculture. A liberal, Harriman acknowledged the end of laissez faire and the desirability of income redistribution away from the corporate sector and toward the farmer and wage earner. He suggested to Wilson devices established in business and legal precedent that could be built into a viable domestic allotment program. A processing tax on millers, Harriman proposed, enjoyed a long history in the form of excise levies. And the use of contracts for acreage limitation had ample precedent in the natural resource industries, such as coal, lumber, and oil. Wilson struck on the avoidance of a huge federal bureaucracy by utilization of county committees, working with county agricultural agents, for the policing of allotments. Finally, he insisted that farmers vote on acreage allotment, giving the word "voluntary" real meaning.[59]

Adoption of the voluntary domestic allotment program, Wilson realized, presaged an enlarged federal role in national economic management, also abandonment for some years of the agrarian sector's traditional reliance on the world market. An exchange with John D. Black is illuminating. In his massive correspondence, which took the form really of a crusade for the allotment scheme, Wilson frequently invoked the imprimatur of the distinguished Harvard economist, a member of the Social Science Research Council and of the Federal Farm Board. But Black became chary. He did not like the application of the plan to hogs, originally suggested by Henry A. Wallace of Iowa and, reflecting the attitude of the Hoover administration, he objected to proposals for acreage reduction and economic nationalism. "I am naturally in favor of having you stress the situation in Europe with increasing tariffs, etc., but I do not like the emphasis which you give to self-sufficiency for the United States." And he desired the elimination from the Hope Bill of its "emphasis on reduction of acreage." [60]

Wilson's reply reflected a characteristic tendency to smooth over rather than exacerbate differences of opinion. He planned to participate in the forthcoming International Economic Conference where he could present to representatives of Australia, Argentina, and Canada "the ideas of the voluntary domestic allotment plan and the possibilities of some pro ratio or quota agreement between these countries as to international shipments and international acreage adjustments." In the meantime he needed "to hook the domestic allotment plan on somewhere" and it seemed that the Hoover administration and the Republican party were "for higher and still higher tariffs which means eventually isolation and if we are to go [?] on that road then production must be curtailed." Black, an economic adviser to Hoover's Federal Farm Board, had been hoisted by his own petard, for Hoover had moved from an internationalist stance, taken in 1931, to one of extreme nationalism under Ogden Mills's tutelage in 1932. Wilson would have preferred the international route: lowered tariffs, cancellation of war debts, and cooperation with Europe in the restoration of international markets. But internationalism reflected the inclination of neither major party, nor that of European nations, nor the mood of the American people including most farmers. Domestic allotment seemed the logical adjustment to existing conditions.[61]

Wilson reiterated his basic conclusions, on the eve of the Roosevelt presidency, for Chester Davis:

> My fundamental philosophy at the present time is predicated on the growth of nationalism in the world and the cutting off of the European markets for our exportable surplus. The more I study this and the more information I get from Europe, the more convinced I am that the difficulties are very deep-seated and that they are not going to be removed immediately by reciprocal tariffs, debt adjustment, etc. In other words, I feel there are about eight chances out of ten that we are in a period of economic nationalism which will probably last for ten years and possibly much longer.[62]

Henry A. Wallace, destined to become Roosevelt's Secretary of Agriculture and one of the more controversial figures of the New Deal era, accepted the realities of these tides by May 1932. Even more reluctantly than Tugwell or Wilson, he accepted domestic allotment with its implications for adoption of economic nationalism. His economic philosophy and political convictions stemmed from several diverse sources—the social Christianity of his grandfather, his reading of the works of Thorstein Veblen, and then, in the 1920s, the political experiences of his father, Henry Cantwell Wallace. Like Tugwell and Wilson, Wallace received exposure in his formative intellectual years to a fundamental economic critique of the laissez faire system, initially through Benjamin H. Hibbard at Iowa State College, then through his reading of Veblen. Wallace, too, embraced institutional economics and the concept of experimentalism.

From Veblen's *The Theory of the Leisure Class* and *The Theory of Business Enterprise*, the young Iowan concluded that the farmer, a producer, became the victim of speculators, who manipulated the market for private gain. Veblen's subsequent work on *Imperial Germany and Industrial Revolution*, published in 1915, and *The Nature of Peace* convinced Wallace that an exaggerated nationalism favored by big business led to high tariffs and protected markets and thereby to a system of high prices for the regulated product of industry. Based on his reading of Veblen and his own agrarian heritage, Wallace espoused the removal of trade barriers and the stimulation of international economic cooperation. A lessening of international tensions would follow and with it the possibility of warfare would be reduced.

Following World War I, Wallace gave his energies, in the mood of experimentalism, to empirical investigations involving hybridization of corn to attain better yields, the securing of greater efficiency in marketing, anticipation of demand for the output of farmers, and a better understanding of the variables that affected farm prices. Also, in the general mold of sophisticated farm opinion, he came to the conclusion that overproduction was the farmers' greatest economic headache. In Veblen-like terms he suggested "sabotage" as a cure, meaning crop reduction, and modification of the laissez-faire system generally following the practices of big business, which limited production when demand declined. Some of these views found expression in his *Agricultural Prices*, published in 1920. Usually Wallace gave vent to his opinions as editor of the family-owned *Wallaces' Farmer*. Though he favored the interventionist state, he deplored the notion of collectivization. An internationalist and a pacifist, he believed in decency and brotherhood. A universalist in his profoundly felt religious convictions, he proclaimed the virtues of single-family ownership of farms.[63]

But Henry A. Wallace was more than the religious-romantic portrayed later by his detractors. Especially through his father's experience in the Woodrow Wilson administration, then in Warren G. Harding's cabinet as Secretary of Agriculture, the youngest Wallace gained insight into agrarian politics in America and particularly, he believed, into Herbert Clark Hoover. The famous clash between Henry Cantwell Wallace, spokesman for agriculture's postwar demand for government intervention, and Herbert Hoover, Secretary of Commerce under Harding and Coolidge, is significant. For it sheds a good deal of light not only on the frustrations of agrarian leadership at a time when most such leaders, outside the South, identified with the Republican party, but also on Hoover's and his party's neglect of its critical base of power in the Midwest.

The Wallaces of Iowa identified as Republicans. While they rejected Populism and the financial nostrums associated with that movement, they did support generally the advanced concepts presented by the Bull Moose movement and specifically Theodore Roosevelt's 1912 campaign. They advocated the social control of business, lowered tariffs, and direct intervention on behalf of agriculture. Henry Cantwell Wallace, appointed to the Harding cabinet as Secretary of Agriculture when the postwar agricultural depression hit full stride, had the makings of an empire builder, much like Hoover who headed the Commerce Department. Under Henry Cantwell's administration, the powerful and influential Bureau of Agricultural Economics (BAE) was created. In that Bureau ideas and careers emerged which would influence agrarian economics and politics for decades to come. William J. Spillman served as a bridge from an older era of agrarian researchers and left as his legacy the germ of the scheme legislated as the voluntary domestic allotment program under Roosevelt. Newer careers launched included those of Henry C. Taylor, M. L. Wilson, Mordecai Ezekiel, Louis H. Bean, and Howard R. Tolley.

With Henry C. Taylor as chief, the BAE, as it was known, undertook a massive compilation of statistics and data and served as a seedbed for new ideas, including McNary-Haugenism. These ideas, the Secretary of Commerce believed, were essentially so-cialistic. The Wallace–Hoover feud, however, originated in the Wilson administration during the war with Wallace's conviction that Hoover as Food Administrator had forced unconscionably low prices on hog producers. Subsequently, when Wallace as Secretary of Agriculture under Harding became a proponent of McNary-Haugenism, Hoover became its principal opponent in the cabinet because of his opposition to the idea of direct intervention in the economy. The Commerce Secretary espoused instead support of the farm cooperative system that flourished in the citrus industry of his adopted state, California.

At stake were opposing conceptions of the government's function in relation to the economy. The recent Hoover historiography, in an attempt to revive the former President's standing, has tended to gloss over inconsistencies of viewpoint and a fundamental conserva-tism that were attributes when he headed the Commerce Depart-ment and later when he served as Chief Executive. Under the Webb-Pomerene Act of 1918, Hoover promoted cooperation by American corporations overseas in the light of the cartelization of Europe's major industries. Internally he encouraged the fortunes and practices of trade associations which represented cooperation by businesses in the domestic market. [64]

Agrarian spokesmen, many of them prominent Republicans from the farm belt, saw an inherent contradiction, for at the very same time the Secretary of Commerce condemned the Norris Export Plan, a dumping proposal which required government subsidy, and its successor, McNary-Haugenism. These measures represented, in Hoover's judgment, unnecessary government intervention in the private sector and bordered on socialism. The solution to the farm problem, he believed, lay in the law of supply and demand. Because of his familiarity with the California citrus operations, he approved of cooperatives, which he equated with trade associa-tions, and of the extension of credit to farmers. He opposed cleverly and fanatically the Bureau of Agricultural Economics, Wallace, and the Farm Bloc as they pushed for passage of the McNary-Haugen Bill in the Senate.

The elder Wallace and Hoover, now bitter enemies, mustered their forces openly in 1923 as Wallace announced his support of the scheme first developed by George N. Peek and Hugh S. Johnson of the Moline Plow Co. and later identified as McNary-Haugenism. Despite its complexities it had two underlying themes: 1) sale of our surplus overseas, at a loss if necessary for the purpose of achieving a ratio price (parity) geared to commodity prices that prevailed prior to World War I; and 2) farmers' payment for losses incurred in dumping through a larger profit from domestic sales at artificially high prices behind a tariff wall. As long as Warren G. Harding lived, Wallace retained some hope for passage in Congress and the President's signature on the measure, despite Hoover's determined and powerful opposition. The sudden death of Harding on the West Coast and the succession of Coolidge to the presidency doomed the scheme, for Coolidge's views on the matter coincided with Hoover's. Wallace fought on, nevertheless, risking the possibility of a forced resignation after the 1924 election. On the eve of that election he died suddenly, at age 58. Henry Agard Wallace became convinced that in substantial measure his father's death was caused by the strain, overwork, and bitterness that accompanied this policy struggle. For this he never forgave Hoover.[65]

Shy, ascetic, remote, Henry A. Wallace, following his father's death, spent the twenties as editor of *Wallace's Farmer*. Despite a growing disenchantment, Wallace remained a nominal Republican but supported Alfred E. Smith in his race against Hoover in 1928. He championed McNary-Haugenism, his father's last major cause, through his editorial columns, lobbying, and the Corn Belt Committee of Twenty-Two, which he helped found in 1926 with George Peek, Frank O. Lowden, and others. With the onset of the depression, he blasted Hoover's high tariff policies, exemplified by Smoot-Hawley, as criminal and insisted on debts cancellation as a stimulus to revived trade.[66] He also developed an interest in M. L.

Wilson's domestic allotment plan, and reluctantly he became convinced of the necessity for an internal market, artificially high prices in that market, controlled production, and temporary acceptance of economic nationalism. Wallace's abandonment of McNary-Haugenism for domestic allotment, his correspondence with Wilson indicates, was rather cautious and deliberate.

In the course of a trip to Washington, early in 1930, Wallace learned from the head of the Bureau of Agricultural Economics, Nils Olsen, later also from Chester C. Davis, that Wilson knew a good deal about collectivization and motorization of Russian agriculture. Wilson had gone over there to render advice on the subject. Would he be willing to write on these developments for *Wallaces' Farmer* as well as their possible implications for the worldwide wheat surplus? "My second curiosity about you," he continued, "is with regard to the domestic allotment plan. It seems to me that this has a lot to be said for it especially with relation to wheat. Have you given the matter any consideration as it relates to corn and hogs?"

Wilson replied that he had been won over to the plan by the Black book "altho I have not yet had time to get it over into the propaganda state." While well received in Montana, millers in Minneapolis and Duluth were lukewarm. In a separate memorandum, evidently part of their correspondence at the time, Wilson conceded a lack of mechanisms needed to make domestic allotment workable, including an inability to find a device for controlling hog production. Neither John D. Black of Harvard, nor Wilson, nor W. R. Ronald, editor of the Mitchell (S.D.) *Evening Republican,* could find a satisfactory application for hogs. [67]

Various considerations impelled Wallace toward abandonment of other schemes in favor of the voluntary domestic allotment plan. Like Wilson, he came to the conclusion that farmers needed to emulate businessmen's practices which limited production in order to get higher prices for their product. Also, by May 1932, Wilson had worked out means whereby production controls could be achieved in a democratic way. This satisfied Wallace as well as the possibility that farmers through their cooperation in enforcing acreage allotments might develop as a more cohesive group. Yet Wallace still had some reservations in the spring of 1932. Wilson nudged the convert into the fold gently. "I believe you will agree," Wilson wrote, "that the philosophy involved in the domestic allotment idea fits in very well with the idea of national economic planning and a few of the business men of the country who are favorable to national planning are now looking with favor towards domestic allotment and using of the allotment fee either wholly or in part for the retirement of land." Wilson revealed that he had finally given up on the possibility of enactment of the equalization fee (McNary-Haugen) or debenture proposals in Congress. "What is your reaction?"

Wallace understood, he replied, that Charles McNary had asked farm leaders to present a united program before the Senate Agricultural Committee. He viewed domestic allotment favorably. But if exposed prematurely "I am afraid that the whole thing is sunk. This does not mean that I think the plan is not practical. I think it can be made practical if we are really going the route of state socialism. And I am very much inclined to think that we are going that route."

Wallace raised another major issue which evidently he had not yet resolved in his own mind. Economic nationalism was at high tide. Even with a Democratic victory in November, it seemed to him that high tariffs would remain. Further, currency controls and the fears of investment bankers made it unlikely that we would be willing to lend European nations funds sufficient to buy our agricultural surplus. Moreover, public hostility toward Europe had been cultivated by a recent investigation conducted by Senator Hiram Johnson of California. Adoption of acreage control seemed to be the only alternative to "long years of low prices for those farm products of which we produce an exportable surplus." [68] Yet there remained the pull of his intense internationalist views.

Wallace broached the alternative approaches to agrarian recovery in a radio address on "Agriculture and National Planning," on

March 22, 1932. National planning, he indicated, in the form of the La Follette scheme for a National Economic Council or the Swope Plan gave little heed to agriculture's needs. He conceded that most farmers opposed the application of planning to agriculture. But he insisted that "City people" were misguided in the belief that planning for industry and labor would work without inclusion of the farm sector.

Wallace could conceive of two types of planning, one based on isolation, the other on world economic cooperation. He made it clear, as he would again in his book *America Must Choose* (1934) that he favored the internationalist route which required reduced tariffs, loans by American investment bankers to facilitate purchases of our commodities, and termination of the millstones of debts and reparations. The internationalist approach, he felt assured, meant elimination of poverty throughout the world and the prevention of war. The alternative was an isolationist economic program, which required acreage controls (domestic allotment), the taking of some 40 million acres of land out of production, and the shifting of some 5 million rural people to new jobs in the cities. Such a program, while feasible, he contended in his radio speech in 1932, would face the dead hand of bureaucracy. Wallace summed up in his radio address:

> Both plans are full of perils but there is no method of escape—we must choose one or the other and act accordingly. . . . If isolation is chosen, the farmers must submit to compulsory control of production [domestic or acreage allotment] or long years of low prices. If world cooperation is chosen, the people of the United States must manifest through the tariff, international money lending, and in many other ways a degree of world consciousness which is altogether new to them.[69]

Toward the end of May 1932, Wilson and Wallace conferred at Des Moines for half a day. Wallace revealed that he favored domestic allotment without equivocation. The Iowa editor was convinced now that it could be made to apply to hogs and, further, that "we are in for isolationist policies." [70] Neither Wallace nor the other agrarian economists of that day, [71] normally internationalists, given the history of farmers' reliance for their prosperity on world markets, could resist in 1932 the harsh realities of the international marketplace.

THE FOREGOING AFFORDED the intellectual setting for Tugwell's meeting with M. L. Wilson and Henry A. Wallace in Chicago at the conference on agriculture and planning on June 23–25, 1932. Each in his own way arrived at the conclusion that a planned economy needed to be substituted for laissez faire in the light of the collapse of our business civilization. Wilson advocated the extension of business techniques to attain planning in agriculture under the aegis of the federal government. Wallace, too, saw the need for a planned agriculture and like Wilson accepted the worldwide drift toward economic nationalism, though he dreamed of international economic cooperation that would lead to the end of poverty and war. Tugwell aspired to a centralized economy, directed from the top, administered by a publicly minded civil service, and the end of our business system as we know it.

At the University of Chicago's impressive campus, Tugwell rhapsodized years later, he and Wallace particularly sensed a community of ideas and ideals that they shared into the era following World War II. Their first encounter, they ate together, wandered about the campus, and exchanged ideas and aspirations for the future. Some of their dreams would be fulfilled under Roosevelt's administration, others would not.

From Wilson, Tugwell picked up at last a clear perception of the details of voluntary domestic allotment as the Montana farm expert envisioned it. The Columbia economist could not contain his excitement and put through a long distance telephone call to Roosevelt at Albany to relay the exciting news. Roosevelt and Rosenman, putting the finishing touches on Moley's draft of an acceptance speech, could not grasp the plan or the nature of Wilson's devices. Tugwell, aroused, testily charged Rosenman with knowing nothing about agriculture. "You were raised in New York. What are you fooling with this for?"

At Chicago, on July 2, in his acceptance speech, Roosevelt indicated his acceptance of domestic allotment in a guarded statement. He wanted the termination of the Federal Farm Board and its program of commodity purchases in the open market, for it had failed. Heeding Tugwell's recommendation and explanation, he proposed as a substitute the planning of production to reduce agricultural surpluses and essential reliance on the domestic market. "I am sure," Roosevelt suggested to the Democratic National Convention, "that the farmers of this Nation would agree ultimately to such planning of their production as would reduce the surpluses and make it unnecessary in later years to depend on dumping those surpluses abroad in order to support domestic prices. That result has been accomplished in other Nations; why not in America, too?" [72]

8

The Brains Trust 3:
Berle and Industry

. . . Within a relatively short space of time something over one-third of the [business] wealth of the country will be controlled by two hundred corporations, or less, who in turn are dominated by less than eighteen hundred men, together with their banking advisers. This involves domination over a large proportion of the savings of the country, of the lives of the employees and, less directly, over the public served. . . .

The only method of preventing this from degenerating into an absolutist system (which is at best unstable and dangerous) must be the development of common law—a sort of informal constitutional law for economic government.

—ADOLF A. BERLE JR. *

WITH THE ENLISTMENT of Rexford Tugwell into the circle of economic advisers, Moley cast about for an expert on the credit collapse, which had begun with the Wall Street debacle of 1929 and soon threatened all of the nation's fiduciary institutions. A disciple of Charles Beard, conscious of creditor/debtor tensions and of the gross inequity of the debtor's position in a deflationary cycle, and a follower of Charles R. Van Hise's acceptance of large corporate aggregates as the wave of the future, Moley felt the need for technical expertise which might reverse the shrinkage of credit manifested by the inability of borrowers to borrow and of lenders to lend. The intial step in reversal of the depression required a

---

* To James C. Stephens, April 24, 1929, Box 11, Berle Papers.

shift in distribution of income and purchasing power from the urban-industrial-financial centers of the East to the rural sector in the West. But the second step could not be delayed—restoration of credit in a capitalist system and recovery were synonymous. Yet, simple restoration of credit and reflation in the industrial sector would hardly suffice. Without elimination of excrescences and fundamental reforms the economic collapse would repeat itself.

A member of the Columbia University Law School faculty, Moley recalled the impressive contributions of a younger colleague at several meetings devoted to curriculum revision. "I rather admired the cleverness of his thinking," he explained Adolf Berle's appeal, "and the sharpness of his expression. I knew that he was a Progressive in his political outlook. And I knew that he knew a lot about corporate finance and finance generally." Moley learned, too, that Berle and an economist, Gardiner C. Means, had collaborated for some years on a major research effort, soon to be published, on the nature and control of the modern corporation. Berle seemed ideally suited for membership in the Roosevelt group.

On the verge of publication of a decade's work on what he suspected might become one of the most prescient analyses of modern economic agregates and their functioning, aware nevertheless that few would read or care to comprehend its import, Berle proved reluctant to seize what seemed an opportunity for the broader exploration of his thought in the political arena. In his customary blunt manner he told Moley that he preferred another candidate. He did not care to elucidate his choice for the party's nomination, though Moley suspected it was Newton D. Baker; nor did Berle indicate that as recently as 1928 he was an active member of the Republican party. Undaunted, Moley pressed the matter in a conference at Berle's law school office. He saw no significance in his colleague's political preferences. "It was his technical assistance that was wanted, not his political support, which carried not the slightest weight in any case, I remarked. He nodded energetically, laughed, and enlisted."

In the weeks that followed others of Moley's colleagues at Columbia University were sounded out and made the journey with him to Albany to converse with the governor, but none passed the test. They proved archetypal academicians, inflated, overspecialized, and irrelevant. With the addition of Berle, the professorial group, later christened the Brains Trust, was completed.[1]

Born in a Boston suburb, Brighton, Massachusetts, on January 29, 1895, to a daughter of a clergyman and a Congregationalist minister, Adolf Augustus Berle, Adolf Jr. grew up in the climate of the Social Gospel. In later years he recalled vividly his father's service as a minister in Chicago during the depression of 1903 and his own experience as he trudged to school past corpses dead of hunger and exposure. It seemed so unnecessary, the ultimate cruelty of the excess and callousness of the age of iron and steel. Excursions with his parents to visit Jane Addams at Hull House and visits to the Berle home of socially conscious reformers also served as formative influences.

The family soon returned to Massachusetts where the senior Berle assumed the stewardship of a church in Salem and young Berle completed his secondary education at age 13. In an era of strict parental direction and in conformity with his own writings on the need for education in the home, the elder Berle shaped the lad's pursuits and mentality in accordance with his own convictions. Adolf Augustus Berle published frequently on the virtues of a Christian education and taught Applied Christianity at Tufts University. Progressive activists frequented the Berle household, among them Louis D. Brandeis, their purpose the achievement of ameliorative legislation at the state level.

"He skipped both adolescence and senility," Max Ascoli recapitulated the lifetime of Adolf A. Berle Jr., in a tribute to one of the geniuses of the twentieth century. Because of his tender years, the youngster's entry to Harvard College was delayed until he reached age 14; he took his B.A. degree at age 18, his A.M. at 19, and his law degree in 1916 at age 21. Berle fulfilled the requirements for a master's essay during his senior undergraduate year by undertaking a study of Alexander Hamilton's Assumption Act (assumption of state debts by the federal government) under the direction of Edward Channing, one of the giants of his generation, then preparing his fourth volume of A *History of the United States* (1917). Berle's research, incorporated in Channing's work,[2] led to his conclusion in 1932 that federal credit which remained sound in the depression should serve as a bulwark for the nation's collapsing debt structure. Although he wanted to become a historian upon completion of his education, he heeded his father's injunction that history as a profession offered no chance at a respectable livelihood. The law seemed eminently more suited to that end and toward their shared conviction that social goals could be achieved only through a major economic reorganization in the United States.

Like Moley and Tugwell, Berle, from the inception of his career, combined scholarly pursuits with participation in the public process. Undoubtedly, this stemmed partly from his training at the Harvard Law School. From Roscoe Pound, he gained perception of the Austrian theory of jurisprudence, which viewed the law as a vehicle for social engineering, a concept regarded as radical at the time. And like Louis Brandeis and Felix Frankfurter, despite later differences over the desirability of atomization or concentration, his education was suffused with the notion, propounded initially by Oliver Wendell Holmes, that economics and legal principles could not be separated in the contemporary world. Disappointed with his failure to make the *Law Review*, Berle spent his leisure time in his final year at Harvard studying Roman law and the Russian economic system. Unable to make a connection with one of the prestigious New York law firms, he believed because of his lack of proper social standing, he secured employment upon graduation with Brandeis, Dunbar, and Nutter in Boston.

Harvard never afforded Berle substantial emotional succor. Although he was scarcely a "loner," his lack of social lineage, perhaps too his tender age, delimited the circle in which he moved. Twenty-five years later, in 1941, having made his mark as one of the leading corporate and financial analysts of his time, he was hooted out of a Harvard Law class reunion. He had been invited as a speaker, but his traditionalist classmates, members of the nation's most prestigious law firms and financial institutions, resented his New Deal affiliations particularly, he believed, his association with securities regulation. Berle never completed the address and never returned. Intellectually independent, he had long since gone his own way in another critical sense. Unlike Felix Frankfurter, one of Berle's instructors at Harvard Law, the precocious youngster early decided that Louis Brandeis' fulminations on the "curse of bigness" simply would not suffice in the twentieth century. Size, he concluded, was organic rather than conspiratorial in origin and the notion of dissolution of large aggregates struck him as a sterile pursuit.[3]

ALTHOUGH OPPOSED to United States entry into the Great War in 1917, the young attorney enlisted in the service after one year with the Brandeis law firm. By sheer chance, in characteristic fashion of the military, he became a Russian economic specialist, and with the signing of the Armistice made his way to Paris—he was a second lieutenant—as part of the coterie assigned to the Versailles Conference. Once in France, Berle found himself in search of a task and fastened onto a Harvard historian, Robert Lord, a specialist in Polish and Central European affairs. Others joined the Russian Section in equally haphazard circumstances, including a stately young gentleman who appeared in striped trousers and cutaway coat and announced himself as Samuel Eliot Morison. It proved a stormy experience for the group tagged the *jeunesse radicale,* the young radicals. For like William C. Bullitt, dispatched to Russia to treat with Lenin, they favored genuine negotiations with the fledgling Soviet regime. Sabotaged in their effort, they believed, by Clemenceau and the French Foreign office, and by the confusion and discord in the U.S. delegation, they returned home disillusioned.[4]

Following the war, Berle joined with Guy Lippitt in forming Lippitt and Berle in downtown Manhattan, then in 1925 resumed

his association with Harvard as a lecturer in finance at the School of
Business. Under the tutelage of William Z. Ripley, a senior colleague, once his teacher, Berle's interests broadened to a probing
of the modern corporation, its financial practices, and the institutional implications. Ripley critiqued the divorcement of ownership
from control and the unchecked power of those who sat in the
boardrooms in a widely acclaimed work published in 1927, *Main
Street and Wall Street*. Others, too, paved the way for Berle's
thought, including the institutionalists, such as John R. Commons,
and his contemporary Walton Hale Hamilton, an economist at the
Robert Brookings Graduate School of Economics and Government
(1923–1928), then, beginning in 1928, a member of the Yale Law
School faculty.

By the 1920s, as he began the publication of scholarly articles in
the law journals, Berle's pursuits represented a fusion of three
schools of thought: the Social Gospel in which he had been nurtured; the new jurisprudence that had taken hold at Harvard Law,
espoused by Holmes, then Pound, Brandeis, and Frankfurter,
which treated the law and economics as intertwined and the law as
an intrument of social action; and institutionalism, which had
caught up the imagination of many bright anti status quo economists such as Tugwell and M. L. Wilson, fascinated by the challenge of an emerging technocratic society.[5]

Convinced that the exposition of corporation law in the law
schools and the courts remained anachronistic, Berle approached
Associate Justice Harlan Fiske Stone of the United States Supreme
Court, formerly dean of the Columbia University Law School.
Columbia's course on corporation law, Berle claimed, was "rotten."
Stone smiled and conceded the issue. The course had too long
been the domain of a former law partner, now over the hill. What
did the young attorney propose to do? Berle suggested a seminar
on securities, bond flotation, and the financial process that had
become so closely related with the functioning of the modern corporation. Thanks to Stone's intercession, the appointment at Columbia Law came through in 1927, and the following year Berle
severed his association with Harvard's School of Business.

A second opportunity opened when Berle learned, about the same time, that the Social Science Research Council, in process of formation, had sufficient funds to cast about for subjects worthy of support. Berle proposed a study of corporations and received money sufficient to recruit a Harvard economist, Gardiner C. Means, then a Ph.D. candidate, as a collaborator. "The attempt I was then making," he reflected in later years, " was to assert the doctrine that corporate managements were virtually trustees for their stockholders, and that they could not therefore deal in the freewheeling manner in which directors and managers dealt with the stock and other interests of their companies up to that time. It was the beginning of the fiduciary theory of corporations," really a conservative, legalistic concept broadened during the depression in its reach and import with Berle's demand for social accountability. The resulting work, *The Modern Corporation and Private Property,* published in 1932, became a landmark in the economic literature of the twentieth century.

When asked in his twilight years about the academic reception accorded *The Modern Corporation,* Berle, characteristically pugnacious, yet somewhat deprecating of his achievement, ventured that "Harvard has never recognized it. I suppose they know it exists. Columbia thought well of it." [6] Over the decades *The Modern Corporation* had been plagiarized, vulgarized, rewritten by Berle himself on several occasions, yet assumed a "sort of canonical quality." Outwardly formidable, it boiled down to a statistical demonstration by Means of the concentration of economic power in some 200 large corporations managed by some 1800 individuals, and Berle's conclusion that the political sector of society must unearth devices capable of imposing upon industry cognizance of its responsibility for the nation's economic and social weal. The premise was easily demonstrable. The difficulty, as Raymond Moley noted in his own copy, was "How to do this?" Berle acknowledged the problem to Louis Brandeis:

> I wish there were some tangible mechanism which could be laid
> hold of to make this tangled economics less master and more servant.
> Since none lies within my grasp (if it exists at all), the obvious job for

the present is to try to understand things a little better. Slowly we
may find ways or light guiding toward a sound solution.

Rereading your own collected essays not so long ago, I was struck
with your opposition to the tremendous corporate concentration. You
were writing in 1915. Now the concentration has progressed so far
that it seems unlikely to break up even in a period of stress. I can see
nothing at the moment but to take this trend as it stands endeavoring
to mold it so as to be useful. If the next phase is to be virtually a non-
political economic government by mass industrial forces, possibly
something can be done to make such government responsible, sensitive, and actuated primarily by the necessity of serving the millions
of little people whose lives it employs, whose savings it takes in
guard, and whose materials of life it apparently has to provide. [7]

It would remain for Roosevelt, Moley, and Berle to make the initial groping effort toward an economic constitutional order in September at the Commonwealth Club in San Francisco. The quest,
inaugurated in 1932, continues.

Berle stated the problem in lucid fashion in his preface. He had
concluded in a series of articles focused on corporate finance that
the nation's industry, through the corporate device, "was being
thrown into a collective hopper wherein the individual owner was
steadily being lost in the creation of a series of huge industrial
oligarchies." Despite the revolutionary implications, Berle did not
condemn the trend toward concentration. It seemed a silent revolution, logical, intelligent, fraught with challenges as readily as
dangers.

Two-thirds of the wealth of the nation had shifted from individual to corporate ownership, with vast implications for workers,
property owners, and methods of tenure. Ownership had become
divorced from control resulting in a new organization of society.
"Manifestly," he challenged, "the problem calls for a series of ap-
praisals." Louis Brandeis and Felix Frankfurter, in his view, desired to turn the clock back on the assumption that the modern
corporate system could not endure. Historically, Berle reinforced
Theodore Roosevelt's views on corporations, according to which
their bigness per se did not concern him as much as the potential

for harm of those who directed them. Berle insisted upon acceptance of the huge economic aggregate, on its study, and on consideration of its relationship to the political state. Would it dominate the political state? Would it be regulated by the state? Or could the two coexist with a minimum of connection? "In other words, as between a political organization of society and an economic organization of society which will be the dominant form?" The question, he ventured, would remain unresolved for some time. [8]

The new corporate system, as Berle viewed it, served as a method of property tenure and a means of organizing economic life. Much like the ancient feudal system it had attached to itself a combination of attributes and power and needed to be dealt with as a major social system. As the product of centripetal tendencies which pulled wealth together into increasingly huge units, it seemed fraught with revolutionary implications. The only limit on concentration was the capacity of human beings for management of large aggregates. The 200 largest corporations as of January 1, 1930, possessed assets of $81 billion or 49 percent of all corporate wealth in the United States and received 43 percent of the income of all nonbanking corporations. Berle and Means estimated further that these 200 aggregates controlled 22 percent of all national wealth. The trend, they predicted, would continue. [9]

As nearly as the authors of *The Modern Corporation and Private Property* offered some resolution of the dilemma, they urged an acceptance of the situation as evolutionary and organic and the development within the business community of a sense of social responsibility. Berle's minimum program urged upon corporate leaders fair wages, employee security, reasonable service to their public and stabilization of business. Ultimately "control" of the giant corporations should evolve into a neutral technocracy balancing a variety of claims within the community. Structurally Berle envisaged the possibility of a new economic state with the socially conscious corporation coexisting with, even supplanting, the political state as the dominant form of social organization.

If *The Modern Corporation* proved intellectually innovative, it reflected nevertheless Berle's departure from his radical origins. A cogent analysis of the contemporary corporate structure, it hardly ventured beyond Andrew Carnegie's "stewardship thesis," also anchored in the Protestant ethic, in its resolution of the dilemma of size and lack of accountability of the modern aggregate. If valid in its critique of Brandeis' naive faith in a return to the small economic unit of an earlier era, the faith it placed in the potential ennoblement of corporate management to social purposes seemed equally jejune. Or perhaps, as has been suggested, it reflected Berle's growing legal practice at the heart of the nation's financial center, his directorship of several large corporations, and his marriage in 1927 to the daughter of a New York millionaire. Berle's conclusions more nearly resembled the thinking of the New Era than the New Deal. If the Social Gospel and institutionalism had pointed the way, worship of management and technocracy in the 1920s, which elsewhere led to the corporative state, seemed to inspire his rationalization of the twentieth-century trend toward size, specialization of function, and huge capital outlay.

Whatever the merit of the argument that Moley, seduced by the fat cats, "had been taken into the Baruch circle" after he left the Roosevelt administration in late 1933, the basic clash of views in the Roosevelt–Brains Trust circle scarcely involved Moley's trust in big business as opposed to Berle's and Tugwell's advocacy of an enlarged federal role. This traditional view breaks down when the record is scrutinized. As Berle recalled in later years, "Tugwell's bent toward collectivism" ventured considerably beyond Roosevelt's philosophy as well as that of "at least nine-tenths of the United States. The country was not ready to accept economic planning and direct action in the measure Tugwell then wanted." Instead, the New Deal promoted an institutional shift in the locus of economic power from the private sector to public institutions. In part, this reflected a shift in Berle's thinking in 1932. But the threat of countervailing power in the form of an enlarged federal presence, enunciated in the Commonwealth Club address, emerged as the compromise struck by Roosevelt and Moley between Tugwell's collectivist views, which relied on a civil service bureaucracy, and Berle's collectivist views, which depended upon the beneficence of corporate management.[10]

THE MODERN CORPORATION, scarcely radical, represented only a slight shift from Berle's earlier conviction, expressed in legal journals, that corporate leaders might need to be restrained by according an enlarged dimension to common law doctrine. But reliance on an enlightened corporate leadership seemed to be contradicted by the depression's growing revelation of the financial and business community's malodorous practices. Remedy, Berle came to realize even before his book appeared in print, might need to be imposed from the outside in order to achieve broader social goals, which he defined as a growing need of the individual for safety—meaning guarantee of employment, security of savings, a reasonable subsistence, and a chance to develop the better things of life, spiritual as well as economic.

As opposed to his willingness only months earlier to rely upon a developing sense of social responsibility by the corporate infrastructure, Berle came by 1932 to advocate federal incorporation for the purpose of imposing some external discipline through a strengthened Federal Trade Commission. "My friends say this is socialism," he complained. "But it does not seem to matter very much. As between a system run by somebody and a system run by nobody, I am all for the former no matter what name you tack onto it; and as between the Government and the National City Bank, the bets are in favor of the Government every time."

Summarizing their collaboration of 1932 in later years, Berle reminded the head of the Brains Trust that they stood "half-way between a philosophy of 'getting the old boat' going again, on the one hand, and the socialist and near-socialist conceptions proposed by some of our friends." In general terms, they rejected the Brandeis–Frankfurter group's dependence on free markets and its stress on a regression to small-scale production. Instead, they preferred

Van Hise's *Concentration and Control* as more logical. In particular terms, they concluded that a larger proportion of the national income should be directed toward the lower income levels, especially the farmer. "This we did consciously, through lowering interest rates, credit arrangements, and so forth. This was not socialist; it was common sense. They needed the money; business needed the customers; everybody needed employment. We thought private organization would do it, but were prepared to do this through public sector expenditures if need be—the result, in any event would be mixed." [11]

Like Tugwell and Moley, therefore, Berle matured as an academician when the depression broke, yet at a time, as he put it years later, when "academic economists did not soil their hands with practical questions." By disparate routes—Moley through Beard and Van Hise, Tugwell through Patten and Veblen, Berle thanks to the Harvard Law School and later Ripley—the three Columbia University academicians fastened on institutionalism and sought its application in the economic crisis of 1932. And Roosevelt in time came to grasp, then as President-implemented, the Brains Trusters' conviction that the fundamental situation demanded a broad spectrum of programs that required a new definition of federal entry. Hoover's passive state needed replacement not on a piecemeal basis, but by an integrated federal program designed to reactivate the economy, then ensure the prevention of a repetition of the post-1929 disaster. This was the task assigned to the Brains Trust. None questioned, however, the finality of the Democratic aspirant's decision as to what constituted a politically acceptable proposition in the national arena. [12]

As Moley requested, Berle contributed a lengthy memorandum on the financial collapse and possible avenues of restoration and recovery in May, drafted in collaboration with Louis Faulkner of the Bank of New York and Trust Company. The Berle–Faulkner memorandum, seminal in its impact on the developments of the campaign and the tenor of the New Deal, contained three parts: an analysis of the major causes of the depression, recommendations for emergency action, and long-range proposals. Depression causation was explained in terms of the sterilization of money and credit through the hoarding of cash and the absence of economic demand. It also stressed the fear of borrowers to borrow or lenders to lend. Loss of confidence resulted in the stoppage of industry and employment and generally of the economic system. Depositors feared for their savings, lenders for the security of their loans, security holders for the safety of their investments. By the same token, no one felt secure enough in his employment to spend beyond his immediate needs, to lend to savings institutions, in the form of deposits, or to corporations, through the purchase of securities. The result was economic stagnation.

Whereas the individual feared for his savings, institutions such as commercial banks, savings banks, and life insurance companies equally feared their own lack of liquidity, considering the state of the equities market. Berle and Faulkner dealt with an array of securities: railroad bonds, public utilities bonds, urban and farm mortgages, industrial bonds, municipals, state issues, and those of the U.S. Treasury. Certain of these securities seemed beyond salvage, particularly real estate bonds, estimated at $12 billion, a traditionally speculative sphere of investment. Yet, a segment of these equities, conservatively drawn home mortgages, some $35 billion, held by individuals and banks, required intervention. Securities of the pyramided holding companies could not be supported and constituted excrescences, as opposed to the obligations of the operating companies, which could be supported by earnings. State, industrial, and federal obligations seemed reasonably secure, but several categories of obligation required intervention through the use of the credit of the U.S. government. These included farm mortgages (because of the millions of farmers involved), salvage of the urban home mortgage market, and rescue of sound railroad bonds (in view of heavy investment in railroad securities by fiduciary institutions). Similarly, for the individual's security, Berle advocated federal insurance of savings accounts.

The Berle–Faulkner presentation represented, in part, a

broadening of the concept of the Reconstruction Finance Corporation, a vehicle now nearly abandoned by the Hoover administration through studied restraint of its activities. It was a forerunner as well of insured personal savings (FDIC), and of federal underwriting of urban home mortgages under the Home Owners' Loan Corporation and farm mortgages via the Farm Credit Administration. Although seemingly simple in retrospect, it was a complex task, as their discussion of railroad debt revealed. Railroad obligations stood at $11 billion, 70 percent held by savings banks, insurance companies, and the like. Interest charges on this debt and operating expenses far exceeded railroad income. Although RFC had adequate financial capacity to enter into the picture, like any creditor, it would need to insist on fundamental long-term changes, particularly a scaling down of high pre-depression fixed interest charges, of wage rates, and of expensive featherbedding practices. Berle also advocated consolidation of weaker rail lines into stronger ones. Similarly, the farm mortgage situation—$9.8 billion outstanding in 1932—required basic readjustments, including the federalizing of marginal operations that needed to be taken out of production and the federal guarantee of mortgages at a reduced interest rate. The credit of the federal government, in short, would be used for the rediscounting of fixed obligations in certain economic sectors at a lowered interest rate. The overall result, Berle hoped, would be the release of sterile credit.

Other emergency measures proposed in the Berle–Faulkner memorandum aimed at affording the individual some measure of economic security, again as a stimulus to activity. Not all were adopted, as in the instance of the suggestion for job security at current wage levels for five years, or the suggestion that federal loans be made to enterprises in return for a guarantee of a stipulated level of employment for a specified period of time. But the basic premise held, namely, that the nation could not wait for the sort of economic windfall that reversed the tide in earlier depressions.

Berle's analysis of long-range requirements hinged on the arguments presented in *The Modern Corporation and Private Property*.

Cycles of depression had worsened in proportion to economic concentration. In simpler times, a downward swing of the economic cycle meant a bad time. But the concentration of business into a relatively few huge economic units and of population in cities meant a dislocation of the entire mechanism. A new situation had emerged in the 1920s:

> Concentration has proceeded to a point at which 65% of American industry is owned and operated by about six hundred corporations; the balance being spread among millions of little family businesses. Nearly 50% of American industry is owned and operated by two hundred large corporations. This means that some six thousand men, as directors of these corporations, virtually control American industry; eliminate the inactive directors, the number of men is reduced to not more than two thousand. These control perhaps 30% of the total national wealth; such wealth being the concentrated industrial wealth which dominates the life of eastern United States.

Concentration, accelerated by the depression, also posed a moral question. Sooner or later, Berle believed, there would be little distinction between the American and Soviet systems, one dominated by a hierarchy of Commissars, the other by a small number of corporate directors. Resolution of the dilemma required a multiplicity of approaches at the federal level, including publicity of corporate accounts at frequent intervals, preferably quarterly, publicity of transactions in securities by officers of these corporations, and creation of a Capital Issues Board (the later Securities Exchange Commission) to extract full information concerning securities sold on the major exchanges. These measures, and one might add the divorcement of commercial and investment banking, were scarcely controversial proposals in the climate of the stock market debacle of that period.

More difficult to attain, because they struck at the heart of the American ethic and congressional fear of Wall Street domination, were Berle's desiderata that encouragement of chain banking and repeal of federal antitrust legislation be undertaken as long-range structural goals. Centralized banking, he believed, could have avoided the worst of our bank failures, as it had in Great Britain and Canada. Repeal of our antitrust strictures would tolerate consolidation and even monoploy situations. But where concentration occurred, defined as 50 percent domination of an industry by one or two units, the federal government should step in and regulate matters of legitimate national concern: prices, security issues, and further consolidation.

As Berle viewed the long-range situation, it seemed, finally, that concentration of control necessitated a national system of insurance against old age, sickness, and unemployment. The individual was at the mercy of a powerful economic system, characterized by uniformity of practices, one that, with few exceptions, notably the Swope Plan, had discerned no social or economic obligations to the mass of its employees. Excess corporate profits had been put into plant investment and might have been used more wisely in terms of society's larger need to care for employees by meliorating for them the downward swings of the economic cycle.[13]

Although Moley incorporated elements of the Berle memorandum in his own presentation to Roosevelt in May, intended as a guide for the 1932 campaign, little discussion of these proposals occurred in the weeks before the national convention. For good reason. The squire's march toward the nomination, once treated by his political intimates as a foregone conclusion, had stalled and revealed signs of imminent collapse. Curiously, Berle typified an important and growing sentiment in the party that another candidate would be eminently more desirable.

As was true of so many of the nation's intellectuals, now alienated by the Great Engineer in the White House, Berle could not countenance four more years of Hoover's antediluvian economics and nostalgic longing for the preservation of the status quo ante regardless of social cost. Something needed to be done. Like most academicians of his generation, despite his offering of economic advice to the Roosevelt entourage, he favored the candidacy of Newton D. Baker. Unknown to Roosevelt and Moley, his activities on Baker's behalf continued through the fateful Chicago convention.

In the weeks before the Democratic National Convention Berle collaborated with Ralph Hayes in a strategem calculated to deadlock the proceedings, then unleash a barrage of telegrams and petitions urging Baker's nomination. Berle's co-conspirators at Columbia included James T. Shotwell, Virginia Gildersleeve, Roswell Magill, and John Hanna, and Arthur N. Newcombe and George K. Gardner at Harvard. The intelligentsia, generally conservative and internationalist, seemed harnessed in a curious alliance with the Jeffersonian Democrats, largely business-financial reactionaries, led by Smith and Raskob, and the Hearst–McAdoo fundamentalist wing of the party, which supported Garner of Texas.

With many other Baker supporters, Berle participated in the stratagem of collaboration with the Roosevelt group by drafting a Democratic platform, conservative and internationalist, appropriate to the Ohioan's candidacy. When the final goal of achievement of a convention deadlock failed, they contented themselves with the squire's candidacy and offered their services. Berle summed up his embarrassment in a letter he believed should ultimately become part of the historical record. "I am thus in the brilliant position," he rued, "of having played both ends against the middle, and I do not like it. But I recall Henry Nevison's remark, 'When you touch politics, you touch the devil.' " [14]

9

Stop Roosevelt Stage 2:
The Struggle for Control of the Party

AS JAMES A. FARLEY and Louis M. Howe set up Roosevelt headquarters at Chicago on the eve of the Democratic National Convention, they mounted a huge map depicting vast areas of the United States, shaded in pink, committed to the governor's nomination. Intended as a psychological weapon, it did not impress the old political pros, who remained unconvinced. When the indomitable Alfred Emanuel Smith learned of the display of Roosevelt's political invincibility, he taunted that the squire's forces had "lots of area" but not "lots of delegates"—an allusion to the geographically huge agricultural and mining states.[1] Most carried little delegate clout at a Democratic enclave and, in the era of the two-thirds rule, little finality in the choice of the party nominee. The large state delegations had fallen to other choices or were badly divided. The Roosevelt candidacy, once regarded as a virtual certainty, had faltered. Smith and the conservative-internationalist coalition gave every indication that with some luck and maneuvering they could suffocate the New Deal at its inception.

Roosevelt's early primary victory in New Hampshire, of initial psychological value, reflected Robert Jackson's political perspicacity, especially in New England politics. But it proved of minor tangible significance after Smith and the urban-Catholic political machines rendered the front-runner a drubbing in Massachusetts, Pennsylvania, Connecticut, Rhode Island, New Jersey, New York, and Illinois. Elsewhere, John Nance Garner gathered up the legacy of the Bryan–McAdoo wing of the party in Texas and California. And "favorite sons," such as Ohio's Governor George White, Maryland's Governor Albert C. Ritchie, Missouri's Senator James Reed, Virginia's Governor Harry Flood Byrd, and Illinois' J. Hamilton ("Ham") Lewis, positioned themselves as dark horse alternatives or for the vice-presidency. Historians in the afterglow of the New Deal made altogether too much of Roosevelt's presumed power in the party and of Howe's and Farley's managerial talents. Amateurish blunders and a lack of grasp of the deeper issues nearly capsized the front-runner's cause. [2]

By the eve of the convention a coalition was forged by Alfred E. Smith and William G. McAdoo, with Bernard Baruch as godfather, with enough votes to check Roosevelt's ambition for national leadership. The interplay of personalities and interests is a lesson in the complexity and ambiguities of the American political process. Underlying this fascinating story of ambitions fulfilled and frustrated and of the political double cross in the summer of 1932, was a powerful clash between diverse visions of the nation's destiny.

The splintering of delegate strength typified Democratic politics of the post-Wilsonian era. Woodrow Wilson's ideals aside, or possibly because of his insistence on them, he had made a shambles of the party and its mechanisms in his second term, and the Democratic party never fully recovered in the 1920s. [3] Suicidal tendencies, endemic in Democratic politics because of the party's heterogeneity, were encouraged by the traditional two-thirds requirement for a nomination. The party was brutally divided by the ugly 1924 conclave at Madison Square Garden in New York. The Houston Convention of 1928 and Smith's nomination did nothing to salve the wounds. McAdoo, killed off in 1924 by Smith's obstinacy and the party's urban Catholic machines, gained sweet revenge four years later when he and his followers, Protestant, rural, and dry, sat on their hands. The third element in the party, the Wall Street internationalists, while less powerful than the other two, had slipped John W. Davis past the rural/urban antagonisms of 1924 and by 1932 became as wary of Roosevelt's urbane Progressivism as it was of McAdoo's rural radicalism. The internationalists, the New York financial community, the utilities magnates, and the intellectuals preferred Baker, another compromise choice.

IN THE MONTHS PRECEDING the national convention the Roosevelt strategy consisted of sapping Al Smith's strength in New England where he had been strongest in 1928. The initial contest occurred in New Hampshire with the wily Robert Jackson in charge. The New England businessman limited the number of delegates committed to Roosevelt's candidacy to the exact number to be selected for the convention as opposed to the considerably larger Smith slate, which divided precious votes. Jackson threatened denial of patronage, played politics to the hilt by maintaining a spy at Smith's New York headquarters, and tended to ignore, with Roosevelt's consent, Howe's political suggestions, which he appraised as "more amusing than practical." Howe, anxious for the result, poured more money into the New Hampshire contest than any other.

Some two weeks before the announcement of his candidacy, on January 26, 1932, Alfred E. Smith summoned Roosevelt's New Hampshire manager to his Empire State office. Old friends, Jackson and Smith met alone. The atmosphere, however, was thick with tension. Smith wanted to know of his chances in the New Hampshire contest if he should decide to enter. Jackson, unhesitatingly, predicted his defeat. "You say so. You're for Roosevelt," Smith shouted accusingly. Jackson reminded him of past loyalties including a $10,000 contribution to the 1928 campaign, but Smith felt deeply betrayed by his old allies:

> He referred to Roosevelt as a good man and he certainly had a right to aspire to the presidential nomination. . . . "But as for Jim Farley, why doesn't he be a man? He crosses to the other side of the street to avoid meeting me face to face. He's timid. What's the matter with him?" . . .
> Al paid his respects also to Louis Howe; his words so blistering I

shall not record them here. . . . He faintly scorns Jim Farley's avoidance of him, . . . but he referred to Eddie Flynn with asperity and the frail Louis bore the brunt of his ridicule.[4]

The two men, calmed, returned to the issue. Smith had been assured by John Curtin that he could defeat Roosevelt in New Hampshire. Jackson disagreed.

Apparently informed by Jackson of Smith's feelings toward him, James A. Farley decided to face the music and arranged for a visit with the Happy Warrior. The date was set for February 1. Farley expressed his gratitude for past favors. Smith, in fact, had promoted his career during his own governorship. The discussion, Farley recalled, remained cordial but aimless. On February 6, 1932, in a private statement to reporters, released to the public two days later, Smith announced availability for a draft, though he would not actively seek the nomination.[5]

As the contest began to take shape, Jackson and Felix Frankfurter, among others, sensed a lack of conviction in the Smith candidacy. Jackson, friendly with the head of the Democratic party's executive committee, mused that Jouett Shouse "hopes to use him [Smith] as a rallying point around which the opposition to Roosevelt can polarize and eventually result in the selection of one with whom Jouett can operate on more friendly terms than with Roosevelt." [6] Frankfurter, a friend and supporter of both Roosevelt and Smith in their political careers, angered by the tactic he divined in the making, telegraphed Joseph M. Proskauer: "Out of a great public figure you fellows are making a small office seeker. With the compliments of Felix Frankfurter." Proskauer taunted, in reply, hinting at the Smith–Baker alliance, "If you knew the whole story you would probably agree what has been done had to be done . . . wait for the last act and when the play is ended you will, I think, admire the plot." [7]

Frankfurter knew the scenario almost from its inception for, in November 1931, Walter Lippmann attempted to recruit him at the Harvard-Yale football game. Lippmann, to Frankfurter's surprise, depicted FDR as "a dangerous man." "I was greatly disposed toward Newton Baker," Frankfurter subsequently explained to an interviewer, "but not for the presidency, and I said, 'Walter, a fellow who has your command of adjectives I should think could use a more felicitous one to describe Franklin than *dangerous*. I can understand anything that might be said about him, but to say that he's a *dangerous man* is straining the word *dangerous*.' " [8]

In his correspondence, especially with Belle Moskowitz, regarded as Smith's most influential adviser, Frankfurter attempted to head off the use of Smith as a stalking-horse for the conservative coalition. The issue was not personal, she insisted; rather the Smith group found Roosevelt's record unacceptable. The contest rested on political principle, not personal pique or party control. The Roosevelt tide had to be stemmed and Smith entered the fray only to keep the convention open to an alternative. [9]

Belle Moskowitz and Joseph Proskauer closed the Frankfurter correspondence, unwilling to supply him with the details of procedure and motivation they believed he wanted. Undaunted, the Harvard professor pursued Ellery Sedgwick, editor of the *Atlantic Monthly*. Favorably inclined toward Baker, Sedgwick conceded the Ohioan's legal association with the Van Sweringen railroad empire, a notorious holding company pyramid, and with the Bethlehem–Youngstown Steel merger. Baker's legal practice was hardly calculated to enhance his political attractiveness. Also, that "Baker looks on the world as a middle-aged man. He has retained the idealism of his youth, but he has lost practical confidence in what can actually be accomplished. In this I feel no little sympathy." As if to reinforce the issue, Frankfurter pressed Sedgwick with copies of his correspondence with Proskauer and Moskowitz with the notation: "bet Joe Proskauer & me re Baker & Al." "From time to time," Ralph Hayes finally taunted Frankfurter as he continued to promote the Baker–Smith strategy, "somebody whispers to me that you think N.D.B. as President might not be so good. Tell me it isn't so." [10]

On March 8, 1932, Roosevelt defeated Smith in the New Hampshire contest by garnering some 14,500 votes to Smith's 9,000.

"Verily," Jackson crowed confidently, "the Lord has delivered the enemy into our hands." Following his custom, Farley predicted a first ballot nomination. Howe, equally sanguine, categorized the Smith movement as a fake. The mood at Albany grew euphoric, careless, even arrogant.[11]

In the weeks following the New Hampshire primary the Roosevelt candidacy took on the attributes of a steamroller running over the opposition. The Albany team now domiciled the New York State Democratic Committee headquarters in New York City, across from the Biltmore Hotel. Following a visit in March 1932, Jackson rendered an extremely colorful picture of its operations and principals:

> The office of the New York State Democratic Committee . . . comprises six or seven rather cramped rooms. Two of these are allocated to the operations of a Women's Division, presided over by an obviously competent professional who might have been drafted from a cosmetic company's sales promotion staff. . . . But the important individual here is Mrs. Eleanor Roosevelt. She has no title or specific duties but operates as a free lance. Nevertheless, she is the dominant personality of the outfit, constantly busy giving orders, dictating letters, and in general supervising all the activities of the small staff.
>
> In the northwest corner is the lair of an implausible little man whose appearance belies his importance in the Roosevelt operations. 5 feet 4 or 5 inches tall, his frail, cadaverous frame is topped by a face that is stretched taut about the skull underneath. His age defies computation; he could be forty, fifty, or sixty. His clothes are a sartorial ruin, disorderly and in need of cleaning. He appears constantly on the verge of a physical collapse. His desk extends the impression of the man himself, cluttered with a litter of letters, memos, and pamphlets. In the corner of a small, adjoining room is a decrepit horsehair sofa, one leg missing so that he who reclines upon it is in constant danger of sliding onto the floor. From time to time the little man replenishes his energies by lying down on this bit of wreckage for ten minutes or so, then rises with strength renewed to tackle the task to which he has dedicated his full measure of devotion.
>
> This inconspicuous figure is the *deux ex machina* of the Franklin Delano Roosevelt campaign for the Democratic Presidential Nomination. He is Louis Howe. Some psychoanalyst could enjoy a field day

explaining the motivations which have inspired his worship of his idol. Is it the instinctive reverence of the physically inferior man for the Apollo? In part, perhaps. But whatever may have been responsible for this attachment it is unique in American political life as I have known it.

In the adjoining room is a small desk assigned to Jim Farley. It is neat and orderly. I am told Jim appears occasionally to sign letters in green ink (What correspondent of his can show a signature "James A. Farley"? They are always "Jim.") He is the roving salesman of the Roosevelt image, travelling here and there throughout the country. This day he made no visit to headquarters and I am told many days frequently elapse without his appearance.[12]

By the first of April, seven states had fallen into the Roosevelt column: Washington, by state convention (16 delegates) in early February; then New Hampshire, Minnesota, North Dakota, Georgia, Iowa, and Maine. The Howe–Farley team, ably assisted by Jackson in New England, seemed en route to a sweep. "Favorite son" candidacies gave the appearance of disintegration. Alben J. Barkley of Kentucky moved into the Roosevelt camp. Joseph Robinson of Arkansas, Smith's 1928 running mate, removed himself from contention. Albert C. Ritchie of Maryland and "Alfalfa Bill" Murray of Oklahoma seemed completely unable to get up a head of steam. The picture looked grim in the Baker camp. Lippmann and Ralph Hayes agreed "that the Roosevelt strength has reached perilous proportions and is in danger of turning into a sweep." Baker's only hope they decided, apparently in concert with Jouett Shouse, was a major address on the issues as he saw them. But Baker refused even to speak on the radio series sponsored by the American Tobacco Company. Jouett Shouse, Hayes conceded to another of the Baker advisers, stood virtually alone "deliberately sustaining a defeat in the hope that he may have enough strength to prevent the nomination falling into undesirable hands."[13] It appeared, in fact, that this last obstacle to a Roosevelt nomination was cleared away at the April 4, 1932, session of the Democratic National Committee's subcommittee on Arrangements.

Roosevelt decided to take on Shouse and Raskob. Exactly what motivated him is not clear. Perhaps it was the Washington gossip and the persistent reports in the New York press that seemed to confirm Robert Woolley's predictions that Smith would be used as a stalking-horse by Raskob and Shouse for a Baker nomination. Or Woolley's further warning that Harry F. Byrd had joined the coalition. Or Robert Jackson's discovery of clandestine meetings in New York that included Byrd, Raskob, Shouse, Maryland Governor Albert C. Ritchie, a conservative protégé of Baruch, James Cox of Ohio, Smith, and likely John W. Davis and Frank Polk. It was known, also that Tammany Boss John Curry flirted with this group.[14] The time had come to take on the stop-Roosevelt movement.

In characteristic fashion, Roosevelt approached the issue obliquely. It was generally assumed that the Arrangements subcommittee meeting in Chicago would be a mere formality with the selection of Jouett Shouse as temporary chairman of the Convention. Roosevelt determined to control the choice. "Frankly, as I told Raskob," he wrote Harry F. Byrd in less than frank fashion, "I am inclined to think that Shouse has become rather an old story throughout the country because of his many speeches, propaganda statements, etc., etc." In similar fashion, he informed Josephus Daniels that "I am doing everything possible to prevent Jouett Shouse from being made Temporary Chairman of the Convention. He has done good publicity work in Washington but is generally regarded as ultra-conservative and most of his reputation is as a mere attacker on the Hoover Administration. I hope on next Monday my friends can definitely select Senator Barkley." Roosevelt was less than candid in the situation. Although it was open knowledge that Shouse had made appearances urging uninstructed delegations, evidently Roosevelt most feared the possibility of rulings from the chair in the opening stages of the Chicago convention which might damage his cause.[15]

James A. Farley and Robert Jackson, dispatched to Chicago as Roosevelt's emissaries at the April 4 Arrangements subcommittee meeting, promptly sensed the functional undermining of their candidate's chances. The party machinery was dominated by Raskob who, in fact, had selected the membership of the subcommittee. And regardless of Shouse's presidential preferences no one could deny his three years' stint as the party's spokesman and propagandist. Nor could it be denied that Raskob had bankrolled the party and many individual campaigns for nearly four years. Cleverly, Raskob selected a Roosevelt majority for the Arrangements subcommittee, but Shouse had acted quickly and secured pledges of support for the Convention's temporary chairmanship and, in fact, by April 4 had the commitments likely of a majority for that post.

Jackson, recently installed as secretary of the Democratic National Committee, a token concession to the Roosevelt forces, was appalled on his arrival in Chicago to discover that Howe and Farley had been completely outmaneuvered. Shouse had already lined up a majority of the Arrangements group, despite the subcommittee's pro-Roosevelt composition. When Jackson telephoned Louis Howe for an explanation, he received only a vague response and the insistence that Shouse's nomination as temporary chairman "be prevented at all costs." Because Farley was ineligible to take part in the proceedings, the burden fell on Jackson, who had managed cordial relations with Shouse to that time. Although acknowledging Shouse's service to the party, he knew through his secret channel that Shouse intended to use the Convention chair to stymie Roosevelt's chances. As he explained years later:

> The importance of both the Temporary and Permanent Chairmanships in this convention was compounded by the lack of a two-thirds vote on the part of the Roosevelt supporters. A ruling by the chair adverse to one of the contestants for the nomination could be overturned only by a two-thirds vote.
>
> In spite of Jim Farley's repeated public claims some of us were only too well aware we were far short of the necessary two-thirds. Whether Jim knew it I cannot say. By temperament a supreme optimist, he radiated confidence at all times. But Roosevelt, Cordell Hull, Louis Howe and I knew we must struggle for additional votes. . . .
>
> It was this awareness of our vulnerability that prompted Governor

Roosevelt, Hull, and Howe to insist that Senator Barkley be named to the temporary chairmanship.[16]

At the close of the Monday morning, April 4, gathering recommendations were made for officers of the forthcoming Democratic National Convention. In a candid address before the closed session, Shouse recited his credentials and proceeded to nominate himself for the Convention's temporary chairmanship, despite, he stated, articles emanating from the "Republican press" that indicated the Roosevelt forces preferred Alben W. Barkley for the post. Jackson conceded that the temporary chairmanship had taken on political significance, especially in the light of a recent movement to prevent Roosevelt's nomination. Both statements were blunt, especially Shouse's claim to the post as a reward for past services. Jackson's motion for an adjournment of the meeting until later that day carried, as many present concluded that a compromise of some sort might avoid an open split in the party.[17]

Following the adjournment, which began shortly after 1 P.M., a small group gathered, including Governor Harry Byrd of Virginia, Jackson, Farley, Arthur Mullen of Nebraska, Mrs. Isabelle Greenway of Arizona, and Bruce Kremer of Montana. Governor Byrd suggested an apparent solution: Senator Alben Barkley would be named temporary chairman (a matter within the purview of the assembled group) and Shouse would be recommended for the permanent chairmanship. Jackson later recalled that he made it clear that the choice of a permanent chairman would remain the exclusive prerogative of the Convention "and Governor Byrd then said he had only suggested a recommendation." When Jackson drafted the compromise resolution, Shouse insisted upon its ratification by Roosevelt.

A telephone call placed to the governor seemingly evoked only a semantic clarification. Jackson proposed in his draft resolution that Shouse be recommended to the permanent committee on Organization for consideration as permanent chairman of the Convention. Roosevelt insisted on the word "commend" instead of "recommend" on the ground that the subcommittee on Arrangements was empowered to choose only temporary officers. At least, Jackson and Roosevelt favored such an interpretation of the compromise.[18] The minutes of the meeting and Shouse's subsequent statement to the press indicate either that he had been led to believe otherwise or deliberately chose to do so.

When the subcommittee on Arrangements reconvened at 4:40 P.M., Jackson explained: "When I sit down, Governor Byrd of Virginia will move that Mr. Barkley can be recommended temporary Chairman of the convention by acclamation, and when that resolution is adopted, I shall offer the following resolution, which has been read to Governor Roosevelt over the telephone and which meets with his approval: 'This committee commends to the Permanent Committee on Organization the consideration as Permanent Chairman of the National Convention the name of Honorable Jouett Shouse of Kansas.' " [19]

The distinction between "recommend" and "commend" apparently had no immediate meaning for Shouse. As the April 4 meeting dissolved, Shouse announced to the press the decision unanimously "to recommend . . . the selection of Senator A. W. Barkley for temporary chairman and the selection of Jouett Shouse as permanent chairman of the convention." Generally the press reported that the Roosevelt managers had been badly outmaneuvered at Chicago, trading off as they did the temporary for the permanent chairmanship.[20]

But Roosevelt had left himself an escape hatch, and technically his position conformed with party custom. In the ensuing weeks statements emanated from Roosevelt headquarters and his Washington supporters that Shouse would be unacceptable to them as convention chairman. Then, on June 5, they revealed their preference for Thomas J. Walsh of Montana.[21] With the emergence of the chairmanship issue, the stage was set for the first clear division at Chicago between the Roosevelt and Smith forces.

BY EARLY APRIL, the burden of projecting a serious candidacy was clearly thrust upon Smith and his followers. Was Alfred E.

Smith a serious contender? Critical primaries and conventions loomed in Massachusetts, Connecticut, Pennsylvania, and California, large-bloc states usually pivotal in a convention. Smith's initial announcement, made on February 8, had been less than satisfactory, for it declared no more than his availability for a draft. It seemed uncharacteristic of the Happy Warrior.

In an interview granted to Arthur Krock of the *New York Times*, April 7, Senator Key Pittman of Nevada, described as a longtime friend, sounded the death knell. Smith, Pittman contended, had been placed in a "humiliating position" by the pleas of "sometimes selfish friends." In what must have been a crushing statement for Smith to read on the front page of the *Times*, Pittman appealed to the Smith intimates to stop his candidacy. Equally galling, one suspects, was the decision made by the Roosevelt group, announced publicly, to abandon an agreement reached with Governor Wilbur Cross of Connecticut, a Smith supporter, to divide that state's convention delegation. "Instead," the Roosevelt managers decided upon "a direct fight for the entire delegation." [22]

But pride alone is not sufficient as an explanation of Smith's decision to abandon the role of reluctant bridegroom. Years later, Joseph Proskauer testified that Smith was profoundly distressed by the threat posed by Roosevelt in the "Forgotten Man" address to "individual liberty and . . . the American federal system." However, complex his reasoning, Smith buttressed his earlier statement of availability for a draft on April 8, 1932, in ringing letters to supporters in Connecticut, Pennsylvania, and California, which denounced as "propaganda" allegations that his candidacy was lukewarm. Roosevelt now faced a serious fight. [23]

Smith's political manager, Frank Hague of Jersey City, made the next move in an attempt at a Roosevelt checkmate. Frank Baker, active in New Jersey politics, and Jersey City's political boss met on March 21, 1932. In short order, the conversation drifted to Frank Baker's brother, Newton, and the mayor demonstrated an unusual familiarity with the Ohioan's record. Hague believed that Newton D. Baker could sweep New Jersey in the 1932 election, "while the state would be doubtful if Roosevelt ran." But, Hague wanted to know, would Baker, in office, "cooperate with, or disregard, the Party organization," meaning obviously the political machines. Newton's brother proved cautious. Although certain that Wilson's former Secretary of War "fully recognized the necessity and approved the functioning of Party organization in a government based upon political parties," he equivocated on the issue of federal patronage. Hague asked Frank Baker to suggest a representative with whom he might confer. And Frank Baker suggested Ralph Hayes as his brother's authorized representative. [24]

Appropriately enough, on April Fools' Day, Ralph Hayes and Frank Hague met at New York City's Biltmore Hotel, across from Roosevelt headquarters. The stop-Roosevelt movement now took on more formidable dimensions. Boss Hague candidly conceded past mistakes, and acknowledged that thus far he was "deeply distressed" with the results. Smith's announcement of availability, made on February 8, had been entirely too tepid. The Maine result, in which Robert Jackson won over the state delegation to Roosevelt, served as a shock, since Hague believed he would get an uninstructed delegation. Indeed, Hague had been forthright. He now wanted to know where Baker stood.

> . . . The feelings of X. [Hague] against R. [Roosevelt] are very strong and he is deeply distressed by the strength that Albany is showing. He is entirely convinced that a situation has been reached in which you [Baker] are the only person in the Party who can save it from having R. as the candidate and from the defeat that . . . the election of either R. or Hoover would constitute. What X. [Hague] is profoundly anxious to secure is an indication of a degree of receptiveness from you that will leave the Party people with whom he is in daily contact less chilled by what they regard as your aloofness from any indication of willingness to submit to a call. He is anxious to have the "draft" project carried out by having a group of prominent individuals sign a statement requesting that you put yourself at the Party's disposition. [25]

Hague's requirements were met. In the ensuing weeks Baker took on a more receptive air, one of willingness to serve if drafted. Although clearly unwilling to take a direct hand in the promotion of his own fortunes, and evidently conscious of the distinct advantages enjoyed by Roosevelt as a frontrunner, Baker indicated willingness to accept the nomination "like any other duty, little as one might be inclined to seek such responsibility." [26] The draft call ultimately fell under Walter Lippmann's jurisdiction. But the immediate need, collection of delegate votes sufficient to check Roosevelt's momentum, could be provided only by Al Smith.

The Hague–Hayes conference concluded with Hague's concession that Smith had absolutely no chance of winning the nomination, despite his ability to command a substantial delegate vote. Smith believed that it would amount to "more than veto proportions." "You," Hayes reported to Baker, expressing Hague's and Smith's sentiment in the matter, "are the only official who can step into the breach, as he [Smith] sees it, and his feeling for the Party and against R. makes him profoundly anxious that you give some indication of your willingness to do so." By April 12, when Hayes and Hague met again, Jersey City's boss seemed even more sanguine concerning Baker's chances for the nomination. Hague had every reason to be. He not only expected to meet Baker personally, but anticipated a Roosevelt defeat in Massachusetts. [27]

As the Smith and Roosevelt forces girded for the pivotal Massachusetts contest, so regarded because the Bay State was one of the few carried by the Happy Warrior in 1928, the stop-Roosevelt coalition increased the tempo of its activity. Hague and Baker conferred twice at Washington's Willard Hotel, with Alfred E. Smith present at least on one of those occasions. Details unfortunately are lacking. But at a still later meeting in New York City Hague pledged he would do nothing to cause Baker embarrassment, presumably open endorsement by the Smith machines. In the meantime, prominent New York Democratic conservatives, such as John W. Davis, Frank Polk, and Nathan Straus Jr., worked on a reluctant Boss John Curry of Tammany Hall, now fearful of what Roosevelt as governor might do with the Walker investigation, to go along with the conservative coalition. [28]

The Massachusetts contest revealed the principal defects of Roosevelt's Albany team, its overconfidence, even arrogance, and lack of familiarity with local, state, and regional divisions which plagued the Democratic party. The Bay State Democrats, deeply divided by factionalism—the state party leaders including Governor Joseph B. Ely, Senator David I. Walsh, and State Chairman Frank Donahue had wrested power from Mayor James Michael Curley of Boston—was wracked by political strife since Smith's 1928 campaign. Anxious to recoup his losses, Boston's mayor latched onto the Roosevelt candidacy in 1931, befriended James Roosevelt, and proclaimed himself head of the Massachusetts draft-Roosevelt movement. Although Roosevelt and the Albany advisers welcomed Curley as an ally, Robert Jackson advised extreme caution. "No Democrat in this state," he wrote Roosevelt months before the primary, "can be against Smith and survive." Roosevelt conceded that "I am perhaps liable to be crushed between the upper and nether millstones through no fault of my own. I do hope that some formula can be found and possibly Mr. Farley can run on and discover one." [29]

Unfortunately for Roosevelt any attempt at compromise in Massachusetts foundered on Curley's presence in the Roosevelt camp. As the primary drew close, Robert Jackson again warned the governor that retreat would be the better part of valor in the circumstances. A Roosevelt victory might well be unnecessary over the long pull, but a defeat, Jackson warned might have wide repercussions for his candidacy. Curley, Jackson insisted in this blunt statement, had absolutely no political clout outside of Boston. The contest seemed disproportionate in its risks for the front-runner. "I hope," Jackson urged, "a miscarriage can be avoided." [30]

In an effort at compromise, Senator Walsh offered the Boston mayor a seat on the Massachusetts delegation provided that he vote for Smith at the convention until it became evident that his prospects for the nomination were nonexistent, whereupon the delegation would be released and members could vote for their second choices. Curley, hardly the diplomat, insisted that at that point the delegation switch en masse to Roosevelt or, alternatively, he wanted to name half the delegation. Walsh never gave Curley the courtesy of a reply.

With the confirmation of Jackson's warnings by a Roosevelt family friend, La Rue Brown, the governor decided to send his own negotiating team to extract himself. Louis Howe and James Roosevelt represented the governor at a meeting with Governor Ely at Boston's Copley Plaza Hotel. Robert Jackson also attended as an intermediary. Unfortunately neither Howe nor Roosevelt's eldest son evinced any sensitivity in the situation, or an awareness that they had few cards to play. When Governor Ely was baldly informed that "he had no realization of the R. [Roosevelt] strength in Massachusetts and that unless they were given half the delegation they would make a contest and take more than half," he erupted. As Jackson recalled the incident, Ely, not known for a long fuse, "plunged into violent personal abuse of Louis. Louis . . . cringed under Ely's brutal attack," which stopped with Jackson's intervention. Previously willing to give Roosevelt some votes after the opening ballots, Ely swore, after Howe's ultimatum "that Roosevelt would get nothing from Massachusetts on the first or fiftieth ballot." [31]

As the April 26 primary approached, the tensions between the two camps erupted into open warfare. Curley and James Roosevelt accused State Chairman Donahue of handpicking the delegates and demanded publicly what they had been denied privately. Curley's bravado culminated in a speech in which he taunted: "What right has Smith to come here at the behest of Donahue?" [32] Smith demonstrated his right by trouncing Roosevelt in the contest by a surprising three to one margin. A stunning defeat for the front-runner, its import broadened with Roosevelt's mediocre showing that same day in Pennsylvania.

The Pennsylvania contest duplicated the Massachusetts experience. The Roosevelt forces allied with former National Committeeman Joseph Guffey, once powerful in Pennsylvania's Democratic organization. But, like Curley in Massachusetts, Guffey oversold himself to the Roosevelt advisers when he claimed in 1931 that he could deliver 66 of the state's 76 convention votes. Guffey took command of the Roosevelt-for-President League, but Raskob and Shouse actively canvassed in the urban-Catholic areas. The April 26 preferential primary gave Roosevelt, presumed to be a favorite, only a slim margin over Smith. The delegate race, distinct from the preference primary, seemed inconclusive. Roosevelt's managers claimed some 60 votes; but when the Pennsylvania delegation cast its first ballot at Chicago only 44½ votes were registered for him.

In quick succession, Roosevelt absorbed a number of defeats. On May 2, 1932, Smith captured the Rhode Island delegation headed by J. Howard McGrath. On May 12, 1932, Maryland's convention opted for favorite son Governor Albert C. Ritchie. On May 17, Connecticut, by state convention, and New Jersey, by primary, fell into the Smith column. Slowly the Smith forces and the favorite sons demonstrated a talent for driving nails into what they hoped would be Roosevelt's political coffin. [33]

WAITING IMPATIENTLY for the Massachusetts results some 3,000 miles distant was Smith's ancient foe, William Gibbs McAdoo of California. "The Roosevelt defeat . . . will help us," McAdoo crowed at the tally. His earlier prediction that Roosevelt by no means had a clear field had come true. The stage was set for California's May 3 primary and for the projection of McAdoo, John Nance Garner, and William Randolph Hearst as a third major element in the 1932 Democratic National Convention.

McAdoo had been appraising his own chances for better than a year. The gist of his communications with old political associates of the Wilson era revealed that he found none of the party's leading contenders acceptable in 1932. Presumably he himself could fill the bill. Despite his 65 years, McAdoo remained vigorous and had been after all a leading contender in 1924 and a major force in the party for better than a decade. From his vantage point, reflective of the old Bryanite-fundamentalist constituency, as well as a new one, rooted in the Southwest, in large-scale farming, ranching, railroads, and oil, Smith and Roosevelt were birds of a feather— New Yorkers, Tammanyites, and wets. The party, he argued, had twice in recent years suffered crushing defeats with New Yorkers (John W. Davis and Smith) at the helm. The performance, he believed, should not be repeated. [34]

McAdoo's association with the Wilson administration and his marriage to Woodrow Wilson's daughter enhanced his availability, but hardly cast him in the role of internationalist. In his memoirs, *Crowded Years*, which appeared in 1931, he insisted, in the mood of the era of postwar disillusionment, that we had been entrapped by a purely European conflagration. The Great War, he stipulated, "grew out of purely European conditions, and was provoked largely by military tension. . . . We were forced into it against our will through Germany's systematic policy of trampling on our international rights." The debts, he maintained, could not be canceled. To McAdoo, who administered the Treasury Department when much of the Allied indebtedness accumulated, they amounted to $11 billions in contractual obligations. It was Europe's war, after all, not ours. As a compromise, in the face of depression and conceivable default, he proposed transfer of the British and French West Indian possessions to the United States in part payment, and the balance to be accounted for by transfer of bonds to us backed by European railroads, steamships, telephone companies, corporations, even real estate. [35]

When invited by Senator Robert M. La Follette Jr. to comment on the financial crisis, McAdoo blamed it, in Bryanite fashion, on contraction of bank credits and circulating medium. His analysis had much validity to it and was reminiscent of the "Cross of Gold" speech. "We have been paying too much attention to Europe," he told the La Follette Committee, "and too little to our own people." McAdoo's view of our economic system, equally Populistic, acknowledged the virtues and economies of large-scale production and massive finance, though he complained in *Crowded Years* that Big Business and High Finance (McAdoo's capitals), motivated by money and power, exercised "a dangerous influence in American affairs." While dissolution into smaller units lacked feasibility, large economic aggregates needed to be restrained and supervised. His own past associations with Wall Street did not trouble him, for he believed himself to be untainted, scarcely among the political and financial "weasels" who had "played hell with the country" in the New Era. In McAdoo's view the primary problem was America; "thus far the White House and the so-called highbrows have been thinking of Europe only." [36]

In 1931 and early 1932, Bryan's heir apparent did everything possible to bring his views on the depression to national attention. The publication of *Crowded Years*, with its stress on his financial acumen, acquired without suffering the loss of his soul to Wall Street, seems more than accidental in its timing. In speeches and press releases, the former Treasury Secretary pressed for a program of money and credit expansion, agricultural relief, Prohibition's retention and enforcement, and repayment of the Allied war debts. When the media ignored him, he pressed for broader coverage of his views which, in retrospect, seem economically and politically tenable. [37]

Vain to a fault, caricatured by many of his contemporaries as something of a bigot and a buffoon, McAdoo has been too summarily dispatched in treatments of the decision-making process which led to Roosevelt's nomination at Chicago. Woodrow Wilson's son-in-law considered himself a force for Progressivism and a spokesman for the little people and in that respect scarcely subject to string-pulling by William Randolph Hearst. Though allied, each pursued his independent interests.

McAdoo's ambitions for the presidency in 1932 were not entirely unrealistic. He had been nurtured in northern Georgia and educated and admitted to the bar in eastern Tennessee, and he maintained his political contacts with and feelings for the South into his maturity. In the prewar period, the peripatetic Tennessee lawyer moved from Chattanooga to New York City with a large family and a few thousand dollars and in short order emerged as the builder of the Hudson & Manhattan Railroad, the first underground connection between New York City and New Jersey. Following his service under Wilson, McAdoo moved his law practice to Los Angeles. In the decade of the twenties he buttressed his Bible Belt constituency with the loyalty and support of the powerful railway brotherhoods, grateful for his role as director-general of the railroads under government operation. His law practice involved him as well with the Southwest's powerful oil and ranching interests. In correspondence with close associates in 1931 and early 1932, he confided that he still harbored the dream of inhabiting the White House. He considered, too, leadership of an independent political movement in the event of Roosevelt's nomination. What he feared most, he wrote, was "four more years of ineptitude and imbecility in government," meaning Hoover, or a "feeble substitute," meaning Roosevelt. Nothing in his huge correspondence suggests even more remotely that he considered Franklin D. Roosevelt qualified for the presidency or worthy of his endorsement.[38]

In their preparations for the California primary contest in 1931, Farley and Howe apparently made the same miscalculation committed in Massachusetts and Pennsylvania. Once again, they turned for assistance to men anxious to recoup their former political fortunes and hardly as powerful as they pretended. In their reliance on Isidore B. Dockweiler and Justus Wardell, Smith supporters in 1928, they fell victim to assurances of an easy triumph, and found allies who had become politically odious in the eyes of the state's dominant figures. "I am convinced we won't even have a contest," Wardell informed Roosevelt in November 1931, after the forging of the Dockweiler–Wardell–Farley relationship in the course of the Elks trip. "But if we do," referring to McAdoo, "the result will be . . . overwhelmingly in our favor."[39] As in Massachusetts, ample warning reached the Roosevelt camp baring the thicket which characterized California Democratic politics.

Somehow a letter written by McAdoo in March 1931 fell into Louis Howe's hands. After ruling out Baker, Ritchie, Smith, and Owen Young, the Californian reached the conclusion that if the

front-runner, Roosevelt, secured the nomination in 1932, he would
be trounced very nearly as badly as Smith in 1928. The letter made
it perfectly obvious that McAdoo regarded Isidore Dockweiler as a
puppet of Smith, Raskob, and Shouse, who had shifted to Roosevelt for personal advantage alone. It was no secret, moreover, that
McAdoo detested the Dockweiler–Wardell group associated with
San Francisco, Smith, and Prohibition repeal. Howe, evidently,
saw no need to act on the information. [40]

William Randolph Hearst's famous New Year's Day statement,
which damned Woodrow Wilson and his followers in the Democratic party and presented John Nance Garner as the party's best
choice as nominee, disturbed McAdoo as it did Roosevelt and
Baker. The California attorney found himself in an ambivalent position, for he had his own hopes in connection with the Texas and
California delegations. McAdoo viewed the Hearst statement as a
"marplot speech," replete with inaccuracies, unfair to Wilson, and
unfounded in its contention that Champ Clark had been cheated of
the 1912 nomination. For a time McAdoo wavered, insisting that
he was being subjected to inordinate pressure "to get into the
[presidential] race again," while also eyeing the possibility of seek-
ing California's seat in the U.S. Senate that would be filled in
November. In the end he proved to be a realist and an oppor-
tunist. For as Garner's candidacy gained support in Texas and California, McAdoo became increasingly "impressed with the arguments and appeals . . . that I ought to be willing to stand [for the
Senate] as a matter of public duty."

Despite his announcement of support of the Garner candidacy,
made on February 18, 1932, McAdoo made himself "available"
should lightning strike at Chicago. Like Newton D. Baker, the
Californian demonstrated his willingness to concede the one issue
that would have crippled his chances for a nomination, in this case
his bone-dry stance on Prohibition. In January, he explained to
Cordell Hull moderation of his previous die-hard position against
repeal on the grounds that it clouded basic problems which confronted the nation. In June, prior to the Chicago gathering, Mc-

Adoo publicized the reversal. "Constant agitation about Prohibition," he announced, "has subordinated economic and social problems of first importance and has distracted the minds of the people from measures which might have ameliorated our present economic distress." McAdoo suggested a national referendum on the question and pledged his willingness to abide by majority rule. [41]

As the California primary approached, Louis Howe sensed trouble. In a telegram to Isidore Dockweiler, Howe suggested that conditions had become "chaotic" in that Pacific Coast state with the entry of Garner into the picture. He proposed a division of delegates equally among Roosevelt, Smith, and Garner. Again the Albany group fell victim to bad advice, when Dockweiler demurred. "Roosevelt delegation will win," he replied. [42] It lost.

On May 3, 1932, John Nance Garner captured the California delegation in that state's primary. The combination of McAdoo's influence in the Los Angeles area, his appeal to the Railway Brotherhoods, the Hearst press, and the Texas State Society (100,000 former Texans belonged) proved too much for Smith and Roosevelt. The final tally showed 214,000 votes for Garner, 169,000 for Roosevelt, and 137,000 for Smith. Herbert Hoover, incidentally received more votes (630,000) in the Republican primary, running unopposed, than all of the Democrats combined. Garner, the returns revealed, had done especially well in Los Angeles County, McAdoo's territory. [43]

In reality, the Los Angeles attorney emerged as the commanding figure in California politics, as indicated by his choice as head of the convention delegation. And in the ensuing weeks he made it abundantly clear that his task consisted of prevention of Roosevelt's nomination. McAdoo followed the classic stop-Roosevelt stratagems: cultivation of uninstructed delegations and retention of the two-thirds rule. [44] He made no secret of the matter. "I think what is most in McAdoo's mind," the newspaper columnist Mark Sullivan wrote after a post-primary interview with the Californian, "is to prevent the nomination from going to New York State. He has a hate against all of New York because of his [Madison Square Garden] experience in 1924." [45]

The Massachusetts fiasco, which led to the loss of most of New England's delegates, the Pennsylvania standoff, the appearance of a mushroom crop of native-son delegations, finally, the California defeat of May 3—these and other defeats suffered by the Roosevelt group opened up new options and created new uncertainties. It was widely acknowledged, as the Chicago contest drew close, that Franklin D. Roosevelt, once regarded as a shoo-in, could be stopped.

BY THE END OF MAY most of the conventions and primary contests had been held. In each of the three major camps, the time seemed propitious for stock-taking, and the confection of stratagems and arrangements required for a convention victory. Roosevelt, with a delegate majority (some 566 votes pledged or instructed), had the strongest hand but lacked by some 200 votes the two-thirds required to dominate the contest. Smith had gathered a substantial number of votes, but not enough on his own to checkmate his Hyde Park antagonist. The trump cards rested in the hands of the California–Texas group headed by the voluble, teetotling McAdoo and the reticent, hard-drinking poker player, John Nance Garner.

As Herbert Bayard Swope, former editor of the *New York World* and crony of Bernard Baruch, and Alfred E. Smith viewed the situation, atop the Empire State Building, in Smith's suite, McAdoo had maneuvered himself into a pivotal position; and the California Populist-Progressive, they surmised, would be as anxious as they to check the Hyde Park squire. Swope placed a telephone call to McAdoo in California inviting Smith's ancient foe to join the anti-Roosevelt coalition. McAdoo indicated his amenability subject to one major condition. "If the opposition to Roosevelt were ultimately to necessitate a conference of Democratic leaders in order that some other nominee might be selected," McAdoo queried, "would Father [Smith] accept Mr. McAdoo as one of the conferees?" Emily Smith Warner recalled that the deed would be sealed at a secret pre-convention conference. [46]

During that era and later in his memoirs, Bernard M. Baruch insisted on his complete neutrality. "I was emphatically not part of any stop-Roosevelt movement," Baruch protested, in reply to James F. Byrnes's recollection that just prior to the convention the New York financier attempted to recruit him on behalf of Newton D. Baker. [47] But the evidence now available clearly indicates Baruch's role as liaison between the Smith and McAdoo groups. Baruch's initial preference was Governor Albert C. Ritchie of Maryland, a conservative whose platform consisted of only one plank, the balancing of the federal budget. By early May, when it became evident that Ritchie had no chance at the grand prize, Baruch informed Walter Lippmann that he now favored Newton D. Baker of Ohio. [48]

Two cryptic telegrams, dispatched in June, indicate the New York financier's arrangement of the McAdoo–Smith meeting at Chicago's Blackstone Hotel on the eve of the convention. [49] Although details of these preliminaries are sketchy, the memoranda of the Smith–Baruch–McAdoo conference at Chicago, which shall be considered later, leave nothing to the imagination. Baruch had managed the improbable, an alliance between the Happy Warrior and the darling of the Bible Belt. There remained, however, one fly in the ointment. McAdoo looked with no more favor on Baker, too closely tied to the power interests to suit the Californian's taste and too anti-union as well, than he did on Roosevelt. It seems likely that McAdoo was unaware of Smith's and Baruch's inclinations toward the Ohioan as the Democratic alternative. [50]

In Cleveland, taken up with a busy and lucrative law practice, and deeply concerned over the illness (initially diagnosed as tuberculosis) of his son, Baker mulled his chances. A mass of correspondence poured in suggesting a broad spectrum of support for the nomination. The nature and quality of that support fell into several categories: 1) the Smith coalition, which relied on the huge

financial resources of the Du Pont and General Motors empire as
well as Pierre S. du Pont's business acquaintances; 2) Wall Street
Democrats, including John W. Davis, Norman Davis, and Russell
Leffingwell of J. P. Morgan & Co. (John W. Davis' organization of
the Minute Men, a group of wealthy contributors to the party, was
regarded as a cover); 3) substantial support from the press, ranging
from the Cleveland newspapers, to the Scripps-Howard chain to
John Stewart Bryan's *Richmond News Leader,* and prominent col-
umnists such as Walter Lippmann and Mark Sullivan; 4) conservative internationalist Democrats, such as Norman Davis, who
stressed international economic arrangements and disarmament as
the major area of priority in the depression; 5) an impressive array
of academicians, in an era when the most prestigious universities
were predominantly conservative and internationalist-minded; 6)
and, finally, widespread support in the South, which preferred
Roosevelt, but which would have shifted to Baker with ease in the
event of a deadlock.

Baker's residual strength lay in the near-universal regard for him
as a statesman, "a second Cleveland or Wilson," a bigger man than
Franklin Roosevelt, short on delegate strength, but capable more
than any other Democrat of healing the wounds of a divided party.
This was true of Robert Woolley, Colonel Edward M. House,
Adolf Berle Jr., and even of Roosevelt himself.[51]

Important in evaluating Baker's chances and the tensions within
the Democratic party are the judgments the Ohioan and the New
Yorker offered in appraising each other's assets and liabilities. Roosevelt, Baker believed, possessed great charm, a good education,
and sincerely desired to serve in the public interest. But the Ohio
attorney found himself disconcerted by Roosevelt's overemphasis
on the mechanics of politics, a tendency toward expediency, and
above all a willingness to let Europe drift on its own. Baker envisaged an impending world conflict, more disastrous than the previous one, rooted in national, racial, and economic tensions. In the
face of this impending crisis, the paramount issue of his time,
"Frank has been silent." The analysis seems cogent.

Roosevelt proved no less perspicacious in sizing up his principal opponent. He predicted accurately in an oft-quoted letter to Josephus Daniels, following Owen Young's declination of candidacy, that "the Smith–Shouse–Raskob crowd . . . will turn with a sigh to Newton and what a wonderful asset he can be to the party during the next four years if we win." But the problem remained, that "in spite of his perfectly legitimate law practice he is labeled by many progressives as the attorney for J. P. Morgan and the Van Schweringens [sic]; he is opposed by labor; . . . by the German Americans; and also by the bulk of the Irish Americans because of his consistent League of Nations attitude up to this year. . . . All of this seems a pity because Newton would make a better President than I would!" [52] Whatever his regard for Baker, all of Roosevelt's political instincts, as the convention approached, were mustered to secure his own nomination as Hoover's opponent.

In the opening days of June, at Hyde Park, the Roosevelt forces took stock of their position and arrived at two conclusions: first, they would contest the Shouse claim to the convention's permanent chairmanship by supporting Senator Thomas J. Walsh of Montana for the post. Second, they planned to eliminate the hallowed two-thirds requirement for the nomination, a decision reversed on the eve of the convention. An analysis of this decision-making process suggests further that the Albany advisers remained less than sagacious in the promotion of Roosevelt's political fortunes.

Present at the crucial June 5 strategy session were the Albany advisers, Farley and Howe; the Democratic National Committee Secretary and liaison between the Albany group and some of Roosevelt's Senate supporters, Robert Jackson; Daniel C. Roper and Homer Cummings, experienced politicians preferred by the old Wilsonians for leadership of the Roosevelt campaign; also, some of the most powerful Democrats in the U.S. Senate, Hull of Tennessee, C. C. Dill of Washington, Burton K. Wheeler and Thomas J. Walsh of Montana. The conference agenda, prepared by Louis Howe, and an exchange between Roosevelt and Jackson in May suggest that Roosevelt and the Albany advisers found Shouse acceptable, if no more than that, as permanent chairman. Had they not been dissuaded by the Senate contingent, Roosevelt would almost certainly have lost the nomination.

Although Farley contended in his memoir of that period that the Albany advisers "had decided upon Thomas J. Walsh of Montana as our candidate for . . . permanent chairman," Howe's agenda and other testimony indicates otherwise. A Shouse intimate, a few weeks later, following Shouse's convention defeat by Walsh of Montana, informed him that Roosevelt and Farley "despite any report to the contrary, had argued earnestly that the agreement should be kept." They had been "over persuaded by the Senatorial group." This account is confirmed by a brief dispatch to the *New York Times* from Washington, which credited Senators Hull, Dill, and Wheeler with responsibility for securing Roosevelt's opposition to Jouett Shouse as the permanent chairman of the convention. Determinant at the secret conference was Burton K. Wheeler's assertion that "if Shouse were elected chairman he [Roosevelt] would never get the nomination." "Finally," Wheeler recalled, the Albany advisers conceded the issue and "decided to put up Walsh for chairman." [53]

When the meeting ended and James A. Farley informed reporters that the Roosevelt group would support Senator Walsh for the permanent chairmanship, Shouse shouted perfidy. One could that month identify the Roosevelt and stop-Roosevelt coalitions by their stance on the question. In a press release, Shouse asserted that his arrangement with Roosevelt constituted a matter of honor. For this charge he mustered support from Newton D. Baker, Herbert Bayard Swope, Bernard Baruch, Alfred E. Smith, John W. Davis, Albert C. Ritchie, Harry F. Byrd, Joseph Proskauer, and William G. McAdoo. In his rejoinder, Robert Jackson took the onus from Roosevelt. The commending resolution originated with himself, he claimed, not Roosevelt, and the governor's sole participation was the substitution of "commend" for "recommend" when informed of the Arrangements subcommittee compromise. [54]

The party's historic two-thirds rule also came up for discussion at the Hyde Park strategy session. Although most of those present favored its abandonment, it seemed best to defer a final decision until the eve of the convention.[55] As the delegates assembled in the Windy City at the close of June, Farley put the question to a meeting of some sixty-five Roosevelt leaders. In short order, he lost control of the proceeding to the indomitable Huey Long of Louisiana. His coat removed, Long introduced a motion to the effect that the Roosevelt forces fight for abrogation of the two-thirds rule. Farley was stunned. Then, in a typical stump speech, Long seconded his own motion and carried the group. Farley candidly acknowledged, in later years, that he had let the situation get out of hand. Badly shaken, pressed by reporters, Farley called Roosevelt in Albany. To back down now, would be a confession of weakness; to persist would cost dearly in the South, which still insisted on its historic veto over the choice of a candidate, and play into Baker's hands.[56]

Sensing his chance, more interested in the nomination than before, Newton Baker released a statement calculated to crystallize the sentiments for him among the Southern delegates. "A nomination procured from a majority riding roughshod over the established traditions of the Party," Baker warned, "would be deeply embarrassing both to the Party and the candidate. Sensitive men would find it difficult to defend a candidate who started out with a moral flaw in his title." The Ohioan then hurled at Roosevelt a principle that the squire had himself enunciated in 1924, when he insisted that the two-thirds rule could not be changed once the convention's delegates were chosen and instructed.[57]

Other warnings of disaster found expression. The conservative Senator Josiah W. Bailey of North Carolina threatened Edward J. Flynn with the defection of that state's delegation and nearly every other Southern delegation. Burton K. Wheeler called Roosevelt to give him the same information, based on conversations with Bailey and Alabama's John H. Bankhead. Roosevelt read the signals and got off the limb. (In his memoir, Flynn conceded that he and

Farley were novices on the national scene and should have prevented the issue from emerging.) [58] In a message to Farley, for release to the delegates, the governor wisely retreated: "This is no time for petty strife and momentary advantage." The two-thirds rule, he asserted, was undemocratic, but the issue had been raised too late, after the delegates had been chosen. "I am accordingly asking my friends in Chicago to cease our activities to secure the adoption of the majority nominating rule at the opening of the permanent organization." This issue waited until 1936. [59]

THE CONSERVATIVE COALITION had a philosophy as well as a candidate well anchored in traditional American fears of the omnicompetent state. The principal alternative in the days when the New Deal took shape came not from a minuscule and impotent Left but from a potent and powerful Right. Depiction of the Baker candidacy and his supporters, subsequently too when the American Liberty League took form, principally as something of a nuisance on the right is to misinterpret and undervalue the conservative coalition egregiously. In the normal times it would have represented a majority view. With allies in the Republican party, the conservatism of the Southern Democrats, and a mild recovery by the mid-1930s, anti-statist conservatives more than matched the Roosevelt–labor coalition of the "second" New Deal period. The Democratic Jeffersonians and Herbert Hoover hated one another passionately, but in the larger perspective of the post-Versailles era to the present theirs represented the nation's traditionalist consensus. With some semblance of prosperity restored following the Hundred Days they blocked further advances along the lines secured by Roosevelt and the Brains Trust.

Put another way, the deliberations of Roosevelt and the Brains Trust in 1932 and the Hundred Days of 1933 are virtually a self-contained moment in the history of this nation. Hoover's minimalism and the Jeffersonian views of the conservative majority within the Democratic party soon put an end to the New Deal venture. In

1932, an old-line Populist-Progressive, William Gibbs McAdoo, anxious for easier credit, an agrarian-oriented administration, and insulation from Europe's affairs swung the tide to Roosevelt. The availability of more radical alternatives represent the fantasies of a later generation of historians.

Newton D. Baker's candidacy needs to be framed in the context of a broader movement and a constellation of views presented by John J. Raskob in the final address of the Lucky Strike radio series on June 9, 1932. Invoking the Constitution, the Declaration of Independence, and the ideas of Jefferson, Raskob insisted on frugality in government and utilization of the state governments as the most competent authority for dealing with the nation's domestic problems. In a clear allusion to Hoover as well as Roosevelt, he decried "false promises" and "indefensible expediencies." "We should do everything to take the government out of business," he urged, "to relieve trade from unnecessary and unreasonable governmental interference and restriction. We should plan to substitute voluntary cooperation for political control, we should clearly define our tariff policies, decry governmental price-fixing schemes and attempts to artificially maintain prices."

Essentially, Raskob desired a return of authority to the states and the rejection of the growing use of the federal government for solution of economic and social problems. Enlargement of federal responsibilities would destroy the fabric of our society. He disapproved the expansion of the federal budget from $2 billion under Coolidge to $3.2 billion per annum under Hoover. Men and women had been placed on the federal payroll who were unproductive, adding nothing to the national wealth, only to the cost of government, a situation, as he saw it, which resulted in the French Revolution. "The greatest security against revolution in the United States sooner or later lies in the restoration of full sovereignty to the States." Raskob and the conservative coalition viewed Roosevelt in 1932 and later the New Deal in decentralist terms and, like Herbert Hoover, felt threatened to the core.[60]

The conservatives' alternative to Roosevelt, Newton D. Baker treated the functions of the federal government in a depression much like the public figure he most admired, Herbert Hoover. Though the Ohioan acknowledged in principle the need for change to meet the requirements of the people, his most radical thoughts sprang from his role as a middle-class reformer of the Progressive era. True, when distressed by signs of collapse in 1932, he conceded the need to graft on to capitalism things once regarded as socialistic. But he had in mind municipal parks and playgrounds, municipal ownership of waterworks, "sometimes light utilities," and highway construction. Baker rejected plans for industrial stabilization such as the Swope Plan because they might stifle competition. The notion of economic equilibrium as a goal worthy of federal endeavor reminded him of the Soviet system. His only reaction to Rexford Tugwell's "Discourse on Depression" was one of utter bewilderment. As the New Deal found expression in his twilight years, like others of the conservative coalition, he became determined to check it if he could. [61]

The world had passed the old Progressive by. Baker's *weltanschauung*, like Herbert Hoover's, derived from nineteenth-century virtues of American society, individualism, competition, voluntary, private activity. Baker's and Hoover's preferences clashed with Roosevelt's acceptance of an enlarged federal role. The squire and his Brains Trust won the initial rounds at Chicago, then in the campaign. But individualist-decentralist views reemerged in a brief space of years to contain the intellectual thrust of the New Deal.

10

The Roosevelt Nomination

A cloud no bigger than a man's hand in the West is forming around the name of McAdoo. . . .

He can't win. A man as dry as McAdoo is doomed in a convention where the great wet states of New York, Pennsylvania, Massachusetts, Illinois, New Jersey, and Maryland control more than a third of the convention.

But McAdoo, none the less, can stop the nomination of Al Smith, or [Ritchie], or any avowedly wet candidate . . . and swing the issues in America upon reality—the economic situation.

McAdoo is in the convention whether his enemies like it or not.

—WILLIAM ALLEN WHITE *

THE INITIAL PRIZE at the Democratic National Convention in Chicago went neither to the Smith–Raskob group nor to McAdoo. Rather the platform committee yielded a set of policy guidelines for the party and its nominee which reflected the convictions of the conservative Wilsonian internationalists. Shaped by the views of Cordell Hull, Newton D. Baker, Walter Lippmann, and A. Mitchell Palmer, the committee's product seemed intended either to serve Baker's candidacy or to forestall Roosevelt's tendency toward an economic program for recovery which would cut the nation off from world tides.

At stake really were two widely disparate conceptions of the wisest course out of the depression. The internationalists aspired to U.S. participation and leadership in multinational arrangements which would gradually eliminate barriers to world trade, reduce ar-

* Editorial in *Emporia* (Kansas) *Gazette*, January 7, 1932.

maments levels, and deflect the continental powers of Europe from policies which might well lead to a resumption of warfare. Roosevelt representatives on the platform committee scarcely fought the issue. Rather the principal opposition to this point of view came from William Gibbs McAdoo.

The product, the Democratic Party platform, represented a fusion of internationalist goals and old-line progressive notions rooted in the Wilson era, designed to open up the marketplace to competition by placing ethical constraints on business and finance. Presumably this course would terminate both the depression and the potential for a second Great War. Internationalists viewed these objectives as inseparable and, given a choice, placed priority on the quest for an enduring peace. McAdoo won a solitary concession in the form of a plank which opposed cancellation of the debts owing to the United States by its wartime allies. Elsewhere the Wilsonian coalition, conservative in its domestic persuasions, won the issue.

The Chicago platform expressed Cordell Hull's conviction that international economic cooperation constituted the preferred route to economic recovery. It urged a competitive tariff for revenue, reciprocal tariff arrangements with other nations, and an international economic conference designed to restore world trade and terminate currency warfare. Although it condemned the Smoot-Hawley Tariff, it endorsed Herbert Hoover's view of depression causation by attributing the collapse to the destruction of the world marketplace. "International economic hostilities," the Democratic platform urged, had "driven our factories into foreign countries, robbed the American farmer of his foreign markets, and increased his cost of production."

On domestic issues the Wilsonian internationalists endorsed Hoover's stricture of "equal rights to all, special privileges to none." Although Louis D. Brandeis rejected the request that he serve as a consultant on the drafting of the domestic planks because of his judicial function, neo-Brandeisian antitrust views found expression through the efforts of Huston Thompson, former chairman of the Federal Trade Commission. Pledges of regulation of securities issuance and securities exchanges, commodities trading, and utilities rates, as well as divorcement of securities affiliates from commercial banks, worthwhile in themselves, seemed as far as the committee would go in considering the federal government's proper role in the nation's economy.

The most liberal pledge that might have emerged, the product of the platform's literary draftsman, A. Mitchell Palmer, Wilson's Attorney General, fell upon a Baker veto. In a near-final draft Palmer urged a federal program of unemployment and old age insurance. Experimentation with these concepts, Baker objected, should best be left initially to the states. Actually, reflecting his conservative constitutional views on the limitations of federal authority, he questioned whether business or industry could be subjected to federal legislation.

Elsewhere, the party's elders condemned Hoover for an excess of zeal in his domestic policies. They insisted on federal retrenchment in the form of agency consolidation and a saving of "not less than 25 percent in the cost of federal government." And they urged a similar policy on the states. Maintenance of the national credit, a balanced federal budget, and of a sound currency "to be preserved at all hazards" were accorded priority, these goals to be implemented at an international monetary conference. Condemned equally were the extravagant fiscal policies of the Federal Farm Board and domestic allotment, defined as "the unsound policy of restricting agricultural production to the demands of domestic markets." [1]

An economic anachronism, reflective probably of a majority view of Democratic legislators in the House and Senate, the Chicago platform would have served Herbert Hoover well in the 1932 contest. McAdoo's Populist-Progressive views scarcely surfaced in the final draft. Little credence was given to domestic priorities. But the Californian, relying on his delegate votes, hoped to do better elsewhere.

THE TWO MOST POWERFUL FIGURES in the stop-Roosevelt movement, William Gibbs McAdoo and Alfred Emanuel Smith, met at the Blackstone Hotel in Chicago on June 26, 1932, the day before the Democratic National Convention opened, at the invitation of a third party, Bernard M. Baruch. According to McAdoo's recollection of the affair little of significance came under discussion. He portrayed himself as a diffident participant, a follower of the amenities, and a loyal supporter of John Nance Garner of Texas, anxious above all to heal wounds and reunite factions.[2] The Smith partisan who leaked the details of the luncheon meeting to Frank R. Kent of the *Baltimore Sun,* probably Belle Moskowitz, painted a more revealing picture. "Bernie," Smith reportedly confided to the financier, "I don't like him [McAdoo], I don't trust him, but in this fight I would sleep with a Chinaman to win and I'll come." [3]

The portrayal of vestal virgins lured by the Wall Street mogul to a potentially compromising conference is contradicted by the eager flow of telephone calls and telegrams earlier in June between Smith, Herbert Bayard Swope, and Baruch in New York and McAdoo in California. These exchanges suggest a prearranged meeting and the principals' eager participation, a view confirmed by a communication from Belle Moskowitz to an intimate in California. "We have every hope," Mrs. Moskowitz confided, "that the California situation [McAdoo's control of the delegation] will turn out favorable to us, and [there is] every indication that it will be so." [4]

As the Baruch–Smith–McAdoo meeting opened, the former enemies shook hands cordially. "How're you, how're you," McAdoo greeted Smith when his old adversary entered the Baruch hotel suite. "Out of sight, out of sight," the Happy Warrior replied. As the love feast commenced, McAdoo disclaimed any remnant of bitter feelings in connection with his treatment at the 1924 convention. "To this," McAdoo later recalled, "Smith merely nodded." At about 1:00 P.M., when luncheon appeared, the trio got down to business. Would California stay with Garner, Smith wanted to know? McAdoo recalled his reply that California would support the Speaker of the House as long as he had a chance. (By taking this position in his November memorandum, following the election,

McAdoo could readily explain his later shift to Roosevelt.) The Kent newspaper article rendered a more plausible version of the opening stages of negotiation.

> . . . There were a few more words [following the opening pleasantry] and they sat down to lunch. "Well," said McAdoo, "what are you going to do out here?" "Well," said Al, "I'm going to be on the level with you. We're both against Roosevelt or you wouldn't be here? Is that right?" To this Mr. McAdoo replied that it was. "All right," said Smith, "if we work together we can beat this fellow."

McAdoo later claimed that he offered no firm commitment when Smith formally proposed an alliance to stop Roosevelt. He was less interested in frustrating the leading contender, he remembered his rejoinder, than in securing the nomination of a man who could win the support of all elements in the party. McAdoo then inquired of Smith whom he and the Roosevelt opposition would put forward in the event the governor could be eliminated from the race. That had not been decided upon, Smith replied. The various candidates could confer at that point and choose a nominee. Dissatisfied with such an accord, McAdoo later claimed, he refused to enter into it. He gave two reasons: first, Smith was an active candidate for the presidency whereas he, McAdoo, was not; also, he would have only one vote in an arrangement of that sort and could easily be outvoted in the choice of a nominee.

Baruch then interjected. Would McAdoo be willing to give notice if California was about to shift its vote away from Garner? Only, McAdoo replied (according to his recollection), if it appeared possible in the circumstances. He gave the example of a floor poll of the delegation, which would preclude such a call. Although he conceded in his memorandum that he pledged his willingness to notify Baruch of a change in California's position, he denied making such a commitment to Smith. On the contrary, he claimed, he refused to limit his freedom of action to do what he believed best for the party.[5]

The Smith people presented a different version of the discussion and carried their bitterness over what they regarded as McAdoo's betrayal very nearly to their graves. "If McAdoo had not broken the pledges he made," Jouett Shouse informed Newton Baker a few days after the convention's close, "Roosevelt would not have been nominated. On the fourth ballot there would have been serious defections from his ranks with the result that some other nominee would have been certain. That nominee would have been you or Ritchie." Norman Hapgood, another Smith intimate who had lobbied behind the scenes for months in Baker's cause, promised Felix Frankfurter, following Smith's abrupt departure from Chicago after Roosevelt's triumph, that the Happy Warrior would make no public charge of treachery by McAdoo. Smith, Hapgood pledged, would not damage the party's chances in 1932 despite the fact "that McAdoo literally double-crossed him in an explicit agreement." [6]

With the election decided in November, the Smith group no longer felt constrained to keep the dirty linen from public view. The Kent newspaper article contended that once Smith gave McAdoo a state-by-state analysis of those delegations willing to break from Roosevelt if given the chance, the Californian became an interested participant in the movement. Kent related:

> Finally McAdoo was convinced and asked, "What then?" "If we go to the fifth ballot," said Smith, "we've got him licked. All right. Then my candidacy is out the window. I can't be nominated, but we can sit down around a table and get together on a candidate." To that the McAdoo query was, "When you sit around the table will I be there?" and the Smith reply was, "If you're not there I won't be there either." That ended the conversation. [7]

McAdoo vehemently denied the charge of perfidy leveled by Smith's associates through the device of a press leak. [8] But the most telling evidence as to the nature of the arrangement and degree of commitment is in a memorandum drafted in February 1933 by Brice Clagett, McAdoo's son-in-law, who served as an aide-de-camp to the Californian in Chicago. Clagett recalled a conversation with his father-in-law at a crucial point in the convention's deliberation. In a revealing sentence, crossed out in Clagett's aide-mémoire, McAdoo announced that he was finished with the "combination" and considered himself a free agent.[9] Indeed, there is ample evidence to suggest that McAdoo willingly joined the coalition on the eve of the convention, perhaps in the hope of emerging as a "dark horse" candidate. His decision to abandon the stop-Roosevelt group needs to be placed in a context of pressures from his old Wilsonian colleagues and his fear of a conservative internationalist as nominee.

From the vantage point of the Albany managers, the stop-Roosevelt combination had to be cracked at some key point. If that could be accomplished the edifice created by the Smith–"favorite-son"–McAdoo–Garner coalition would quickly crumble. James A. Farley's initial effort in this direction took him to Illinois, Indiana, and Ohio. In a hurried trip, made on the weekend of June 11–13, 1932, it became evident that he could make no headway in those states. Mayor Anton Cermak of Chicago held fast. When, in fact, Senator James Hamilton ("Ham") Lewis withdrew as Illinois' "favorite son" on the eve of the convention, to Farley's chagrin Cermak simply trotted out another dark horse, Chicago banker Melvin Traylor. Farley's hopes for Indiana were frustrated by the party's gubernatorial nominee, Paul V. McNutt, and by Roy Howard of the Scripps-Howard newspaper chain. The delegation split, with its leadership bent upon securing Newton D. Baker's nomination. Ohio's delegation proved unyielding too. Nominally the Buckeye State supported its "favorite son," Governor George White, who aspired to the vice-presidency. In reality James Cox controlled the group in the hope of checking the Roosevelt candidacy and then launching the Baker candidacy as a means of breaking a convention deadlock.[10] As the convention opened, Farley found himself compelled to turn to Garner, McAdoo, and Hearst. His sense of desperation heightened particularly with the ballot count following the Democratic enclave's initial major contest.

The first indication of the comparative strengths of the Roosevelt forces and of the opposition came in connection with the dispute which had festered since the spring concerning the convention's chairmanship. On the second day of business, June 28, Jouett Shouse's and Thomas J. Walsh's claims came forward in the form of minority and majority reports. James A. Byrnes of South Carolina extolled the political accomplishments of the Montana Senator, who had headed the Teapot Dome inquiry and stood as a Progressive bulwark in the Congress for a generation. John W. Davis countered that Shouse had labored unrewarded in the party's behalf for the previous three years and deserved recognition. But the real issue emerged with Senator Clarence C. Dill's outspoken claim on Walsh's behalf that the real contest involved "the progressive forces of this country on the one side," as opposed, here he grew vague and uncharacteristically diplomatic, to those who wished to displace him. The meaning seemed clear enough, however, and cries of "Boo" greeted Dill's remarks from the galleries, packed by Cermak with Smith partisans.

Walsh defeated Shouse for the permanent chairmanship by a close vote, 626 to 528, offering evidence in the convention's preliminary stages that Roosevelt could be overtaken considering the two-thirds requirement for nomination. It could be argued, with validity, that some of the votes for Shouse had been cast by Roosevelt supporters who felt morally bound by Raskob's and Shouse's services to the party and their own commitments made early in the year. While evidently Roosevelt could do better than 626 votes on the first ballot, it seemed equally clear that Farley's first-ballot predictions would not materialize. Roosevelt appeared to be vulnerable, some 100 votes short of the nomination.[11]

THE LENGTHY, sometimes bitter struggle for the nomination, in its final stages, took on an air of desperate maneuvering on both sides. In a widely distributed broadside, actually a reprint of Heywood Broun's June 29 column in the Scripps-Howard press, the charge surfaced that "If Franklin D. Roosevelt is nominated he will go before the country as the corkscrew candidate of a crooked convention." Cited as evidence was Roosevelt's fight against the convention's two-thirds rule, then its abandonment, and his devious behavior in connection with the Shouse chairmanship issue. Also, Broun deplored Roosevelt's alliance with the reactionary A. Mitchell Palmer and Louisiana's Kingfish, "who makes speeches about the poor and oppressed in the legislative halls of Washington and $1,000-dollar election bets in the hotel corridors of Chicago." Broun plumped for the Scripps-Howard stalking-horse for Baker, Alfred E. Smith, as nominee.[12]

Walter Lippmann proved no less diligent if somewhat more temperate. In a last ditch effort to head off the Roosevelt candidacy, the nation's most influential journalist openly presented "Baker for President" in his June 29 column. "Smith," he reasoned, "is not here to win the nomination for himself, and Roosevelt's supporters are in the main people who like him, . . . who thought he was probably the most available candidate, but are in no sense fanatically devoted to him." The way out of a convention deadlock, Lippmann proposed, "is Newton D. Baker of Ohio." The presentation rested on Baker's ability and character, his appeal as a unifying force in the party, and his ability to attract independent Republicans. "Newton D. Baker," the columnist urged, "is the man of the hour."[13]

The Roosevelt managers, on June 29, 1932, sensed their desperate position. The moment arrived, Farley realized, to abandon the strategy of winning over Illinois, Ohio, and Indiana and to concentrate on Texas and California; Garner, Hearst, and McAdoo represented the last hope of the Roosevelt forces. In the course of the convention proceedings, the chairmanship dispute, the reading of the platform, the interminable nominating speeches, working eighteen hours a day, grabbing sandwiches on the run and occasional naps, attempting to hold the Roosevelt delegations in line, Farley concentrated on William Randolph Hearst of San Simeon and John Nance Garner in Washington.

Hearst, Farley knew, harbored an enmity toward Smith that extended back to the press magnate's earlier involvement in New York state politics, and would be deeply disturbed by the growing current that ran through the gathering to the effect that a dead-locked convention would turn to Baker. The newspaper publisher, contacted by Joseph Kennedy among others, learned of Baker's potential as a compromise candidate. Hearst listened courteously to Farley's depiction of "the menace of the Baker movement," but would make no commitment. At that point, Farley recalled, he played his last big card.[14]

Convinced that John Nance Garner represented his last and best hope, and that the Speaker of the House desired above all avoidance of a repetition of the 1924 convention fracas, which rended the party almost beyond repair, Farley sought out Sam Rayburn, Garner's close political associate and campaign manager at Chicago. Rayburn and Silliman Evans, a member of the Texas delegation, heard Farley's appeal, then assured him that "We don't intend to make it another Madison Square Garden." Just prior to the balloting, Farley sought out Rayburn again and asked if the Texas delegation would be willing to switch to Roosevelt after the first ballot. Garner would then have received the compliment of a convention vote, and the switch to Roosevelt would end the matter. Rayburn refused. Texas felt bound to support its favorite son through two or three ballots, but Rayburn did want to know how long Farley could hold the Roosevelt delegations for his man. "Three ballots," came the reply, "four ballots, and maybe five." Realistically, Rayburn had committed himself to no particular course of action.

"Completely satisfied," as Farley saw the picture in his customary optimistic cast, he reported these negotiations to the wizened Howe. Virtually incapacitated by asthma, possibly emphysema, and the Chicago heat, forced usually to lie gasping for air on the floor of his hotel room with an electric fan as his only relief, Louis listened to Farley's recital of his contacts with Rayburn. Unimpressed, Howe argued that Farley had requested the meeting with Rayburn, not the reverse, that Rayburn and Evans had made no commitments, and their pro-Garner strategy paralleled his. They had met with Farley, the ancient warrior concluded, only to keep their own avenues open. Farley remained convinced, however, that Garner and the Texas delegation remained the coalition's most vulnerable point.[15]

Farley's estimate of the situation, in fact his conviction in later years that he had pursued the course that resulted in Roosevelt's nomination, seems only partially correct. A party man to the core, Garner did not wish to be responsible for a stalemated convention. Yet, he scarcely coveted the tendered vice-presidential plum, for he preferred the Speakership of the House to the role of supernumerary. When, in fact, two of Garner's closest cronies in Washington, Senators Harry B. Hawes of Missouri and Key Pittman of Nevada, boomed a Roosevelt–Garner ticket in a pre-convention telegraphic blitz, the Speaker, infuriated, made it plain to them as well as Farley that he had no interest in the nation's second highest office. In short, Garner, his own man in the situation, made no move until the fateful twelve-hour recess between the third and fourth ballots.[16]

A critical flaw revealed itself in Farley's approach. William Gibbs McAdoo, not Garner, held the key to the convention's outcome. The Texas delegation, while loyal to Garner, demonstrated widespread antipathy to the New Yorker. As events proved, only California's switch led to a shift by Texas to Roosevelt by two (perhaps four) votes at a rump meeting held when most of the Roosevelt opposition was absent. By necessity, however, Farley could scarcely treat with McAdoo. Although the matter is not broached in the Farley memoirs, the McAdoo papers leave no doubt that the Californian resented deeply the Howe–Farley alliance struck with his bitter political enemies, Isidore Dockweiler and Justus Wardell, former Smith supporters who had shifted to the Roosevelt camp as a matter of expediency. As a result, negotiations with McAdoo on Roosevelt's behalf fell into the hands of those old Wilsonians who championed the squire's candidacy, among them, Breckinridge Long, Robert Woolley, and Daniel Roper.[17]

In their contacts with McAdoo, the old Wilsonians, prior to the actual balloting at Chicago, proved no more successful than Farley in his pursuit of Garner, as typified by Breckinridge Long's experience with the Californian. A devoted supporter of and financial contributor to the Roosevelt campaign (later ambassador to Mussolini's Italy), Long reached Chicago three days before the convention opened, determined to win over McAdoo. "He was obdurate," Long reported to Key Pittman after the convention's close. "I had two long conversations with him. . . . But from McAdoo I got the distinct impression he was playing his own game and could not be counted on to help at all—or unless Baker became a real threat. But, in that case, a deadlock would already have developed." [18]

As the balloting began it appeared that the Roosevelt forces had been stymied. Garner, who professed no serious interest in the presidency, gave no indication, either, of a willingness to take second place on a ticket headed by Roosevelt. Although the promise of his refusal to permit a repetition of the 1924 situation buoyed Farley, this easily could have led to endorsement of a compromise choice. William Gibbs McAdoo entertained his own ambitions. And Frank Hague of Jersey City, Smith's campaign manager, had won a respectable showing for his candidate in New England and several of the large urban states, principally those with large Catholic and ethnic constituencies, some 200 delegates in all. In conjunction with "favorite son" candidacies, there appeared to be ample delegate votes needed to prevent Franklin D. Roosevelt from attaining the nomination. This seemed to be the essence of the initial balloting held during the night of June 30 and early morning of July 1.

On the first ballot Roosevelt received 666.25 votes, a clear majority, principally from the Southern states, the farm belt, the Rocky Mountain area, and the Pacific Northwest, but 100 votes shy of the required two-thirds, or 768. (The total votes cast were 1,154.) Smith had 201.75 votes, mainly from New England, New Jersey, New York, and Pennsylvania. Garner showed no strength outside of California's 44 votes and Texas' 46 votes, The balance fell to "favorite sons," among them, Ritchie of Maryland, Traylor of Illinois, Byrd of Virginia, and White of Ohio. [19]

Aware of his predicament, Roosevelt permitted his lieutenants at

Chicago to lure delegate votes with promises of cabinet posts as well as second place on the national ticket. Governor Ritchie of Maryland, offered a chance at the vice-presidency, refused, as did Governor White of Ohio. Robert Jackson recalled that he suggested the post of Secretary of the Navy to Virginia's Admiral Richard Byrd, brother of Governor Harry Byrd, in exchange for that state's delegation. The admiral seemed receptive, "but Harry embarrassed me," Jackson reminisced, "by saying he had considered me a friend who should have known he would never be a party to so contemptible a maneuver. As I recall his words, he added, 'I couldn't deliver them and I wouldn't if I could.' I was appropriately abashed." Later, Jackson learned that Byrd in reality "was playing both ends against the middle," in the form of a Baker–Byrd ticket. Nor was Jackson any more successful when he proffered the Treasury post to Melvin Traylor of Illinois. The Chicago banker claimed that he could not afford the financial sacrifice. Farley met a similar rebuff at the hands of Mayor Anton Cermak of Chicago. Rumors of other proposed deals abounded in the late night hours of June 30.

A second ballot followed the first, despite the late hour, likely in the hope that the Roosevelt managers could penetrate the two-thirds barrier. But the leading contender mustered only an additional 11.50 votes for a total of 677.75, these votes having come from a minor shift in the divided Missouri delegation. The coalition, Farley sensed, had Roosevelt on the run.

In the morning hours of July 1, Roosevelt's floor leader, Arthur F. Mullen of Nebraska, aware of his candidate's predicament, rose to move that the convention adjourn until four o'clock in the afternoon. Loud cries of "No!" reflected belief that Farley had no more votes to produce. Dudley Field Malone of New York pressed, "We have been held here all night at great inconvenience and we are prepared to stay here all day." Mullen withdrew the motion, for if he had lost on that question, the Roosevelt candidacy was ended. His very withdrawal of the motion could be interpreted as a sign of weakness. Not without reason, for Roosevelt, thanks to Senator Pat Harrison of Mississippi, held that delegation's 20 votes against the

Baker forces, led by Governor Martin ("Mike") Sennett Conner by only one vote, 10.5 to 9.5, under the unit rule. The loss of Mississippi to Baker, now regarded as a momentary possibility, represented a potential turning point.[20]

The third ballot carried the proceedings to 9:15 A.M. on Friday, July 1, and confirmed the inability of the Roosevelt forces to produce a two-thirds vote without a major psychological shift. This time, as morning broke in the steaming Chicago Auditorium, Farley could manage only five new votes for a total of 682.79. Necessary to a choice was 768. By an agreement reached with Roosevelt's floor manager, William Gibbs McAdoo rose to move a recess until 8:30 P.M. Arthur Mullen, breathing a sigh of relief, gladly seconded. Upon a voice vote, which some challenged unsuccessfully, Walsh, the presiding officer, hammered the gavel, walked off the platform, and gained twelve critical hours for Franklin Roosevelt. For the slightest decline in FDR's delegate strength, now a possibility, would have been fatally damaging.[21]

THE INITIAL THREE BALLOTS demonstrated the coalition's ability to hold Roosevelt some 80 to 90 votes short of the nomination. On the conviction that the Roosevelt candidacy had been checked, the Baker forces went into high gear. Ralph Hayes had surmised that the Ohioan must emerge only as the alternative to a stalemated convention and at no point as a threat to the leading contender. Even if completely stymied, the Roosevelt forces after all could veto the choice of an alternative candidate. It now appeared appropriate, gradually, during the course of the next two or three ballots, to unfold Baker's nomination to the exhausted delegates as a suitable escape. Walter Lippmann circulated a round robin petition among eighty prominent Democrats, most of them conservative internationalists, including Norman Davis, Frank Polk, former Supreme Court Justice John H. Clarke, Stanley King, and Hamilton Fish Armstrong, director of the Council on Foreign Relations, urging Baker's nomination. Although reluctant to sign a declaration criticizing Hoover, Norman Davis cabled from Switzerland, while representing the government in Europe, "would gladly declare for Baker whose nomination offers best chance of uniting party and achieving success." [22]

The Lippmann effort, as well as Adolf Berle's round robin among the Columbia and Harvard faculties, had been designed to coincide with important delegation shifts to Baker on the ensuing ballot. The contest long waged within the Mississippi delegation between Senator Harrison and Governor Conner, actually rooted in the issue of control of state politics, took on a pivotal cast. James Farley dashed by cab to Pat Harrison's hotel room, and dragged the Senator, half-clothed, to a Mississippi caucus to hold the delegation for Roosevelt. But, following the third ballot recess, the Mississippi delegation capitulated to Conner and voted to switch to Baker on the next ballot. As Governor Conner ruefully observed after the convention's close, "This would have been done but for the action of California and Texas." [23]

Considerable Baker potential could be found elsewhere. Throughout much of the South, where loyalty to Roosevelt was skin deep, Baker's conservatism and internationalist convictions offered no handicap. Ralph Hayes, who managed Baker's fortunes at Chicago, arranged with John Stewart Bryan, editor of the *Richmond News-Leader*, for a swing to Baker, with Governor Byrd's consent. "What a tragedy," Senator Carter Glass later confided to Baker, "was enacted at Chicago in the failure not to nominate you and Byrd as our national standard bearers! The folly of it, even should we succeed at the election, depresses me more than my illness." Baker replied cordially, "Now that I am not in danger of having to bear the burden and responsibility, I am frank to admit to you that a ticket of Baker and Byrd would not have been a bad combination from my point of view." Later in February 1933, wary of the President-elect's flexibility in fiscal attitudes, Glass declined the post of Secretary of the Treasury in order to preserve his right to act as a critic. [24]

Other delegations also considered Baker as the convention's best alternative. During the twelve-hour recess, eight North Carolina delegates, restive under that state's unit-rule voting for Roosevelt, declared themselves for the Ohioan. Characteristic of the attitude of Southern moderates, Josephus Daniels conceded to Bernard Baruch on the eve of the convention: "If it turns out at Chicago that Roosevelt cannot be nominated, we must all strain our nerves to get Baker." After the proceedings had ended, Daniels confirmed Walter Lippmann's view that Baker was the party's ablest man but, he argued, "Newton would not turn a hand over in his own behalf." [25] Elsewhere, Wendell L. Willkie, then practicing law in New York and a Democrat, had made headway with the Alabama delegation; Governor Ritchie of Maryland, likely with Baruch's assent, prepared to go over to the Ohioan; Oklahoma, which gave up Governor Murray's cause, evinced satisfaction with Baker as a compromise; and Kansas, Iowa, Minnesota, and a portion of the Pennsylvania delegation also indicated willingness to shift to Baker. John W. Davis and Judge Samuel Seabury tackled the New York delegation, which proved so badly factionalized that the Empire State contingent turned out to be a cipher in the Chicago proceedings. From Paul V. McNutt, Baker learned later, "If the battle had lasted twenty-four hours longer it would have been possible to bring up the army to what Roy Howard called 'The Lost Battalion,' " an allusion to Indiana's lonely early votes for Baker. Dispirited, convinced that Baker lost only because of bad management at Chicago, James Cox contended: "The disheartening thing about the convention's result is that it could so easily have been something different." [26]

Sometime during the late afternoon of July 1, 1932, the keenest politician of them all, keeping his vigilance in Albany, began to see the handwriting on the wall. Franklin D. Roosevelt called the party's alternative choice, Baker recalled, at about 5:20 P.M. on that fateful day. It appeared to the leading contender that "the Chicago convention is in a jam and that they will turn to you. I will do anything I can to bring that about if you want it." Genuine in his wish to serve only if drafted, Baker claimed ignorance of the proceedings at Chicago. He did not want Roosevelt "to do anything of the kind [endorsement of Baker] on the basis of any such information as I had." As he later explained his response to one of his oldest and closest friends, "after all I am sixty and have had a warning experience [in reference to a heart attack suffered four years earlier], so that it may well be that the burden of a candidacy and the responsibility of the presidency would have been more than I could expect to find left in me after so active a life." [27] Unknown to Baker and Roosevelt as they conferred, the matter had been settled, principally by Daniel C. Roper and William Gibbs McAdoo.

Although never mentioned in the Roper–McAdoo negotiations during the July 1 convention recess, a telegraphic bombardment organized by Ralph Hayes surely entered the picture. As Judson King viewed the situation, "When it appeared, after the third ballot, that a deadlock was in prospect a literal flood of telegrams from all over the nation deluged the individual delegates, urging Baker . . . I have never seen an attempted coup fall flatter." Hayes overplayed his hand. It appeared to King, who headed the National Popular Government League's crusade for public power, as well as others, that "the utility and banking interests" saw their opportunity to name the Cleveland attorney as the party's nominee. As William E. Dodd of the University of Chicago, active in Illinois politics and an admirer of Baker, put it: "I think Roosevelt's nomination was the very best thing that could have been done. The behavior of the utility people . . . so annoyed and irritated delegates to the convention that very many of them lost their faith in Baker, whose candidacy was in the back of many people's minds throughout the convention. . . . I do not know how it happened that he allowed so many interests of anti-social objectives to figure in his behalf." Even the conservative ex-Governor of Ohio, James Cox, who anticipated that he could swing that state's delegation to Baker, stood incensed at the flood of telegrams which seemed so patently engineered by the utilities and the financial community. "This was a terrible mistake," he complained to Baker in a postmortem, which questioned the Baker leadership at the convention's critical moment. [28]

As Breckinridge Long, Robert Woolley, and Daniel C. Roper

knew, the possibility of Baker's candidacy might lead to McAdoo's willingness to do business with them. Certainly, Daniel C. Roper decided, after days of fruitless negotiations with Brice Clagett and McAdoo, one last desperate effort should be made. Earlier, following the Garner primary victory in California, Roper and Woolley came away from a conference with McAdoo confident that the California delegation would swing to Roosevelt on the second ballot in the event Garner could not be nominated. Upon arriving in Chicago, however, they found McAdoo in a totally different frame of mind. Woolley suspected that McAdoo had his own ambitions. As he explained to Colonel House,

> On the opening day of the Convention we discovered that our friend from California treasured the idea that we didn't have all the votes we claimed and that, a deadlock resulting, a dark horse could walk away with the nomination—he being the dark horse. He confided as much to a United States Circuit Judge from New York (M. B. M.), who promptly imparted the information to me. [29]

Daniel C. Roper, at one time Commissioner of Internal Revenue in the Wilson administration, and one of McAdoo's staunchest supporters in the twenties, finally wrenched the Californian away from the coalition. Following the third ballot, on Friday, July 1, Roper conferred with McAdoo's son-in-law, Brice Clagett, insisting that Baker would be the beneficiary of the imminent collapse of the Roosevelt candidacy. (In a bitter letter, sent that day to McAdoo, Woolley charged his old friend with "making common cause with the worst elements in the party.") [30] According to Roper, Roosevelt was "through" unless California and Texas switched on the fourth ballot when the convention reconvened that night.

Late that afternoon, in a conference with McAdoo, Roper again raised the specter of Baker as nominee. McAdoo, urged to name his price for conversion, insisted on control of patronage in California, a veto over the choices of Secretary of State and Treasury, and the selection of Garner as the vice-presidential nominee. He desired, McAdoo insisted, not usurpation of the president-elect's right to choose his own cabinet, but assurance, through his own veto power, that key posts would be filled by progressives. After communicating with Roosevelt and Howe, Roper gave McAdoo the assurances he sought.

But William Randolph Hearst had not yet been accounted for. In the absence of documentation, it has been traditionally assumed by Hearst's biographers that the lord of San Simeon functioned as the senior partner in the Hearst–McAdoo alliance. And it is legend among those who have probed Hearst's career that telephone calls from Hearst to Garner and McAdoo terminated the stalemate.[31] Yet the evidence associated with these negotiations indicates otherwise. At 5 o'clock in the afternoon, some four hours before McAdoo's dramatic announcement of the California shift, Roper, McAdoo, Amon Carter of Texas, George Creel, and Hearst's personal secretary and representative in Chicago, Joseph Willicombe, gathered at the McAdoo suite in the Sherman House. Willicombe announced that he had spoken with the newspaper magnate, who could envisage a shift by Texas and California to Roosevelt on a later ballot. (Roper recalled that it was the eighth ballot, Brice Clagett, the sixth.) Roper insisted that such a decision would ensure the nomination of Smith or Baker. The contention that Hearst shifted his position has never been documented.

At 6 o'clock a delegation dispatched by Smith, unable to reach McAdoo on the telephone, tracked down his ostensible ally. Would California stay with Garner until the sixth ballot? What, McAdoo inquired, would the coalition do at that point? They did not know. McAdoo became testy. Suspicious of Smith's motives, he announced unwillingness to remain in the coalition and go up a "blind alley." He could support the combination only if he knew its choice as nominee. They could not say. A sentence crossed out in the Clagett memorandum reveals that McAdoo then concluded, shortly after 6 o'clock, that he was through with the "combination" and considered himself a free agent. Desperate phone calls made by Smith and his entourage to McAdoo at his hotel and Garner in Washington went unanswered.[32]

Evidently McAdoo's pointed inquiries reflected a growing sentiment at Chicago that Newton D. Baker would be the beneficiary of the combination.[33] For at about the same time that McAdoo confronted the Smith representatives, two of his most trusted political allies in California, Hamilton Cotton and Thomas Storke, arrived at the same conclusion in a candid conversation with James A. Farley. Farley expressed his conviction that the Roosevelt candidacy could not remain viable beyond the fourth ballot. He had exhausted every available delegate vote. Choked with emotion, Storke recalled in a memorandum written in 1934, "tears literally flooding his eyes," Farley told the two California delegates, known to be McAdoo intimates, "Boys, Roosevelt is lost unless California comes over to us on the next ballot." Storke volunteered his feeling that California would eventually go over to Roosevelt, but that the delegation intended to stay with Garner for another ballot or two. "Well, then," Farley countered, "Newton D. Baker will be nominated. He is the interests' candidate, and you will be playing squarely into their hands if you wait. I tell you, unless California comes over on the fourth ballot, Roosevelt is lost and Baker will win!"

The California delegates related the exchange to McAdoo, who conceded that the "boys in the smoke-filled back room" had apparently settled upon Baker as their choice. (He did not mention his earlier negotiations with the coalition.) Garner, McAdoo informed them, expressed his willingness to concede. Wary of Hearst's feelings in the matter, however, the trio decided to convene the California caucus at 7:00 P.M. At the chaotic delegation meeting, a chorus of shouts expressed the predominant sentiment to stay with Garner. The cry of betrayal greeted McAdoo, when delegates sensed that Roosevelt was the intended beneficiary of the caucus. "No vote was ever taken," Storke recalled, contrary to McAdoo's post-convention statement that the California shift had been voted unanimously. Rather, Storke related, a majority preferred to support Garner for at least another ballot. Beyond that consensus, the California delegation, like the convention, appeared hopelessly divided. At that moment John B. Elliott of Los Angeles, a former newspaperman who had struck it rich in oil and became powerful among state Democrats, proposed the creation of a steer-

ing committee that would determine when and if California would
leave Garner. McAdoo, Elliott, C. C. McPike of San Francisco,
and National Committeewoman Nellie Donohue of Oakland were
chosen. As the convention reconvened, Storke recalled, the steering committee decided to switch to Roosevelt on the fourth ballot.
He explained:

> A deadlock in 1932 would undoubtedly have nominated Newton
> D. Baker, and his running mate would have been chosen from Rit-
> chie of Maryland, Byrd of Virginia, or more probably Garner. All
> three of these men were conservatives. In any case, none of them
> was capable of fathering a "New Deal."
>
> The political philosophies of Roosevelt and Baker were worlds
> apart; so was their approach to domestic and world problems.[34]

Following McAdoo's decision to opt for Roosevelt, John Nance
Garner, never a die-hard contestant, called Sam Rayburn in Chicago. "Sam, I think it is time to break this thing up. . . . Roosevelt
is the choice of the convention. He has had a majority on three
ballots. . . . The nomination ought to be made on the next roll
call." But the task proved difficult. As Bascom Timmons, long-time
Washington correspondent and Garner intimate related the situation, when the Texas caucus convened at about 6:30 P.M. on July 1,
to hear Garner's decision, only 105 of 180 delegates could be mustered. The vote to go to Roosevelt, Timmons relates, was 54 to 51.
Another newspaperman, R. G. Sucher of the Washington Press
Service, learned from Texas Senator Tom Connally as they rode
home on the train that the margin was actually two votes. Of the
seventy-five absentees, most had scattered in search of Garner
votes from other delegations. Many had been die-hard opponents
of Roosevelt, including Ralph W. Morrison, a powerful and
wealthy rancher, hotel operator, and utility magnate, who had financed the Garner campaign and the expenses of the Texas delegation. As William E. Dodd viewed the scene, the result was purely
adventitious.

> An ex-governor of Texas informed me [Dodd wrote Illinois Judge
> Henry Horner] how many utility men were here and working upon
> the Texas delegation with one object in mind, namely, the defeat of

Roosevelt. One of my students was with the Mississippi delegation and he reported the same thing there. [Senator] J. W. Bailey and Governor Gardner of North Carolina, both utility sympathizers, were working in that state to change the delegation. Any one of these moves might easily have been made the night of the final decision had it not been for the attitude of California, and the attitude of California was certainly curious and close.

The Texas delegation remained deadlocked as the convention reconvened. "Actually there is some question," Bascom Timmons concluded, "whether the Lone Star delegation ever voted to go to Roosevelt." It is doubtful in fact, as one views the evidence, that a poll of the Texas delegation, once fully assembled in the Chicago Auditorium, would have sustained the rump vote for Roosevelt engineered by Sam Rayburn and Tom Connally. But the contest ended just after 9 P.M. as delegates still assembled and caucuses of various states attempted to decide where they would now go. [35]

Tension and a sense of history filled the Chicago Auditorium as California was called. Rumors circulated that McAdoo intended to break the deadlock. From the floor the veteran of other convention fights asked to explain his state's vote before casting it on the fourth ballot. "California," the darling of the Bible Belt intoned from the rostrum in one of the most dramatic moments in convention history, "came here to nominate a President of the United States. She did not come here to deadlock this convention or to engage in another disastrous contest like that of 1924." In a clear allusion to the injustice he felt eight years earlier when, despite the attainment of a majority vote, he could not secure the needed two-thirds because of Smith's bitter opposition, he proclaimed his "belief that when any man comes into a Democratic National Convention with the popular will behind him to the extent of almost seven hundred votes. . . ." The implication was clear and pandemonium broke loose, McAdoo drowned out by Smith's partisans who jammed the galleries controlled by Chicago's mayor. Thirty minutes went by before order could be restored. "I intend to say what I propose to say without regard to what the galleries or anybody else think." This time, unlike Madison Square Garden, he would be heard. He intended to put the knife all the way in. "As I was saying when this demonstration began, when a man comes into this convention with 700 votes in his favor, I take it as indicative of the public sentiment in this country for that candidate. I believe in democracy and in the rule of the majority. . . . California casts forty-four votes for Franklin D. Roosevelt." As state after state fell into the Roosevelt column the galleries roared their disapproval.

On the fourth and final ballot Roosevelt gathered 945 votes, Smith 190.5, a handful scattered among Ritchie, Baker, White, and Cox.[36] "I am grateful to you," Roosevelt telegraphed McAdoo as he prepared for his flight to address the convention, "for your generous and patriotic statement to the convention and I hope to see my old friend tomorrow." "You did the wise and patriotic thing and democracy owes you a debt of gratitude," Garner, the reluctant vice-presidential choice, reassured his political ally.[37]

Scores of accounts of these historic events in the sweltering early summer heat of Chicago, ranging from correspondence to press reports to memoirs and full-scale historical treatments, exist, all with considerable variation in the theme. Some will remain convinced that Farley, Rayburn, and Garner were pivotal; some that Garner and Hearst, who never attended the convention, decided the issue on the telephone; Arthur Mullen, that his negotiations with Senator Tom Connally and Edgar Howard, Garner's Washington poker-playing crony, proved decisive; others that it was "a sham battle" with Roosevelt's nomination determined even "before the gavel fell to call the first session in order." [38] Yet, there is ample evidence that McAdoo perceived in Roosevelt's candidacy and election the best chance for a progressive resurgence in the midst of the agonies of a horrendous economic depression. Surely there will never be any final interpretation of the myriad events, details, and deals which surrounded the 1932 Democratic festivities. But, after several decades, with the New Deal a concluded chapter in not-so-recent American history, some new attention needs to be given to those who lost the battle. For it is questionable that they entirely departed the American political scene or that they became permanently disabled.

The conservative coalition, bitter, wary of Roosevelt and his newly won "radical" allies, whom they held responsible for the denouement, never, in fact, capitulated. For Smith, Raskob, Shouse, and their business allies, the fight waged at Chicago in 1932 constituted a battle in a patriotic effort at preservation of the Jeffersonian tradition of minimal government in Washington. For a time, Roosevelt's and the Brains Trust's conceptualizations of new and expanded governmental functions designed to attain a degree of central management of economic and social goals, dubbed the New Deal, emerged as a major theme. Although the new administration was virtually unopposed by a nearly defunct Republican party, within a year after the famous Hundred Days, many of the former conservative coalition that had opposed Roosevelt's nomination in 1932, regrouped under the banner of the American Liberty League, bent upon repealing the New Deal's economic and social philosophy. Theirs was the first of a mounting conservative opposition to what was regarded as Roosevelt's fundamental transformation of the American way of life, away from its historic stress on individualism, self-reliance, free enterprise, and emphasis on the virtues of local and state government, toward excessive dependence upon and domination by central government, its measures and its bureaucracy.

Symbolically the initial expression of conservative discontent within Roosevelt's own party was Alfred E. Smith's refusal to turn over his 190.5 delegate votes to the winner as the Happy Warrior stalked out of Chicago. He never listened to Roosevelt's acceptance of the nomination, in reality Roosevelt and Moley's reaffirmation of the "Forgotten Man" address. In correspondence, in leaks to press, later in their recollections, Smith's supporters in the conservative coalition claimed perfidy on McAdoo's part. Indeed, they claimed more. Shouse, Raskob, and Baker complained bitterly of the demise of "responsible" party leaders such as John W. Davis, Ritchie, Carter Glass, Virginia's Governor Byrd, the reactionary James Reed of Missouri, later a bitter opponent of the New Deal, Pierre S. du Pont, Cox of Ohio, and others, and their replacement in the party's councils by a group of radicals, Long, Wheeler, Dill, Garner, McAdoo, and Hearst, who seemingly held Roosevelt in tow. "It is certainly too bad," Raskob concluded in a letter to Virginia's Harry F. Byrd, "that we did not have a general in charge of our forces, and thus . . . save our Party from the radical element which is now in control." [39]

Although the conservative coalition did not desert Roosevelt during the 1932 campaign—in fact, the Pittsburgh speech and its firm pledge of cuts in federal spending and the balancing of the budget represented an attempt to appease it—with the singular exception of Bernard Baruch, who throughout his lifetime showed more dedication to participation than ideological commitment, it played no role in the Roosevelt victory. Loyalty to the Democratic party and its candidate, admittedly begrudging in tone, was its advice to other dissidents who saw the end of an era. [40] Toward the middle of the campaign, through the offices of Felix Frankfurter and Herbert Bayard Swope, the Smith advisers agreed to allow the Happy Warrior to show the colors on Roosevelt's behalf. [41]

But the fissure between the two camps rested too firmly on fundamental philosophic differences to be smoothed over for long. Restive during 1933, Smith, Raskob, and Shouse, with Du Pont–General Motors support, formed the American Liberty League the following year to mount a renewed attack on the centralist tendencies of the modern state. The Liberty League, transparently reactionary in its defense of property rights, laissez faire, and its assertion of Jeffersonianism and constitutionalism, proved unable to recruit Herbert Hoover in its opposition to the New Deal—not because of its tenets, incidentally, but because Shouse and Raskob had persistently propagandized the public against his administration during the depression.

Generally viewed as a minority or fringe group on the Right in the Roosevelt years, the Liberty League quickly took on a more viable approach, alliance with the Republican party and Southern Democrats, who dominated the Congress. Roosevelt's turn to organized labor marked the demise of the New Deal majority and its transformation into a minority party in Congress. By the mid-to-late 1930s, the conservative coalition represented the majority view in the legislative branch of government. [42]

ROOSEVELT'S DRAMATIC FLIGHT to Chicago and delivery of the address that pledged a "new deal" for the American people was designed to serve several purposes. One, immediate, reflected the candidate's sense of melodrama, his love of the hustings and the noise of the crowd, instincts diametrically distinct from the retiring and crusty White House incumbent. Further, he intended to dispel the notion that he was incapacitated. He had done that before when he toured New York State in the 1928 gubernatorial campaign. Then again, Roosevelt intended to offer a viable economic program in the course of the presidential quest. The acceptance speech had as its aim a statement of broad economic principles, from which there would be elaborated during the campaign concrete remedies for the depression. Raymond Moley's May 19 memorandum had been drafted for that purpose.

With a railroad trip out of the question because of the time element, arrangements had been made even before the convention for a possible plane flight. Secretly the governor's secretary, Guernsey Cross, contacted the general traffic manager of American Airlines, Colonial division, at Albany. Could the governor be flown to Chicago at a moment's notice? American Airlines flew only tiny Stinsons and Pilgrims out of Albany as far as Cleveland, but publicity value effected the transfer of a Ford tri-motor from the Dallas to Los Angeles run. "It was a rough ride along the Mohawk Valley," Goodrich Murphy of American Airlines recalled; "flying against the prevailing winds at low altitude was rough, and that Ford was a balloon." The plane, he noted, "rode like a blimp." But the nominee seemed unaffected by the flight.

On board the lethargic and bouncy prototype of the modern era of transportation were the governor, Eleanor Roosevelt, two of their children, John and Elliott, Guernsey Cross, Grace Tully, Margaret "Missy" Le Hand, Samuel I. Rosenman, and two state police officers, Earl Miller and Gus Gennerich, who served as bodyguards. After lunch on the plane, the Democratic nominee took out the acceptance statement and entered last minute corrections. Mrs. Roosevelt knit a sweater for a grandchild. As Franklin finished each page he handed it to his sons, then Eleanor, and finally Sam Rosenman for comment and a final check. It was a dramatic flight and a ringing statement. [43]

In the decades since the historic pronouncement of a "new deal" in the Chicago auditorium, authorship of the address and the catchphrase that came to symbolize an era of American history has been a matter of contention. The earliest claim was put forward by Raymond Moley when he reprinted in his 1939 memoir, *After Seven Years,* an excerpt from the May 19, 1932, document in which it appeared. "It may easily be argued," Moley suggested, "that this material foreshadowed not only most of the campaign speeches but much of the New Deal itself." [44] Since that time historical scholarship has tended to reject the Moley argument.

Arthur Schlesinger Jr., this generation's most distinguished New Deal specialist, disputed Moley's claim of authorship. Instead, he credited the governor's counsel, Samuel I. Rosenman, with principal authorship and the famous emblem of liberal reform in the 1930s.

> Moley [Schlesinger wrote] had completed the first draft of an acceptance speech by the third week in June. . . . The Moley draft was too long, and Roosevelt worked away at odd moments with Rosenman to cut it down. The speech also lacked a conclusion. After listening to the all-night balloting, Rosenman, nervous and restless, retired with hot dogs and a pot of coffee to try his hand at writing the peroration which he half thought would never be used. It was then that Rosenman, jogged perhaps by the title of a Stuart Chase article in the current *New Republic* ("A New Deal for America") but without noting any special significance (any more than Roosevelt did when he came to deliver the words), set down the sentence, "I pledge you, I pledge myself, to a new deal for the American people."

In a lengthy footnote Professor Schlesinger acknowledged Moley's use of the "new deal" phrase in his May memorandum. But, curiously, he insisted on its appearance in the address as having

come from another source. Possibly, he suggested, it emanated
from the *New Republic* series, which began on June 29, possibly
from Henry James's *The Princess Casamassima* (chapter 34) published in 1886, or even more likely from Roosevelt's favorite novel,
Mark Twain's *A Connecticut Yankee in King Arthur's Court*
(chapter 13). "But there can be little doubt," Schlesinger concluded, "that Rosenman contributed the actual words; and that the
press, so to speak, created the phrase 'New Deal' by endowing the
words with a significance that neither Roosevelt nor Rosenman intended." [45] Upon Rosenman's death, in 1973, the nation's newspaper of record, the *New York Times*, rendered this interpretation its
coveted imprimatur when it, too, attributed "the historic phrase
New Deal" to the governor's counsel. [46]

Such an interpretation ignores convincing evidence that on the
eve of delivery of the acceptance speech, Rosenman, hot dogs and
coffee in hand, worked from Moley's final draft. Of greater import,
the Schlesinger interpretation ignores the role of the Brains Trust
in the 1932 proceedings. The "New Deal" symbolized more than a
slogan in Moley's mind. Put another way, because Rosenman remained at the periphery of the Brains Trust's economic deliberations, he took no special note of the "new deal" catchphrase as he
inserted it in the reading draft, hence its near elimination.

There are extant two drafts of the acceptance speech written by
Raymond Moley in the period before the convention. The final
Moley draft remained in use as the Democratic Convention
opened its proceedings in Chicago, actually as late as June 28. The
third paragraph of the final Moley draft, as well as the third paragraph of the final Rosenman–Roosevelt draft, the reading copy
which Roosevelt carried to the podium in Chicago, proposed, in
Moley's words, "a new deal" as "an emblem—a happy emblem of
new purposes, renewed life, rededicated devotion . . . to the
sorely tried people of this country." That paragraph was excised at
the last moment as the consequence of a curious incident. As Roosevelt's motorcade wended its way through the streets of Chicago
toward the auditorium, he substituted the first page of a speech

authored by Louis Howe in the Windy City for the first page of his reading draft. After all, it seemed the least he could do as a tribute to his faithful mentor. As a result the "new deal" as an emblem of his purpose remained only in the peroration. Fortunately, the press perceived what had very nearly been deleted from the address. [47]

As is true of the New Deal slogan, much of the historic peroration originated with the final Moley draft:

Acceptance Speech, Chicago, July 2, 1932

Moley draft (page 24)

My program is based upon a simple moral principle. It assumes that the welfare and soundness of a nation depends upon what the people want and whether they are getting it. And what do the people want more than anything else? To my mind, two things: first work, with all the moral and spiritual values that go with it. Idleness is stagnation. Stagnation is disintegration. And disintegration is death. Second, they want a reasonable measure of security for themselves and for those who depend upon them.

Work and security are the spiritual values toward which our efforts for reconstruction should lead. These are the values that this program is intended to gain. These values have not been achieved by the leadership we now have.

It is all very well for those who speak for the present administration to speak of economic laws. But men starve while economic laws exist which cannot be controlled by the laws of men. Our economic system is a human thing, built by human beings. I believe it can likewise be controlled by human beings, and for the general good. Emerson, long ago, said this in words of common sense. . . .

Roosevelt (Rosenman) reading draft (pp. 15–16)

My program, of which I can touch on but a few points today, is based upon this simple moral principle: the welfare and soundness of a nation depend first upon what the great mass of its people wish and need, and second whether they are getting it.

What do the people of America want more than anything else? To my mind two things: work, with all the moral and spiritual values that go with it, and, with work, a reasonable measure of security for themselves and for those who depend upon them.

Work and security—these are the spiritual values, the true goal toward which our efforts for reconstruction should lead. These are the values that this program is intended to gain. These are the values we have failed to achieve by the leadership we now have.

Our Republican leaders tell us of economic laws—sacred, inviolable, unchangeable,—that these laws cause panics which no one can prevent. But while they prate of economic laws, men are starving. We must lay hold of the fact that economic laws are not made by nature, they are made by human beings. . . .

Whereas Moley concluded with words from Emerson and the prophet Isaiah, Rosenman in a stirring and vibrant rewrite of Moley's third paragraph concluded:

I pledge you, I pledge myself, to a new deal for the American people. Let us here assembled constitute ourselves prophets of a new order of competence and courage. This is more than a political campaign; it is a call to arms. Give me your help not to win votes alone, but to win in this crusade to restore America to its own people.

The acceptance statement pledged a reorientation of the party and its program toward the middle and lower classes, specifically, labor, the farmer, and the small businessman. In the decade following the death of Woodrow Wilson, the Democratic party had been preempted by the business community, much like a bankrupt corporate shell. Roosevelt and Moley desired a return to the party's traditional role, as they saw it, of "liberal thought, of planned action, of international outlook, and of the greatest good to the greatest number of our people." To a party that had shifted far to the right and appeared virtually barren of social and economic issues, Roosevelt, in words taken directly from the Moley memorandum of May 19, 1932, insisted on posing a liberal alternative to the Republican "Normalcy" of the 1920s:

There are two ways of viewing the government's duty in matters affecting economic and social life. The first sees to it that a favored few are helped and hopes that some of their prosperity will leak through to labor, to the farmer and to the small businessman.

This theory belongs to the party of Toryism—now the party of ruined prosperity. But it is not, and should never be, the theory of the Democratic party. This is no time for fear, for reaction for timidity. . . .

The people of this country want a genuine choice this year, not a choice between two names for the same reactionary doctrine. Ours must be a party of liberal thought, of planned action, of enlightened international outlook, of the greatest good to the greatest number of our people.

In its economic thrust the acceptance speech excoriated the cycle of overexpansion and underconsumption, fed by excess corporate profits, which led to the depression. Solutions included budget balancing and economy in government, an axiom of the era; work spreading in the form of a shorter work day and week; and conversion of millions of acres of abandoned and marginal land, through reforestation, to a future natural resource. This last scheme, Roosevelt claimed, would afford employment to a million men.

Echoing, too, the determination of the group of academicians which shaped the New Deal in its broad outline, Roosevelt asserted that a depressed agriculture lay at the core of the economic collapse. Cleverly, the Democratic nominee spoke of the restoration of rural America's purchasing power through domestic allotment in McNary–Haugen terminology. Direct reference to the new and controversial scheme was shunned. He wanted, he stated, a higher return for the farmer and proceeded to outline what eventually became the New Deal agricultural program. He called for the bestowal upon agriculture of the same reasonable tariff protection enjoyed by industry, control of production to reduce surpluses and avoidance of dumping of that surplus abroad and, without mentioning the processing tax, which would redistribute income from urban to rural America, he promised that this would be done at no cost to the government.

It should have followed from the vantage point of Rexford Guy Tugwell, who listened closely with Moley in Chicago as Roosevelt spoke, that the nominee would proceed to the enunciation of his scheme of industrial organization. Moley had accepted the proposal for an advisory Economic Council to the President, "an organized planning body," that would give direction to the nation's industrial and financial sectors. The proposal, incorporated into the May 19 memorandum, had been retained in the final Moley draft. But it did not surface in the Rosenman draft, the speech read by Roosevelt. Was it simply one of the many deletions made by Sam for economy of time? Tired and hot delegates would not listen to a lengthy address. Or did the omission promise abandonment of economic planning for industry? Tugwell soon raised the issue.

A second dilemma required resolution. The speech contained internal economic contradictions which became evident as the campaign got under way. The economic logic of the Roosevelt–Brains Trust collaboration intended the restoration of farm purchasing power and higher farm prices by artificially reducing output. Presumably a restored agriculture would make increased purchases of the product of industry and labor. The approach represented a filtering up of prosperity through the stimulus of an artificial balance of supply and demand and a government-created reflation. Yet, Roosevelt condemned ruinously high tariffs and, to the delight of the party's internationalists, pledged his adherence to the party's plank which endorsed: "A competitive tariff for revenue . . . ; reciprocal tariff agreements with other nations; and an international economic conference designed to restore international trade and facilitate exchange."

At that point, Roosevelt and his principal economic advisers had no difficulty in subscribing to both the maintenance of artificially high domestic prices (the restoration of purchasing power) and a low tariff—reciprocal trade agreements philosophy in the international arena. As the economic contradiction became evident during the 1932 campaign, Roosevelt and Moley, compelled to choose, opted for domestic priorities.

By default, Herbert Hoover remained relatively unchallenged as he maneuvered the nation's economic diplomacy on a course calculated to abort the New Deal before its inception. In the summer and early autumn months of 1932, the incumbent President set in motion a course of events that led to the interregnum crisis and the catastrophic London Economic Conference of 1933. Herbert Hoover and the Democratic internationalists who drafted their party's platform—Walter Lippmann, Newton Baker, A. Mitchell Palmer, and Cordell Hull—preferred the international route to economic recovery. For, regardless of party label, as domestic conservatives and classical liberals, they became wary of the interventionist state and the reforms symbolized by the New Deal. They preferred the route of international economic rapprochement. For the internationalist conservatives the avoidance of war was the paramount issue of their time; domestic recovery would follow. Fundamental economic and social reform seemed tertiary.

11

The State of Hoover's Union

THREE THEMES, which figured prominently in the election campaign, dominated the closing fifteen months of the Hoover presidency (December 1931–March 1933): return by Great Britain to the gold standard served as the guidon of its diplomacy; maintenance of the credit of the United States by adherence to the gold standard and a return to budget balance governed its domestic policies; and the Reconstruction Finance Corporation (RFC) surfaced as a vehicle for avoidance of institutional change and reliance on the private sector for economic regeneration. RFC constituted a mirage as the Hoover–Mills fiscal program plunged the nation still deeper into the quagmire.[1]

PRESIDENT HOOVER'S EXPLANATION of the depression in his December 8, 1931, State of the Union message to the second session of the 72d Congress fits perfectly the sense of *American Individualism*. Its chauvinism, its belief that the depression originated in Europe, that Americans, on the other hand, as individuals, voluntarily, through their communities and private organizations, would lift themselves from the depths, pervaded the communication. Governmental assistance in the financial crisis would be temporary, and supportive primarily of private financial instruments of credit, in order to avoid further contraction. Nowhere in the proposed legislation was the individual to be touched directly by the dread hand of the federal government. Once this government's willingness to balance its budget and redeem dollars for gold became evident here and abroad, the President explained, the worst would be over. Hoover offered no alteration of existing institutional arrangements. On the contrary, the Hoover proposals relied on the autoregenerative abilities of the American system.

"The chief influence affecting the state of the Union during the past year," the President maintained, "has been the continued worldwide economic disturbance." He acknowledged no fundamental imbalances in our own economic system. As he viewed his past accomplishments, the President boasted: "We have striven to mobilize and stimulate private initiative and local and community responsibility. There has been the least possible Government entry into the economic field, and that only in temporary and emergency form." He credited employers with work spreading and the maintenance of reasonable wage levels, and the Red Cross with enormous accomplishments in the administration of relief to 2.5 million sufferers the previous winter. He claimed as government's contribution to the effort its expanded public works program, curtailment of immigration, and the promotion of the National Credit Corporation, a mechanism created by private bankers with resources purportedly of $500 million to support banks under the pressures of deflation of assets and withdrawal of deposits.[2]

Like so many of Hoover's lengthy and dreary lists of his achievements, repeated endlessly in his presidential utterances and his *Memoirs,* this one was obfuscatory rather than enlightening. The National Credit Corporation had proven a grievous failure, neither the Red Cross nor other private relief agencies could cope with the burden of needed relief efforts, and his proposed budget for fiscal 1933, presented the next day, curtailed public works expenditures. He did, however, propose a bevy of measures intended to ameliorate the devastating credit contraction that had crippled the economy. As one examines these proposals, offered by some Hoover historians as heralding interventionism, it seems that they actually were intended to accomplish exactly the opposite purpose, for they shifted the burden of economic regeneration from the federal government, as in the instance of abandonment of Federal Farm Board activities, to private institutions.

The domestic program urged by Hoover in his December 8 message gave priority to the reestablishment of confidence in the credit of the United States government. Disturbed by huge gold withdrawals in September and October following Great Britain's abandonment of the gold standard, he desired Europe's confidence in this nation's ability to meet its obligations. The situation demanded elimination of budgetary deficits, accepted dogma in the financial community. Budget surpluses of the 1920s, managed by Andrew W. Mellon's and the Congress' parsimonious attitudes toward governmental expenditures (regarded as essentially nonproductive), gave way in the depression to increased deficits. In part, Hoover's unbalanced budgets reflected a decline in tax revenues; in part, substantial expenditures for public works, agricultural relief, and veterans benefits.[3] Fiscal 1931, ending on June 30, 1931, had yielded a deficit of $903 million; the projected deficit for fiscal 1932 promised to be $2.1 billion; and for fiscal 1933, extending from July 1, 1932 to June 30, 1933, a deficit of $1.4 billion was anticipated, widely regarded as untenable in relation to a total federal budget which ranged in the neighborhood of $3 billion to $4 billion annually. Hoover desired increased taxation and the curtailment of federal expenditures in order to bring the federal budget into balance. Restoration of confidence would follow. Specific proposals, he promised, would soon be made in his budget message, delivered actually on December 9, and in a statement that would emanate from the Treasury Department.

Increased utilization of the credit of the United States to shore up private lending (credit) mechanisms served as the second major element in Hoover's domestic program for 1932–1933. The package included expansion of the capital of the Federal Land Banks; also, the creation of Home Loan Discount Banks, which would discount mortgage loans made by building and loan associations, savings banks, and other lenders of money for home construction. Most important, the President urged institution of the Reconstruction Finance Corporation. Although superficially RFC seems to have served as a harbinger of New Deal interventionist policies, in reality it appears to have been intended to foil demand for enlargement of federal programs and activities. [4]

The Reconstruction Finance Corporation, proposed in Hoover's December 8, 1931, message and legislated late in January 1932, aimed at checking the pyramiding rate of bank closings in the United States caused by a crisis in liquidity. Bank failures and desperate pursuit of cash by fiduciary institutions dried up credit availability for industry, exacerbating the depression. Although bank insolvencies had loomed large in the 1920s, amounting to very nearly 7,000 in the period 1921–1930 (deposits affected totaled some $2.6 billion), the situation drew little attention. The preponderance of institutions affected were small "country" banks, located in rural areas, tied too heavily to a depressed staple crop agriculture, often lax and unsupervised in their operations. Some 90 percent of these failures involved banks of less than $100,000 in capital. Many, it could be argued, needed to be absorbed by larger, sounder institutions.

The closing months of 1930, however, offered a radically new picture, as bank failures intruded on the urban scene and numbered 1,345 for the year. The closing of the huge Bank of the United States, a New York City institution, with $200 million in deposits, in December 1930, the largest failure in the nation's banking history, seemed especially ominous because of the unwillingness of the New York Clearing House banks to rescue a relatively strong and large institution. Rather than afford weaker banks relief, as in the bankers' panic of 1907, stronger institutions sought to improve their own liquidity. A contraction of loans and investments by some $9.1 billion between the autumn of 1929 and the close of 1931, failed to produce the desired liquidity and stimulated a deflation of unprecedented proportions. The dumping of sound assets, especially medium grade corporate bonds, drove down values to an extent that remaining assets, badly undervalued, could not insure solvency. The economic results were broad and centrifu-

gal in tendency: deflation of values, price declines, inability to
meet fixed obligations, business and commercial bankruptcies, and
large-scale unemployment.

Conditions improved in the opening months of 1931, but the
Creditanstalt failure, the German banking collapse, and Britain's
abandonment of gold in the period May to September 1931
triggered off another round of bank closings. "Once bitten, twice
shy," depositors began the hoarding of currency and bankers pursued liquidation with a vengeance. Foreigners who converted dollars to gold, in anticipation of U.S. currency devaluation following
the devaluation of the pound, added a new dimension to the crisis.
Between September 16–30, 1931, the nation's gold stock declined
by $275 million, then by an additional $450 million in October. In
the months of August and September, banks with deposits of $414
million shut their doors. All told, 2,298 closings in 1931 involved
deposits of $1.6 billion.[5]

This confluence of events occasioned the gathering, at Hoover's
request, at the lavish Washington residence of Treasury Secretary
Mellon, of nineteen of New York's financial leaders. To avoid public panic the conferees met secretly on the evening of Sunday, October 4, 1931. Among those present were Hoover, Mellon and
Mills representing the Treasury Department, George L. Harrison,
governor of the Federal Reserve Bank of New York, Eugene
Meyer, governor of the Federal Reserve Board, Thomas W. Lamont and George Whitney of J. P. Morgan & Co., Albert H.
Wiggin of the Chase National Bank, Charles E. Mitchell of the National City Bank, and William C. Potter of Guaranty Trust.

The President opened the conference with a bleak portrait of the
nation's banking picture. Since January 1, 1930, there had been
2,560 bank failures involving $1.8 billion in deposits. An estimated
$800 million in withdrawals revealed currency hoarding. Resulting
fears in the banking community had led to the dumping of securities in a quest for liquidity. Larger banks, particularly those of New
York, Hoover noted, had attained the desired liquidity. (The New
York Clearing House banks, for instance, were on an average 60

percent liquid.) But smaller, weaker banks, removed from the
large urban centers, had suffered as their assets declined in value.
"Such a process," the President admonished the Wall Street magnates, "cannot be continued indefinitely."

Hoover continued with the lecture on the failure of the stronger
banks to fulfill their responsibilities in the crisis. Prior to the establishment of the Federal Reserve System, the President remon-
strated, larger banks in the principal financial centers provided assistance in similar crises to their out of town correspondents. But
since the creation of the Federal Reserve System, the burden
shifted to the Federal Reserve banks whose eligibility requirements were so restrictive that a good deal of sound paper held by
troubled banks could not be discounted. Hoover conceded the
need for legislation to remedy the situation, but the liquidity crisis
could not await congressional action.

Determined upon the principle of voluntarism, Hoover pressed
the New York bankers to take the lead in the formation of a cooperative association of private bankers, the National Credit Corporation, with resources of $500 million. Its principal function would be
"the rediscount of bank assets not now eligible in the Federal Reserve System in order to assure the stability of banks throughout
the country from attacks by unreasoning depositors. That is to
prevent bank failures." The New York Clearing House Association
should put up $150 million of the needed half billion. In return,
the President pledged: "(a) The extension of rediscount eligibility
in the Federal Reserve System. (b) If necessity requires to recreate
the War Finance Corporation with available funds sufficient for any
emergency in our credit system. (c) To strengthen the Federal
Farm Loan Bank System."

The bankers balked. They preferred reliance on a reconstituted
War Finance Corporation, created in the Wilson administration
and headed at one time by Eugene Meyer, as a device for expansion of capital. After Hoover's departure from the meeting, according to Meyer's recollection, only his pledge that he would continue
to press the President for WFC revival, secured the bankers' con-

sent for the pool. The next day, on his return to New York, George L. Harrison informed Mills and Hoover that a committee of New York bankers had agreed to form the pool and that the New York Clearing House Association's twenty-four member banks would put up their share ($150 million), approximately 2 percent of their net demand and time deposits.

As Harrison later conceded to a Senate subcommittee, the pool advanced only $10 million that fall. Even the Treasury Secretary turned the President down when asked for $1 million from Pittsburgh's Mellon National Bank to rescue the Bank of Pittsburgh. Whatever Hoover's reluctance in the matter, the large banks' unwillingness to jeopardize their own positions compelled him to accept the notion of a revived WFC, renamed the Reconstruction Finance Corporation, proposed in his December 8 message to Congress. [6]

The Reconstruction Finance Corporation, enacted into law in late January 1932, inaugurated its activities with a capital of $500 million subscribed by the U.S. Treasury Department, Further, it received authority to borrow an additional $1.5 billion in tax-exempt obligations guaranteed by the government. The new agency could make loans, secured by sound assets, to banks, insurance companies, agricultural associations, and with Interstate Commerce Commission approval, to the railroads, then one of the nation's largest employers. Disturbingly, railroad bankruptcies threatened the securities portfolios of banks and insurance companies. [7]

What Hoover gave with one hand, he took away with the other. When considered in conjunction with Hoover's and Mills' parallel proposal for financial retrenchment by the federal government in expenditures for agriculture and public works and for a steep increase in taxation, RFC takes on the character of a shift away from limited government financial measures aimed at recovery to total reliance on the private sector. The Hoover policies of late 1931 and 1932, financially regressive in character, stimulated the downward economic spiral. Reconstruction Finance Corporation loans to banks, totaling $900 million in 1932, were of dubious value, since RFC took only the soundest assets of a troubled institution as security, leaving "little . . . to meet any further demands by depositors." Nor can it be demonstrated that RFC loans stimulated economic activity in 1932. What is demonstrable is the contraction of the federal government's already limited role in attempts at recovery.[8]

The shift to retrenchment and minimalism is intelligible only in the context of Ogden L. Mills's influence in the Hoover administration. Mills had become the President's principal adviser by 1931, even as Undersecretary of the Treasury. And the wealthy and conservative New Yorker, in turn, reflected the views of the New York financial community, which insisted on these policies and desired as well the elimination of wartime debts and reparations. Mills's career was a paradigm of the Street's influence in the nation's domestic policies and financial diplomacy in that era.[9]

Although Andrew Mellon, the Pittsburgh financier, presided over the Treasury Department until February 1932, when Mills formally replaced him, Mellon had long since become a figurehead. Age was a factor. More important, Mellon, never attuned to politics, despite a lengthy tenure that began with his appointment by Warren G. Harding in 1921, an unabashed reactionary, had become too much of a political liability. Widely quoted is Hoover's recollection that the Pittsburgh banker and art collector, one of the nation's wealthiest men, had advised him, as the depression set in: "Liquidate labor, liquidate stocks, liquidate the farmers, liquidate real estate." Perhaps Hoover required a reactionary contrast for his own self-portrait as an activist President, when he wrote his *Memoirs*. A practitioner of the art of public relations and management of the appearance of substantive policy change as opposed to the realities, Hoover decided a new visage was required at Treasury in 1931. Mellon, packed off for a vacation in the south of France, was assigned to various conferences in Europe, then parked in London as our ambassador in 1932. (Mellon replaced Charles Dawes, who took over RFC.) But when one examines Mills's convictions, they

represented no departure from those of his former superior at
Treasury. He simply was a shrewder politician. [10]

Ogden Mills, like his Hyde Park neighbor, Franklin D. Roosevelt, born to wealth, chose politics as his lifetime avocation. Until
his premature death, in 1937, at age 53, the hard-living, ambitious
New Yorker, long powerful in Republican circles, earned consideration as a possible successor to Hoover. Tough, arrogant, pugnacious in his younger years, he plunged into politics and law in
New York City, won two terms to the New York state senate in
1914 and 1916, served as a captain in the American Expeditionary
Force, then represented New York City's "silk stocking" district
(upper Fifth and Park Avenues) in the House of Representatives
beginning in 1920.

During the course of his congressional service, which lasted from
1921 through 1926, Mills became expert in the field of taxation and
the national budget, and he emerged as one of the conservative
luminaries on the powerful House Ways and Means Committee.
Tapped to oppose the popular Alfred E. Smith in the New York
gubernatorial campaign of 1926, he fought a hard, some claimed an
unethical, battle. Badly beaten, Mills received an appointment as
Undersecretary of the Treasury. There was an arrogance about
"Little Oggie," as FDR loved to call his Harvard classmate (Mills,
in turn, regarded the squire of Hyde Park as a traitor to his class)
in the twenties and he treated his Washington colleagues with a
strong measure of social contempt. By 1931, he had matured. "Age
has mellowed him," *Time* noted in an article when he was 46. Mills
had become a buffer for his superior at Treasury in his contacts
with the press and Congress. By early 1932, the pretense ended as
Mills took over Treasury and emerged openly as the President's
principal adviser in foreign as well as domestic affairs. [11]

Mills proved no less reactionary than his predecessor at the helm
of the Treasury Department. Indeed, his record in the 1920s
showed support in the House of the Mellon tax reductions and the
Fordney–McCumber protective tariff of 1921, as well as consistent
opposition to "the present tendency to centralize all authority in

Washington." Mills categorized progressive Democrats and Republicans "as a disorganizing and disintegrating force, incapable themselves of affirmative results, and not even useful as constructive critics." Like Hoover, he opposed McNary-Haugenism and flaunted his opposition to the scheme as "a test of economic soundness." In 1924 and again in 1928, the Undersecretary of the Treasury, as a harbinger of their future intellectual and political collaboration, drafted the Republican party platform jointly with Herbert Hoover.[12]

In 1931 and 1932, Mills served as Hoover's economic and financial emissary to the New York financial and business community. Hoover had never related well to the Wall Street establishment, but Mills's wealth, his family connections, the obvious confidence he had won over the years on the Street, served the President's needs particularly well in securing the cooperation of the Wall Street bankers and the powerful Federal Reserve Bank of New York as allies in the administration's domestic and foreign policies. The financially and politically troublesome intergovernmental debts and reparations, unbalanced national budgets, the collapse of international trade and currency exchange, and the threat to the traditional gold standard were mutually shared concerns, treated as interconnected and central to domestic and international recovery.[13]

The principal thrust of the Hoover–Mills collaboration in domestic affairs (December 1931–March 1933) took the form of curtailment of federal expenditures and increased taxation. Although deflationary in its consequences, they gaged retrenchment as pivotal to the attainment of their domestic and diplomatic objectives. Mills tackled the issue of mounting federal deficits (some $4.4 billion for the fiscal years 1931–1933) in a major address before the Economic Club of New York on December 14, 1931. Federal income had declined, he explained, because of the government's narrow tax base. Two-thirds of revenues derived from corporate and individual incomes; 16 percent from customs duties; and 17 percent from miscellaneous taxes, principally on tobacco and securities' issuance and transfers. The Treasury official proposed a broadening of the tax base so as to stabilize federal income, in effect, to make it depression proof, and eliminate deficits in the budget.

Mills, capable of deep emotion on the subject of "preservation, unimpaired, of the credit of the United States," defined the essence of the domestic policy of the Hoover administration in the last year of its stewardship:

> In this period of deep uncertainty the unimpaired credit of the Federal Government is the most priceless possession of the people of the United States. We must assume its existence as we assume the continuance of unlimited supplies of air and sunlight. . . . Human lives stop. Promises go on. The civilized world today is run on the basis of a belief in promises. Whatever our doubts about the meaning of modern civilization, we may at least take some comfort in the trust which men show in each other's promises.
>
> Now, this belief in promises, this credit structure of ours, depends to a very great extent upon the confident belief that the Government will meet its financial obligations. . . . Our currency rests predominantly upon the credit of the United States. Impair that credit and every dollar you handle will be tainted with suspicion. The foundation of our commercial credit system, the Federal reserve bank, and all other banks which depend upon them, are inextricably tied into and dependent upon the credit of the United States Government. Impair that credit today, and the day after thousands of development projects . . . will stop; thousands of business men dependent upon credit renewals will get refusals from their bankers; thousands of mortgages . . . will be foreclosed. Merchants who would buy on credit, will cancel orders; factories that would manufacture on part capacity at least will close down.

Mills's program for recovery from the financial panic of 1931 required new taxation that would produce in excess of $900 million in revenues in fiscal 1933 as well as some added revenues for fiscal 1932. He rejected the introduction of a general sales tax, which he regarded as regressive and bearing no relationship to ability to pay. And he rejected, too, the Canadian limited manufacturers' or producers' sales tax, at that time of some interest to conservative legislators in the Congress. The Canadian tax, levied on the manufacturer, based on his sales price or on the import value of goods, seemed too cumbersome for introduction in the United States. Mills proposed instead a return to taxation policies of the revenue act of 1924: an increase in existing excise taxes, the reinstitution of an assortment of levies ranging from automobiles, trucks, and accessories, to telephone and telegraph messages, and an increase in corporate, personal income, and estate taxes. The tax rate on corporate incomes would be increased only slightly, from 12 to 12.5 percent; income taxes would rise more steeply and exemptions diminished so as to subject more persons to income tax payments. His recommendations, Mills estimated, could yield an additional $60 million from corporations, $185 million from individual taxpayers, $11 million from estates, and $514 million from miscellaneous excise taxes. [14]

Financial retrenchment also served as the theme of the President's budget message, sent to the Congress on December 9, 1931. Hoover advocated a reduction of $365 million in federal spending in fiscal 1933, with savings to be achieved by huge cuts in agriculture and public works. A $100 million reduction in Federal Farm Board expenses eliminated that program; and an additional $49 million cut in the Agriculture Department's budget left all but a shell of attempts to alleviate the farm depression. Total public works expenditures, some $780 million for fiscal 1932, were to be reduced to $575 million in the 1933 fiscal year, affecting river and harbor improvements, the development of internal waterways, merchant shipping, navy, army, and aviation expenditures, Interior Department programs, and highways. Hoover explained in his budget message and in his State of the Union address that the burden of employment should be the function of private enterprise, not of the federal government:

> I am opposed to any direct or indirect Government dole. The breakdown and increased unemployment in Europe is due in part to such practices. Our people are providing against distress from unemployment in true American fashion by a magnificent response to public appeal and by action of the local governments. [15]

The draconian Hoover–Mills program of December 1931–March
1933, which rested on the twin pillars of voluntarism and fiscal retrenchment, constituted the Republican legacy in domestic policy
to the New Deal. It precipitated the banking collapse of February
and early March 1933, and generally accelerated unemployment,
the farm depression, and the downward economic spiral. Since
banking institutions actually contracted credit in 1932, refusing
loans even to the most creditworthy customers, and continued
where they could the conversion of assets to cash, using RFC loans
principally for that end, Mills's insistence on adherence to the gold
standard and a balanced budget simply exacerbated deflationary
tendencies.[16] The final phase of the Hoover administration, in
short, which began in December 1931, precipitated the most en-
nervating and demoralizing stage of the Great Depression. Hardly
a legacy for the modern era, it represented the application of nineteenth-century convictions to twentieth-century dilemmas.[17]

FOR A TIME, as the year 1932 opened, it seemed that the administration would secure congressional enactment of its priorities,
despite the fact that the House of Representatives shifted to Democratic control under Speaker John Nance Garner. Passage of the
RFC law and the Glass-Steagall Act, designed to achieve greater
liquidity in the nation's banking structure, demonstrated the continuation of the virtually unchallenged leadership Hoover enjoyed
since his inauguration as President. The Congress, dominated by
conservatives, including aging Republican reactionaries (many
would be defeated in the November landslide), and Southern
Democrats, rejected programs offered by a minority of Midwestern
progressives and urban liberals. McNary-Haugenism, Muscle
Shoals development, and large-scale public works projects, occasionally able to muster a majority in the past, could be dam-
pened by Hoover's intransigence. The threat of a presidential veto
usually terminated demonstrations of legislative independence.[18]

Congressional support for the Mills budget seemed assured

when Hoover, on January 8, 1932, decreed that "We cannot squander ourselves into prosperity," with the endorsement of the Republican and Democratic leadership in the House and Senate. "Rigid economy," the President proclaimed, "is a real road to relief, to home owners, farmers, workers, and every element of our population. . . . Our first duty as a nation is to put our governmental house in order, national, state, and local. With the return of prosperity the Government can undertake constructive projects both of social character and in public improvement." While superficially plausible, Hoover's statement reveals a tendency toward deception. He had preached in the 1920s the desirability of storing up public works projects for periods of economic decline. Now, instead, like the establishment of RFC, the Great Engineer revealed a fatal tendency to offer only the appearance of action in vain hope that the private sector would manage recovery on its own. In this instance the limiting element proved to be his insistence on projects which were self-liquidating.[19]

Initially, the situation went well for Mills, who negotiated with the conservative and friendly Charles Crisp, acting chairman of the House Ways and Means Committee. On February 10, the Georgia legislator asked the Treasury Secretary to suggest sources of additional revenues and Mills complied. Treasury and Ways and Means, Mills exulted, were in total accord on the "necessity of balancing the budget during the next fiscal year so as to eliminate any further increase in our public debt. There can be no question as to the soundness of this position. It admits of no compromise."

Matters had worsened since December, Mills explained, and the deficit for fiscal 1933, estimated at $920 million (exclusive of statutory debt retirements) in the figures he had originally submitted to the Congress, now appeared to be $1.241 billion, owing principally to a decline in tax receipts. The Secretary of the Treasury estimated that expenditures of about $4 billion could be reduced by $118 million, leaving $1.123 billion to be raised through increased taxes. On top of his December proposals, Mills wanted an additional .5 of 1 percent increase in corporate rates, modification of in-

come surtax tables to yield some $50 million, a 7 percent tax on
consumption of electricity and natural gas, and a 1 cent increase on
capital stock sales and transfers making the total tax 4 cents. These
supplementary proposals, he estimated, should yield some $337
million in added revenue in the fiscal year beginning July 1, 1932.

In view of the congressional rebellion against the proposal of a
general sales tax, which emanated from the House Ways and
Means Committee, Mills's views seem pertinent. In his December
14 address before the Economic Club of New York, the Treasury
Secretary termed a manufacturers sales tax as "regressive" and destructive of purchasing power; in his letter to the Ways and Means
Committee chairman he reiterated his "original opinion that a limited group of selected excise taxes is a preferable method of raising
the required revenue, not only from the standpoint of administration but also from that of basic economic considerations." Mills insisted on a balanced budget, and if Crisp wanted to know the revenue potential of a general sales tax, as Treasury Secretary he felt
obliged to supply the information. This he did, estimating that a 2
percent sales tax might yield $600 million.[20]

On February 16, the day he informed Crisp of a looming budget
deficit of $1.32 billion, the Secretary of the Treasury conferred
with Speaker Garner on the Hill to inform him of the gravity of the
nation's financial situation. The conservative Texan promptly
formed a Democratic Economy Committee, instructing it to slash
government expenditures. Garner concurred with the Ways and
Means chairman on the necessity for a sales tax to bring in added
revenue. In the opening days of March, with only Robert
Doughton, Democrat of North Carolina, dissenting, the Democrat-
controlled House Ways and Means Committee reported out a revenue measure which incorporated a general sales tax.[21]

The sales tax proposal won the support of Democratic party
bigwigs, considered the powers behind many of the House and
Senate conservatives, Baruch, Raskob, Shouse, and Hearst. But for
a variety of reasons, ranging from progressive insurgence led by
Doughton and Fiorello La Guardia against a levy that would have

borne down heavily on the laboring class, to traditionalists' fears that the states would be deprived of an essential revenue base, the House balked and the sales tax went down to defeat. The Speaker, a seasoned politician, aware he had lost control of the lower chamber, looking worn and tired, stepped down from the rostrum to the floor on March 29, and made an impassioned appeal to his colleagues.

The galleries were jammed and Mrs. Garner found herself seated in an aisle on the floor, Bascom Timmons recalled the dramatic occasion; Senators scurried over to hear what many anticipated as one of the rare dramatic moments of the 72d Congress. Garner reminded his colleagues that he had served on the House Ways and Means Committee for eighteen years, also that he and President Hoover had collaborated on the attainment of a budget balance since October 1931. "I believed then as I do now, that it was the duty of our government to sustain its credit and to ask Congress to balance the budget." The House applauded. He explained, further, that he and Senator Joseph Robinson of Arkansas had chosen the Senate House Democratic Policy Committee, which on January 6, 1932, agreed unanimously that it was "of primary importance that the budget be balanced promptly."

Garner explained his earlier endorsement of the sales tax, when Crisp's Ways and Means Committee produced it, in terms of his obligation as a legislative leader and because of his commitment to the balanced budget. Restoration of confidence in the ·United States government constituted his prime commitment, however, not the sales tax which he had opposed throughout his legislative career. "I appeal to you," he urged his colleagues, "not only in the name of my party but my country, that in view of the fact that there has been stricken from this bill more than $500,000,000 of taxation, it is your duty, your paramount duty, to help this House and this committee restore some taxes to this bill in order that this country's financial integrity may be maintained." Foreigners, Garner indicated, were converting dollars to gold and withdrawing gold from the United States. "As sure as I stand in the well of this

House, I believe that if this Congress today should decline to levy a tax bill there would not be a bank in existence in the United States in sixty days that could meet its depositors." The banker from Uvalde, Texas, warned of "a financial panic such as has never been equaled in this Republic since its organization."

In an extraordinary move, Garner insisted on a vote of confidence on the issue of the balanced budget. "I want every man and every woman in this House who hopes to balance the budget . . . to rise in his seat." Very nearly the entire membership of the body rose. No one stood up when Garner asked for those "who do not want to balance the budget." He had saved his political career. Ways and Means brought in a new revenue bill offering a balanced budget and it passed.

The new revenue bill, signed by Hoover on June 6, 1932, contained higher taxes on incomes and corporations than Mills and Hoover wanted, with rates raised nearly to wartime levels. Basically Mills secured what he wanted, increased income and corporate taxes and the wide-ranging application of excise taxes on items that ran the scale from soda pop to automobiles. As Mills viewed the picture, he emerged unscathed and lacked only $200 million, which could be trimmed from federal expenditures to balance his budget. [22]

The basic economic and intellectual limitations of both the Hoover administration and the Congress in their understanding of the dimensions of the Great Depression is demonstrated by the fracas over the Emergency Relief and Construction Act of July 21, 1932. Not that it was unimportant in terms of the dire economic straits of millions of despairing people, but balancing the federal budget and the level of public works expenditures consumed the energies of the President, the press, and the Congress in the spring and summer of 1932 rather than a more fundamental discourse on the causes and remedies of the depression. Leadership and the level of economic sophistication proved sadly lacking. Proposals like M. L. Wilson's domestic allotment scheme scarcely stirred a ripple in the 72d Congress. Relief and public works received definition as a purely urban issue, though farmers had become so specialized and dependent on single crop production that they, too, could not feed their families or buy the goods of industry. Although long-term problems required discussion and resolution, the national budget had become an obsession.

With millions unemployed and the appearance of "Hoovervilles," pressure built up in the Congress for a massive public works program. Progressives such as Robert La Follette Jr. of Wisconsin, Bronson Cutting of New Mexico, and Edward P. Costigan of Colorado, joined the Senate's earliest and principal advocate of a large-scale effort, Senator Robert A. Wagner of New York. Supporters of self-liquidating schemes financed by bond sales, including the Senate's Democratic leader, Joseph Robinson of Arkansas, Bernard Baruch, Al Smith, and William R. Hearst, added to the clamor, hoping that relief would blunt pressures for more fundamental change. Hoover and Mills resisted. They insisted on self-liquidating projects which by definition limited their amount to some $1.1 billion. Hoover abhorred the "dole" (relief), which he identified with Great Britain's social and economic decay. He assigned relief and public works to state and local government for fear of individual dependence on the central government, a condition he dreaded.

Conceding in a press statement of May 12, 1932, that certain localities or states might be lacking the financial wherewithal to afford relief, Hoover proposed RFC loans totaling some $250 million to $300 million to those states that had exhausted their own financial capacities. Also, RFC capital should be made available to private and public bodies willing to undertake "self supporting projects of a constructive replacement character," provided private banking institutions refused to provide the needed capital. These and other proposals for the expansion of RFC functions, Hoover suggested, required the stretching of its authorized borrowing capacity to $3.3 billion but, he insisted that "unproductive" public

works, those that did not generate revenue, funded by the federal
budget at taxpayers' expense, not be expanded beyond the amount
allocated in the Mills' budget, some $575 million.[23]

Congress was now in a combative mood. As the campaign approached, Democrats lacked an issue to distinguish themselves
from the increasingly unpopular President. Even Garner, sniffing a
Democratic victory for the first time since the Wilson era, one of
the most passionate of budget balancers, joined the advocates of
increased federal spending for direct relief in the form of public
works. These took the shape of river and harbor improvements,
road and trail construction, erection of post offices and other federal buildings, categorized by Hoover as "pork barrel" spending
beyond the $500-odd million already projected for fiscal 1933.

On June 24, the Republican President warned of a veto of the
Wagner–Garner Relief bill if it trespassed the formula he outlined.
As Mills wrote Walter Lippmann privately in rebuttal to the columnist's endorsement of the legislative position, the Wagner proposal would add $500 million to outstanding bonds for nonproduc-
tive public works, a sum that would be charged to the Treasury
Department. "Once we abandon the principle of a balanced
budget, our defenses are down. If it is all right to unbalance the
budget by $500,000,000 why not a billion dollars; and if a billion
dollars, why not a billion and a half or two billion dollars? . . . The
only safe and wise course to pursue is to stand or fall on the principle of a balanced budget and the integrity of the National finances.
If the Administration ever attempts to compromise this principle,
my best judgment is that the dam will go out and the flood will
follow." The Treasury Secretary would accept, however, Wagner's
proposal for $300 million in relief bonds in the form of loans to the
states made through RFC, since RFC loans were not a direct
charge on the budget. Also, as he explained to the Senate Committee on Banking and Currency, he could accept other elements of
the Wagner bill, totaling $1.8 billion in RFC loans for self-liquidat-
ing projects. This figure embraced $1.46 billion for loans to politi-
cal subdivisions and quasi-public corporations for self-liquidating

projects (including public housing) and $40 million to be made available to the Secretary of Agriculture for the sale of surplus commodities overseas.

The $500 million construction fund proposed by Wagner and Garner, involving the sale of Treasury securities, required creation of a special or emergency budget. Mills countered that other nations' experience with extraordinary budgets had proven unsuccessful. It would not hide the reality of a deficit, Mills explained to the Senate Banking Committee, and would offer employment to only 59,943 men at an expense of $265 million in fiscal 1933. The costs were too high for the limited employment involved and the "shock to public confidence" that would result from "unsound" financial practices would be devastating.[24]

The Congress persisted, some conservatives collaborating apparently with the Wagner–Garner forces, with the confident belief that Hoover would veto the measure if it required a $500 million charge to the federal budget for additional nonproductive works. The President obliged and on July 6, 1932, released a blistering warning followed by a veto message on July 11. The chief executive found inadequate the tests imposed by the law in connection with loans to the states by the RFC. In effect, he wanted the states to demonstrate complete exhaustion of their own resources before they could resort to RFC loans for relief purposes. Also, he restated Mills's argument that the creation of a several hundred million dollar budget deficit for federally financed public works would scarcely affect the level of employment. Hoover would countenance the proposition only if legislated in a form that would permit the Secretary of the Treasury to certify that funds were available. In his July 6 warning message Hoover blasted Garner, moreover, for his "insistence upon provision that loans should also be made to individuals, private corporations, partnerships, states and municipalities on any conceivable security and for every purpose." It would put the Reconstruction Finance Corporation in "the most gigantic banking and pawnbroking business in all history."[25] Doggedly, he insisted on preservation of one of his central tenets, avoidance of direct financial relief by the federal government to the individual.

The veto was sustained and the Emergency Relief and Construction Act of July 1932 emerged basically as Mills and Hoover desired. Whatever provisions they did not care for, in fact, they ignored once Congress adjourned for the campaign. In practice, the new law had minor economic impact. Although it expanded the borrowing power of RFC to $3.3 billion and, therefore, its capacity to lend funds, there was little demand from banks which feared the onus of an RFC loan especially with the threat of congressional insistence, led by Speaker Garner and Senator James Byrnes of South Carolina, that RFC loans be publicized. That threat became a reality in the interregnum, precipitating bank closings in February 1933. RFC's authority to lend $300 million to the states for relief was rendered meaningless by the requirement that a state prove virtual bankruptcy before it could qualify for such a loan. Up to October 1, 1932, when RFC activity nearly halted under Hoover's and Mills's aegis, loans to states for relief and public works totaled only $35 million. Nor was the agency more generous in its other undertakings or even successful. Its minuscule agricultural provisions had no impact on commodity prices in the closing months of the Hoover administration. Overall, the administrative wheels ground slowly once Congress adjourned as Mills and Hoover hoarded their household cash. [26]

The economic and financial snail's pace induced by the Hoover–Mills's policies was described by the testy young Irishman, RFC counsel, and Harvard Law protégé of Felix Frankfurter, Thomas G. ("Tommy the Cork") Corcoran, later of "second New Deal" fame. "Very little stuff of half decent economic feasibility has come in from private enterprise," Corcoran complained to his Harvard mentor. Sound loans had already been made by the banks and the microscopic examination by Hoover administration officials of loan applications to RFC hardly poured money into the dying economy. Then, too, valid proposals by state and local government for public works ran into the conservative biases of Hoover appointees. Corcoran cited the example of RFC treatment of the application of Seattle, Washington, for a loan to construct a municipal power plant, which evoked the fear that it would compete with private enterprise or displace it altogether. [27]

Corcoran had cut to the core of the matter. Legislation, authorization, speechmaking, and posturing for the 1932 campaign aside, the Hoover administration had little fundamental faith in RFC to accomplish anything except bolster public psychology until the private sector could regenerate itself. Although Hoover taunted Mellon by quoting him on the need for liquidation of virtually all values, that is exactly what happened in the closing months of 1932. RFC had really served as camouflage for the achievement of federal fiscal retrenchment of a catastrophic nature. The continuity thesis crumbles in the end because it ignores the principal thrust of the Hoover–Mills prescription for domestic recovery and Hoover's fundamental convictions. These were expressed clearly enough in the 1932 presidential campaign.

HERBERT HOOVER'S CAMPAIGN for the presidency urged voluntarism and individualism, freedom from federal economic interference in the marketplace, and reliance on local government as basic to the economic exigencies of the early 1930s. For the Great Engineer they constituted immutable guidelines which transcended immediate circumstance. He was engaged, he believed, in a nonpartisan mission, a life-or-death struggle for the salvation of the American System from the preachments and objectives of "irresponsible and ignorant men." Proudly, he boasted in his memoirs that he had authored all of his campaign speeches (which were dull and repetitious) as opposed to his opponent's reliance on academicians who favored a planned economy, Brains Trusters, "expert in semantics but grievously undernourished on truth." His acerbity, two decades after the event, reflected accurately his lifelong adherence to the dogmas pronounced in *American Individualism* as enduring (he hoped) features of American life, and his conviction that

Roosevelt's New Deal, as formulated in the 1932 contest, threatened an intolerable departure.

Although the Republican incumbent delivered nine major addresses in the 1932 campaign, as was his custom, his acceptance statement, presented at Constitution Hall in Washington, D.C., on August 11, covered the range of his argumentation. As he viewed the depression, it originated with circumstances beyond his control: the legacy of the World War, speculation, economic overexpansion, the European collapse of 1931, and the subsequent financial repercussions and decline in consumption. No effort, to Hoover's credit, was made to gloss his basic convictions on the limited functions of the federal government in the resolution of the economic crisis that had befallen the nation. Federal powers should be reserve powers to aid private citizens and local government in overcoming "forces beyond their control. It is not the function of the [Federal] Government to relieve individuals of their responsibilities to their neighbors, or to relieve private institutions of their responsibilities to the public, or of local governments to the state, or of state governments to the Federal Government." A decentralist credo, it persisted in the American ethos even beyond the New Deal era, embraced recently almost as readily by the New Left as by the Right.[28]

Hoover reiterated the precepts of his *American Individualism:* ordered freedom, equality of opportunity, release of initiative. He opposed what he categorized as "haphazard experimentation" and proposed instead "cooperative action which builds initiative and strength outside of government. It does not follow," the Republican spokesman contended, "because our difficulties are stupendous, because there are some souls timorous enough to doubt the validity and effectiveness of our ideals and our system, that we must turn to a State-controlled or State-directed social or economic system in order to cure our troubles. That is not liberalism; it is tyranny. It is the regimentation of men under autocratic bureaucracy with all its extinction of liberty, of hope, and of opportunity. . . . The movement of a true civilization is toward freedom rather than regimentation. This is our ideal."

As a champion of the old order of rigidly delimited governmental function, Herbert Hoover asked the American people in 1932 to refuse to be stampeded by "demagogues and slogans," meaning Roosevelt and the New Deal, which, he believed, would destroy our democracy in the momentary pressures of an emergency. Accordingly, he opposed the creation of agencies and mechanisms that might survive the termination of what he described as a temporary condition. These were the guidelines of the Hoover era. The American people were given a clear alternative in the 1932 campaign, between passivity for fear of jeopardizing historic relationships and restrictions, or a more active responsibility by government for economic and social conditions.

Unwilling to tolerate interventionism, Hoover spoke vaguely of banking and securities reforms, revision of railway legislation (primarily because banking and insurance institutions were large holders of railway bonds of dubious value), and of conservation of natural resources, in which he seemed genuinely interested. But he stood squarely for the protective tariff, which he had supported for a dozen years, and for reliance solely on the cooperative movement for alleviation of the farmers' plight.

Hoover's position on agricultural prices and the limits of government intervention on behalf of the agrarian serves as the key to an understanding of his difference, fundamental in nature, with Roosevelt and the Brains Trust. "No power on earth," he argued, "can restore prices except by restoration of general recovery and markets. . . . There is no relief to the farmer by extending government bureaucracy or to control his production and thus curtail his liberties, nor by subsidies. . . . I shall oppose them." Indeed, he did.

"No regimented mechanisms but free men is our goal. Herein is the fundamental issue." It was Herbert Hoover's battle cry as he set out on the American road in 1932 to prevent the coming of the twentieth century. [29]

Initially, Herbert Hoover anticipated victory in 1932, perhaps as a display of bravado for his intimates, when he appraised Roosevelt as intellectually unable to sustain the rigors of a national contest.

But as the campaign progressed, the President showed increasing signs of disturbance once he sensed a basic challenge to the American System. Ready to concede the immediate contest, he determined to fight for his own conceptualization of the American dream. As the defender of *American Individualism* grew increasingly aware that more than a customary shift in political management at the White House was in store for the nation, he took full aim and let loose at Madison Square Garden on October 31.

The American System, Hoover explained to his audience, "had been builded up by 150 years of the toil of our fathers." It was the unique accomplishment of our race and its experience. We had created on this continent a civilization superior to any other in the history of mankind. He disparaged the Old World's rigidity of class structure, preferred our own social and economic fluidity. The depression, he insisted, was a fleeting phenomenon, nearly ended. To enter at that point on a course proposed by his opponent would undermine and destroy our basic institutions and accomplishments.

Voluntarism, Hoover proposed, constituted "self-government by the people outside of Government," the wisest approach to the nation's malaise. It preserved freedom and opportunity, our basic values. And voluntary cooperative action would readily dissolve with the end of the crisis. Roosevelt's proposals, to the contrary, portended the enlargement of the federal bureaucracy, its power, and its budget at the expense of the people, local government, and the states. Tyranny and incompetence would ensue. "You cannot extend the mastery of government over the daily life of a people," Hoover protested, "without somewhere making it master of people's souls and thoughts." Free speech would die with the suffocation of free enterprise. More by implication than by concrete proposals, he warned ominously, his opponents planned a profound change in American life. "Dominantly in their spirit they represent a radical departure from the foundations of 150 years which have made this the greatest nation in the world." [30] Defeated at the polls in November 1932, the Great Engineer devoted the balance of his life in an effort to undo the New Deal, not, it needs to be concluded, without some measure of success.

Short-term, Hoover's analysis proved deficient when applied to the urgent needs of our society. Self-help and regeneration of the economy required a spiritual attitude sorely lacking at the depression's depth, and the willingness of banks to lend and individuals to spend—which they were not. The rush to liquidity evidenced widespread fear in the nation. Only in the central government, by 1932, could serve as a reservoir capable of restoring activity in the marketplace and individual self-confidence. Long-term, Hoover's prognosis perceptively warned of the potential dangers and excesses of the welfare state, which Roosevelt and the Brains Trust had not intended, but which characterized the post-New Deal era.

AS THE HOOVER ADMINISTRATION drew to a close, the President and Mills, despite electoral defeat, determined to continue the fight. Mills looked to the future, which he defined as fiscal 1934, and pleaded the outgoing administration's case to two intimates. Venting his aspirations for the nation's future course and its destiny, Mills addressed identical letters, marked personal and confidential, in November 1932: one to Owen D. Young of General Electric because of the regard he enjoyed in financial circles and likely, too, because of rumors that Roosevelt would select him or Carter Glass as his Treasury Secretary; the other to George Leslie Harrison, who would stay on at the vortex of the nation's financial activities as head of the New York Federal Reserve Bank.

"I am coming to you now," Mills summoned his innermost convictions, "as I have in the past, because I am anxious about the situation which seems to be developing." Congress, he complained, as he prepared for the fiscal year beginning July 1, 1933, demonstrated scant willingness to make "the essential reduction in expenditures, or to provide the necessary revenues to bring the budget into balance. They seem to be still living in a little world of their own without genuine realization of the gravity of the fiscal problem and of its relationship to the general economic situation." The federal deficit, Mills explained, incurred in the three previous fiscal years increased the national debt by $5 billion, an invitation to national disaster. Mills then explained his own and Hoover's priorities in national and international affairs:

> If I were a dictator and could write my own ticket, the first two goals which I would reach for would be the balancing of the budget of the United States government and the return to the gold standard by Great Britain. . . . Clearly it is comparatively easy today to bring our budget into balance, and from what Day and Williams [31] tell me I believe that if we can reach a reasonable settlement with Great Britain on the matter of the governmental debt, that as part of that settlement directly or indirectly, we might obtain an understanding from them to assist in the stabilization of currencies and exchanges, which of course would mean their return to the gold standard. Once currencies and exchanges are stabilized, the artificial trade barriers that have been set up to protect exchanges should automatically come down, world prices will almost inevitably rise, and there is real ground for belief that a general forward impulse might result. The coming Economic Conference furnishes a promising instrumentality through which these aims might be attained.

With the budget in balance, the credit of the United States established beyond question, and Hoover's financial diplomacy brought to fruition in the form of a return to the gold standard and currency stabilization, Mills believed, the nation could sustain "the foolish experiments" contemplated by Franklin D. Roosevelt. [32]

During the interregnum (November 1932 through early March 1933), Hoover and Mills hoped, in fact, with the assistance of Henry L. Stimson, Hoover's Secretary of State, and of conservative Democratic internationalists such as Norman Davis, to fasten their economic diplomacy on the President-elect. It had been fashioned painfully since the central European financial collapse and Great Britain's abandonment of gold in 1931, and interlinked with the Hoover–Mills domestic priorities. If they could convince Roosevelt and his "neophyte" academic advisers, of the wisdom of their internal policies, of a general debts settlement, and the restoration of the gold standard, the New Deal could be aborted and the American System might be preserved.

12

Defining the New Deal

THE NEW DEAL fashioned by Franklin D. Roosevelt and the Brains Trust represented elements both of continuity and change in its treatment of the nation's tradition and future. Though the continuity/discontinuity thesis has been debated to a point of near suffocation, examination of post-convention decisions of the Democratic nominee and the deliberations of his advisers should resolve the nature and content of the New Deal venture. As best as one can summarize their accomplishment, they did not completely repudiate the nation's Jeffersonian tradition evoked by the Hoover strictures. They aspired to a balanced federal budget, shunned the notion of a vast bureaucratic overhead, and rejected the idea that a vast long-range public-works/relief program would prove of lasting value. They neither envisaged nor promoted the welfare state. Later developments proved a corruption of the New Deal.

Unlike Herbert Hoover, Roosevelt and the Brains Trust felt that past prescriptions needed to go into discard. Interventionism and planning seemed usable concepts, not for their own sake, but for the achievement of broad, socially desirable purposes. Although they preferred budget balance and the gold standard, they had no fear of their abandonment in the search for recovery and, while internationalists in spirit, they proved willing to insulate this nation from world economic tides. [1]

During the summer months of 1932, alternatives were discussed and scrutinized, sometimes authored by the Brains Trust, sometimes solicited from experts on the subject matter considered for the campaign. Reform of certain basic institutions seemed essential to the promotion of permanent resuscitation. The interplay of ideas appears to have been relatively uninhibited. Yet, the luxury of an ideal commonwealth never received consideration. The economic thinking of Moley, Berle, and Tugwell, while ranging in originality and usually accepted by Roosevelt, nevertheless met the test of the candidate's political judgments. Roosevelt sought opinions elsewhere and evidenced sensitivity to the conservative political climate in which he functioned. Although the "squire thesis" has been exhumed as the Hyde Park aristocrat fell from favor in the post-New Deal era, the evidence indicates that he had complete grasp of the situation as he forged ties with the conservative coalition and shaped his economic program.

Roosevelt as compromiser, oriented toward concrete goals, will never satisfy those with transcendent ideological commitment. The governing motif of the 1932 campaign reflected the longing of the mass of the American people for the attainment of economic recovery and some measure of security. In tandem, the Democratic candidate aspired to achievement of majority status for his party by forging a liberal coalition that would outlast the immediate crisis. Through his service in the Wilson administration, Roosevelt had witnessed the impalement of the Princeton University academician on unbudging principle. Anxious for recovery, Roosevelt insisted on the presentation to him of concrete analysis and goals and viable mechanisms. He did not accept or promote intervention for its own sake, as an abstraction.

Franklin D. Roosevelt's New Deal, Rexford Guy Tugwell concluded in later years, "had glamour, not substance." It represented, he argued, a carrying on of the Hoover years, not a reconstruction. The Democratic candidate had been taken over by the party elders as well as the simplistic economic views of Louis D. Brandeis and Felix Frankfurter. Much of Tugwell's later writing on the subject, while sympathetic, was, nevertheless, a lament, almost poetic in its expression of disappointment with lost opportunities. "The power in men to escape, to break down walls and build new systems of collective living, had not been appealed to; and when it was all over, the establishment was more solidly planted than ever. Its functions had not been nationalized nor had its elite been disciplined." More radical critics have gone further. "Marxism was in the air all around him," Howard Zinn has asserted. Although one is tempted to wonder at such an observation rather than contend with it, it is true that Roosevelt and his advisers steered clear of public ownership as readily as the Hoover folklore, leaving, as Professor Zinn claimed, only "a vast middle ground of which Roosevelt explored only one sector." [2] That middle ground requires some clear definition.

THE COMING of the New Deal pledged, the dozens of wellwishers and politicians gone from the candidate's hotel suite late that night, Farley and Howe off for their first decent respite in days, Raymond Moley prepared for his own exit. His task seemed accomplished. For days he had defended the literary and intellectual product of the Brains Trust from Louis Howe's dogged determination to substitute his own document. "The die was cast," Moley recalled some years later. There could be no turning back. "The doctrine of a potentially great political movement had been proclaimed." As he turned to depart with the last of the crowd, Roosevelt signaled him to remain. Moley observed with amazement that the squire, hardly ennervated by his flight to Chicago or the day's proceedings, wanted to discuss the campaign.

It is scarcely surprising that the head of the trio of academicians tapped for economic advice by the governor in the pre-convention months, as well as Tugwell, who waited anxiously outside, wondered what their roles would be now. Would the Columbia group be discarded in favor of the Albany advisers and the conservative party warhorses? Moley, particularly, was conscious of his secondary role in the political melodrama that unfolded in the Windy City. Like most academicians, he judged the political system as dominated by the smoke-filled room where principles yielded to expediency. The conclave that produced the party's available man seemed a debasing spectacle, one which corrupted men in public life, eroded their fundamental decencies and convictions, made opportunists of them all. Just what had been ceded by Howe and Farley to nail down the elusive two-thirds vote? What compromises had been made? Who would be charged with the formulation of the campaign's intellectual content? "Tugwell, Berle, and I never spoke of it to one another," he reminisced, "but each of us, I know, in his innermost being was watching for it to materialize out of the political ectoplasm around us."

Tugwell's and Moley's suspicions had been triggered actually when Bernard Baruch, acknowledged leader of the stop-Roosevelt coalition, sauntered into Louis Howe's Congress Hotel suite, with General Hugh Johnson in tow, and reviewed Moley's acceptance speech. While Moley felt relieved when Baruch approved of it, he remained wary of the reputed power of the financier's checkbook in Democratic politics.

When Moley emerged from the late-night conference with Roosevelt, he offered Tugwell reassurance. The Columbia group, augmented by additional advisers, would be entrusted with the preparation of a half dozen or more major subjects for Roosevelt's consideration, including taxation, efficiency in government, internationalism, Prohibition, inflation, the issuance of securities, the role of women in politics, all in a framework of the need for statesmanship and realism ("a little of each"). But, above all, Moley assured his associate, the campaign would deal with the need for economic adjustments. "This is the basic thing," Moley scrawled on a yellow pad, reflecting Roosevelt's view.

With Roosevelt's and Moley's agreement upon the academician's management of the substance of the campaign, they decided on a series of overtures to the party's conservatives (the Smith–DuPont–Raskob wing) and the Wilsonian internationalists, principally Cordell Hull, Norman Davis, and Newton D. Baker. The task of reconciliation began immediately following the Chicago proceedings, when Roosevelt dispatched Moley to Cleveland to confer with his adviser's old associate of Cleveland Foundation days, Newton D.

Baker. Moley sensed antipathy on Baker's part, dating back perhaps, he suspected, to the Foundation's internecine quarrels involving himself and Ralph Hayes. But Moley possessed a genuine regard for Wilson's Secretary of War and shared Baker's veneration of the former Democratic leader. Above all, Roosevelt's emissary determined to convey his own impression that neither William Randolph Hearst nor Huey Long possessed the candidate's soul. [3]

As they conferred in Baker's law office, Moley gained the impression that Roosevelt hardly represented the sort of man Baker envisaged as the nation's executive head. The attorney expressed no disappointment that he had not been nominated, rather a sense of relief that he would be spared the burdens of the presidency. But he pressed the issue of Roosevelt's seeming abandonment of the Wilsonian ideal. Earlier, in New York, Moley assured Ralph Hayes that the Albany address represented Colonel House's confection rather than a capitulation by Roosevelt to Hearst. Moley's blandishments would not do. Baker and others of the old Wilsonians desired some public assurance from Roosevelt of his independence from isolationists and radicals such as Hearst, Long, and McAdoo. There seemed only one pathway to placation of the elders, public endorsement by the candidate of the party's Chicago platform, accomplished in a radio address delivered from Albany on July 30, 1932, the first of his campaign. [4]

Tugwell and Rosenman initially, then Roosevelt and Moley, tried their hand at the July 30 statement, which emerged as a scissors-and-paste version of the conservative-internationalist platform. There was one crucial decision. Stricken from the earliest draft of the Albany radio address, written by Rosenman and Tugwell, in bold strokes of a pen wielded by Roosevelt, was a restatement of the view uttered in the February Albany address that "all just national debts are 'debts of honor,' " that no debtor could honorably repudiate his obligations. "Europe owes us. We do not owe her." The internationalists had made their point.

In his address to the nation, on July 30, Roosevelt repeated the platform's attribution of the depression to disastrous economic policies pursued since the World War, to our economic isolation, and the fostering of monopoly. The remedies he proposed, quoting the platform, included:

> An immediate and drastic reduction of governmental expenditures by abolishing useless commissions and offices, consolidating departments and bureaus and eliminating extravagance, to accomplish a saving of not less than 25 percent in the cost of the Federal Government. . . .
> Maintenance of the national credit by a Federal budget annually balanced. . . .
> A sound currency to be preserved at all hazards. . . .

Recovery from the depression would be achieved, again the candidate echoed the Chicago pledges, through the extension of federal credit to the states for unemployment relief, the restoration of agriculture through better financing of farm mortgages, extension of the farm cooperative movement, and effective control of crop surpluses. In obeisance to Cordell Hull's views, Roosevelt promised a competitive tariff for revenue, reciprocal tariff arrangements with other countries, and the promotion of an international economic conference designed to restore trade and facilitate currency exchange. Herbert Hoover could readily have endorsed the statement.[5]

Bernard Baruch, too, and his factotum, General Hugh Johnson, pressed the conservative view in July. For a time, very briefly, there seemed to be an ominous potential in terms of undermining the efforts of the Brains Trust. Baruch, reactionary on domestic issues, wielded substantial power among the most powerful Democrats in the Congress. As one examines the relationships forged by the financier with the legislative conservatives of the South, they appear to have been anchored in mutual conviction as much as the largesse of his purse and the vaunted hospitality of his South Carolina plantation. Baruch and much of the Democratic party's congressional leadership, convinced that the Hoover deficits were intolerable, gaged federal deficits as the President's principal area of vulnerability in the forthcoming campaign. Their formula for recovery represented a throwback to the rigorous economic policies of the Cleveland and McKinley administrations in the 1893–98 depression. Federal fiscal retrenchment, the sanctity of contractual obligations, and maintenance of a sound currency seemed the logical path to follow. Americans had gone on a wild spree in the 1920s. Now the piper would be paid his due. It was as simple as that. [6]

Bernard Baruch and Franklin D. Roosevelt, experienced party warriors, waged a skillful contest in 1931–32 for control of the party and its orientation. Baruch had been burned badly in 1924 when he endorsed William Gibbs McAdoo in the Madison Square Garden bloodletting. He declared afterward he would never again participate in one of the Democracy's quadrennial brawls. Yet, temptation overcame reluctance when Franklin Roosevelt took an enormous lead in 1931 and prospects for a Democratic victory swelled in direct proportion to the nation's growing economic woes. The financier had regarded the squire as a lightweight, coined the "boy scout" opprobrium, disseminated his view widely that the governor was unqualified for the presidency, and that Albert C. Ritchie of Maryland or Newton D. Baker would be clearly preferable.

For all of the behind-the-scenes machinations, despite the stakes, Roosevelt and Baruch remained cool professionals. Unknown to his privy council Roosevelt proved willing, even before Chicago, to show deference to Baruch's power and philosophic strictures. Baruch's visit to Louis Howe's Congress Hotel suite to approve Moley's acceptance speech represented no chance incident. Roosevelt and Baruch commenced their political minuet in December 1931, when Baruch chided the governor for inquiries emanating from the Roosevelt camp concerning his political views in reference to the nomination. "I always felt," the financier lectured, "if you had any interest in my views that our relations were so close that you would personally make the inquiry, as our long-standing friendship requires no intermediary." Baruch denied interest in any candidate. He declared total neutrality. He had entered no combination with Smith and Raskob to head off the governor's chances.

Roosevelt played the same game. Like his old friend he found himself "in the position of one who sits on the side lines and has little personal interest but a great deal of concern as a Democrat and a citizen." Still, he could not help knowing of the "conversations of some people who profess friendship but nevertheless emit innuendos and false statements behind my back with the blissful assumption that they will never be repeated to me." Each pursued his own path toward Chicago, Roosevelt in quest of the main prize, Baruch in search of a conservative alternative. Each, also, hedged his bets. In the period before the Convention they exchanged views through correspondence, then conferred at Hyde Park in May.[7]

Baruch pressed on several issues. He viewed a balanced federal budget as obligatory, requiring a $1 billion cut in the Hoover–Mills outlay projected for fiscal 1933. The draconian measures instituted by the conservative Secretary of the Treasury left him unsatisfied. And in the spring of 1932 he waged war on the Mills budget through powerful Democrats in the Congress, testimony before congressional committees, and a dogged correspondence, even personal visits, with the Treasury, the White House, and the Federal Reserve. Mills, Baruch claimed, had overestimated projected Treasury receipts. "Personally, I believe," he instructed the President, "the budget ought to come down this year to less than $3,500,000,000, including statutory debt retirement, or $3,000,000,000 without that." Such a plan would prove unrealistic, Hoover rebutted, since $2.5 billion of the federal expenditure constituted fixed contractual obligations. Baruch's plan "would leave only $500,000,000 with which to conduct the Army and Navy at one-half their present strength; it would necessitate turning our prisoners out of jails, a reduction in the fundamental services to public health and other activites that just simply cannot be abandoned." The prospect of putting most federal agencies out of business scarcely dismayed the millionaire.

Bureaucrats resembled Janizaries in Bernard Baruch's scale of values, leeches on the body politic, who had "drawn so much of our life's blood from us that the whole economic structure has become anemic." He invoked the judgment of the English historian-statesman Thomas Macaulay:

> Our rulers will best promote the improvement of the people by strictly confining themselves to their own legitimate duties—by leaving capital to find its most lucrative course, commodities their fair prices, industry and intelligence their natural reward, idleness and folly their natural punishment, by maintaining peace, by defending property, by diminishing the price of law, and by observing strict economy in every department of the state.

In concert with other Democratic conservatives, Baruch conceded the need for minimal gestures toward the depressed state of the economy. He favored limited aid to agriculture in the form of McNary-Haugenism, restricted to wheat producers, in reality the dumping of our surplus on the world market, clothed in terms of the tariff equivalent and the equalization fee. He could countenance the Reconstruction Finance Corporation as a mechanism for the preservation of certain equities and the liquidity of our banking system. In company with most conservatives, he acknowledged that massive urban unemployment required enactment of the Smith–Hearst–Wagner–Robinson proposal of a multibillion dollar public works effort, managed by the states and municipalities, including bridge and tunnel construction and public housing, capable of being amortized over a brief span of years. These projects, he lectured Roosevelt, would pay for themselves. The budget could be balanced by a 25 percent cut, by a sales tax, and a tax on legalized beer, in effect taxation of the lower classes as opposed to those who were the job-makers. The nub of the Baruch argument for recovery, urged upon Roosevelt in April and May, and again shortly after the Chicago convention, assumed the form of federal fiscal retrenchment as a stimulus to business confidence.[8]

In early July, following Roosevelt's nomination, Baruch offered a $50,000 contribution to the campaign as a peace offering, conditioned on inclusion of Hugh Johnson in the coterie of Roosevelt's speech writers. Roosevelt and Howe accepted. Moley became infuriated. "This is the process," the head of the Brains Trust bristled, "of getting campaign contributions. . . . Then after the money is in the bag the West will be appeased. So it goes—first the radicals will be betrayed then the conservatives. So everyone is ultimately sold out. . . . The Republicans of course are selling out just the same." [9]

Moley, Tugwell, and Berle calmed quickly. After several conferences with Baruch and Johnson, agreement, they decided, could be reached on specific measures without sacrifice of principles. The Baruch–Johnson memorandum, Moley advised Roosevelt, represented a "most excellent document," which could serve as the basis for his opening campaign speech at Columbus, Ohio, intended as a forceful indictment of the Hoover administration. On issues such as the tariff, the budget, and foreign debts the Baruch memorandum coincided "approximately . . . with what Tugwell, Berle, and I believe. With regard to agriculture, the difference is not great. . . . In my opinion, Mr. Baruch's memorandum is a distinctly valuable contribution to the campaign." Berle, more discerning, urged caution in treating with the financier:

> When he gets under principle, B.M.B. poses the essential issue between the two wings of the party. Like most eastern businessmen, B.M.B. wants to permit free play to business, which in practice means freedom to six or eight hundred large corporations and banks to fight out among themselves the ultimate mastery of the situation. He believes individuals must suffer for and rectify their own mistakes. Unfortunately, the result reached is that the "forgotten men" suffer for the mistakes of the industrial leaders, who come off relatively unhurt.
>
> The obvious line is to agree on definite measures without committing on questions of philosophy or principle. [10]

The Baruch–Raskob axis of the party remained mollified for the duration of the 1932 campaign. Moley's "battle plans" now contained the notation: "Include Gen. Johnson." "I hope," the financier wrote the embittered Raskob on July 22, "that in your way and with your spirit of fair play you will find a way to give Franklin Roosevelt the aid and comfort which you can give so well and which would be so effective in this election." Roosevelt followed up with a telephone call to the deposed party leader, "and I told him," Raskob reported to Baruch, "I would run up to Albany to see him some day next week." In the ensuing weeks Raskob received a check from Baruch for $5,000 which was credited toward the substantial sum still owed to him by the Democratic National Committee.[11] And Roosevelt, in turn, made conservative statements on the excesses of intervention by Hoover, at Columbus, and on the requirement of a balanced budget, at Pittsburgh, in October.

Was it a compromise or an intellectual sellout? A truce or a permanent peace? Had the Jeffersonian Democrats, as they called themselves, the business-financial group that commandeered the party's machinery commencing with the Smith nomination, won the contest after all? And how does one square the agreement expressed by the Brains Trusters, following their discussions with Baruch and Hugh Johnson in mid-July, with Rexford Tugwell's later charge of intellectual defalcation by Roosevelt and Moley? In retrospect, Tugwell's appraisal of the impact of these statements on the New Deal appears exaggerated. The platform and Columbus addresses were mid-summer preludes to the 1932 campaign, and Tugwell had collaborated in their drafting. Yet, as one examines them, they do strike a discordant note. In tandem with the Pittsburgh pledge, they were fabricated in an effort to retain a hold on the party's conservative wing. As Mark Sullivan observed in October 1932, Roosevelt could not manage to juggle so many balls interminably. While it lasted, it was a glorious feat to behold—Huey Long damning the wealthy and Owen Young, John Raskob, and Bernard Baruch in support of the squire. The wild men of the West, Louisiana's Kingfish, and the moguls of New York were bewitched for a moment by Roosevelt's artistry. Sooner or later, one or another of the party's constituent elements would desert.

When the campaign ended and its pledges redeemed in the form of the legislative record of the early New Deal years, the "gold bugs" and budget balancers, the financiers, and Grover Cleveland Democrats bridled; some defected to form the American Liberty League. More importantly, southern Democrats and Republicans forged the conservative coalition and checked the New Deal program by the mid-1930s. Liberal intellectuals defected decades later, in the Vietnam/Watergate climate of frustration with the compromises of liberal government. In the interim, during the period 1932–1935, the Brains Trust synthesis emerged as the dynamic of the modern era. Rexford Tugwell's later ruminations to the contrary, it emerged as much his own product as any other's.

CONFUSED AND TROUBLED by the omissions and contradictions of the Chicago acceptance speech, by Roosevelt's unqualified endorsement of the party platform (the work of its conservative establishment), by Samuel Rosenman's mishmash of Moley's effort, by the sudden entry upon the scene of one of the party's foremost reactionaries in the person of Bernard Baruch, Rexford Tugwell retreated following the convention for a few days' reflection to the quiet of his family home on the shores of Lake Ontario. He had become painfully aware of the reality that he was a political novice, shocked by the compromises inherent in a presidential nomination, dependent upon Roosevelt's law partner, Basil "Doc" O'Connor for a Baedecker to Democratic politics. Distressed by the apparent conservatism of Roosevelt's following in the party, its insistence upon victory in November rather than on institutional change, he wanted a device for social and economic management, a commitment to planning for agriculture and industry. Speculation needed to be curbed, production regulated, investment allocated. As he ruminated on these matters in the idyllic setting of his father's home in upstate New York, the economist drafted a memorandum for Roosevelt's consideration.

An analysis of Tugwell's proposals of the post-convention period is crucial to an understanding of what Franklin D. Roosevelt was and was not willing to undertake and how he functioned in relation to the advice he received. In later years, Moley shrugged off the Tugwell presentation as too extreme for serious consideration and credited instead the primacy of Baruch's and Hugh Johnson's conservative views in the 1932 effort. Moley insisted on limiting Tugwell's intellectual input, in retrospect, to Roosevelt's requirements for agricultural planning in the form of domestic allotment. Tugwell concurred. In several articles, then *The Brains Trust*, the economist asserted that the campaign became muted in deference to the party's elders and their traditionalist views, especially those of Baruch and the neo-Brandeisian atomists. [12]

When one departs from the participants' recollections and turns to the contemporary documents, a different picture emerges of the deliberations of July-August 1932. Moley, not Tugwell, bitterly protested Baruch's intrusion. Accommodation was reached quickly once the Brains Trust realized that Baruch could retreat gracefully from his archaic views on federal intervention in exchange for a pledge of a balanced budget, a matter on which all agreed. Tugwell's principal proposals were incorporated and adopted with the notable exception of creation of an Economic Council, bypassed upon Adolf Berle's recommendation. Nor did Bernard Baruch have it all his way either. When the campaign closed, the President-elect artfully informed the financier that he contemplated charging only interest and amortization, as opposed to whole expenditures, to the federal budget in connection with capital outlay (emergency projects). Baruch protested the device as an artifice, known as a supplementary budget, also the domestic allotment plan for agriculture. In the interplay of these hectic months, Roosevelt emerged as the determinative figure. [13]

The memorandum drafted by Tugwell at his Lake Ontario retreat takes on the attributes of a Corporatist society, in perspective, rather than a Collectivist one. Presented to the Roosevelt entourage in the Albany–Hyde Park discussions of early July, it found initial acceptance as evidenced by Moley's frequent reference that summer in his notes to a speech on an "Economic Council." In a modification of views presented to the American Economic Association at its winter 1931-32 meeting, he proposed creation of a Federal Economic Council which would serve in an advisory capacity to the President.[14] It would consist of professional economists and industrial representatives who would anticipate the average of demand, coordinate production in relation to demand, and regulate the flow of goods into the marketplace accordingly. Reasonable planning and persuasion, Tugwell hoped, would filter to industry's executive levels. He did not propose, the economist insisted, "to have government run industry; it is proposed to have government furnish the requisite leadership; protect our resources; arrange for national balance; secure its citizens' access to goods, employment and security; and rise to the challenge of planning that concert of interests."

To facilitate these tasks, Tugwell urged the repeal of the federal government's anti-trust legislation and encouragement of the organization of industry on a regional and national basis. Oversight of the nation's economic activity should be given to an advisory council to the President, made up of nine functional divisions:

(1) Statistical, with the duty of gathering and interpreting information relative to current production, distribution, capital issues, monetary supplies, domestic and foreign trade, and consumption;

(2) Production, with the duty of planning the national output of staple goods, agricultural and manufactured;

(3) Consumption, with the duty of estimating future needs of the population;

(4) Domestic trade, with the duty of estimating the ability of distributive resources to care for the streams of commerce;

(5) International trade, with the duty of formulating policies with respect to our international economic relations;

(6) Prices, with the duty of watching and advising concerning the general and specific relationships among various prices for the preservation of balance;

(7) Capital issues, with the duty of encouraging or discouraging the flow of capital into various industries;

(8) Natural resources, with the duty of estimating the rate of use and efficiency with which resources are used;

(9) Finance, with the duty of coordinating the work of the Council with that of the national banking system.[15]

Considered in tandem with the Tugwell proposals were those of M. L. Wilson for agricultural planning. Wilson was summoned to Albany by Moley for a luncheon with the governor and his advisers. In typical Roosevelt fashion it seemed time, now, having endorsed the domestic allotment scheme in his acceptance speech, to get a crack at its author. The governor conducted most of the questioning, Wilson recalled, rather than any of his advisers (which included Moley, Berle, Tugwell, Henry Morgenthau Jr., and Marvin MacIntyre), demonstrating remarkable familiarity with the various proposals for agricultural planning before the Congress. When the discussion concluded, the candidate suggested to those assembled what he wanted done.

Both presentations were accepted. Wilson would remain at Albany for further discussions with Tugwell and Moley, then consult Henry A. Wallace en route to Montana. The first draft of the Topeka address, on the resolution of the decade-old agricultural crisis, charged to Wilson, would be submitted by August for Morgenthau's and Moley's consideration. Tugwell's analysis of the need for industrial planning, including the Economic Council, would serve as the basis for a subsequent campaign statement. Upon Wilson's recommendation Henry I. Harriman, President of the United States Chamber of Commerce, came into the picture. Harriman, regarded as a maverick in the business community, had already contributed key ideas to Wilson's formulation of the domestic allotment scheme and concluded that in industry, too, laissez faire needed to be replaced by planning. Wilson took on an additional assignment, the recruitment of Ralph Budd, president of the Chicago, Burlington, and Quincy Railroad, still another of the Montana State College professor's Republican acquaintances known to be unhappy with the Hoover administration, for assistance in a third major campaign speech on the railroads. This latter became Adolf Berle's assignment. [16]

Moley and Tugwell summarized the Hyde Park–Albany discussions on July 11, 1932, for the benefit of Sam Rosenman and "Doc" O'Connor, revealing the clarification of basic domestic programs, and foreshadowing the tenor of foreign economic relations in the

1930s. The recent settlement of the reparations question by Europe's major powers at Lausanne pointed toward the need for some response by the United States on the debts. The Brains Trusters enunciated a tough position, later defended against Norman Davis and Henry Stimson during the interregnum. As a generalization, accommodation seemed desirable; but not by bolstering up private indebtedness owed to American bankers at the expense of public indebtedness. The Wall Street bankers, the Brains Trusters insisted, "will attempt to get unconditional cancellation [of intergovernmental obligations] into the Democratic program. We think this ought to be resisted and that a wider policy ought to be looked forward to."

On the issues of public expenditures (budget balance) and relief of unemployment, Moley and Tugwell indicated willingness initially to follow either the path favored by conservatives of a balanced federal budget, heavy taxation, and the financing of public works through bonded indebtedness, or by the inflationists (ranging from tinkering with the gold content of the dollar, favored by the Cornell School, to monetization of silver, or the printing of fiat money). Yet, their own inclinations propelled them toward the views argued by Baruch. Inflationism, associated in that era with the irrationalities of the Populist crusade and the devastating potential of printing-press money, seemed disadvantageous for the nation's monetary system and threatened demoralization of the banking and business communities. Moley and Tugwell, in time, rejected the tendency of cheap-money advocates to overlook problems which required thoughtful resolution, and favored tackling the fundamentals. [17]

Only one substantial change occurred in the formulation of domestic priorities as the 1932 campaign took shape, abandonment of Tugwell's proposed Economic Council. The address on planning for industry, ultimately the Commonwealth Speech, fell to Berle and mention of a coordinating body at the national level dropped. This action requires further explanation. Despite contrary recollection by the participants in later years, reference to an Economic

Council appears as early as Moley's May 19 memorandum and as late as August 2 ("Ec. Council—Tugwell to confer w. Harriman"), in the campaign plans drafted by Roosevelt and Moley. Whatever Franklin D. Roosevelt's reputation for capricious behavior, the evolution of the Commonwealth Club address, basic to an understanding of the nature of the New Deal, indicates that the candidate weighed the situation carefully and perceptively as he checked the opinions of one adviser with another.

Toward the end of July, Tugwell presented Roosevelt with the projected campaign address on industrial planning and the necessity of an Economic Council, characterized as a device that had been tried and found successful in Europe. In his customary, almost lyrical, way the economist urged the substitution of cooperation for competition, a true concert of interests as opposed to the traditional safeguarding of individual privilege. He wanted the creation of general economic insurance funds for the long-run security of industrial workers. And he attributed the depression, at least in part, to the huge corporate surplus of the twenties diverted to overseas investment and stock market speculation.

Roosevelt turned to Adolf A. Berle for a verdict. Tugwell's observations were acceptable to the expert in corporate law and structure, and the notion of an Economic Council, Berle explained, held appeal among liberal Democratic intellectuals. Modifying the conclusions he reached in *The Modern Corporation and Private Property*, Berle suggested that "most responsible students agree that the present industrial system, if it survives, can reach only one of two results. Either the government steps in through some form of economic administration; or business and banking units, by consolidation, merger, etc., evolve an irresponsible government of their own."

Yet, Berle advised against the candidate's espousal of an Economic Council in the course of the campaign. Tugwell had assigned it a Herculean task, its equivalent nonexistent except in wartime. Campaign explication did not seem feasible. "I think," Berle urged alternatively, "the best line is the creation of a group of existing government officials (without setting up another bureau) which will collect economic information, rendering general opinions to the President and the Congress at intervals, and reporting on the effect of specific measures on national economy as a whole." If such judgments proved wise, Berle believed, the group would gain authority and public confidence.[18]

Whatever might have developed as a consequence of the Economic Council and the duties envisaged for it by Tugwell, Collectivism as he later suggested, or conceivably a Corporatist society, it was scrapped. Although it appears to have been the forerunner of the National Emergency Council, created by Roosevelt in 1933 to monitor and coordinate emergency economic measures aimed at recovery,[19] still later of the Council of Economic Advisers, a development of the Truman administration, it is equally obvious that no centralized agency, including NIRA, which depended on state and local authority, has been accorded the wide-ranging economic powers contemplated in the Tugwell memorandum. The limits of intervention in the shaping of the New Deal were imposed by the squire of Hyde Park in consultation with Berle in the summer of 1932.

Elsewhere, Tugwell's views proved decisive. Shortly after the Convention, the Democratic candidate asked for a written critique of the Berle–Faulkner analysis of May 1932, on the depression's origination and possible remedies, as well as Bernard Baruch's proposals, also submitted as a memorandum. Tugwell's response, drafted with the aid of Robert K. Straus (son of Jesse I. Straus of New York's Macy's department store), "Money and the Financial Complex," Moley informed Roosevelt on July 16, 1932, had successfully synthesized varying viewpoints into a coordinated economic program. Planning never stood at the core of the "first" New Deal, but rather served as one of several means to more sophisticated ends.

Tugwell's "Money and the Financial Complex" led to the salient feature of the New Deal program: selective economic treatment by the federal government as a means of attaining economic balance or equilibrium. The money or financial issue appeared crucial even to the lower classes, the economist reasoned, because of the existence of so many debtors. Influenced by Charles Beard, Tugwell and Moley viewed the division of society into debtor and creditor classes, the preponderance debtors who had been hit hardest by the depression. This was particularly true, according to the Tugwell–Straus analysis, of primary materials producers (farmers), whose incomes had fallen 30 to 40 percent. Their expenses, interest, taxes, cost of electric power and implements, had not fallen proportionately. As a consequence, their profit margins had been wiped out. Tugwell proposed restoration in the form of a better, more equitable distribution of income as opposed to simple inflationism.

> It is not the collapse of prices but the collapse of some prices and the rigidity of others which has resulted in the present untenable predicament. Some groups in the nation have a claim on a larger real income than they had in 1929 at the expense of the vast majority who are receiving a much smaller real income. . . .
> All commodities have fallen 33.7% below their 1926 price level in February, 1932. All farm products had fallen 49.4%, whereas agricultural implements had only fallen 14.9%.

Undesirable disparities existed elsewhere. Iron and steel products had declined 20.7 percent in the 1926–32 period; motor vehicles only 4.7 percent; building materials, 26.6 percent; chemicals 19.2 percent; gas 1.4 percent. The cost of electricity had risen some 7.5 percent and interest on long-term debt had remained unchanged. Wage rates had fallen substantially in some industries and scarcely at all in others. Whereas millions were unemployed, those fully employed enjoyed a higher standard of living in 1932 than at the depression's inception.

Tugwell pushed toward certain generalizations. The privileged groups were those who sold on contract or rented at old price levels for a period of years—the landlord, the banker, or some municipalities which sold future services and raised tax rates for their construction, undertaken at lower than anticipated costs. The monetary problem could be resolved by restoration as far as possible of price relationships which existed in 1929, or, conceivably, the creation of new, more desirable ones. This could be accomplished, he believed, either "through crushing the forces which now prop up the privileged groups, or through putting price props under the underprivileged groups."

Reduction of claims of the privileged groups, accomplished in part by substantial private default, could be facilitated further through general legalized public default under the auspices of the central government. The Hoover administration policies, according to Tugwell's analysis, had chosen an opposing course under the National Credit Corporation, RFC, the Glass–Steagall Act of 1932, and with the help of Federal Reserve open market policies, namely, that of propping up the privileged creditor groups. As a corollary, it determined further, according to the Republican platform, to maintain the gold standard and avoid currency inflation.

Gaging the alternatives available to Roosevelt, Tugwell opposed a broad inflationary program that would escalate wholesale prices through resort to currency devaluation. It was a route, we might note, that Roosevelt later followed with no visible success. Tugwell preferred a position taken in the Berle memorandum, which he characterized as "selective devaluation," under the auspices of federal instrumentalities using the credit of the national government. This would afford a measure of security, as Berle suggested, concomitant with the deflation or reduction of creditor claims. But Tugwell insisted on more.

Prices were out of line, and the Tugwell memorandum stressed the need for the elimination of price and income inequities. Balance was a prerequisite for the revival of industrial activity. "Shortages of income for some groups involves their inability to buy from others. Surpluses for some groups involves their uses of income in such ways as to make the disproportion greater." General inflation, broadly and unselectively undertaken, would exaggerate inequities and might prove disastrous over the long haul. Once begun, inflation would be difficult to end, and he questioned it as a device for stimulation of industrial production or employment. Tugwell urged instead a program that would limit the income of the favored groups through a variety of devices such as refinancing at lower levels and higher taxation of income and inheritances. He proposed, as well, extreme retrenchment in federal expenses, avoidance of bond issues, the giving of relief directly rather than indirectly, and the salvaging of savings institutions and insurance companies.

Tugwell recapitulated his proposals as follows:

> (1) selective deflation, the bringing down of income in the most favored groups, and (2) increasing the advantages of those groups which are the least favored. Workers and farmers are the worst—extensive property owners are the best [off]. We ought, therefore, to undertake more income to workers and farmers, and ought to reduce (by taxation and refund operations) the incomes of large property owners. With these corrections made, activity would at least have an opportunity to resume.

Finally, contrary to his recollection in *The Brains Trust* of insistence on Collectivism in the summer of 1932, also to Moley's portrait of Tugwell as a radical dreamer, Tugwell urged, in one of the key memoranda of the early New Deal years, deliberate disavowal of a doctrinaire approach, or as he put it, of "principle." The Hoover administration, he observed in his July memorandum, had been bogged down by the strictures of individualism, which it nevertheless felt compelled to violate by yielding to the demands of the larger property-owners for protection of their investment. Having violated the basic tenets of its belief, it refused to extend the attempt at federal protection of vested interests equally to all classes. Roosevelt was advised to follow a pragmatic course, pursuit of recovery by the shortest route with a minimum of distress. The avoidance of structural theories emerged as the keystone of the Roosevelt era.[20]

IT BECAME Raymond Moley's responsibility to translate the broad economic goals of the Brains Trust into a series of campaign addresses that would be intelligible to the voter and acceptable to a popular majority.[21] Subsequently, under Moley's management, these served as the basis for the legislative proposals submitted by the President during the Hundred Days. Obviously, unforeseen emergencies came along, most importantly the bank crisis of the winter 1932–33. Compromises and adjustments would need to be made as in the premature legislation of NIRA and greater concessions than originally anticipated to the labor movement, but these could readily be subsumed within the tenets outlined by mid-summer 1932 when the New Deal was fashioned. If Roosevelt had little contact or sympathy with organized labor in the early years of the New Deal, the labor movement's concrete goals harmonized with the Brains Trust's aspirations and his own for a better economic balance and attainment of certain economic minima. Though emergency relief measures and the development of a broad public-works/relief program unbalanced the Roosevelt budgets, balancing federal outlay with its income nevertheless remained a long-range objective in the pre-Keynesian era.

The goals outlined in 1932 were realized in the early Roosevelt years: the restoration of the nation's private credit structure, propping up of income of farmers and industrial workers as part of a broader goal of creation of a new base of purchasing power, acknowledgement of concentration of control and consequently of the need for enlargement of the federal government's role as umpire—further, in certain instances, its assertion of national priorities, the institution of basic reforms in the banking system and in the sale and issuance of securities, and the melioration of the economic cycle and of individual economic insecurity through an assortment of insurance schemes. These emerged as the priorities of the Age of Roosevelt.[22]

The legislation of the Roosevelt administration hardly constituted an improvisation. The deliberations and memoranda of the Brains Trust led to conclusions which guided the New Deal's subsequent course. First, whatever the credibility of arguments directed toward the resolution of international dislocations, internal imbalances, fundamental to our own dilemmas, required priority. International economic cooperation would wait given the state of intergovernmental relations.

The principal requisite of internal recovery was the achievement of a better economic balance fostered by legislative and executive management at the national level. The nation's economic system, the Brains Trust decided, could no longer tolerate Hoover's limiting adherence to the notion of individualism. Corporate concentration and concentration of control had made it an outmoded concept. Economic imbalance, fostered principally by an inequitable and undesirable distribution of wealth, income, and purchasing power, required remedy. While the nation's productive capacity was enormous, thanks to the advent of technological innovation, it could not be consumed by the farm population, which had been pauperized, or by industrial labor, whose wages had been outdistanced by productivity. Farm income and the wages of labor needed to be boosted by artificial means. This required federal intervention both for short-run or emergency purposes as well as long range objectives. Where necessary, individualism would need to be abandoned and collective methods substituted under the aegis of the federal government. But, as Adolf Berle pointed out in later years, "Serious consideration, so far as I know, was never given toward Socialization—that is, government takeover—of production in general."

It was agreed, further, on Berle's and Tugwell's recommendations, to use the credit of the U.S. government through quasi-public mechanisms such as the Reconstruction Finance Corporation to halt a situation in which credit had become sterilized. This needed to be done selectively. Certain private debt situations, such as utilities empire pyramids, had been so speculative as to require a catharsis. Other situations, however, such as high-grade railroad securities, home and farm mortgages, required federalization at scaled down values. Through extension of the RFC principle, now nearly abandoned by the timid attitudes of the Hoover administration, far beyond its original dimension, the decision was reached to rescue fiduciary institutions which held depreciated paper and to prevent the railroads and farming community from going under.

Growing interdependence of the various segments of our society and concentration of power in large economic aggregates dictated an expansion of the federal role. The problem revealed two dimensions; one, of scale, locus of power, and ultimate social responsibility; the other, a continuation of the Wilsonian effort to stem the free-wheeling, buccaneering tactics of the post-Civil War era which wreaked so much havoc in the marketplace. Regulation of securities issuance and exchanges, of the size and complexity of utilities holding companies, and of banking practices, which enjoyed a conceptual understanding in Congress, proved difficult only in its legal execution. But control or regulation of the nation's corporate giants remained elusive in practice despite the fact that Roosevelt set it down as a goal in the Commonwealth address.

It has been argued that the "first" New Deal attempted to tackle the problem of regulated monopoly, the "second" New Deal, frustrated by its experience and the Supreme Court, reverting to the regulation of competition. Both are really interrelated, and the memoranda of the Brains Trust and the record of the Hundred Days shows no such exclusivity. Concentration of control has been organic and remains the fundamental reason for an enlarged federal presence in the nation's economy.

Finally, there occurred a coalescence of the long-felt need embraced by the Progressive remnant for a larger measure of social justice and the conclusion reached by the Brains Trust that some measure of economic security required introduction to terminate the depression. Economic anxiety had undermined individual confidence resulting in stagnation. It seemed socially desirable that the peaks and valleys of industrial employment be meliorated through unemployment insurance, that child labor be curbed, that old age be made more tolerable. Although such ideas originated with the social justice objectives of the progressive movement, they made sense from the perspective of the Brains Trust also as an "economic

bill of rights." Anxious to stimulate economic activity and to provide the social minima as a floor, an irreducible base of purchasing
power, against future downward thrusts of the business cycle, the
Brains Trusters promoted the origination of the modern welfare
state in American society.

If the New Deal did not emerge as an improvisation, neither was
it as revolutionary as described by Herbert Hoover. It avoided the
violent ideological tendencies abroad in Europe and Asia in the
depression decade.[23] Roosevelt advocated government intervention, not ownership. He sought to accommodate the American System to the twentieth century, not to liquidate it. He captured the
tattered remnant of the Progressive movement, scarcely welcomed
by Hoover and Mills, for the Democratic party. His appeal, broad-
based, reached the middle class, hard-pressed and bewildered by
the collapse, the farming community, and the urban-industrial
workers unemployed in the millions. Although conscious of our society's economic pluralism, he tended to avoid its racial and ethnic
diversity. The nature of his party's history and structure and the
realities of congressional leadership compelled him to deal with
conservative Southern Democrats, who controlled the legislative
process. Ultimately he wrung more fundamental alterations of
American life than they would have initially conceded. His willingness to compromise and the rejection of ideology, however,
made the New Deal less appealing to a later generation nurtured
on the assumption of prosperity and accustomed to ideological
commitment as the measuring rod of academic acceptance. But in
the Great Depression dogma seemed a luxury. "Our danger is neither from radicalism nor conservatism," Walter Lippmann observed in the summer of 1932, "but from incoherence and paraly-
sis. What we have to fear is the inability of government to
determine policies and to execute them." [24]

Other caveats need to be entered. Keynesian options did not
exist, since Keynesian mechanisms emerged some years later. The
British economist's views had not fully matured, comprehended
only in terms of inflationism by the American academic commu-

nity, and the balanced budget viewed as axiomatic by academicians. "We are . . . starting out with a notion of correcting price disparities," Tugwell declaimed in early 1933. "Inflation is like going after the bird with a shotgun when the operation really requires a rifle." Roosevelt's subsequent departures from the precept of budget balance, like his predecessor's, reflected the need for emergency expenditures rather than economic dogma.[25]

The conviction that Felix Frankfurter and Louis D. Brandeis, with the able assistance of their strategically deployed Harvard Law School protégés, undermined the holistic or organic approach of the Brains Trust lacks credibility. The New Deal encompassed a panoply of approaches. Invariably when Frankfurter commented on domestic remedies that required planning in the campaign or later in the Hundred Days, in the form of the Agricultural Adjustment Administration and the National Industrial Recovery Administration, he expressed only approbation. "I am not for a planned society *en gros*," Frankfurter explained during the Hundred Days. "I am prepared to get these by *ad hoc* treatment of specific problems." This dramatic and nondoctrinal approach to exploring social and economic solutions perfectly summarizes the New Deal.[26]

13

Campaign Milestones 1932

WITH FEW EXCEPTIONS, the economic innovations of the Roosevelt era were broached by the Brains Trust, so dubbed by *New York Times* writer James Kieran on the eve of the squire's campaign trip to the West Coast as correspondents and advisers relaxed at a Hyde Park picnic catered by Eleanor Roosevelt. " 'The harvest is past, the summer is ended, and we are not saved,' " Raymond Moley recapitulated seven years later. "Vastly important reforms remain to be achieved." Such is the nature of man's limited accomplishment. But the Brains Trust ventured bold, new ideas in an era fettered by traditionalist views unsuited to a horrendous economic crisis. These ideas have become a part of our permanent past, the substance of the nation's contemporary economic practice. This emerged as their unique and Franklin D. Roosevelt's lasting contribution.

The suggestion of recent scholarship that Herbert Hoover pioneered the New Deal, or at the very least deserves recognition as a "forgotten progressive" rends the delicate fabric of history beyond recognition and affords the Great Engineer's views a disservice. Hoover qualifies as a progressive in the postwar era only in the sense that business conservatives and reactionaries dressed their views in the language of that movement. Whereas Roosevelt and the Brains Trust broadened the social contract to include an economic constitutional order, Hoover persisted in traditionalist views that restricted the federal government and its functions and insisted on reliance upon local and state government, as well as private voluntary (associative) endeavor, in the depression crisis.

Indeed the interwar period requires redefinition not, however, as dominated by liberal-progressive currents nurtured by reverence for the advances of science and technocracy, but as dominated by a coalition of conservatives in business and government, including the Congress, anxious for the avoidance of statism. Hoover's *American Individualism*, his stress on private, associational activity found subsequent expression in Barry Goldwater's *Conscience of a Conservative*, not in Franklin D. Roosevelt's New Deal. The Age of the Conservative Coalition, with Herbert Hoover as spokesman has, since Versailles, governed the nation's attitudes as readily as the New Deal, in its suspicion of centralism and bureaucracy, in its insistence on minimalism at the federal level, its stress on the Jeffersonian tradition.

The Hoover/Roosevelt campaign was the basic confrontation of the post-Versailles era. It was not a pivotal or turning point campaign in terms of patterns of voting behavior on a national or regional basis, but rather because of the economic rationale developed by the Brains Trust. Since its statement of alternatives, some 40 percent of the electorate can be mustered in any presidential contest either for the American System or for interventionism. The swing vote maximizes at 20 percent in time of economic crisis, as in 1932, or when either major party candidate, as in 1964 (Barry Goldwater), and in 1972 (George McGovern), hews too rigidly to one or another ideological view.

Interventionism won the day in 1932, then peaked in the early New Deal years. But the economic collapse was temporary, not permanent. As the nation adjusted, then regained a measure of confidence, the Hoover ethic enjoyed a recrudescence. In the long run, the Great Engineer and his American System, like Banquo's ghost, managed to prosper as a potent antistatist political force. It is in this sense that stress on Hoover's origination of the New Deal is most egregiously misleading.

Equally disconcerting is the assertion of a realistic radical alternative, one that could muster a sizable suffrage. Even at the depression's depth, the Socialist and Communist parties commanded

an insignificant minority of the electorate. All minor parties gar-
nered only some 1.1 million votes in 1932, and 1.5 million votes
four years later. The individualist-voluntarist alternative to Roosevelt's statist proposals, on the other hand, remained potent even
during the depression. Hoover, scarcely popular even within his
own party's ranks, massed 15.7 million votes in the 1932 contest,
or 40 percent of those cast. Roosevelt's 22.8 million votes (57.4 percent), represented a smaller percentage than the suffrage for
Hoover in 1928 or Harding in 1920. Nor does the 1932 voter
breakdown account for the conservative views of the Democratic
party's Eastern business interests. Unable to check the squire's
nomination, they supported him with some reluctance. But in the
years that ensued, many of the Jeffersonian Democrats, as they
depicted themselves, departed from the New Deal, and allied
openly or surreptitiously with the Republicans and the Southern
Democratic legislative leadership. By the mid-1930s, the Conservative Coalition dominated the Congress and halted the New
Deal.[1]

The 1932 campaign and the origins of the New Deal require consideration in a frame of reference considered both by Hoover and
Roosevelt. Each sensed the economic crisis of the early thirties as a
potential turning point in our nation's post-Civil War industrial and
financial development. The Republican incumbent, particularly in
his August acceptance speech and at Madison Square Garden on
October 31, 1932, urged adherence to established values in the
face of the storm. Underestimating its depth and range, he portrayed the depression as fleeting in the perspective of our experience, the omnicompetent state as a permanent danger.

Roosevelt pointed to an altered set of realities in our economic
society, particularly at Topeka, in the Commonwealth Club
speech, and in a radio talk to the party's Business and Professional
Men's League. Growing corporate concentration, concentration of
control in few private hands, and severe economic unbalance called
for overhead management or social control. On Berle's advice,
Roosevelt chose a course of organic evolution of federal mecha-

nisms in the industrial sector. Rexford Tugwell placed greater faith in the contemporary state of the governmental arts. But the farm crisis and its threatening shadow of peasantry required immediate resolution. Millions of small farms had gone under in the previous decade. Those who remained to till the soil could not consume the output of the industrial sector. The mechanisms for remediation seemed available, and federally directed planning introduced. The interventionist program fashioned by Roosevelt and the Brains Trust also included a more active role for existing federal agencies and, where needed, the creation of new ones in the checking of excrescences in the marketplace for protection of the public interest. Insistence upon corporate and financial accountability, the development of public power, federal provision on an enlarged scale for relief and urban rehabilitation, and income redistribution away from the Eastern-industrial sector toward the Western and Southern agrarian rounded out the Roosevelt–Brains Trust objectives.[2]

Abandoned by his own party as a political liability, the once vaunted Great Engineer, symbol of our society's technocratic achievement, ventured out onto the American road in the autumn of 1932 on a trek that lasted to the end of his days. Absolutely certain that Roosevelt and his academic consorts would undermine a hundred and fifty years of progress toward individualism, overworked, depressed, booed and jeered at by the menacing crowds, Herbert Hoover seemed obsessed, driven as Raymond Moley suggested, "by some damned sense of mission and duty." Toward the end of the campaign, Rexford Tugwell recalled, the Republican standard-bearer seemed a stricken man, often disoriented, stumbling over his words. Too often Hoover crammed his speeches, as he would later his memoirs, with a litany of dreary economic facts and his administration's questionable achievements.[3]

Whatever the state of his psyche, almost overcome by the burdens of office, Hoover determined to have his say about the ominous portent of the New Deal, as he saw it, for the nation's future. He would be heard. The Great Engineer not only outlived the squire of Hyde Park but, in time, with the depression's subsidence, he witnessed the recrudescence of his American System as an alternative to statism.

AT VERY NEARLY MIDNIGHT on September 12, 1932, the Democratic standard-bearer boarded the "Roosevelt Special" at Albany for a 9,000-mile campaign tour of the Middlewestern and Pacific Coast states. In a very genuine sense it would have been more appropriate to this contest than that conducted four years later if Raymond Moley, who accompanied the governor, would have summoned his "rendezvous with destiny" catchphrase. For, together, the squire and his chief Brains Truster forged one of our history's most striking collaborative enterprises, the economic and political catchall they dubbed the New Deal.

One feature, taken for granted by an older generation, now virtually ignored, requires rehabilitation—Roosevelt's Christian capitalism and his appeal to the masses as a man who had bravely overcome his physical infirmity:

> . . . In every age a guide is found,
> The Choice of God, whose love profound,
> Doth help all those in bitter need,
> Where famine stalks from earth-born greed.
>
> A leader now again appears
> Who quickly drives away all fears.
> He'll never leave his work undone,
> For God upholds his Chosen One. [4]

Two Franklin Roosevelts traversed the nation from Albany to San Francisco and back. One, the thoughtful politician, who turned to academe in the spring of that year as the Albany advisers crumbled under the intellectual demands of the economic crisis, planned now to elaborate the Brains Trust's economic program as a viable approach toward the Great Depression. The other Roosevelt, capable of inspiration and infusion of hope, the foremost political artist of his time, the troubadour, the *Reise*-Roosevelt, seemed as eager to travel and influence people as to pursue a cause. The squire excelled at the ritual demanded of our national aspirants, and delighted in the approbation of the crowds.

From its inception the Western tour assumed a dualistic format. Enunciation of major policy statements, shaped in outline in July and August, were interspersed with back-platform appearances and countless railroad car discussions with local and regional politicians, businessmen, farm spokesmen, senators, governors, journalists, and welfare workers. As statesman, Roosevelt preached an ordered society before thousands of farmers under the scorching sun at Topeka and businessmen at San Francisco's elegant Palace Hotel; as the optimistic squire, he joked incessantly about his "little boy Jimmie" who stood "only six-foot three-inches tall, that is all," and reassured thousands threatened by the loss of their farms, their jobs, their businesses. Over and over again Roosevelt explained that he, too, had taken his lumps with the rest on his Hyde Park and Georgia farms, and was anxious to tackle and resolve, now, the nation's economic dilemma. If it represented partly an effort toward psychological reassurance, there emerged, too, a broad formulation of approaches and priorities.[5]

The back-platform format took shape quickly at Bellefontaine, Ohio. After introducing his family, the Democratic candidate discussed with the crowd of some 500 persons the election of the State Democratic ticket in Maine.* He was on his way to Topeka, Roosevelt related, for an "agriculture speech" and working hard at it. An admirer let him know, "We are glad you are going to be elected instead of Hoover. I keep your picture in my room, Governor." "Isn't that grand!" Roosevelt exulted. Asked about Prohibition, "I think we are going to repeal it."

As the train pulled away, someone shouted from the crowd, "You are not going to make them all lie down on park benches like Hoover." The train halted and the exchange resumed. It concluded with another anonymous admonition: "Brother Roosevelt, you are a distant relation to old Teddy. Have you got one joint of his back-

* Maine's state election, held in September, was regarded as a bellwether for the November result.

bone?" Later, at a small Missouri town, a tiny woman, elderly, attired in a faded black dress, clutched a bouquet of flowers and pressed toward the candidate. "Pound Hoover!" she shouted as she presented her gift, "Pound him hard!" Roosevelt intended that and more. [6]

The farm states required more than the emotional outlet afforded by a messiah. Indeed, for two generations they had witnessed a plenitude of panaceas and platitudes and now required a program which would afford relief and long-range recovery from the exploitation of urban society, as they saw it, and the collapse of domestic prices. Promises would no longer suffice. Alfred E. Smith's endorsement of McNary-Haugenism four years earlier, Roosevelt had been cautioned, suffered rejection because of suspected insincerity. Smith had conveyed neither a sense of genuine commitment nor one of real understanding of farm belt problems in the 1928 effort, nor did farmers trust any longer even their own leadership. In Iowa, one informant reported, "we have distances of 75 miles without a single bank open," and scarcely a single dollar of loan money available for any purpose. Those who still owned their farms outright could not secure a few hundred dollars for a time to avoid selling oats at nine to ten cents a bushel. [7]

Roosevelt's "agriculture speech" at Topeka, Kansas, as he described it, reflected several desiderata broached initially in the "Forgotten Man" and St. Paul speeches, further developed by M. L. Wilson, Henry A. Wallace, and Henry I. Harriman. The ramifications proved widespread, affecting our economic diplomacy as well as our domestic priorities, the first step in a developing series of interlocking economic conclusions. Roosevelt and the Brains Trust attached priority to the achievement of a better balance between rural and urban-industrial income and purchasing power. This, in turn, required federal planning for control of our surplus production of basic agricultural commodities. The internalizing of the nation's economy emerged as the final requirement, pending achievement of better world market prices. For as matters stood commodity prices had become too low in the international marketplace to cover production costs and drove domestic prices down as well. It led to Roosevelt's abandonment in the campaign of his prior low tariff position, then in the 1932–33 interregnum to the conceptualization labeled "intranationalism."

In the evolution of mechanisms, M. L. Wilson's role as progenitor and publicist proved crucial. An astute judge of the Plains farmers' mentality and a genuine student of wheat husbandry, knowledgeable in the intricacies of the international grain trade, cognizant of the resistance of grain millers to higher grain prices, Wilson perceived as well the damage that might be done by a low tariff program which could undermine every gain achieved on the domestic front. His principal strength, overall, was a finely tuned political sense. He feared most in July and August of 1932, the tendency of Henry Morgenthau Jr., and other of the governor's New York state agricultural "experts," to rest content with advocacy of reforestation and withdrawal of marginal land from production, in effect, Hoover's program, one which aroused scant interest west of the Appalachians. Farmers, Wilson prodded Morgenthau in July, suffered from wheat prices so low—hard spring wheat brought only 25 to 30 cents a bushel—that harvesting often proved unprofitable. Neither party's platform would do, considering the huge surpluses which swamped the marketplace and depressed farm income.

While nudging Morgenthau, Wilson struck a cautious note with Roosevelt and Moley, who appeared prone to direct intervention. Since Eastern business interests would oppose a program based on federal controls, the Montana professor-farmer urged a discrete route toward domestic allotment. Word must be passed to farmers and the farm belt leadership that Roosevelt would be responsive once in office and would "do more than you propose in the platform and your speeches," but they must be given to understand "that you cannot say in your speeches all that you will do."

The Wilson memorandum for the Topeka address, dispatched to Moley in early September, followed lines forged at a group discussion (Wilson, Moley, Tugwell, and Wallace) in August in New York, subsequently revised at a Wilson–Wallace meeting at Des

Moines. But it lacked punch and clarity, Wilson observed ruefully, as he put it in the mail. "I am not sufficiently accomplished a speech writer to correct these defects." The task, he apologized, fell in Moley's lap. Yet, the logic and structure of the presentation formed the basis for the New Deal farm program.

Wilson's proposals embraced two integral elements—production controls and a domestic market economy. Farmers, he observed, though prepared for a program geared to reduction of surplus commodities, favored restoration of the European market, their normal outlet for excess output. Privately, however, Wilson conceded the impracticability of attaining a better international climate in the foreseeable future and he equated domestic allotment with autarchy. "If the Ottawa Conference puts a preferential tariff of 6¢ a bushel on wheat entering Great Britain," Wilson concluded, "the Equalization Fee and Debenture are both automatically eliminated." [8]

Moley also relied upon a presentation made by Henry I. Harriman, President of the U.S. Chamber of Commerce, at the University of New Hampshire on August 5, 1932. Harriman elaborated in some detail domestic allotment's principal features for a round table on production control. These included not only acreage allotment, but the levying of an excise tax on processors with distribution of the receipts to farmers and, generally, the attainment of parity for the wheat producer in the form of restoration of his 1910–1914 purchasing power. Not insignificantly, Harriman pointed as well to the need for an internalized market. The rise of nationalism had developed pressure for self-containment in Europe, and every nation evidently determined to raise its food supply and avoid dependence on imports. The United States had no choice but to accommodate to the situation. [9]

The Roosevelt Special entered Topeka at 9:30 A.M. on September 14, 1932. It was a full day, highlighted shortly after noon with the candidate's speech to thousands of farmers gathered around the state capitol building. In an hour and a quarter, his face red, sweating from the heat, the troubadour broached the principal features of his New Deal agricultural program. Roosevelt conceded that he possessed no sure cure for the agrarian's woes. But some determined effort needed to be made. "We have poverty, we have want in the midst of abundance." Millions of farmers toiled in "the shadow of peasantry," their children deprived of a decent education. Grim statistics revealed that some 6.5 million farm families, or 22 percent of the nation's population in 1920, received 15 percent of the national income, 9 percent in 1928, then only 7 percent in 1932. Another 50 to 60 million were affected indirectly. Agriculture must be restored through national planning, otherwise industry and our cities would continue to languish.

Long-range, an agricultural program required the planned use of land, elimination of marginal land from production and its conversion to tree crops, tax reduction, and the resettlement of displaced persons in small towns sustained by a decentralized industry. The need for immediate relief called for emergency measures, including the refinancing of farm mortgages at lowered rates of interest over an extended period of time. Federal credit for this purpose would be made available to private lending agencies.

Roosevelt promised an effort at the negotiation of barter agreements with individual nations based on the exchange of our farm surplus for their industrial goods. But, until the international marketplace could be restored, he observed, other means would be required to achieve the elusive tariff equivalent so long desired by the agrarian. Roosevelt envisaged a program containing several basic features, the essence really of the Wilson–Harriman proposals. It would need to afford the producers of certain staple crops (wheat, cotton, tobacco, and corn in the form of hogs *) the equivalent of the tariff benefit enjoyed by the manufacturing community in order to assure prices higher than production costs. Production controls would avoid stimulation of output. The plan should be self-financing, though Roosevelt purposefully avoided mention of Har-

---

* Corn-hog ratio figures represented an effort by hog producers to determine accurately their cost of production. Corn-hog ratio charts included items such as corn prices, cost of shipment, labor costs, etc.

riman's processing tax for income redistribution. It would shun dumping schemes that might invite Europe's retaliation. Dependence on existing agencies and on cooperative action and emphasis on decentralization was promised lest the plan weigh agriculture down with a stultifying bureaucracy. Finally, Roosevelt pointed up its voluntary character. "I like the idea that the plan should not be put into operation unless it has the support of a reasonable majority of the producers of the exportable commodity to which it is to apply." [10]

Topeka met M. L. Wilson's aspirations. He secured Roosevelt's imprimatur for his domestic allotment program without arousing the Eastern conservatives and the nation's business community. Typically, Walter Lippmann declaimed that no concrete scheme existed that met the specifications outlined at Topeka. True, Wilson learned that the grain millers comprehended the message. "Everyone here who knows of the allotment plan (and that now includes most of the grain men)," he heard from his allies, "immediately recognized FDR's speech in Topeka as a complete endorsement of the plan." However, most of the potential opposition remained in the dark into the interregnum, affording Wilson's National Domestic Allotment Committee sufficient opportunity to educate farmers and the farm leadership to the allotment program's purpose and possibilities. Producers could be organized by an educational effort. Group action, in the tradition of John R. Commons' institutionalist views, constituted an integral element of decision-making and enforcement. Central planning would follow. Domestic allotment, Wilson believed, would confirm the conviction of John Maynard Keynes and those liberal economists who subscribed to the view that laissez faire had come to an end. [11]

Rexford Tugwell was less sanguine, though generous in his acknowledgement of Wilson's contribution. "You—not I—deserve the credit," he declared. Content that something at last had been done for the farmer, Tugwell desired more. "I am not impatient," he claimed, "and I feel that things ought to grow gradually into national policies but I wish there were more prospect that a *real beginning with industry* would be made too. About that I am doubtful, even discouraged. Still something may happen—anyway we must work for it ceaselessly." The Commonwealth Club address, delivered on September 23, only partially met Tugwell's specifications.[12]

Herbert Hoover, in a rage, summoned Henry I. Harriman to the White House. Harriman's role in the creation of domestic allotment had been an open secret. (Various chambers of commerce, in fact, threatened to withdraw from the national organization headed by the New England utilities magnate because of his urging of a greater measure of planning in the economy.) Hoover, visibly perturbed, characterized the domestic allotment scheme as a challenge to our liberty. Harriman's scheduled fifteen-minute meeting with the nation's chief executive dragged out interminably, it seemed. "Mr. Harriman," the defender of the American System fumed, "What kind of *God* dam(n) wild idea is this that you are supporting in farm relief?" It was unconstitutional, Hoover raged. Harriman claimed otherwise. At the close of two hours neither had convinced the other of the merit of his position.[13]

The Republican standard-bearer attempted a public rebuttal of Roosevelt's farm proposals at Des Moines, Iowa, on October 4, in a foray intended to salvage his crumbling chances. The statement meandered from a moving reminiscence of his Iowa boyhood to a recapitulation of measures instituted on behalf of the rural sector during his custodianship. Hoover attributed the depression to external dislocations stemming from the Great War, all beyond his control, and offered the farmer succor through maintenance of the gold standard and a high tariff system. His agricultural position represented a replay of his earlier anti-interventionist struggle waged against Henry Cantwell Wallace. Now the gold standard joined the list of his traditionalist values. The Great Engineer abhorred interventionism to the end.[14]

THE NEW DEAL's agricultural priorities shaped its early economic diplomacy. Raymond Moley's account of the drafting of the Sioux

City tariff speech is often brought to bear as illustrative of Roosevelt's casual manner in effecting diplomatic decisions. But the discussion in *After Seven Years*, published in 1939, seems to have been motivated by Moley's adherence to Charles Beard's continentalism and his opposition to U.S. involvement in Europe's power conflicts. Explanation of the New Deal's economic diplomacy in the early thirties requires a more substantive replication of the tensions surrounding Roosevelt than is generally suggested in examinations of the Hull/Moley controversy or the squire's tendency toward evasion. Shifts did occur, responsive to the formulation of alternative economic interpretations of the depression's causation and the surest route out of the economic abyss.

Sooner or later, Franklin D. Roosevelt would have to resolve the question of priority for an internalized economy, pending a changed international climate, or attainment of recovery by means of international accords. The issue had been broached by the candidate in his first Albany address, in February 1932, when he took a nationalist stance, then by Cordell Hull when he thrust an internationalist party platform down Roosevelt's throat at Chicago. Apparently, Roosevelt conceded the matter in his second Albany address of July 30, 1932, with his commitment to a competitive tariff for revenue purposes only. Seemingly, Hull drove the lesson home in an exegesis on the Democratic party platform presented at Charlottesville, Virginia, on July 14, 1932.

Economic isolationism, which marked the Hoover era, keynoted by a high tariff environment, the Senator from Tennessee lectured, had wrought fearsome economic consequences for ourselves and the world. Hull could be emotional on the subject, to a point of near-religious conviction. The Hoover policy was "half insane," suicidal, absurd, the major factor in the breakdown of international confidence, credit, finance, exchange, and trade. It had destroyed our position as a major creditor and surplus-producing society, caused exports to decline, and resulted in massive unemployment. Business had become prostrate and agriculture impoverished.

Hull plumped for a policy reversal by the United States directed toward the opening up of channels of world trade through reciprocal tariff arrangements and tariffs for revenue only. More broadly, he envisaged a world economic order which would benefit us through absorption of our surplus. The depressed state of the nation's and the world's economy raised the terrifying specter of "war breeding commercial strife." No nation in history, Hull urged, had been more favorably equipped for "world leadership and domination, financially, industrially and commercially, as ours." The United States, he enjoined, "must gird itself for world trade conquest." The consequence, he sincerely believed, would be a world more tranquil, better fed and clothed, less prone toward warfare.[15]

Charged with orchestrating the economic thinking of the Brains Trust into a synthesis that would afford recovery, Raymond Moley gradually moved toward an opposing interpretation of causation and remedy, focusing on internal priorities. Moley was influenced in his thinking by Rexford Tugwell, by M. L. Wilson's analysis of agriculture's needs, and by Alexander Sachs, an economist who served as research director for the Lehman Corporation. Also, by the example of Britain's quest for economic independence through the Ottawa Agreements. As he came to the conclusion that "as to *necessities* we *are* self-contained," the political scientist abandoned his Wilsonian commitment as inappropriate and shifted to the notion of intranationalism, the giving of priority to economic recovery on a domestic basis. "The problem," Moley decided in the course of the campaign, "[is] starvation amid plenty. The solution is to get control of the two ends of the equation; but you can't if one end is abroad."[16]

The issue was bruited about privately and publicly in a fashion that typified Roosevelt's style as a politician. Scarcely willing or able to dump the Democratic internationalists, he courted Hull and Norman Davis during the campaign and encouraged their hopes for a renewed Wilsonian vision. Yet, the nation's agricultural needs and domestic recovery demanded priority, and Roosevelt resolved the dilemma by practical considerations. While he never completely closed out the hopes of the free traders, oriented toward a large role by the United States in world leadership (which he may well have shared), Roosevelt veered toward internal priorities.

The issue surfaced in the early stages of the Western tour. Two contradictory lines of approach emerged as appropriate to the New Deal, one pressed by Hull in collaboration with Charles William Taussig, president of the American Molasses Company of New York. The sugar and molasses importer entered the Brains Trust's periphery in a casual way just before the Chicago conclave. Upon meeting Roosevelt on a train headed north from New Orleans and Warm Springs, Taussig proffered his services to the candidate. When Roosevelt transmitted the request to Moley, the Brains Truster, harried by the awesome burdens he assumed, recruited Taussig as a go-between with Cordell Hull, whose views were solicited on a tariff speech.

At Moley's request, Hull and Taussig conferred in Nashville, Tennessee, on the eve of the Western tour. Upon Taussig's return to New York, then through much of the Western tour, he urged on his own behalf and Hull's two campaign commitments: attribution of the depression to the nation's high tariff policies, and a pledge of an immediate 10 percent reduction in the Smoot-Hawley Tariff. Prosperity, Taussig and Hull argued, would follow from the restoration of a world market for our surplus. The quintessential issue of the era, Hull declaimed, was nationalism (revenue tariffs) versus sectionalism (protectionism), a pre-Civil War, free trader's view of the complexities of the modern era.[17]

By this time a second broad line of analysis of the depression had opened up, that developed by the Brains Trust. It accorded priority to internal recovery, and the remedies which evolved required insulation from external pressures; and it relied, initially, on Kemper Simpson's tariff advice, an economist recommended by Senator Edward P. Costigan of Colorado. Simpson warned Moley of the danger of dependence on any [single] theory of what caused the depression. Economists themselves could not agree. Beyond this cautionary note, he ventured that Republican stewardship had intensified the downward spiral. Our problems originated with the worldwide collapse of commodity prices, which commenced in 1919, followed by international maladjustments in production and trade. As matters stood in 1932, the difficulty was not overproduction, so commonly believed, but instability of commodity prices. Once prices could be stabilized, increased consumption would resolve the problem of apparent overproduction. Though Simpson preferred a low tariff system, a high-tariff climate had evolved since the Great War, and he warned that Democrats who placed faith in international conferences for tariff reform would be disappointed.[18]

When Taussig returned to New York City from his conference with Hull, a low tariff speech draft in hand, the Western tour about to begin, the Brains Trusters balked. Unwilling to go along with a campaign commitment to tariffs for revenue only, General Hugh Johnson, now part of the Roosevelt entourage, drafted his own version of a tariff speech. The Smoot-Hawley tariff appeared vulnerable to political attack in Johnson's view, but the world's high tariff system constituted a formidable economic reality. There could be no assurance, Johnson inveighed, that reductions in our own tariff structure would have a favorable impact on world trade or yield us any measurable economic benefit. He cited the example of Great Britain, short of gold, deeply in debt to the United States, which created a protective system for the Empire in response to Smoot-Hawley. "We have our trade barriers. They have theirs." Unilateral sacrifice by the United States could not secure a reversal.

Johnson described Hull's proposed immediate cut in our tariffs by 10 percent as absurd. But there remained a basis for bargaining at the council table to reciprocal advantage. Negotiated tariff reduction on a step by step basis conducted in "good old Yankee trading fashion," reflected a condition, not a theory. "What is here proposed," Johnson stressed for Roosevelt's consumption, "is that we sit down with each great commercial nation separately and independently and negotiate with it alone . . . for the purpose of reopening the markets of these countries to our agricultural and industrial surpluses."[19]

As Roosevelt and Moley departed from Albany on September 13, the head of the Brains Trust put the dilemma to Lindsay Rogers, Smith's tariff adviser in the 1928 campaign. "Nothing," he confided, "with which we have been dealing has been subject to such wide differences of opinion and it will help clarify the atmosphere to get your impression." Rogers' reply confirmed Moley's fears, questioning the efficacy of the Hull–Taussig proposal and the wisdom of a 10 percent across the board tariff reduction.[20] Confirmation quickly arrived from two other sources, Senators Claude Swanson of Virginia and Edward P. Costigan of Colorado.

These powerful Senate Democrats—their views later reinforced by Thomas J. Walsh and Key Pittman, who even more vehemently rejected Hull's low tariff philosophy—favored "tariff by negotiation" as opposed to flat reductions or even reciprocity. When international conditions assumed some semblance of normalcy, Swanson reasoned, this nation could return to its historic most-favored-nation posture in tariff legislation. Costigan, a powerful Progressive ally of Robert La Follette Jr. advised equivocation. Dangerous times ahead would void all preconceptions, and firm commitment on a tariff policy would restrict the new administration to its disadvantage, especially in relation to agricultural requirements. Costigan, not Roosevelt, proposed to Moley that he weave the Hull–Taussig and Johnson speech drafts into a single statement that would leave wide room for future maneuver.[21] M. L. Wilson, in conference with Roosevelt and Moley at Butte, Montana, sealed the matter.

Roosevelt arrived at a clear decision after a conference with the apostle of domestic allotment on September 19, 1932. Moley was present. At the bottom of a typed page of remarks on the need for an international economic conference under our leadership, Moley noted: "America first!" At Seattle, on September 20, Roosevelt took an unequivocal stand. Although he condemned the consequences of Smoot-Hawley, Grundyism he dubbed the measure, since it induced other nations to retaliate, it explained the current situation. "To remedy that kind of fact," Roosevelt stated, "I have advocated and continue to advocate [a] high tariff policy, based on reason, on good old-fashioned horse sense."

"Horse-sense" and "Yankee trading" seemed less ominous, more delicate politically, than "America first." But they amounted to the same policy. Roosevelt pledged a tariff program based on profitable exchange for each nation, with benefit to each nation, but never at the expense of a "violent and general shake-up in business." As the head of the Brains Trust chortled in later years, he had woven Hull's free trade views right out of the 1932 campaign.

The tenor of Wilson's advice at Butte, repeated in a letter sent to Moley on September 21, served as the basis for Roosevelt's tariff speech delivered on his return from the West Coast, on September 29, at Sioux City, Iowa. "It is my judgment after sleeping on the two speeches," Wilson wrote Moley, one the Hull–Taussig statement, the other Hugh Johnson's, "that the 'tariff by negotiation' is by *all means* the speech which the Governor should make." Farmers had been traditionally Republican and high tariff in philosophy in the past decade, and Hoover would cater to protectionist sentiment in his own statement at Des Moines. Negotiated tariffs offered farmers assurance that protection would remain until markets could be reopened. [22]

Wilson did not urge an "America first" position, accepted by Moley and Roosevelt, without considerable sensitivity to the internationalist viewpoint. When in late September the Department of Agriculture economist, Mordecai Ezekiel, and the State Department's economic adviser, Herbert Feis, urged upon him endorsement of unilateral blanket tariff cuts by the United States, however, he demurred. Specifically, Feis wanted a 10 percent annual reduction in our tariffs for ten years until full free trade could be achieved. Wilson's rejoinder is instructive: agricultural recovery required priority, not free trade. Elsewhere in his correspondence he pointed to Europe's opting for self-sufficiency. Nor could the major European nations abandon such a course, thanks to powerful nationalist political and economic pressures. On a more optimistic note, Wilson hoped ultimately for the formation of an international wheat cartel with export quotas assigned to the United States, Canada, Argentina, and Australia. Export ratios, geared to world market demand, could be formulated on a basis of previous experience, as in any pooling arrangement. Internal controls abroad would emulate our own domestic allotment program. But he did not anticipate restoration of the world marketplace for a decade or more.[23]

Roosevelt's Sioux City address, billed as a major tariff speech, not insignificantly emerged as a confirmation of domestic agricultural priorities. Moley and Wilson, aided by Senators Thomas J. Walsh and Key Pittman, won the day. In no uncertain terms, at Santa Barbara, California, as Taussig prepared to present his and Hull's viewpoint, Walsh dismissed the molasses importer as an interested party, directly affected by tariff rates. Moley and the two powerful Democrats took the Johnson statement as the basis for a tariff policy. Indeed, though Grundyism was denounced, tariff reduction, Roosevelt promised, would impair no legitimate interest, and would be secured by Yankee horse-trading intended to open markets for our surplus. As the campaign closed Roosevelt beat a total retreat on the issue.[24]

Roosevelt's 1932 performance projected the New Deal's reluctance to go beyond advocacy of restoration of international comity as a desirable condition while giving precedence to domestic priorities. When Hoover demanded during the campaign that Roosevelt specify which tariffs appeared too high, the Democratic nominee backed off. Farmers and farm organizations also pressed for a concrete response. Toward the close of the campaign, in the urban East, Roosevelt pledged continued protection for the industrial sector. Then, on November 4, in a statement to the leadership of five major farm organizations, Roosevelt explained that he stood for a tariff policy that would protect the domestic marketplace for our own farmers.[25]

In the Moley/Hull struggle, of major import for the 1930s, the tariff question was the tip of an iceberg. Whatever the nature and dimension of Roosevelt's deep-seated Wilsonian view of the world, the realities of the post-Versailles years dictated a course shaped by nationalist priorities. Herbert Hoover, in an unguarded moment, outside the political arena, had explained the fundamental economics of the situation. In a statement delivered before the Indiana Republican Editorial Association, on June 5, 1931, Hoover debunked his own attribution of the nation's depression to international economic unsettlement. Our exports totaled some $5 billion per annum at the time or 10 percent of gross national product. The world disruption cut exports by $1.5 billion, about 3 percent of GNP, then some $50 billion, as opposed to an internal shrinkage of $12 billion. The key to recovery lay at home, a conclusion reached by the Brains Trust and by Roosevelt as the campaign closed.[26] Gradually they moved toward a view more sophisticated than simple economic nationalism, dubbed intranationalism.

INTRANATIONALISM, formulated for Moley and Roosevelt by Alexander Sachs, Ralph Robey, and William W. Cumberland, economists associated with the New York financial community, dismissed internationalist objectives as beyond achievement in the current climate. These included disarmament agreements, abolition of trade restrictions, attempts at international currency arrangements (stabilization) and coordinated central bank policy, adherence to the League of Nations or World Court, reparations and debts cancellation, and active support of world economic conferences. Intranationalism viewed as practicable the regulation of our own central bank policy with a view toward meeting domestic needs, aid to railroads, attainment of a better equilibrium between the farming and manufacturing sectors, and avoidance of new weapons of international economic warfare such as import quotas and still higher tariffs.

Broadly conceived, Roosevelt and the Brains Trust perceived restoration of a sound economy within the nation's borders as a prerequisite to efforts at international economic equilibrium. Initially, each nation must put its house in order by internal adjustment. International agreements might then become feasible. A reversal of priorities would not work. "We believed," Rexford Tugwell recalled, "recovery would only be possible in a nation shut off temporarily from the influences that would exploit every advance that was made—foreign influences. The debts, the handling of monetary problems, and tariffs, etc., were all involved. We could only carry out a relief and recovery program for our own benefit instead of others if we were thus isolated. We wanted recovery, we wanted a balanced economy, we wanted to institutionalize the balance and prevent future depressions. We had to shut off interference."

Intranationalists, including the Brains Trust, defined our problems as rooted in relationships between various groups and classes that had become skewed. It followed that internally balanced arrangements were required between agriculture and industry, producers and consumers, creditors and debtors, the availability of employment and the work force, wages and living costs, income and expenditures, meaning the balancing of the federal budget. There could be no return to prosperity, nationwide or worldwide, until the achievement of internal equilibrium by all major nations.[27]

ROOSEVELT URGED intranationalist concepts on several occasions in the 1932 campaign, as in his reaffirmation of the "concert of interests" in a broadcast to the Democratic party's Business and Professional Men's League, made from Albany on October 6. He opposed a return to the freewheeling prosperity of the 1920s, preferring instead the achievement of economic balance among productive processes and among all sections and economic units, including agriculture, industry, mining, commerce, and finance. When an imbalance developed, as in the drying up of purchasing power, government should step in. Business, he hoped, would prove capable of maintaining cooperation and stabilization without government interference. Agriculture required federal intervention. The "new deal," as he put it, "is plain English for a changed concept of the duty and responsibility of government toward economic life." [28]

Roosevelt also equated restoration of economic equilibrium with a greater measure of security for workers in the form of "old age, sickness, and unemployment insurance," pledged at Detroit on October 2, and reiterated at Albany on October 13. "Social justice through social action" symbolized his endorsement of progressive goals as opposed to "the jungle law of the survival of the so-called fittest." But estimates of unemployment ran as high as 12 millions in a civilian labor force of 49.5 million or very nearly 25 percent. What was to be done until a restored agricultural purchasing power could set the wheels of industry rolling? [29]

Interest in the problem of unemployment as an undesirable social accompaniment of cyclical downswings began with the depression of 1919–1921, when Senator William S. Kenyon of Iowa proposed federal public works programs which would contract and expand in response to employment levels. Presumably an impetus should have been provided by the conclusions of President Harding's Conference on Unemployment, headed by Commerce Secretary Hoover, which pointed to the need for collection of statistics on joblessness and for a planned program of public works as a counter-cyclical device. But nothing happened in the decade of Normalcy under Hoover's aegis at Commerce. And though he endorsed the concept as President-elect, in 1929, of a $3 billion reserve fund for public construction, once the depression set in he abandoned the notion as federal income declined. Instead, he resorted to expedition of self-liquidating or "productive" projects already on the drawing boards, opposed "nonproductive" spending, and remained adamant in his opposition to direct federal relief. Equating federal relief to individuals with the dole, he considered it a function of the state and local community.

During 1932, as unemployment jumped from 7 to nearly 12 millions, congressional public-works/relief advocates, led by

Senators Wagner, La Follette, Costigan, Cutting, and Norris, secured passage of the Emergency Relief and Construction Act, which appropriated $2.3 billion for public works and $300 million through RFC to the states for relief projects. But Hoover won the issue in a bitter contest with the Congress. Public works expenditures were subject to availability of funds in the Treasury Department and states required to demonstrate exhaustion of their own resources. It is doubtful that Hoover, in any event, would have spent the money.

Although Roosevelt as governor of New York criticized the inadequacy of federal efforts in resolving the unemployment crisis, the squire gave little evidence of following different practices. His principal accomplishment was limited to securing a paltry $20 million from the state legislature for the Temporary Emergency Relief Administration despite the fiscal solvency of the Empire State. His 1932 campaign utterances, principally the Pittsburgh Address of October 19, condemned the incumbent president as a spendthrift and pledged economies at the federal level. Much like Hoover, in speeches Roosevelt delivered at Detroit and Albany, the Democratic nominee stressed that the initial burden for relief and public employment belonged to localities and the states. Both candidates, at least in principle, advocated budget balance.

In the last analysis, Hoover and Roosevelt differed on the public-works/relief issue and the balanced budget, as in so many others, not in principle but in the squire's willingness to jettison received dogma when reality dictated its abandonment. Hoover refused to alter his fundamental position, as revealed to an intimate during his contest with the 72d Congress on relief legislation, for fear that direct federal relief to the people would lead to "socialism and collectivism with its destruction of human liberty." Roosevelt had no such ideological fears. As he explained at Pittsburgh, he intended to introduce economies in order to achieve budget balance, but he left an important loophole: "If starvation or dire need on the part of any of our citizens make necessary the appropriation of additional funds which would keep the budget out of balance, I shall not hesitate to tell the American people the full truth and ask them to authorize the expenditure of that additional amount." True, Roosevelt and the Brains Trust had rejected inflationist-monetarist solutions and equated the balanced budget with equilibrium. Yet, they were keenly aware, as Moley's May memorandum indicated, of the escape hatch afforded by an emergency budget.[30]

Anne O'Hare McCormick's interview with Roosevelt, published in the *New York Times,* captured the man and his views perfectly. "Until unemployment is cured, we're sick, and will get sicker. Unemployment insurance is necessary," the squire explained, "but it's the second step, not the first. It cannot meet the present emergency. I believe we could spend $2,000,000,000 in construction work, partly self-liquidating, without bankrupting the country. . . . But that's not enough either. Unemployment was increasing long before the depression. It's inevitable when half the population had lost its purchasing power." The first step, Roosevelt claimed, in securing a healthy industrial civilization was restoration of the purchasing power of the farm. "That's the fellow you've got to start building up, the farmer." [31] The governor's views seemed reminiscent in a deeply philosophical way of Jefferson's idealization of the rural sector and Bryan's effort to salvage the rural dream from domination by the increasingly urban East.

At Portland, Oregon, on September 21, then a week later at Mc-Cook, Nebraska, Franklin D. Roosevelt made further promises to the nation's rural population and common political cause with George W. Norris and the public power progressives. Much of the remnant of the Progressive movement identified with the cause of public development of the nation's waterpower resources and stricter regulation of private utilities. Some, gas and waterworks socialists, aspired to government ownership of transmission lines and ultimately community ownership of utilities on a local or even regional basis. In December 1930, as Roosevelt's public power policies clarified at the state level, Norris rejected an appeal by John Dewey, who chaired the League for Independent Political Action, to head a third party movement. Hoover, Norris believed, represented the "money trust" and the "power trust." Roosevelt, he became convinced, would sign legislation for federal development of Muscle Shoals. In May 1932, he declared his support for the New York governor if he were the nominee of his party. [32]

Yet, even following Roosevelt's nomination, Norris, Judson King, who headed the National Popular Government League, and others of the public power advocates retained some nagging doubts. Many of the Progressives, Norris confided to Basil Manly, desired to know where Roosevelt stood on the Muscle Shoals question. Private assurances would no longer suffice. "I have received many inquiries from Progressives who do not want to support Hoover and who would be glad to support Roosevelt if they were satisfied he was alright on the power question. They ask me the concrete question as to what Roosevelt would have done with the Muscle Shoals bill which Hoover vetoed." [33] Roosevelt cleared the air, initially, at a conference with Judson King, Norris' ally since the postwar years when Republican administrations attempted to convey the Muscle Shoals complex to private ownership. King reported to Norris:

> I said in effect that if you [Roosevelt] were elected President we would expect as a *minimum* that you would sign the Norris Muscle Shoals Bill and that means transmission lines and all;
> 2nd: That you would appoint a real commission to enforce the Federal Power Act;
> 3rd: Same for the Federal Trade Commission. . . .
> 4th: That you would fight for a genuine Act regulating interstate transmission holding companies and that you certainly would not be the chief mouthpiece to the Power Trust. How's that?
> He followed me closely, intelligently, and said: "Bully, that's fine."

Roosevelt and King expanded on public power development at Muscle Shoals. Initially, Roosevelt argued, it might be desirable to sell some power to private companies for resale. But he could insist on the same terms he had proposed for transmission in New York, a reasonable profit of about 7 percent on actual cash invested in transmission facilities. Preference, however, would be given to farm districts and cities which desired public ownership. When King inquired if three-cent electricity would be the goal, Roosevelt concurred, expressing the hope that it might even cost less. "Outside yourself," King reported to Norris, "I have never met an official in public life that has a firmer grasp upon the technical requirements of the electrical fight." [34]

At Portland, Roosevelt insisted upon enforcement of the common-law principle that privately owned utilities, vested with a public character, be held accountable to government for quality of service and reasonableness of rate structure. Public utility commissions had fallen short of their responsibilities. Too often those intended to be regulated dominated the regulators. Citing the example of the New York State Public Service Commission, which had become a referee between complainants and companies, he lectured that such agencies should serve the public interest in securing rate relief and better service. Rates were excessive nationwide, utilities collecting some $4 billion in 1931, or $133 for each family. Conceding that he had been attacked as a radical for such views, the candidate challenged: "If that be treason, my friends, then make the most of it!"

Moving squarely into the Norris camp, Roosevelt proposed full publicity for all capital issues, regulation and control of holding companies by the Federal Power Commission, and abolition by law of the reproduction cost theory of rate making, which led to excessive charges, and substitution of the actual money or prudent investment principle. While he did not favor government ownership of all utilities, preferring regulation to federal operation, he did believe, he told his audience, in the right of a community (a city, county, or utility district) to provide public service. Its rates and quality of service could function as a valuable "birch rod" in the cupboard. Then, in relation to the Muscle Shoals controversy, which had raged for over a decade, Roosevelt endorsed federally owned power site development. "The natural hydroelectric power resources belonging to the people of the United States, or the several States," he pledged, "shall remain forever in their possession."

Private capital, he believed, should be given the initial chance to transmit and distribute such power at the lowest rates commensurate with quality service and a reasonable profit. Again, invoking the "birch rod" principle, he threatened federal and state transmission where private service proved unsatisfactory.

Finally, in the Portland address, Roosevelt went beyond Norris' aspirations to proclaim a dream which foundered later on conservative resistance to the New Deal. He desired public development of the St. Lawrence power site, Muscle Shoals, Boulder Dam, and the Columbia River, as a "national yardstick to prevent extortion against the public." In his peroration, the expert campaigner taunted the fallen utilities magnates: "Judge me by the enemies I have made. Judge me by the selfish purposes of these utility leaders who have talked of radicalism while they were selling watered stock to the public." [35]

The Portland address appeared satisfactory on every count "except as to transmission lines," Norris informed Judson King, meaning Roosevelt's preference for giving corporations the initial opportunity to construct transmission facilities and to contract for reasonable rates and quality service, a policy followed during the governorship period. [36] But Norris felt assured that Roosevelt would sign the Muscle Shoals bill, which Hoover had vetoed. Accordingly, the Nebraska Republican awarded the Democratic nominee his coveted embrace at McCook, where he resided, on September 28, 1932, urging others of his party to forego traditional loyalties. "I stated in my remarks introducing Governor Roosevelt here," Norris recalled to King, "that I did not agree with him on power one hundred per cent, but that his position on public utilities was the most advanced, the most logical, and the most progressive that had ever been taken by any candidate for President at any time. Altho it was not in the advance copy which I gave to the press, I stated in that speech . . . that I had no doubt whatever that the election of Roosevelt meant a victory for Muscle Shoals."

Moley, inspired by a brief visit to the Senator's modest home and by the humanity and simplicity of the man, drafted a fitting

reply for the Democratic party's standard-bearer, characterizing
Norris as "the very perfect, gentle knight of American progressive
ideals," from Chaucer's Prologue to the *Canterbury Tales*. Roosevelt, touched by the scene—more than 20,000 persons crowded
the Red Willow County fairgrounds as twilight fell—gestured toward the giant of the Progressive movement, "Our cause is common, I welcome your support. I honor myself in honoring you."
Then:

> History asks: "Did the man have integrity?"
> "Did the man have unselfishness?"
> "Did the man have courage?"
> "Did the man have consistency?"
> And if the individual under the scrutiny of the historic microscope
> measured up to an affirmative answer to these questions, then history
> has set him down as great indeed in the pages of all the years to
> come. [37]

Roosevelt's stand on power, Judson King observed in *The New
Republic*, was one of the principal factors responsible for his nomination at Chicago in July. TVA, the child of the gentle knight from
Nebraska, George W. Norris, became one of the major symbols of
the humanitarianism of the New Deal.

ROOSEVELT'S AGRICULTURE SPEECH at Topeka and his statement
on industry before San Francisco's Commonwealth Club, on September 23, 1932, portended the interventionist state and the limitations he would impose on it. Agriculture, judged unable to fend
for itself because of the existence of millions of small units, evidently required direct government intervention to facilitate production controls and income redistribution. Industrial concentration enabled planning in that sector without direct intervention;
but business irresponsibility in the previous decade, if continued,
presaged a new measure of social control.

The Commonwealth Club speech proclaimed broad purposes
and eschewed definitive solutions. Its economic observations

proved insightful in the notation that frontier individualism was a thing of the past, supplanted in the twentieth century by concentration and control of 50 percent of our industry by some 200 aggregates and a small group of individuals. Yet, Roosevelt avoided imposition of potentially rigid, restricting features of overhead management favored by Tugwell in his July memorandum, further developed in his *The Industrial Discipline and the Governmental Arts* (1933). The tendency of the historical literature is to misinterpret the underlying factors in the Commonwealth compromise. The "squire thesis" leads to the suggestion that Roosevelt likely did not understand what he had read. Discussions between Roosevelt and the Brains Trust regarding Berle's conclusions, followed by telegrams between Roosevelt and Moley (on the campaign tour) and Berle (in New York), led to a satisfactory middle ground on government-business relations.

Berle's basic premises are scarcely contradicted in Tugwell's *The Industrial Discipline*. They differed, fundamentally, as they would in later years in their evaluation of the New Deal's aims and achievements, in their judgment of the desirability of instituting specific measures and mechanisms of social control. Berle favored organic development. Tugwell pressed for immediate imposition of overhead or statist devices. Berle placed considerable faith in the modern corporation's capacity to accept the discipline of societal responsibility. Tugwell proved pessimistic in the matter. He wanted experimentation before it became too late, though in his own metaphor, he did not want to blow up the railroad station and forego rail service while building a new structure.

Both Tugwell and Berle agreed that government should intervene to afford a measure of security and access to employment. Both rejected the dogma, as Tugwell put it, "that government should take over completely all economic functions." But Tugwell regarded regulation as unworkable. He preferred a national plan for equilibrium, surveys which would measure demand for goods and services, the rearrangement of industry to suit the plan, supervision of the flow of capital, control of prices, protection of certain vital interests. In his judgment, the farmer, the worker, and the consumer were disadvantaged in the marketplace in relation to the large economic unit. These functions, Tugwell insisted, should be assigned to a National Economic Council or an Industrial Integration Board with planning, integrative, and stabilizing responsibilities.

Berle's refusal to go the whole way with Tugwell is perhaps best understood by brief examination of a memorandum he prepared in 1938 representing a summary of his views for Jerome Frank and Thurman Arnold, about to launch the Temporary National Economic Committee investigations. Berle scoffed at the notion that small economic scale could be equated with competition. The nineteenth-century village store, the blacksmith, and the grist mill were monopolies by dint of isolation. Until the transportation revolution and the emergence of large-scale economic enterprise no genuine competition existed. The concept of nineteenth-century price competition constituted an exercise in nostalgia. Where it did exist, in the major commercial centers, it bred sweatshops. The principal advantage of small business as the functioning unit in small isolated communities was the locality's capacity to bring to bear public opinion for the general advantage. By extension, Berle applied the principle to the twentieth-century aggregate and the central government.

Convincingly, Berle dismissed as sterile the conviction of those who followed Brandeisian views that past a certain size, large-scale operations became inefficient. No one knew optimum size or could know it. It was based on market conditions, methods, and technology and became subject to overnight change in the event of new innovations. The most efficient economic unit imaginable, because it allowed worthwhile endeavor to all ages and talents, had been the much disparaged family farm. The genuine issue was the potential for large-scale enterprise to "outrun the moral and mental stature of man or men who run it." Vital to an understanding of Commonwealth, then the New Deal's abortive venture into NIRA, and its abandonment, was Berle's rejection of any standard approach or preconception. It explains, further, Berle's and Roosevelt's rejection of Tugwell's rigidly structured proposals in 1932.

While Berle conceded that large-scale industry stimulated want for goods and services, it appeared equally true that studies by Stuart Chase of society's wastefulness, popular at the time, presumed the impartiality of the commentator. Who, indeed, should stimulate or dictate want? The advertiser? The idealist? The planner? The matter, Berle insisted, defied clear resolution. But one thing seemed evident. Dictation of want by federal mechanisms constituted "tyranny pure and simple." In the thirties, as Ellis W. Hawley concluded, the New Deal's approach to the problem remained one of studied ambivalence. Quite consciously, Roosevelt and Berle preferred the evolution, organically, of mechanisms suited to the situation at hand. Commonwealth is understood in this context.

The Commonwealth Club speech, in one vital respect, went beyond Berle's *The Modern Corporation and Private Property* in its appraisal of government's role in the enforcement of corporate responsibility. Moley sensed the chance for an historic declaration which would expand the definition afforded the social contract by Jefferson's generation. The Declaration of Independence had imposed limitations on the excesses of government. Now, it seemed, grave danger emerged from excessive concentration of private economic power. "New conditions," Moley wrote, "impose new requirements upon government and those who conduct government. . . . I feel that we are coming to a view through the drift in the last quarter century that private economic power is (to enlarge an old phrase, [added in FDR's hand]) a public trust as well. . . . The power of the people," Moley concluded, "is always a reserve power." The principle seemed as applicable to the twentieth-century corporation as to the eighteenth-century state.

Speaking before a large business audience at San Francisco's Palace Hotel, Roosevelt proclaimed that the day of enlightened administration had arrived. He did not wish the dissolution of powerful private aggregates. He preferred, instead, the counterpoise of

government. Together the two should forge a new "economic declaration of rights, an economic constitutional order," consisting of a
better economic balance, better distribution of purchasing power,
restoration of wages, the end of unemployment, and a return to agricultural prosperity.

In their quest for a broadened interpretation of the social contract, Roosevelt and Moley reached back to their initial collaboration. Public office, they insisted in the dismissal of Sheriff Tom
Farley months before, constituted a public trust. Now, they explained, private power was equally a public trust. "I hold," Moley
added to the Berle speech draft for Roosevelt's utterance, "that
continued employment of that power by any individual or group
must depend upon the fulfillment of that trust." Private advantage
must give way, where required, to public advantage. Hopefully,
the Democratic candidate moderated, business would put its own
house in order. But should it use its collective power contrary to
the nation's requirements, government would intervene for protection of the public interest. [38]

The Commonwealth speech fell on a receptive society. Walton
H. Hamilton of the Yale Law School, later a member of the National Recovery Administration, observed in *The Nation* that our
antitrust legislation reflected the wisdom and needs of an earlier
generation. The new industrialism, he believed, dictated an economy of scale. Even Supreme Court Justice Louis D. Brandeis,
Hamilton noted, conceded in 1932, in a dissenting opinion, that
many persons attributed the depression to unbridled competition.
Traditionally, Americans distrusted size. The task, it seemed, was
not dissolution of the industrial system but an effort at social control. No panacea, he conceded, as did Berle and Roosevelt, existed. No single approach or set of solutions would suffice. Producers
of luxuries could be left to the market. Necessities, such as transportation or electric power, required stringent overhead management. The coal and steel industries, already highly integrated,
could well organize from within, subject to a system of public accountability.

Public control seemed inviting to industry, caught in the vise of depression, as well as to academe. As Max F. Burger of the Congress of Industries pointed out to Roosevelt, unfair methods of competition had run rampant and proven ruinous. He had heard much of the "Forgotten Man." Five hundred thousand independent business units required inclusion in the concept. The way was paved for NIRA. [39]

HERBERT HOOVER'S VIEWS, firmly anchored in the American ethos, could not be totally submerged by the Age of Roosevelt. The immediate crisis ended, the spirit of normalcy, defined so accurately in *American Individualism*, reemerged. But in the early 1930s, especially the Hundred Days, the Roosevelt leadership incorporated the formulations of his Brains Trust into our society's political and economic fabric. To his credit, Franklin D. Roosevelt accomplished what he believed feasible, discarded what did not work, rejected dogma, left to a later generation the fulfillment of its own destiny. FDR intended to adjust the outmoded American System of private initiative to modern conditions, not to destroy it. Hoover's doctrinaire blindness prevented him from conceding that the New Deal's shift in economic approaches and governmental responsibilities merely tried to restore the nation's prosperity that had fallen victim to evidently outdated and socially insensitive policies. Fearful that the Roosevelt–Brains Trust proposals of the 1932 campaign would subvert the American System, the Republican President attempted to forge an alliance with conservative internationalists of both parties to check the New Deal at its inception.

14

The Effort To Abort the New Deal

THE NEW DEAL proposed by Franklin D. Roosevelt in the 1932 campaign, based on the program prepared by the Brains Trust, Raymond Moley, Rexford Guy Tugwell, and Adolf A. Berle Jr., gave precedence to domestic reforms, reflation, and recovery as opposed to international economic action. In their estimate, recovery would be possible only in a nation shut off temporarily from the foreign influences that might exploit every advance made on the domestic scene. Specific measures designed to accomplish recovery included aid to agriculture in the form of the domestic allotment principle, correction of price and income disparities in the economy, federal regulation of securities and exchange practices, banks, and public utility holding companies, a public works program, a limited degree of industrial planning, a system of employment exchanges, unemployment insurance, relief measures, aid to the railroads, a balanced budget, and utilization of the "yardstick principle" for regulation of utility rates.

It was a program whose central theme, "intranationalism," precluded at least for a time international economic cooperation in certain areas. Elimination of abuses in the American economic system might well be accomplished without reference to external affairs. But establishment of a structured economy with an artificially induced rise in price levels, especially of farm products, and therefore a drop in the purchasing power of the dollar, required for a time insulation of the American economy from the vicissitudes of the world market. "We wanted recovery, we wanted a balanced economy, we wanted to institutionalize the balance and prevent future depressions. We had to shut off interference." [1]

Intranationalism, with its domestic emphasis, had a political appeal as well. It was a program certain to please the Western progressives, Republicans as well as Democrats, who had supported Roosevelt in the campaign and whose continued support would be essential in Congress. And it seemed to have been sanctioned by an electorate in the November election which was by and large ill disposed toward the European powers.

Yet the winter of 1932–33 saw a fierce contest behind the scenes between those who tried to reshape the President-elect's thinking and those who struggled to keep him on the road marked out during the campaign. It was not so much a struggle between Hoover and Roosevelt as between two sets of advisers, Moley and Tugwell on the one side and Norman Davis and Henry L. Stimson on the other. Nor was it mere competition for the favors of a man who had been chosen for the presidency. Rather it was a contest between the advocates of alternative paths to recovery, the one stressing domestic remedies for economic ills as the first need and the other giving priority to international agreement on such questions as monetary stabilization, restoration of the gold standard, reparations, debts, tariffs, and disarmament. At stake was the course of the New Deal.

AT FIRST GLANCE, the aspirations of the international-conservatives in the closing months of the Hoover administration seemed reasonable enough. Disarmament, monetary and trade agreements, and attainment of relief from the reparations–debts millstone bore the stamp of rationality in a world increasingly bent on warfare. For a moment the results of the Lausanne Conference of June–July 1932 offered a ray of sunshine through dark clouds, albeit ominously the moderate Brüning government had given way to that of the crafty Franz von Papen and the Nazis emerged as the Reich's third largest party. The major source of frustration for Secretary of State Henry L. Stimson and Norman Davis, this nation's principal diplomatic representative in Europe, emanated from the Hoover–Mills tendency toward nationalistic poses, their principal hope that the Democratic nominee would favor a major role for the United States in effecting a general European rapprochement.

Hoover's diplomacy in the closing months of his presidency reflected purely domestic political considerations. The Lausanne (reparations) and Geneva Disarmament Conferences of the early summer, 1932, were separated by sufficient Swiss real estate to convey the fiction that the United States remained uninvolved with the reparations issue. When it became bruited about in the early stages of the Lausanne discussions that a secret arrangement had been made for a reparations–debt quid pro quo, Secretary Stimson, upon Hoover's insistence, issued the customary denial of any connection between the two.[2] Yet, the previous autumn Hoover had encouraged the origination of such an arrangement. The Republican President's hostility toward what came to be known as the "gentlemen's agreement" of July 8, 1932, rested on his intention to effect his own up-dated version of a quid pro quo. On June 22, he had proposed to the Geneva group a wide-ranging disarmament agreement in the hope that its acceptance would make a debts accord more palatable to the American public. It might well have proven, in his estimate, a campaign coup.[3]

Great Britain's Prime Minister J. Ramsay MacDonald let it be known that his own domestic problems dictated a prompt reparations settlement. (Disarmament, he felt, would follow.) The Chancellor of the Exchequer, Neville Chamberlain, told a Cabinet meeting that he could not raise the war debt payment of 40 million pounds due the United States in December. "In order to avoid the onerous position of a separate default," Chamberlain argued (MacDonald was hospitalized at the time), Great Britain "should form a united front with the other debtors to deal with this problem as a whole." MacDonald explained to Hugh Gibson, who represented the United States at Geneva, that he disagreed with Chamberlain's position, but the British Foreign Secretary, Sir John Simon, "without authority . . . committed himself to the French to join in the formation of a united front." As the Prime Minister related the situation, he had learned of Simon's agreement with the French upon leaving a nursing home. "If you want," MacDonald later apologized to Norman Davis, "you can tell Stimson I am sitting out on a rock and I haven't got any clothes on right now." [4]

After considerable haggling Great Britain and France reached an accord on July 8, reducing Germany's Young Plan payments by 90 percent to some $700 million. Reparations reduction became conditioned, however, on the "gentlemen's agreement," an informal decision by Germany's creditors to act jointly in wringing a proportionate concession on war debts from the United States. Actually the Lausanne agreements were neither ratified nor executed by the participants, and Great Britain made a final, token payment to the United States in December 1932. France "deferred" her debt payment and subsequently defaulted. [5]

Perennial optimists, Norman Davis and J. Ramsay MacDonald peered into the future. Now, the Prime Minister informed our chief negotiator at Geneva, "We may really do something remarkably for the people of the world." If Davis would only come to London "we will sit down and reach an agreement on the navy!" Davis, ever the proponent of the "Geneva spirit," promised his superiors in Washington that the demise of reparations heralded a new era of interdependence among nations. "They have got to have political appeasement . . . and it is going to work out here." [6]

Hoover initially weighed the end of reparations as a campaign advantage. Although he instructed the Undersecretary of State, William R. Castle, to issue the usual denial of any change in his attitude toward the war debts, he commended the Lausanne agreement as a great step forward in the stabilization of Europe's economy. But Hoover became infuriated when news leaked of the "gentlemen's agreement." Hoover and Stimson conferred. The President argued for a public disavowal, the Secretary that the Lausanne settlement offered some promise of a price recovery.

Hoover lectured the Secretary that they differed in fundamentals.
The debts ought to be paid, he claimed, and "the European nations were all in an iniquitous combine against us." Stimson countered that perhaps he ought not to be Hoover's adviser, likely a
conscious recognition that Ogden Mills predominated in foreign as
well as domestic affairs. The antagonists calmed and Stimson departed convinced that the President would not issue a hostile public statement. [7]

When news arrived in Washington that Neville Chamberlain
claimed in Commons on July 11 that U.S. representatives knew in
advance the substance of the reparations agreement, Hoover could
no longer be contained. To Stimson's dismay:

> He wanted to make some statement himself or myself, but I man-
> aged to cool him down and persuade him not to interfere with the
> good work of the reparations settlement. But he is taking a very dras-
> tic and radical view now, which I find more and more difficult to
> square myself with, and I have had several talks in which I find
> myself very far apart from him and have told him so. Today he said
> that he and I were not on common ground, and I agreed with him
> and said that if he remained on that ground, it would be very difficult
> for me to continue to give him advice. He looks upon everybody with
> suspicion in the foreign field and in domestic politics they are all
> reptiles. He regards the other nations as having conspired against us
> in this Lausanne agreement instead of the fact being, as I know it
> was, that MacDonald has made a most gallant fight to do what he
> thought we wanted done. [8]

In an effort to soften Hoover's hostility toward Britain and
France—Stimson observed privately that MacDonald had every
reason to believe he had followed a course encouraged by the
Hoover administration—the Secretary pursued two lines of communication. One led to Edward M. House, at the Colonel's instance, in an effort to take the question of debts and reparations out
of the campaign through an agreement with Roosevelt. But Hoover
saw difficulties in the scheme and it got nowhere. Stimson then
decided on a similar appeal to Treasury Secretary Mills, now proposing instead a unilateral statement removing the issue from poli-

tics. It would be a great stroke for the world, the Secretary of State pleaded, and would benefit Hoover as well. Mills demurred.

Stimson's pleas culminated in a compromise. Originally Hoover and Mills contemplated a tough declaration that we would not be pressured by our debtors into any line of action inimical to our will. They relented in the form of a letter dispatched by the President on July 14 to Senator William E. Borah of Idaho, Chairman of the Foreign Relations Committee. It expressed gratification with the Lausanne settlement, but insisted that we would not be forced into any action by the "gentlemen's agreement." Nine days later the isolationist senator, scarcely known for his affection for our debtors, suggested in a major address the possibility of revision or cancellation of Europe's debts to the United States. For the Secretary of State, at least until the interregnum, the matter seemed closed with his observations to Hoover and Mills that Hoover's July 14 letter was unfair to MacDonald, who had accomplished a "magnificent piece of work" at Lausanne. Borah's radio address, he pointedly told Mills, represented a step in the right direction.[9]

In his formal acceptance of the Republican nomination, on August 11, Hoover had offered a compromise aimed especially at Great Britain in the form of purchase of some of our surplus agricultural output in lieu of the forthcoming debt payment. It was categorically rejected. When Roosevelt made a similar offer during the interregnum, the British Foreign Office scoffed at it as a repetition of Hoover's "harebrained scheme for obtaining debt payments *from us* by selling *to us* surplus American commodities—a scheme which . . . is clearly complete and absolute nonsense. . . . Do the United States administration think it possible that we should be ready to jettison the whole Ottawa settlement within six months or a year of its conclusion?" The question seemed obviously rhetorical.[10]

For the internationalists early hopes turned to despair as aspirations for debts reduction, other than in the form of repudiation by our debtors, and for disarmament evaporated. The U.S. position that debts and reparations had been legally separated at their inception, while technically correct, proved economically and psychologically unrealistic. Since the Balfour note of 1922, a position reasserted by MacDonald in late 1931, Great Britain had conditioned debts payments to us on her reparations receipts, and France had long since joined her wartime ally in similar argumentation. The Young Plan agreements of 1929, the work of American financiers, accorded de facto recognition to the Allied contention by matching German payments with those made to us. When Franz von Papen and General Kurt von Schleicher succeeded Brüning to Weimar's chancellorship, in the last game of musical chairs played in Germany before the advent of Hitler, each anxious to outdo the other in their nationalism and their courtship of the Right, they made it clear that they regarded reparations a dead issue. The debts appeared equally doomed except as a glimmer in Hoover's and Mills' aspirations to balance the national budget.

Disarmament, too, seemed a losing battle. The Geneva Conference reached an impasse in July when Edouard Herriot described the Hoover disarmament proposal, an oblique form of according Germany arms parity with the other major nations, as unacceptable unless accompanied by Anglo-American guarantees against aggression. At the same time, General von Schleicher asserted, in violation of the Versailles agreements, that the Reich would settle for nothing less than arms equality. Actually, British military experts believed, Germany, through an assortment of subterfuges, including weapons research, the creation of prototypes, and outright violations, had very nearly reached its goal. Economic autarchy accompanied military resurgence.

Whatever the merit of parchment guarantees, Stimson, a believer, pressed Hoover for a consultative pact with France, one that would take cognizance of an aggressive act and require consultation by the signatories without prejudicing our decision in advance. Hoover rejected the proposal, Jay P. Moffat of the State Department, a career officer, concluded, on entirely political grounds. Perhaps, the President suggested to Stimson, he could have joined in such a proposal with the Democratic candidate if

Newton D. Baker had been the nominee, but never with Roosevelt. His contempt for the squire of Hyde Park was too complete to entertain such a notion.

Although willing, Hoover explained in his August acceptance speech, to consult with other nations in times of emergency to promote world peace, he opposed agreements committing the United States to any future course of action "or which call for the use of force to promote peace." Herriot's warning in September, that German Minister of Defense General von Schleicher openly boasted at military maneuvers in East Prussia that Germany was in the process of rearming, went unheeded. Ruefully, for his own benefit, Norman Davis prepared a detailed memorandum that noted the Reich's growing preparation for another war. "I can smell blood. The issue this time is: Democracy against Militarism. . . . The duty of democrats of all nations is to unite in a demand that German militarism shall be curbed before it is too late." The best that could be achieved at Geneva, on December 10, 1932, was an agreement by the former wartime Allies, including the United States, with Germany which recognized the validity of the Reich's claim to equal military rights, restrained vaguely by "a system which would provide security for all nations." [11]

Gradually, as realistic aspirations for accords in other areas evaporated, internationalists pinned their hopes on Anglo-American economic cooperation. Presumably with the stimulation of recovery through international agreements, a new climate of cooperation would engender a changed attitude toward the flagging disarmament discussions. These aspirations, part and parcel of the origins of the World Monetary and Economic Conference of 1933, legitimate as they may have appeared on the surface, threatened the goals outlined by the Brains Trust for domestic recovery and reform. As Rexford Guy Tugwell explained, years later:

> The fact was we had deeper reasons and convictions we were fighting for. We believed recovery would only be possible in a nation shut off temporarily from the influences that would exploit every advance that was made—foreign influences. The debts, the handling of mone-

tary problems, and tariffs, etc., were all involved. We could only
carry out a relief and recovery program for our own benefit instead of
others if we were thus isolated.[12]

ALTHOUGH THE NOTION of a world monetary and economic conference had been aired by J. Ramsay MacDonald in 1931, Hoover
and Mills displayed little interest until May 1932. Perhaps Hoover
believed the moment had arrived to press Britain's return to gold,
part of the Hoover–Mills program for international economic recovery.[13] One can only surmise, for the President gave Henry L.
Stimson no explanation of his interest on May 20, 1932, when he
broached the MacDonald proposal for the lessening of economic
tensions in the international arena. The President simply stipulated
that there should be no discussion of tariff rates or debts and that
silver be considered as an agenda item. When Stimson explored
the possiblility of an international conference on money, tariffs, and
other economic questions with his principal economic adviser,
Herbert Feis balked. He could not make bricks without straw.
Stimson persisted. He required a report for the President. On May
24, Stimson telephoned MacDonald. Was the Prime Minister still
interested in the proposal he had made earlier? "The President
thinks that it might have a good psychological effect." [14]
    Following a preliminary exchange of views between the two gov-
ernments, the conference was scheduled for the close of the year.
Significantly, Mills rather than Stimson dominated the picture.
Mills's selection of Treasury advisers, among them the principal
New York bankers and Chicago banker, Melvin Traylor, indicated
his determination that the outgoing administration should secure
its interpretation of the causes and cure of the depression. The appointment in October of Professor John H. Williams of Harvard's
Graduate School of Business Administration, an occasional Treasury adviser, and Edmund E. Day of the Rockefeller Foundation
as U.S. representatives on the Preparatory Committee seemed to
wrap up the situation. The squire of Hyde Park and his academic

coterie could now be pointed in the right direction, toward budget balance, monetary stabilization, and preservation of the gold standard as priorities. [15]

At this juncture Norman Davis projected himself into the picture in a quest to enlarge the scope of his operations beyond Geneva and to present himself as a bridge between the Hoover and Roosevelt administrations. An intimate of Wall Street's principal financiers, he sensed the import of the planned monetary conference and insisted in a lengthy telephone conversation with Stimson that his presence as U.S. representative on the Organizing Committee (Day and Williams would become his subordinates) was desired by Britain's Foreign Secretary. [16] Stimson yielded. The silver-haired Democrat, however, had more on his mind. When he visited with State Department career diplomat Jay Pierrepont Moffat in September, Moffat grasped the larger picture. "He hopes now," the Department's Western European specialist noted, ". . . as soon as the Organizing Committee is over, to start in his naval talks with the British and French. . . . I gained the impression that he hoped to widen the scope of his soundings even further than disarmament,—possibly even in the direction of debts or Manchuria. This would assimilate him to Colonel House." Correctly, Moffat guessed that Davis aspired to become Franklin D. Roosevelt's Secretary of State. [17]

Following the defeat of Newton D. Baker at Chicago, Davis, with the encouragement of Walter Lippmann, carried the conservative-internationalist gospel to Roosevelt. A lengthy memorandum stressed the desirability of a low tariff policy as the road to economic recovery. Another communication, dispatched as the campaign drew to its conclusion, detailed Davis' efforts in connection with the monetary and economic conference's Organizing Committee, with disarmament, and toward an Anglo-American entente that would serve as a balance between France and Germany in Europe and as a check on Japanese ambitions vis-á-vis China.

Quite the political showman in his own right, anxious to move to the center of the stage as Roosevelt's intermediary with Europe,

the Democratic diplomat finally appealed to the squire's well-
known instinct for surprise and the theatrical. Davis urged a trip to
Europe by the President-elect, likely to divert him from the campaign's domestic emphasis. Davis' communications took on an
urgent and informed tone. The Disarmament Conference, he
wrote Roosevelt, had reached a crucial stage. MacDonald wished
to exchange assurances with Roosevelt of Anglo-American cooperation in world affairs. Talks with Europe's heads of government
(needless to say with Davis in the limelight as Roosevelt's con-
fidant), Davis assured Roosevelt, would head off Europe's impending disaster.[18]

Davis pressed his views relentlessly, enlisting Adolf A. Berle's
support through Columbia University's James T. Shotwell, an active supporter of the League of Nations. On the eve of the election, Berle submitted a memorandum to Roosevelt on foreign affairs:

> Professor Shotwell telephoned me last night. He acted as informal
> mediator, with Stimson's knowledge and consent, between the
> French and German governments, opening the way for Norman
> Davis' negotiations in disarmament. Yesterday the French govern-
> ment offered a disarmament proposal designed more or less to meet
> the views of the American government. It created a stir in Europe.
> Premier Herriot, through his agent, Cassan, cabled Shotwell to know
> whether you were likely to say anything disapproving the negotia-
> tions as they now stood; Shotwell was to cable his private views. I
> told Shotwell that in my personal opinion no statement of any sort
> would be made upsetting things, certainly for the time being.
> Shotwell's reaction was also asked as to your attitude towards a
> proposal to settle the foreign international debts for one billion dol-
> lars cash next December; as to which I expressed no opinion. The
> French government contemplates some such proposal.
> These negotiations have some bearing on Stimson's negotiations for
> Anglo-French support in our attitude toward Japan over Manchuria.
> The situation might raise the question of a statement, presumably
> informal and private, from you after election; which perhaps could be
> made only after conference with say Davis, who is accurately in-
> formed. All European governments assume your election; have been

negotiating on Stimson's lines; do not wish to look foolish if having made concessions to that line your government repudiates the whole structure. The course of negotiations would probably be adapted to accord with your supposed views; a method of expressing these views (if you express any) would have to be worked out. If you express none, I imagine the European settlements pending will probably languish, fearing an ultimate upset.

When Berle broached the Stimson–Davis concerns with the candidate, he drew only a vague response.[19] Davis managed nevertheless to keep his own lines open to Roosevelt.

Two letters sent in mid-November 1932 are particularly significant since they reveal an awareness on the part of Davis that key members of Roosevelt's "inner circle" did not accept the thesis of domestic recovery via international cooperation. In one dated November 15, Davis delegated to Edmund E. Day, American representative to the Preparatory Commission of the forthcoming Economic Conference, the task of educating Roosevelt's advisers toward "getting over ultimately something constructive. I have had a thorough talk with him [Day] as to what our strategy and policy should be and I have given him a letter to you [Roosevelt] as I think it would be a good idea for you to have a talk with him and then let him thrash out these matters in detail with some of your economic advisers."

Davis presented substantive proposals in a letter dispatched only three days later. He reminded Roosevelt of the merits of a visit to Europe; his [Davis'] efforts to "get France and Italy . . . to agree to enter the London Naval Treaty"; of possibilities regarding attainment of a preliminary disarmament agreement; of the need to reach "some important decisions" on the Manchurian question; of the relationship between the debts, disarmament, and the tariff question; and, "of utmost importance," the need to "maintain a continuity of policy along general fundamental lines." Although Roosevelt rejected Davis' suggested trip to Europe ("while there is much to be said for it, the difficulties are such that I have concluded to stay here"), he nevertheless invited Davis into the "inner circle" by soliciting a "confidential letter in the diplomatic mail bag" on the "whole situation" and by inviting Davis to call upon him when he returned from Europe.[20]

When Davis debarked in New York on December 22, 1932, he furthered the growing impression that he had become Roosevelt's spokesman on foreign affairs by his definite announcement that the World Monetary and Economic Conference would meet in London in April, following a final organization meeting of the committee of experts in January, and by his remarks about monetary stabilization, a return to the gold standard, and the need for tariff reduction. An appointment was made by Davis to see the President-elect on December 26. Roosevelt, meanwhile, had agreed with Tugwell, Day, and Williams (Moley, taken ill, had returned to his home in Cleveland for a rest) that the final meeting to decide the agenda of the Conference would be delayed until March 15 and that the Conference itself would not convene until about July 1. Tugwell sought also—and Roosevelt agreed—to delay the sailing of Day and Williams (hence the work of the organizing committee) until mid-February. In this way work begun by Hoover appointees would be completed after inauguration.[21]

Tugwell became so concerned about Davis' dockside statement to the press and the possibility that Day and Williams might return to Europe uninstructed in the policies of the incoming administration that he called Hyde Park on Christmas Eve. Roosevelt preferred not to interrupt his family party. When Roosevelt returned the call the next morning Tugwell learned to his dismay that "our plans for postponing the conference until the storm is over seem all to have gone wrong." Davis had succeeded in preventing Day and Williams from seeing Roosevelt and, amazingly, for a time blocked Tugwell as well from Roosevelt.

> I determined to go to Albany in the afternoon [December 26] hoping to arrive before Davis to tell the Governor what I have been able to learn. But when I arrived at the executive mansion Davis was al-

ready closeted with him and I was told to come back at 9:30 in the morning. . . .

At 9:30 [December 27] I went to the Governor's bedroom and found Davis there. The Governor apologised handsomely for not having me in on the conference of the night before, saying he wanted to make up his mind about Davis by letting him talk alone. I was naturally anxious about whether Day and Williams were to be seen. They were not. Davis and I were to go to New York together and see Day at Davis' house; Davis had his way about this too.

The first stage of the Davis interlude resulted in a compromise. "Davis had his way about the preliminary meeting of the experts," meaning that Day and Williams were to depart for Europe immediately, and neither was to see Roosevelt for orientation in the philosophy of the new administration. On the other hand, Davis was unable to bring Roosevelt around to support his statement that the conference would convene in April. "He told reporters last night it would not come until summer."

To Tugwell's chagrin Davis told reporters even more. "I was rather pleased when I picked up the morning paper," Tugwell recorded sarcastically in his diary, "to note that Mr. Davis has been the medium through which Mr. Hoover and Governor Roosevelt had been brought closer together in their foreign policy. The cleverness with which these diplomats learn to forward their interests in the press is perhaps their chief accomplishment." [22]

Thus began the "unseemly scuffling behind closed doors" that service in Roosevelt's interest seemed to require for the next few days. [23] At stake was not merely a timetable for the projected Conference. Rather both Moley and Tugwell believed that if the internationalists had their way, through a speed-up in the meeting of the Conference and through the premature raising of irritating international questions, the only result would be in angering the Congress and thereby endangering the passage of Roosevelt's legislative program. True enough it had been hoped originally that a special meeting of Congress might be avoided. But all hopes of remedial legislation bogged down in the anarchic winter lame-duck session, and by late December it was evident that the new Congress would be summoned after inauguration to carry out the pledge of a "New Deal."

THE CONTEST between the intranationalists and internationalists intensified with Felix Frankfurter's management of a meeting of minds between Roosevelt and Stimson early in the new year. The Harvard Law professor was anxious for an Anglo-American entente because of Japanese expansion in the Far East and the increasing probability of a renewed conflict between France and Germany in Europe. He was well aware, through Herbert Feis, of France's insistence on political guarantees by the United States in exchange for a softened position toward Germany on reparations and arms parity. He desired forgiveness of the debts, he wrote Henry L. Stimson, because of the "larger implications for a cooperative spirit between Great Britain and ourselves." What Frankfurter deplored most was the failure of the Hoover administration "to take the nation to school [educate the American people to their international obligations] in the past and even now!"

During much of 1932, Frankfurter, while aware of the deliberations of Roosevelt and the Brains Trust, focused much of his attention on Stimson and Feis in the State Department. Then, with Roosevelt's election, he attempted to educate the President-elect toward what Frankfurter believed were Roosevelt's internationalist responsibilities. At issue between Frankfurter and the Brains Trust was not the reality, which Frankfurter acknowledged, of nationalism run rampant, but Frankfurter's conviction concerning "the necessarily limited consequences of any merely local national economic program so long as the international situation is untouched." In this respect Frankfurter was much less sanguine than Henry Stimson or Norman Davis concerning the possibilities for international cooperation, but he desired that Roosevelt be exposed to Stimson's weltanschauung and acknowledge, at least privately, the international responsibilities of the United States.[24]

Roosevelt had deep respect for the Republican internationalist statesman and eagerly welcomed Frankfurter's suggestion on December 22, 1932 (following the first abortive Hoover–Roosevelt meeting), that the President-elect should have the benefit of Stimson's counsel. "Why doesn't H.L.S. come up and see me," Roosevelt reacted. After strenuous effort at overcoming Hoover's objections, the Harvard law professor arranged for the meeting at Hyde Park on January 9, 1933.[25]

The Roosevelt–Stimson discussion began at 11 A.M., lasted through luncheon, and continued on late that afternoon as they were chauffered down the beautiful Hudson Valley to New York City. Stimson, according to his diary, convinced Roosevelt to embrace the entire internationalist panoply: endorsement of the previous administration's Far Eastern policy (including the Stimson Doctrine), continuation of the disarmament talks (which were really a quagmire), accommodation on the debts question, the holding of a monetary and economic conference in London (meaning the stabilization of the pound to the franc to the dollar at a fixed gold ratio). Roosevelt, as Stimson noted later in his diary, appeared to be wobbling on the key issues. When Tugwell protested that commitment to Stimson's policies might well lead to war with Japan, Roosevelt's rejoinder was startling. He enjoyed his newfound cooperation with Stimson, called the Secretary "on the phone every day lately and says furthermore, that he is quite prepared to see his policy through. . . . He admitted the possibility of war and said flatly that it might be better to have it now than later. This horrifed me and I said so." [26]

It is tempting to speculate on Roosevelt's veering toward the conservative-internationalist view in December and January. Was he an old Wilsonian after all, really more at home with Davis and Stimson than the Brains Trust? Or simply eclectic, unconcerned by intellectual consistency, Hoover's greatest virtue and principal failing as a statesman? Academicians cherish consistency. Shrewdly, Roosevelt, a politician to the core, preferred to keep his options open. In the course of his presidency, Roosevelt's advisers became consistently frustrated by his willingness to consider contradictory views that seemed to negate one another. Perhaps, as Walter Lippmann suggested, he was at times too eager to please, too malleable, too facile at private assurances; perhaps on the other hand, having escaped his mother's embrace no one would again, ever, have a complete lockhold on Franklin D. Roosevelt.

Whatever the President-elect's rationale, which might have included a willingness to follow the international route to recovery in other times and circumstances, he made up his mind, finally, following the January 20, 1933, White House meeting of Hoover, Roosevelt, Davis, Moley, Mills, and Stimson, which occasioned a last-ditch battle by the head of the Brains Trust for the nationalist priorities enunciated in the 1932 campaign. Hoover clung to the confidence theory, determined to check Roosevelt's flexibility toward the gold standard and the balanced budget. He argued that a public pledge by Roosevelt to tamper with neither of these sacred cows of the Hoover–Mills administration would stem the economic downturn. Stimson and Davis stressed the internationalist priorities they had been urging on Roosevelt in the previous weeks. For a time Roosevelt wobbled and Moley, quite isolated, fought the 1932 campaign all over again. It developed as a discouraging moment for the Brains Truster, perhaps, as he suggested later in *After Seven Years*, the germ of his disillusionment with Roosevelt's way of doing business. As the meeting closed, however, and in the days and weeks that followed, Roosevelt swung back to the domestic program.[27]

Moley's demand that Davis be discarded as an adviser in the Roosevelt circle, enforced one might add by the growing gossip concerning Davis' ties to Wall Street and the Morgan preferred list, secured Roosevelt's private pledge that he was "through with Norman Davis." By mid-February, to Oswald Garrison Villard's and Felix Frankfurter's dismay, the squire blithely informed a group of visiting progressives "that the only thing for the United States to do as far as Europe was concerned was to withdraw into its shell and sit still until we regain our economic power." Tugwell and Moley had won the contest. [28]

When, on the evening of February 27, 1933, Moley and Roosevelt turned to the final drafting of the inaugural address, a process they had begun at the Palace Hotel in San Francisco during their Western campaign tour, the commitment to domestic priorities enunciated in the 1932 campaign received reaffirmation. It was translated into legislative history in the Hundred Days: "Our international trade relations, though vastly important, are in point of time and necessary secondary to the establishment of a sound economy. I favor as a practical policy the putting of first things first. I shall spare no effort to restore world trade by international economic adjustment, but the emergency at home cannot wait on that accomplishment." [29]

FROM THE VANTAGE POINT of the Brains Trusters in the post-campaign months, Roosevelt proved less than totally reliable, subject at whim to the pulls of old friends and traditionalist ideas, or even pursuit of financial nostrums. From their point of view relatively little distinguished the Hoover–Mills policies from those of Stimson and Davis. As the bank crisis intensified on the eve of Roosevelt's inauguration and Hoover pressed again for a pledge that budget balance and the gold standard would remain inviolate, the outgoing President acknowledged "that if these declarations be made by the President-elect, he will have ratified the whole program of the Republican administration; that is, it means abandonment of 90% of the so-called new deal." [30] A program of international economic accommodation or of collective security, or both, would further cripple the new administration's maneuverability on domestic economic issues. The likelihood of its failure, Tugwell and Moley believed, would convert a potentially cooperative Congress into a hostile camp.

The early months of the New Deal served as a replay of the 1932 campaign. Moley, as principal economic adviser to the new President, was bent upon the execution and articulation of the program outlined in the 1932 contest. Like Roosevelt, he felt the Wilsonian longing for an ordered world in the post-Versailles years, and believed that this nation should provide moral leadership in economic reconstruction and the political reconciliation of international problems. But the depression radically altered priorities and required a return to economic fundamentals. Agricultural collapse lay at the vortex of the crisis and agricultural recovery, serving in turn as a stimulus to the urban-industrial sector, merited priority. Accordingly, once the emergency banking legislation and the Economy Act had been dispatched, the first long-range recovery measure introduced was the Agricultural Adjustment Act. Later, despite his sponsorship of the World Monetary and Economic Conference, when compelled to make a choice, Roosevelt replicated the interregnum decision for intranationalism. As the President explained to the stunned J. Ramsay MacDonald, whose plans, nurtured since 1931, for international economic accommodation lay dashed to the ground, he could not forfeit internal gains to the chances of international arrangements.

U.S. domestic and diplomatic objectives of the 1930s were shaped by the Brains Trust in 1932, despite the disappearance in time of the Columbia group from the political arena. The domestic economy received priority. A better distribution of income, achievement of the social minima, and federal intervention where necessary for social and economic purposes became part of our permanent past. This has remained the legacy of Roosevelt and the Brains Trust.

Abbreviations and Locations
of Collections Cited in Notes

Baker Papers	Library of Congress, Washington D.C.
Barkley Collection	University of Kentucky Library, Lexington
Baruch Papers	Princeton University Library, Princeton, N.J.
Berle Papers	Franklin D. Roosevelt Library, Hyde Park, N.Y.
Brandeis Papers	University of Louisville Law School Library, Louisville, Ky.
Daniels Papers	Library of Congress, Washington D.C.
John W. Davis Papers	Yale University Library, New Haven, Conn.
Norman Davis Papers	Library of Congress, Washington D.C.
DNC (Democratic National Committee) Papers	Franklin D. Roosevelt Library, Hyde Park, N.Y.
Dodd Papers	Library of Congress, Washington D.C.
FDRL	Franklin D. Roosevelt Library, Hyde Park, N.Y.
Frankfurter-Feis Correspondence	Library of Congress, Washington D.C.
Frankfurter Papers	Library of Congress, Washington D.C.
Glass Papers	Alderman Library, University of Virginia, Charlottesville
GOF (Governor's Official File)	Franklin D. Roosevelt Library, Hyde Park, N.Y.
GPF (Governor's Personal File)	Franklin D. Roosevelt Library, Hyde Park, N.Y.
Hamlin Papers	Library of Congress, Washington D.C.
Harrison Papers	Columbia University Library, New York City
Hayes-Baker Correspondence	Library of Congress, Washington D.C.
Hoover Papers	Hoover Presidential Library, West Branch, Iowa
House Papers	Yale University Library, New Haven, Conn.
Howe Papers	Franklin D. Roosevelt Library, Hyde Park, N.Y.
Hull Papers	Library of Congress, Washington D.C.
Hiram Johnson Papers	Bancroft Library, University of California
Judson King Papers	Library of Congress, Washington D.C.
Lippmann Collection	Yale University Library, New Haven, Conn.
Long Papers	Library of Congress, Washington D.C.
McAdoo Papers	Library of Congress, Washington D.C.
Mills Papers	Library of Congress, Washington D.C.
Milton Papers	Library of Congress, Washington D.C.
Moffat Diary	Harvard University Library, Cambridge, Mass.
Moffat Papers	Harvard University Library, Cambridge, Mass.
Moley Diary	Hoover Institution on War, Revolution, and Peace, Stanford University, Palo Alto, Calif.
Moley Papers	Hoover Institution on War, Revolution, and Peace, Stanford University, Palo Alto, Calif.
Moskowitz Papers	Connecticut College Library, New London
Norris Papers	Library of Congress, Washington D.C.
Pittman Papers	Library of Congress, Washington D.C.

Plaut Papers	Franklin D. Roosevelt Library, Hyde Park, N.Y.
PPF (President's Personal File)	Franklin D. Roosevelt Library, Hyde Park, N.Y.
Rainey Papers	Library of Congress, Washington D.C.
Raskob Papers	Eleutherian Mills Historical Library, Greenville, Del.
Rosenman Papers	Franklin D. Roosevelt Library, Hyde Park, N.Y.
Seligman Papers	Columbia University Library, New York City
Shouse Papers	University of Kentucky Library, Lexington
Stimson Collection	Yale University Library, New Haven, Conn.
Stimson Diary	Yale University Library, New Haven, Conn.
Taussig Papers	Franklin D. Roosevelt Library, Hyde Park, N.Y.
Tugwell Papers	Franklin D. Roosevelt Library, Hyde Park, N.Y.
Frank Walsh Papers	New York Public Library, New York City
Thomas Walsh Papers	Library of Congress, Washington D.C.
M. L. Wilson Papers	Montana State University Library, Bozeman
Samuel Wilson Manuscript Collection	University of Kentucky Library, Lexington
Woolley Papers	Library of Congress, Washington D.C.

Notes

1. Albany Days, Albany Advisers

1. Alfred B. Rollins Jr., *Roosevelt and Howe* (New York: Knopf, 1962), pp. 233 ff.; Bernard Bellush, *Franklin D. Roosevelt as Governor of New York* (New York: Columbia University Press, 1955), pp. 3–36; Frank Freidel, *Franklin D. Roosevelt: The Triumph* (Boston: Little, Brown, 1956), pp. 17 ff.; Robert Jackson Diary, June 11, 1931, copy in author's possession.

2. Bellush, chs. 10 and 11; Freidel, *FDR: The Triumph*, parts of chs. 1, 2, 6, and 8; *The World*, editorials of January 2, 3, 4, and 13, 1929, authorship noted in pencil in Walter Lippmann Collection, Yale University Library; Samuel I. Rosenman, comp., *The Public Papers and Addresses of Franklin D. Roosevelt* (New York: Random House, 1938), I, 75–83, 91–92, 171–79, 186–93, 197–202; Governor's Official File (GOF) 197; folder, "Public Service Survey Commission," GOF 147; Judson King to George W. Norris, July 20, 1929, Tray 69–Box 3, Norris Papers; "Statement of Senator Norris," March 14, 1929, Tray 70–Box 5, Norris Papers; Roosevelt to Norris, January 6, 1930, GOF 198; Frank Walsh to George Norris, June 5, 1931, Tray 70–Box 1, Norris Papers; Norris to Walsh, September 4, 1931 Norris Papers; Josephus Daniels to Roosevelt, April 8, 1931, Box 15, Daniels Papers; Thomas Walsh to Roosevelt, April 15, 1931, Box 382, Thomas Walsh Papers; Daniel Roper to Roosevelt, April 9, 1931, Governor's Personal File (GPF) 146; Roosevelt to Frank Walsh, August 23, 1929 and April 23, 1930, and Edward Keating to Walsh, April 26, 1930, Box 69, Frank Walsh Papers; and generally Boxes 64 to 77, Frank Walsh Papers; Randolph J. LeBoeuf Jr., "The Contract Method," William A. Prendergast, "Fact Finding and Judicial Function in the Work of State Commissions," and William E. Mosler, "A Quarter Century of Regulation by State Commissions," in *Proceedings of the Academy of Political Science*, vol. 13 (May 1930); Judson King, "Roosevelt's Power Record," *The New Republic*, September 7, 1932, is a summary of King's invaluable discussions in the publications of the National Popular Government League, Judson King Papers; and Morris L. Cooke, "Taking Stock of Regulations in the State of New York," *Yale Law Journal*, November 1930.

3. See Roosevelt's personal correspondence with dirt farmers in "Farm Relief" folder, GOF 66.

4. "A Program for Farm Relief," *American Agriculturalist*, December 28, 1928, pp. 5, 20.

5. "Farm Relief and Reduction of Rural Taxes," part of a series of leaflets issued for the 1930 gubernatorial campaign, copy in Moley Papers; *Public Papers and Addresses of FDR*, I, 485–95; Bellush, pp. 94–98; interview with Rexford G. Tugwell, August 1968; interview with Raymond Moley, December 6, 1968; Freidel, *FDR: The Triumph*, pp. 13, 35–36.

6. Bellush, chs. 6 and 8; Freidel, *FDR: The Triumph*, chs. 13 and 15; the Roosevelt–Gifford Pinchot correspondence, in GOF 74, and generally GOF 190.

7. Rollins, pp. 452–53.

8. Walter Lippmann, "The Candidacy of Franklin D. Roosevelt," *New York Herald Tribune*, January 9, 1932; William Gibbs McAdoo to George Fort Milton, January 19, 1932, Box 348, McAdoo Papers; David F. Houston to Josephus Daniels, May 8, 1932, Box 665, Daniels Papers; Allan Nevins to Newton D. Baker, April 15, 1932, Baker Papers; Carl Becker to William E. Dodd, November 29, 1932, Box 39, Dodd Papers; Moley tape-recorded interviews, author's possession; Adolf A. Berle Jr. to Ralph Hayes, July 6, 1932, Box 8, Berle Papers; Walter Lippmann, "The Permanent New Deal," *Yale Review*, 24 (June 1935), 649–67; Paul K. Conkin, *The New Deal* (New York: Crowell, 1967), ch. 1.

9. James A. Farley, "Selling Roosevelt to the Party," *The American Magazine* (August 1938), *Behind the Ballots* (New York: Harcourt Brace 1938), and *Jim Farley's Story* (New York and Toronto: Whittlesey House, 1948). The most detailed account of the Howe–Farley exploits, state delegation by state delegation, is in Earland I. Carlson, "Franklin D. Roosevelt's Fight for the Presidential Nomination, 1928–1932," doctoral dissertation, University of Illinois (Urbana, 1955).

10. James A. Farley to Franklin D. Roosevelt, July 6, 1931, and Farley to Louis M. Howe, n.d., Box 53, Howe Papers; Memorandum, Farley to Howe, July 1, 1931, and Justus Wardell to Farley, August 4, 1931, copies in Box 42, folder 1326, ser. 1, Selected Correspondence, House Papers; Farley, *Behind the Ballots*, pp. 80–88.

11. The earliest record of correspondence between the two men is dated June 7, 1916, Box 95, folder 3283, ser. 1, Selected Correspondence, House Papers. See also House to Roosevelt, March 10, 1925, March 22, 1925, and undated note, March [?], 1925, Roosevelt to House, October 8, 1928, and House to Roosevelt, November 4, 1930. The proposed party conference is discussed in Frank Freidel, *Franklin D. Roosevelt: The Ordeal* (Boston: Little, Brown, 1954), pp. 210–13.

12. The strategy is outlined in Robert Woolley to E. M. House, December 20, 1928, Box 124, folder 4375, ser. 1, Special Correspondence, House Papers. It was a reversion to the old Wilsonian strategy of 1912; see House to McAdoo, November 5, 1928, Box 74, folder 2464, *ibid.*

13. House to McAdoo, January 6, 1931 and McAdoo to House, January 10, March 6, and March 18, 1931, Box 74, folders 2464–65, ser. 1, Selected Correspondence, House Papers. The generalizations reached stem from a reading of portions of the McAdoo Papers.

14. Freidel, *FDR: The Triumph*, pp. 201–9; Scott Bullitt to Breckinridge Long, March 21, 1931, and Long to Bullitt, April 10, 1931, Box 95, Long Papers; Robert Woolley to House, March 23, 1931, Box 124, folder 4378, ser. 1, Selected Correspondence, House Papers; House to Roosevelt, July 6, 1931 and July 28, 1931, and Roosevelt to House, July 13, 1931, Box 95, folder 3285, Ser. 1, Selected Correspondence, House Papers.

15. Roosevelt to House, June 23, 1931, Box 95, folder 3284, House Papers; Freidel, *FDR: The Triumph*, pp. 201–4; Carlson, pp. 386–87.

16. Robert Jackson Diary, June 11, 1931, copy in author's possession.

17. Roosevelt to House, June 23, 1931, and House to Roosevelt, June 26, 1931, Box 95, folder 3284, ser. 1, Selected Correspondence, House Papers.

18. House to Roosevelt, July 17, 1931, Box 95, folder 3285, ser. 1, Selected Correspondence, House Papers; Roosevelt to House, July 21, 1931, and House to Woolley, October 1, 1931, Box 125, folder 4382, ser. 1, Selected Correspondence, House Papers.

19. House to Woolley, September 2, 1931, Box 125, folder 4381, and House to Howe, September 18, 1931, Box 63, folder 2002; House to Roosevelt, July 6, 1931, and July 18, 1931, Box 95, folder 3285; Bingham contributed $1,000 to Roosevelt's primary campaign on October 31, 1931. Bingham to House, October 31, 1931, Box 15, folder 449; and House to Howe, November 3, 1931, Box 63, folder 2002; also Bingham to House, September 19, 1931, Box 15, folder 449; Woolley to House, August 19, 1931, and House to Woolley, September 11, 1931, Box 125, folder 4381; and Howe to House, August 31, 1931, Box 63, folder 2001; all in ser. 1, Selected Correspondence, House Papers.

20. Woolley to Roosevelt, September 18, 1931, Box 17, Woolley Papers; Woolley to House, September 29, 1931, Box 125, folder 4381, ser. 1, Selected Correspondence, House Papers.

21. House to Woolley, October 1, 1931, Box 125, folder 4382, ser. 1, Selected Correspondence, House Papers.

22. Woolley to House, March 23, 1931, Box 124, folder 4378, ser. 1, Selected Correspondence, House Papers.

23. House to Judge Robert W. Bingham, November 21, 1931, Box 15, folder 449, ser. 1, Selected Correspondence, House Papers; Roosevelt to House, November 16, 1931, GPF 84, FDR Private Correspondence, 1928–1932; Roosevelt to Woolley, November 16, 1931, Box 17, Woolley Papers; "F. D. R. Thwarts Al; Rejects League; Wins!" pp. 5–13, Memoir, Box 44, folder 33, Woolley Papers.

24. Woolley to Roosevelt, January 11, 1932 [incorrectly dated 1931]. Copy in Box 124, folder 4378, ser. 1, Selected Correspondence, House Papers.

25. Woolley to House, January 9, 1932, Box 125, folder 4382, ser. 1, Selected Correspondence, House Papers.

2. Stop Roosevelt Stage 1:
The Democratic Conservative Coalition

1. Interview with Eddie Dowling by Ruthanna Hindes, May 1, 1968. On deposit at the Eleutherian Mills Historical Library, Greenville, Del.

2. Samuel Lubell, *The Future of American Politics* (New York: Harper, 1952), pp. 35–49; Bernard Sternsher, "The Emergence of the New Deal Party System: A Problem in Historical Analysis of Voter Behavior," *Journal of Interdisciplinary History*, 6 (Summer 1975), 127–50, especially 142–44, challenges the view that individual elections mark major turning points in electoral history. Focusing on the Smith/Hoover contest of 1928, Allan J. Lichtman, too, agrees on behalf of "a broader vision of electoral change and stability in the United States" in "Critical

Election Theory and the Reality of American Presidential Politics, 1916–40," *The American Historical Review*, 81 (April 1976), 317–48.

3. Irénée du Pont to John J. Raskob, May 5, 1920 and Raskob to Irénée du Pont, April 16, 1920, folder: Irénée du Pont, Raskob Papers. Also, anonymous source.

4. C. L. Chapin to John J. Raskob, November 1927 and W. H. Stayton to general membership of the Association Against the Prohibition Amendment (AAPA), November 7, 1927, Box: AAPA, Correspondence, 1920–1930, Raskob Papers. The 1926 revenue of the federal government from all sources was $3.6 billions. Stayton's letter contended that a tax on beer, at the same rate as the cigarette tax, "would permit of a 50% reduction in all miscellaneous taxes and *income taxes* [Stayton's emphasis]. What such a reduction would mean to individuals and corporations—increased prices of securities and decreased taxes—is obvious." For a slightly different emphasis on dates, see George Wolfskill, *The Revolt of the Conservatives: A History of the American Liberty League, 1934–1940* (Boston: Houghton Mifflin, 1962). Professor Wolfskill relied on the hearings of the Senate Judiciary Committee, *Lobbying Activities: Hearings*, 71 Cong., 1 and 2 Sess. (1929–1930), and on the *Annual Reports of the President of the Association Against the Prohibition Amendment.*

The hypothesis that the Du Ponts were interested in the AAPA principally for the purpose of shifting the burden of taxation is rejected by William H. A. Carr, *The du Ponts of Delaware* (New York: Dodd, Mead, 1964), pp. 303–5. Carr prefers the argument, frequently made by the Du Ponts and Raskob, that they rejected Prohibition as a failure and because it promoted gangsterism.

5. W. H. Stayton to John J. Raskob, June 5, 1920, Box: AAPA, Correspondence, 1920–1930, Raskob Papers; "Acceptances to Membership in the Board of Directors," April 23, 1928, *ibid.*; Wolfskill, p. 39; see *Who Was Who in America* for corporate affiliations. The following were members of the AAPA Board of Directors: Rodolphe L. Agassiz, chairman of the board of Calumet & Heckla Consolidated Copper Co. and a director of the State Street Trust Co., Old Colony Trust Co. and Edison Illuminating Co.; Nicholas F. Brady, chairman of the board of New York Edison Co. and Brooklyn Edison Co.; Samuel H. Church, president of the Carnegie Institute and former vice-president of the Pennsylvania Railroad Co.; Lyman Delano, chairman of the board of the Atlantic Coast Line Railroad Co.; Frederick P. Fish, retired president of AT&T; Frederic J. Fisher, chairman of Fisher & Co. (Fisher Body) and a General Motors executive; Haley Fiske, president of the Metropolitan Life Insurance Co.; Charles Hayden, senior partner of Hayden, Stone & Co. and chairman of the board of International Nickel; Cornelius Kelley, president of the Anaconda Copper Co.

6. See, e.g., Pierre S. du Pont to John J. Raskob, March 25, 1929, Box: AAPA, Correspondence, 1920–1930, Raskob Papers. Du Pont asked Raskob for a list of AAPA contributors in order to better measure their giving capacity to the Democratic Fund. Also Raskob to Jouett Shouse, October 6, 1931, Box: Democratic National Committee (DNC), 1931–1937, Shouse Correspondence, Raskob Papers.

7. Raskob to Irénée du Pont, July 19, 1928, folder: Irénée du Pont, Raskob Papers.

8. Raskob to Jouett Shouse, December 4, 1930, Box: DNC, April 1929–December 1930, Raskob to Jouett Shouse March 13, 1931, Box: DNC, 1931–1937, Shouse Correspondence, Raskob Papers. In addition to his salary of $50,000 per annum Shouse was to benefit from the earnings of a business syndicate created by Raskob which, as it turned out, made no profit because of the crash.

9. "Radio Address by John J. Raskob . . . October 27, 1930," File 1917 (Personal File), Raskob Papers, and Julius H. Barnes to John J. Raskob, November 18, 1930, plus memorandum attached, *ibid.*; John J. Raskob, "Radio Address, May 1932," Jouett Shouse Papers.

10. Raskob to Roosevelt, October 10, 1928, Raskob Papers.

11. Jouett Shouse to James M. Cox, October 27, 1930, Jouett Shouse to John W. Davis, October 27, 1930, and Shouse to Raskob, December 1, 1930, Shouse Papers. Raskob originally contemplated a January meeting, then decided to wait until the winter session of the Congress ended.

12. Bernard Baruch to Raskob, n.d., Box: DNC, January–February 1931, Raskob Papers; William Gibbs McAdoo to Raskob, March 2, 1931, Box: DNC, March–April 1931, *ibid.*; "Statement of Cordell Hull, March 2, 1931," Group 12, GPF, FDR Private Correspondence, 1928–1932; Joseph T. Robinson to Jouett Shouse, January 9, 1931, Raskob Papers; Jouett Shouse to Raskob, Michelson, and Tumulty memoranda attached, January 21, 1931, Box: DNC, 1931–1937, Shouse Correspondence, Raskob Papers, Joseph P. Tumulty to Raskob, January 21, 1931 and February 6, 1931, Box: DNC, January–February 1931, Raskob Papers; *Proceedings, Democratic National Committee at Washington, D.C., March 5, 1931*, pp. 12, 23–30; Arthur Schlesinger Jr., *The Crisis of the Old Order, 1919–1933* (Boston: Houghton Mifflin, 1957), p. 277; Freidel, *FDR: The Triumph* (Boston: Little, Brown, 1956), pp. 177–82.

13. Raskob to Dr. E. A. Alderman (President, University of Virginia), March 9, 1931, and Raskob to John H. McCrahon, April 9, 1931, Boxes: DNC, March–April and April–June 1931, Raskob Papers; Raskob to Shouse, April 23, 1931, Box: DNC 1931–1937, Shouse Correspondence, Raskob Papers. See, for instance, "Radio Speech of Jouett Shouse," April 1931. Shouse, speaking on the Dixie Radio Hookup of the Columbia Broadcasting Company, attacked the high "Hoover-Grundy" tariff that was anathema to Southerners who suffered from a falling off in trade because of foreign economic retaliation. In reality Raskob favored high tariffs, but expressed willingness to compromise by proposing a tariff designed to account for higher production costs in this country. See the Raskob–Harry Byrd correspondence in Raskob Papers.

14. Harry F. Byrd to Raskob, April 8, 1931 and April 18, 1931, and Raskob to Byrd, April 9, 1931 (two letters), Box: DNC, March–April 1931, Raskob Papers.

15. Harry F. Byrd to Raskob, April 8, 1931 and Raskob to Byrd, April 9, 1931 (two letters), Box: DNC, March–April 1931, Raskob Papers; Byrd to Raskob, April 18, 1931, *ibid.*; Byrd to Raskob, August 20, 1931 and Raskob to Byrd, August 24,

1931, *ibid.;* Robert Woolley to Edward M. House, March 23, 1931, Box 124, folder 4378, ser. 1, Selected Correspondence, House Papers; interview with Jouett Shouse.

16. Raskob to Newton D. Baker, July 28, 1931 and Baker to Raskob, August 5, 1931, Box: DNC, July–October 1931, Raskob Papers. Ralph Hayes, though considerably younger than Baker, was a long-time friend who had served under him in the Wilson administration.

17. Ralph Hayes to Newton D. Baker, September 3, 1931, Box 4, Hayes–Baker Correspondence. Hayes to Judge John H. Clarke, September 17, 1931, and Hayes to Baker, September 10, 1931, Box 115, Baker Papers. In most such letters Hayes and Baker used a code system denoting persons as "X," in the case quoted, Shouse; "Y," meaning Raskob; and "Z," meaning Smith. There is no consistency from letter to letter and Hayes no longer recalls who is represented by those code letters. Names were attached to a separate strip of paper which was removed when the letter was read. Ralph Hayes to author, November 9, 1964. I have supplied names in these and other letters that follow from internal and other evidence.

Hayes was hardly naive when entering negotiations with the Smith group. He recognized the essential loyalty to Smith of Belle Moskowitz, Shouse, and Raskob, and decided that they turned to Baker as their alternative only because they recognized that Smith had little chance in the contest for the nomination. Hayes to John H. Clarke, September 17, 1931, Box 115, Baker Papers.

18. Jouett Shouse to Mrs. Newton D. Baker, December 28, 1937, Shouse Papers; Josephus Daniels to John Stewart Bryan, December 14, 1931, and Bryan to Daniels, December 15, 1931, Box 654, Daniels Papers; Ralph Hayes to Newton D. Baker, November 13, 1931, and Baker to Hayes, December 24, 1931, Box 115, Baker Papers; Hayes to Raskob and Raskob to Hayes, September 15, 1931, Box: DNC, July–October 1931, Raskob Papers; and Clarence H. Cramer, *Newton D. Baker* (Cleveland: World, 1961), pp. 229, 247–48.

19. Walter Lippmann, "The Democratic Party: IV, Roosevelt, Smith, and Baker," *New York Herald Tribune*, February 12, 1932.

20. Byron R. Newton to Newton D. Baker, March 26, 1930, Box 162, Baker Papers; Edith Bolling Wilson to Baker, March 26, 1930, Box 235, *ibid.;* Cary Grayson to Baker, August 6, 1932, Box 108, *ibid.;* H. F. Drugan to William Gibbs McAdoo, January 10, 1932, Box 363, McAdoo Papers.

21. Moley interview, tape recorded, September 1963.

22. Tugwell interview, August 1968. Tugwell's observations were limited to Baker and were a reaction to the author's "Baker on the Fifth Ballot? The Democratic Alternative: 1932," *Ohio History* (Autumn 1966), pp. 226–46, 273–77.

23. Norman Davis to Newton Baker, April 7, 1932, Box 83, Baker Papers; B. Howell Griswold to Baker, April 28, 1931, Box 109, Baker Papers; Ralph Hayes to Baker, February 6, 1932, March 18, 1932, and June 7, 1932, and Norman Hapgood to Baker, February 16, 1932, Box 116, Baker Papers; Hayes to Baker, November 12, 1931, Box 4, Hayes–Baker Correspondence, Melvin Traylor to

Josephus Daniels, July 9, 1932, Box 667, Daniels Papers; D. F. Houston to Daniels, March 8, 1932, Box 665, Daniels Papers; John W. Davis to John J. Raskob, January 6, 1932, Charles E. Peddicord to John W. Davis, April 23, 1932, John W. Davis to W. Jett Lauck, September 21, 1932, Philip C. Nash to John W. Davis, January 28, 1932 (Davis accepted the honorary vice-presidency of the League of Nations Association), John W. Davis to Hon. Clem L. Shaver, May 10, 1932, Davis to Arthur F. Cosby, August 12, 1932 (accepting membership in the New York State Committee of the National Economy League), Davis to Byron R. Newton, May 3, 1932, in John W. Davis Papers.

"When I was in New York the other day," Griswold reported to Baker in April, 1931, "I talked . . . with several bankers—fortunately ones of fine character and patriotism—and somewhat to my surprise (because I thought of their local predilections) they spoke of you as to their minds the most satisfactory candidate the Democrats could find."

24. Hayes to Baker, March 24, 1932, and April 25, 1932, Box 116, Baker Papers; Hayes to Baker, January 27, 1932, Box 4, Hayes–Baker Correspondence; Mark O. Watson to Baker, April 6, 1932, Box 226, Baker Papers; Mark Sullivan to Baker, April 14, 1932, Box 214, Baker Papers; George Creel, *Rebel at Large: Recollections of Fifty Crowded Years* (New York: Putnam, 1947), p. 268; Cramer, *Newton D. Baker*, p. 236; Robert Woolley to Edward M. House, October 6, 1931, Box 125, folder 4382, ser. 1, Selected Correspondence, House Papers; James Cox to Ralph Hayes, October 30, 1931, Box: DNC, July–October 1931, Raskob Papers.

25. Burton K. Wheeler to Raskob, November 17, 1931, Box: DNC, November–December 1931, Raskob Papers.

3. Hoover: First of the New Presidents?
or Last of the Old?

1. Carl Degler, "The Ordeal of Herbert Hoover," *The Yale Review*, vol. 52 (Summer 1963); Hicks, 3d ed. (Cambridge, Mass.: Houghton Mifflin, 1955), ch. 26, "The New Deal Begins."

2. For recent scholarly opinions which differ in their interpretations of voluntarism, the American System, and/or Herbert Hoover's approach toward the depression from those presented in this work see: Albert U. Romasco, *The Poverty of Abundance: Hoover, the Nation, the Depression* (New York: Oxford University Press, 1965), especially the conclusion; Joan Hoff Wilson, *Herbert Hoover: Forgotten Progressive* (Boston and Toronto: Little, Brown, 1975), which consistently treats Hoover as a progressive; Ellis W. Hawley, "Herbert Hoover, the Commerce Secretariat, and the Vision of an 'Associative State,' 1921–1928," *The Journal of American History*, 41 (June 1974), 116–40; and generally the essays in Martin L. Fausold and George T. Mazuzan, eds., *The Hoover Presidency: A Reappraisal* (Albany: State University of New York Press, 1974), and J. Joseph Huthmacher and Warren I. Susman, eds., *Herbert Hoover and the Crisis of American Capitalism* (Cambridge, Mass.: Schenkman, 1973). A contemporary statement,

which purports that Roosevelt was intellectually incapable of fostering the New Deal program, is found in Walter Lippmann, "The Permanent New Deal," *Yale Review*, 24 (June 1935), 649–67, a view presented originally in "The Candidacy of Franklin D. Roosevelt," *New York Herald Tribune*, January 9, 1932. The original Lippmann piece questioned Roosevelt's qualifications for the presidency. The 1935 statement attributed much of the innovative qualities of the New Deal program to Hoover's imagination.

3. Herbert Hoover, "Crisis to Free Men," address delivered to Republican National Convention, Cleveland, Ohio, June 10, 1936. Copy in New York Public Library.

4. Herbert Hoover, *American Individualism* (Garden City, N.Y.: Doubleday, Page, 1922). Hoover's effort at blending corporatist and antitrust ideals is explained in Ellis W. Hawley, "Herbert Hoover and American Corporatism, 1929–1933," in Fausold and Mazuzan, eds., pp. 101–19, also Introduction, pp. 7–9.

5. See Hoover's *American Individualism*, and Joseph Brandes, *Herbert Hoover and Economic Diplomacy* (Pittsburgh: University of Pittsburgh Press, 1962), chs. 2, 3, 6 and 7 as sources for the conclusions reached.

6. Brandes, pp. 38–39.

7. Brandes, pp. 213–20 and section 2.

8. Romasco, pp. 42–44; John D. Hicks, *Republican Ascendancy: 1921–1933* (New York: Harper, 1960), p. 12; Frank Freidel, *America in the Twentieth Century* (New York: Knopf, 1965), pp. 251–52.

9. Herbert Hoover, *Memoirs: The Cabinet and the Presidency, 1920–1933* (New York: Macmillan, 1952), pp. 167–73 and p. 173 fn.

10. Edward L. and Frederick H. Schapsmeier, "Disharmony in the Harding Cabinet: Hoover-Wallace Conflict," *Ohio History*, 75 (Spring and Summer 1966), 130–34.

11. Memorandum drafted by Herbert Hoover and sent to Odgen L. Mills, May 31, 1924, Container 2, Mills Papers.

12. Schapsmeier and Schapsmeier, "Disharmony in the Harding Cabinet," pp. 130–34; Edward L. and Frederick H. Schapsmeier, *Henry A. Wallace of Iowa: The Agrarian Years, 1910–1940* (Ames, Iowa: Iowa State University Press, 1968), p. 102.

13. Eugene Lyons, *Herbert Hoover, A Biography* (Garden City, N.Y.: Doubleday, 1964), pp. 174–76; Arthur Schlesinger Jr., *The Crisis of the Old Order: 1919–1933* (Boston: Houghton, Mifflin, 1957), pp. 87–88; William Allen White, *A Puritan in Babylon, The Story of Calvin Coolidge* (New York: Macmillan, 1938), pp. 308–9, 374ff., 398–402.

14. Hoover, *Memoirs: The Great Depression, 1929–1941*, (New York: Macmillan, 1952), Introduction and pp. 1–37.

15. *The New Day: Campaign Speeches of Herbert Hoover, 1928* (Stanford, Calif.: Stanford University Press, 1928 and 1929), pp. 17–22, 190–91.

16. Romasco, pp. 106–18; Broadus Mitchell, *Depression Decade: From the New*

Era through the New Deal, 1929–1941 (New York and Toronto: Rinehart, 1947), pp. 69–72; Harris Gaylord Warren, *Herbert Hoover and the Great Depression* (New York: Oxford University Press, 1959), pp. 168–76.

17. Warren, p. 176.

18. L. Ethan Ellis, *Republican Foreign Policy, 1921–1933* (New Brunswick, N.J.: Rutgers University Press, 1968), p. 22.

19. M. L. Wilson Papers. See citations below.

20. M. L. Wilson to James C. Stone, April 9, 1932, and Stone to Wilson, April 16, 1932, Domestic Allotment Correspondence, April 1932, CD F30, M. L. Wilson Papers.

21. Ezekiel to Stone, Memorandum, May 24, 1932, M. L. Wilson Papers; William D. Rowley, *M. L. Wilson and the Campaign for the Domestic Allotment* (Lincoln, Neb.: University of Nebraska Press, 1970), pp. 138–41.

22. Alexander Legge to M. L. Wilson, May 24, 1932, Legge to Representative William Williamson, James C. Stone, and Arthur M. Hyde, May 27, 1932, CD F63A, M. L. Wilson Papers; Mordecai Ezekiel to Rexford Guy Tugwell, October 20, 1939, CD F40A, *ibid.*

23. M. L. Wilson to Mordecai Ezekiel, January 11, 1933, CD F58, Wilson Papers; Frank Freidel, *Franklin D. Roosevelt: Launching the New Deal* (Boston and Toronto: Little, Brown, 1973), p. 34, citing Hoover Memorandum, November 22, 1932; "Address of President Hoover Accepting the Republican Nomination for President of the United States . . . ," August 11, 1932, p. 9.

24. George Soule's *New Republic* articles on a planned economy are elaborated in his *A Planned Society* (New York: Macmillan, 1932); the evolution of Tugwell's thought is described later in this work; see also Ellis W. Hawley, *The New Deal and the Problem of Monopoly: A Study in Economic Ambivalence* (Princeton, N.J.: Princeton University Press, 1966), pp. 44–45.

25. Gerard Swope to Herbert Hoover, September 11, 1931, Swope, "Discussion of 'Stabilization of Industry,'" Container 1-F/754, Hoover Papers, and Thomas D. Thacher to Hoover, October 1, 1931, Container 1-E/87, *ibid.*

26. Herbert Hoover to Felix Hebert, September 15, 1931, and September 22, 1931, and Hebert to Hoover, September 18, 1931; also, "Statement of United States Senator Felix Hebert on the Subject of Stabilization of Industry," Container 1-E/87, Hoover Papers.

27. Thomas D. Thacher to Herbert Hoover, October 1, 1931, Hoover Papers.

28. Herbert Bayard Swope to Ogden L. Mills, April 16, 1932, and Mills to Swope, April 20, 1932, Container 9, Mills Papers.

4. The Disharmony of International Cooperation

1. Henry L. Stimson and McGeorge Bundy, *On Active Service in Peace and War* (New York: Harper, 1947, 1948), p. 191.

2. President Hoover wrote Senator Joseph T. Robinson, Democrat of Arkansas, after his announcement of a one-year moratorium on intergovernmental payments

of debts and reparations: "The response in the rise of the commodity markets including cotton and wheat, seems to corroborate my view that this movement would have a large effect in the restoration of confidence and the building back of the whole economic situation." Hoover to Robinson, June 22, 1931, Foreign Affairs File: Financial, 1-G/880, Hoover Papers. Ogden Mills, Undersecretary of the Treasury, advised Hoover that a two-year moratorium on intergovernmental obligations would restore Europe's confidence and "might well turn the economic tide. In any event, in the limited field in which government can act, here is something that would be a definite contribution to the restoration of confidence." Mills to Hoover, June 18, 1931, *ibid.*

3. Herbert Hoover, *Memoirs: The Great Depression, 1929–1941* (New York: Macmillan, 1952), pp. vi, 61.

4. David Williams, "The 1931 Financial Crisis," *Yorkshire Bulletin of Economic and Social Research*, 15 (November 1963), 106; Edward W. Bennett, *Germany and the Diplomacy of the Financial Crisis, 1931* (Cambridge: Harvard University Press, 1962), pp. 100–1, 113–14, 122. An excellent analysis of the factors responsible for the worldwide depression may be found in Charles P. Kindleberger, *The World in Depression, 1929–1939* (London: Lane, 1973). Agricultural surpluses and slippage of prices followed by massive widespread deflation, he observes (p. 107), provided the "fateful mixture."

5. Bennett, pp. 155–56; L. Ethan Ellis, *Republican Foreign Policy, 1921–1933* (New Brunswick, N.J.: Rutgers University Press, 1968), pp. 308–9; Dawes Diary, July 3, 1931, Foreign Affairs File: Financial, 1-G/891, Hoover Papers.

6. Hoover, *Memoirs: The Great Depression*, pp. 64–65; Hoover Diary, May 7, 1931, June 2, 1931, and June 5, 1931, Foreign Affairs File: Financial, 1-G/879 and 1-G/880, Hoover Papers. Hoover's optimistic appraisal of the potential economic impact of a moratorium and of arms reduction rested on several memoranda drafted by J. F. Dewhurst for Dr. Julius Klein of the Commerce Department. Of our principal debtors, Dewhurst's tables demonstrated, France' debt payments during 1930 constituted 47.7 percent of U.S. imports from France ($54 millions in debt payments as opposed to $113 millions in U.S. imports of French goods); and Great Britain's debt payments ($160 millions) were 76.6 percent of U.S. imports of British goods ($210 million) in 1930. In a second table Dewhurst calculated that U.S. imports of goods from debtor countries had declined since 1928 and in another table that debt payments were but a small fraction of national defense budgets. In a fourth table Dewhurst calculated that the funded war and postwar indebtedness of our debtors in relation to total government debt of these nations amounted to 27.5 percent for Belgium, 26.2 percent for France, 58.1 percent for Italy, and 12.2 percent for Great Britain. See J. F. Dewhurst to Dr. [Julius] Klein, May 9, 1931, and three memoranda dated May 12, 1931, 1-G/879, Hoover Papers.

7. Thomas W. Lamont to Martin Egan (for President Hoover), July 9, 1931, 1-G/880, Hoover Papers; Bennett, pp. 122, 155, 241, and *passim*. A customs union was generally regarded as the first step toward political union of Germany with Austria. The proposition, though discussed for some years and in some

quarters regarded as the logical outcome of the excessive political fragmentation which emanated from Versailles, was in 1931 the work mainly of Germany's Foreign Minister Dr. Julius Curtius. It was publicly announced by Germany and Austria in late March 1931 and abandoned because of the economic crisis and French pressures. Curtius resigned in October when the plan fell through. See Bennett, pp. 44–58, and pp. 92–98.

8. Atherton to Secretary of State, June 8, 1931, 2 A.M., Foreign Affairs File: Financial, 1-G/880, Hoover Papers.

9. Atherton to Secretary of State, June 8, 1931, midnight, Hoover Papers.

10. Hoover, *Memoirs: The Great Depression*, p. 68; Hoover Diary, June 18–20, 1931, Foreign Affairs File: Financial, 1-G/880 and 1-G/891, Hoover Papers.

11. President's Press Release, June 20, 1931, 1-G/891, Hoover Papers.

12. American Embassy, Paris [Walter Edge] to Secretary of State, No. 1343, June 24, 1931, Hoover Papers. Ogden L. Mills, Acting Secretary of the Treasury, estimated in a memorandum prepared for President Hoover, that the net effect of the moratorium would be the postponement during the fiscal year beginning July 1, 1931, of net receipts amounting to $17.5 million for Great Britain, $77.6 million for France, $7.3 million for Italy, $21 million for Belgium, and $262.3 million for the United States. Germany would be the major beneficiary through the postponement of $394.4 million in payments, principally to France ($188.1 million), Great Britain ($89.4 million), Italy ($42.7 million), Belgium ($29 million), Yugoslavia ($8.8 million), and the United States ($15.7 million). Mills to Hoover, June 23, 1931, 1-G/880, Hoover Papers.

13. The "unconditional payments" were those funds which were to be used by the Bank for International Settlements for the amortization of bonds sold under the German External Loan of 1924. Although under the Young Plan Agreements Germany unilaterally could declare postponement of conditional payments for two years after giving 90 days' notice, she was obliged to make the unconditional payments regardless of economic circumstances. Bennett, p. 6; Harold G. Moulton and Leo Pasvolsky, *War Debts and World Prosperity* (New York: Brookings Institution, 1932), pp. 189–90, 225–31. Ch. 10 of the Moulton work describes the Young Plan Agreements.

14. Mills and Stimson to American Embassy, Paris [Edge], June 25, 1931, Foreign Affairs File: Financial, 1-G/880, Hoover Papers.

15. American Embassy, Paris [Edge] to Acting Secretary of State [Castle], June 28, 1931, 1-G/881, Hoover Papers.

16. American Embassy, Berlin [Sackett] to Secretary of State, June 28, 1931, 1-G/881, Hoover Papers.

17. American Embassy, Berlin to Secretary of State, June 29, 1931 and June 30, 1931, 1-G/881, Hoover Papers.

18. Sackett to Secretary of State, July 2, 1931, Hoover Papers.

19. Hoover Diary, July 5, 1931, Castle to Stimson and Department of State Press release, July 5, 1931, Castle to Edge and Mellon, July 5, 1931, all 1-G/881 Hoover Papers.

20. State Department Press release (two), July 6, 1931; Hoover Diary, July 6, 1931, 1-G/881, Hoover Papers.

21. Jean Parmentier to Charles Dawes, June 24, 1931 and July 8, 1931 in Extracts from the Diary of General Charles Dawes, June 22–July 21, 1931, Foreign Affairs File: Financial, 1-G/891, Hoover Papers. Felix Frankfurter to Herbert Feis, June 29, 1931, Box 54, Frankfurter Papers. Governor Eugene Meyer of the Federal Reserve Board also contended that Hoover had in fact reversed himself as to the relation between debts and reparations. Charles S. Hamlin Diary, June 26, 1931, 19:61, Hamlin Papers. Alanson Houghton, former U.S. ambassador to Germany (1922–29) predicted that the moratorium would help Germany for only a few weeks and that if things went badly the Hitlerites would come to power and "would not pay another dollar" in reparations. Ibid., July 5, 1931, 19:68 and Index-Digest [to] Diaries, 19:144.

22. David Williams, "The 1931 Financial Crisis," Yorkshire Bulletin of Economic and Social Research, 15 (November 1963), 97–100.

23. Ibid., pp. 98–102; Hoover, Memoirs: The Great Depression, pp. 21–23. Most United States banks which closed were small "country banks" located in rural communities.

24. Bennett, pp. 100–1; Williams, "The 1931 Financial Crisis," pp. 102–7.

25. Bennett, p. 241.

26. Eugene Meyer, Governor, Federal Reserve Board, to the President, July 9, 1931, and enclosure, George Harrison to Montagu Norman, July 8, 1931; in folder: Meyer, Eugene, Correspondence, 1930–1933, Secretaries File, 1-G/971, Hoover Papers.

27. Walter Edge to Secretary of State, July 11, 1931, Foreign Affairs File: Financial, 1-G/881, Hoover Papers.

28. Sackett to Acting Secretary of State, July 11, 1931 and July 13, 1931, 1-G/881, Hoover Papers. Hjalmar Schacht, former president of the Reichsbank, told Sackett that Brüning's government was finished, since the Catholic Center Party (Brüning) could not avoid a break with the Social Democrats. Its only recourse, an alliance with the Rightist parties, would not last long. The only solution, Schacht believed, was a directorate or dictatorship of five industrial leaders. Idem.

29. Treasury Secretary Mellon was in Europe on vacation when drafted by Hoover to negotiate in Paris on the moratorium. He was joined by Stimson and then both went to London to attend the financial conference of July 20–23, 1931. Mills, an extreme conservative in matters of finance and a nationalist, was becoming increasingly influential in the Hoover council. William R. Castle was Hoover's man in the State Department though technically Stimson's Undersecretary. Stimson later regretted the choice since Castle did not share his "basic attitudes." See Stimson and Bundy, On Active Service in Peace and War, p. 192.

30. Proposed statements from Mills and Castle, July 12, 1931, Foreign Affairs File: Financial, 1-G/881, Hoover Papers.

31. Williams, "The 1931 Financial Crisis," pp. 106–7.

32. Castle to American Embassy, Paris, July 16, 1931; Hoover–Stimson–Edge–

Mills telephone conversations, three transcripts, July 16, 1931, Foreign Affairs File: Financial, 1-G/882, Hoover Papers; Elting E. Morison, *Turmoil and Tradition: A Study of the Life and Times of Henry L. Stimson* (Boston: Houghton Mifflin, 1960), pp. 362–65; Hoover, *Memoirs: The Great Depression, 1929–1941*, pp. 74–78. At a White House Conference on July 20, Governor Eugene Meyer of the Federal Reserve Board rejected a proposal for additional short-term credits for Germany to be extended by the Federal Reserve System; see Charles S. Hamlin Diary, July 21, 1931, 19:98–99 and Index-Digest [to] Diary, 19:183–84, 204.

33. David Williams, "London and the 1931 Financial Crisis," *The Economic History Review*, 2d ser., 15 (No. 3, 1963), 514–27.

34. W. Randolph Burgess to Ogden L. Mills, "Summary of the Principal Measures Adopted Since September, 1931, which Affect World Trade and Balance of Payments, January 30, 1933," and preliminary tables for "Analysis of Proposal for Devaluation of the Dollar," Container 11, Mills Papers.

35. Henry L. Stimson to Herbert Hoover, August 11, 1932 (p. 18); Walter E. Edge to Henry L. Stimson, September 18, 1931; Stimson to Edge, September 19, 1931; and Stimson to Department of State, Memorandum of Conversation with the Italian Ambassador, Nobile Giacomo de Martino, September 24, 1931; in Foreign Affairs File: Financial, 1-G/883, Hoover Papers.

36. "Subjects for Laval Conversation," September 1931, Foreign Affairs File: Financial, 1-G/883, Hoover Papers.

37. Office of the Economic Adviser, Department of State, Memorandum of Exchange of Views at Meeting in Federal Reserve Bank of New York, October 19, 1931, Foreign Affairs File: Financial, 1-G/884, Hoover Papers.

38. Ellis, pp. 211–12.

39. Lawrence Richey to William R. Castle, October 28, 1931, for transmission to Ambassador Dawes [England], Foreign Affairs File: Financial, 1-G/884, Hoover Papers.

40. Dawes to Secretary of State, October 29, 1931, 1-G/884, Hoover Papers. Interestingly enough when the London Monetary and Economic Conference opened in 1933 MacDonald launched into a public statement on the debts contrary to prior understanding that the touchy issue should be avoided.

41. Herbert Hoover to Secretary of State, dated in brackets October 1931?, probably November or December 1932, 1-G/884, Hoover Papers.

42. Stimson Diary, October 23, 1931 and October 24, 1931, 1-G/890, Hoover Papers.

43. *Idem*. Garrard Winston's proposals, known to the French as well as Hoover and Mills, rested on these assumptions: 1) debts reduction (not cancellation) was an economic necessity because of the depression; 2) France could no more abandon reparations willingly than the United States could abandon debts; 3) Germany would be unable to make external payments as long as the depression continued. Winston proposed that the Reich continue to make reparations payments in marks to the Bank for International Settlements, as it was doing under the moratorium. The BIS in turn would loan the marks to German industry, public utilities,

railroads and possibly private borrowers in exchange for long term obligations payable in gold. The BIS could use these obligations to repay the war debts. Finally, Winston proposed, German borrowers could use BIS loans to reduce their short-term obligations to the banks, thus replenishing the banks' assets. Garrard Winston to Ogden L. Mills, October 22, 1931, Container 9, Mills Papers.

Mills believed Winston's proposal a workable one provided our debtors guaranteed the bonds received by the United States from the BIS. Jean-Jacques Bizot, the French Treasury representative, who accompanied Laval to Washington, informed Mills that the plan was similar to one worked out in the French Treasury. Mills to Garrard Winston, October 27, 1931, Container 9, Mills Papers.

44. Charles G. Dawes, *Journal as Ambassador to Great Britain* (New York: Macmillan, 1939), p. 409.

45. William Starr Myers, ed., *The State Papers and other Public Writings of Herbert Hoover* (2 vols.; Garden City, N.Y.: Doubleday, Doran, 1934), II, 20; Herbert Feis to Felix Frankfurter, November 5, 1931, and Note on the Present Status of the International Debt and Reparations Negotiations, November 2, 1931, Box 54, Frankfurter Papers.

46. American Embassy, Berlin [Ambassador Sackett] to Secretary of State, November 6, 1931, and November 12, 1931, Foreign Affairs File: Financial, 1-G/884, Hoover Papers; *New York Times*, November 21, 1931.

47. Erich Eyck, *A History of the Weimar Republic* (Cambridge: Harvard University Press, 1962, 1963), I, 253–54; Andreas Dorpalen, *Hindenburg and the Weimar Republic* (Princeton, N.J.: Princeton University Press, 1964), chs. 6–9; Fritz Stern, "The Collapse of Weimar," in *The Failure of Illiberalism* (New York: Knopf, 1972), especially pp. 207–9.

48. *New York Times*, November 27, 1931; Eyck, II, 309; American Embassy Berlin, to Secretary of State, December 1, 1931, Foreign Affairs File: Financial, 1-G/884, Hoover Papers.

49. Myers, ed., *Hoover State Papers*, II, 73–75; Hoover, *Memoirs: The Great Depression, 1929–1941*, pp. 171–72; Harvey Bundy to Theodore Joslin, December 7, 1931, 1-G/884, Hoover Papers; Herbert Feis to Felix Frankfurter, December 8, 1931, and "Copy handed to Secretary [Stimson] at 4 P.M., December 4th," Box 54, Frankfurter Papers.

50. *Congressional Record*, vol. 75, 72 Cong., 1 Sess., December 7, 1931 to January 19, 1932, pp. 297, 794, 1081–82; Arnold J. Toynbee, ed., *Survey of International Affairs: 1931* (London: H. Milford, 1932), p. 140.

51. American Embassy, London [Dawes] to Secretary of State, December 16, 1931, and American Embassy, Paris [Edge] to Secretary of State, December 17, 1931, 1-G/884, Hoover Papers.

52. H.J. Res. 147, December 17, 1-G/884, Hoover Papers; Hoover, *Memoirs: The Great Depression, 1929–1941*, p. 172.

53. Hoover, *Memoirs: The Great Depression*, p. 172; Dawes to [Stimson], December 21[1931], No. 467, 1G/885, Hoover Papers; Toynbee, ed., *Survey of International Affairs: 1931*, pp. 141–42.

54. Memorandum of Conversation Between Secretary Stimson and the British Ambassador, Sir Ronald Lindsay, December 24, 1931; Aide Memoire handed to French Chargé d'Affaires by Secretary of State, December 29, 1931; and Memorandum of Conversation between Secretary Stimson and the German Ambassador, . . . December 25, 1931, in 1-G/885, Hoover Papers; also, Diplomatic Journals, December 16, 1931, vol. 30, Moffat Papers.

55. American Embassy, Berlin to Secretary of State, January 9, 1932, No. 7 and No. 8; American Embassy, London [Atherton] to Secretary of State, January 9, 1932, No. 8; Summary of Cables from U.S. Embassy at Berlin formulated by the Division of Western European Affairs, Subject: German Policy on Reparations, n.d.; American Embassy, Berlin to Secretary of State, January 12, 1932; Despatch 1397 from the Embassy at Berlin to the Secretary of State, January 12, 1932, in 1-G/885, all in Foreign Affairs File: Financial, Hoover Papers.

56. Edge to Secretary of State, January 10, 1932, and Memorandum of the Undersecretary of State of a Conversation with the French Ambassador, January 14, 1932, 1-G/885, Hoover Papers.

57. Herbert Feis, Memorandum on the Drift of the World Economic Situation, February 4,, 1932, Box 54, Frankfurter Papers; Stimson to Hoover, Memorandum on the Respective Positions of Germany, Britain and France on the Present Negotiations Respecting Reparations and Debts, January 21, 1932, in 1-G/885, Hoover Papers; Stimson Diary, January 17, 1932, Yale University Library.

58. Quoted in Elting Morison, p. 383.

59. New York: Harper, 1971, pp. xv, 243.

60. Morison, p. 407; Ellis, pp. 182–89; Robert H. Ferrell, *American Diplomacy in the Great Depression: Hoover–Stimson Foreign Policy, 1929–1933* (New Haven, Conn.: Yale University Press, 1957), pp. 194–214.

5. "A Pleasant Man Who . . .
Would Very Much Like To Be President"

1. William G. McAdoo to George F. Milton, January 19, 1932, Box 348, McAdoo Papers; Houston to Josephus Daniels, May 8, 1932, Box 665, Daniels Papers; George Creel, *Rebel at Large: Recollections of Fifty Crowded Years* (New York: Putnam, 1947), p. 270; Robert Jackson Memorandum to author, February 24, 1966; Allan Nevins to Newton D. Baker, April 15, 1932, Box 162, Baker Papers; William E. Dodd to Baker, March 24, 1932, Box 87, Bakers Papers; Carl Becker to Dodd, November 29, 1932, Box 39, Dodd Papers; Moley tape-recorded interviews, September 1963, author's possession; Adolf A. Berle Jr. to Ralph Hayes, July 6, 1932, Box 8, Berle Papers; Index-Digest [to] Diaries, 20: 18–20, and Hamlin Diary, December 14, 1931, 20: 15–16, and February 13, 1932, 20: 71, Hamlin Papers; Jonathan Daniels to Josephus Daniels, February 19, 1932, Box 660, Daniels Papers; Thomas J. Walsh to Hon. E. G. Norden, November 17, 1931, Box 382, Thomas Walsh Papers.

2. "The Candidacy of Franklin D. Roosevelt," *New York Herald Tribune*, January 9, 1932.

3. Paul K. Conkin, *The New Deal* (New York: Crowell, 1967), ch. 1; Barton J. Bernstein, "The Conservative Achievements of Liberal Reform," in Bernstein, ed., *Towards A New Past: Dissenting Essays in American History* (New York: Vintage edition, 1969), pp. 263–68.

4. William Randolph Hearst, "Who Will Be the Next President?" *New York American*, January 3, 1932.

5. "Address by Newton D. Baker during Democratic National Convention, Madison Square Garden, June 29, 1924," Box 9, Hayes–Baker Correspondence; *New York World*, June 30, 1924; Moley interviews.

6. Baker to F. R. Coudert, November 18, 1931, Box 77, Baker Papers.

7. Ralph Hayes to Newton D. Baker, November 7, 1931, and January 27, 1932, Box 4, Hayes–Baker Correspondence; Norman Hapgood to Baker, October 22, 1931, Box 109, Baker Papers; Hayes to Baker, February 6, 1932, April 8, 1932, and April 11, 1932, Box 116, ibid.

8. Folder: "League of Nations Statement: 1932," Box 146, Baker Papers. "A New Boost for the Baker Boom," *Literary Digest*, February 6, 1932, p. 8; Baker to John H. Clarke, January 16, 1932, and February 22, 1932, Box 59, Baker Papers.

9. Baker to Byron R. Newton, October 7, 1932, Box 162, Baker Papers.

10. In the New Deal historiography the lines between internationalism and intranationalism are drawn most sharply in the publications of Herbert Feis, Raymond Moley, and the author. See particularly Herbert Feis, *1933: Characters in Crisis* (Boston: Little, Brown, 1966); Moley, with the assistance of Elliot A. Rosen, *The First New Deal* (New York: Harcourt, Brace, 1966); Rosen, "Intranationalism vs. Internationalism: The Interregnum Struggle for the Sanctity of the New Deal," *Political Science Quarterly*, 81 (June 1966), 274–97; and Feis's review of *The First New Deal*, "Looking Backward," in the *New York Times Book Review*, December 11, 1966, pp. 3, 77.

11. "The Week in the World," Mark Sullivan's column, January 30, 1932; *New York Herald Tribune*, editorial, January 27, 1932; Springfield (Mass.) *Republican*, editorial, January 28, 1932; and Providence (R.I.) *Journal*, editorial, January 28, 1932. Clippings are in Box 10, Hayes–Baker Correspondence.

12. Roosevelt to Woolley, January 29, 1932, and Woolley to Roosevelt, January 28, 1932, and February 2, 1932, Box 17, Woolley Papers.

13. Frank Freidel, *Franklin D. Roosevelt: The Triumph* (Boston and Toronto: Little, Brown, 1956), pp. 250–51.

14. Isidore B. Dockweiler to Louis Howe, telegram, April 19, 1932, and Franklin D. Roosevelt to Charles McClatchy (editor, *San Francisco Bee*), April 20, 1932. In Democratic National Committee Papers, Before Convention, Mc-MacC; See Hiram Johnson to Charles K. McClatchy, April 9, 1932, Part III, Box 13, Hiram Johnson Papers.

15. "Address of Governor Franklin D. Roosevelt before members of the New York State Grange, . . . Albany, February 2, 1932." Copy in Box 662, Daniels Papers.

16. David Burner, *The Politics of Provincialism: The Democratic Party in Transition, 1918–1932* (New York: Knopf, 1968), p. 168.

17. James MacGregor Burns, *Roosevelt: The Lion and the Fox* (New York: Harcourt, Brace, 1956), pp. 74–75; Frank Freidel, *Franklin D. Roosevelt: The Ordeal* (Boston: Little, Brown, 1954), chs. 5 and 8.

18. Copies of Roosevelt's and Mills's *Foreign Affairs* articles are in Box 211, Mills Papers.

19. Norman Davis to Roosevelt, April 12, 1928, and April 17, 1928, Box 51, Norman Davis Papers.

20. Davis to Roosevelt, November 7, 1930, Box 51, Norman Davis Papers.

21. Statement of Cordell Hull, February 23, 1931, in FDR Private Correspondence, 1928–1932, GPF, Group 12 (Cordell Hull); Hull Memorandum, January 17, 1931, Series 1, Folder 55, Box 31, Hull Papers; and Cordell Hull to Scripps-Howard Newspaper Alliance, telegram, June 24, 1931, ser. 1, folder 55A, Hull Papers. See also, for Hull's economic views: "Some Phases of a Democratic Fiscal Program," Statement of Cordell Hull, November 29, 1931, in Box 192, Baker Papers, in which he urged fiscal entrenchment by state, local, and federal governments and labeled Raskob and others he opposed as "Bourbon isolationists." For a particularly thorough exposition of his views on the causes and remedy of the Great Depression see his Senate speech of February 8 (legislative day of February 5), 1932, appended to Cordell Hull to Josephus Daniels, February 11, 1932, in Box 665, Daniels Papers.

22. Russell Leffingwell to Cordell Hull, December 22, 1932, Box 32, ser. 1, folder 56A, Hull Papers. See also Leffingwell's introductory address, "Causes of the Depression," in Academy of Political Science, *Proceedings*, 14 (June 1931), 331–32.

23. Hull, *Memoirs* (New York: Macmillan, 1948), p. 141; Howe–Hull Correspondence, Box 31, Hull Papers.

24. William Randolph Hearst to E. D. Coblentz, January 21, 1932. Copy in Part VI, Box 10, Hiram Johnson Papers; Freidel, *FDR: The Triumph*, p. 250.

25. Authorship of the speech at Albany should be determined, since it marks the end of the Howe–House collaboration as consultants in matters of broad public policy. In the light of the deep antagonism among the internationalists toward the Grange address, House entered a demurrer in his papers for the record. A copy of a nearly final draft by Louis Howe to Edward M. House, now in the House Papers at Yale University, has the following entry in the Colonel's hand: "My addition to Gov. F. R. [*sic*] Roosevelt's speech delivered at Albany Febry 1932 before the Agricultural Society. I disapproved of the entire speech & in particular what he says and did say about the League of Nations. EMH." The historian, however, is compelled to enter his own demurrer. House's disclaimer may well have been an afterthought following the internationalists' condemnation of the address. Howe consulted him every step of the way. Also, it needs to be noted that the most draconian statement in the Albany address was House's contribution: "Europe owes us. We do not owe her." In a letter to Robert Woolley the day the speech was delivered House simply summarized its content. He gave no sign of disap-

proval. See the following: House to Woolley, February 2, 1932, Box 125, folder 4386, ser. 1, Special Correspondence, House Papers. Albany speech drafts are in Box 95, folder 3282, House Papers; and Baker to Ralph Hayes, July 6, 1932, Box 5, Hayes–Baker Correspondence.

26. Woolley to House, February 4, 1932, Box 125, folder 4386, ser. 1, Selected Correspondence, House Papers; Woolley to House, February 9, 1932, Box 17, Woolley Papers.

27. House to Woolley, February 8, 1932, Box 8, Woolley Papers; House to James A. Farley, February 10, 1932, Box 42, folder 1327, ser. 1, Selected Correspondence, House Papers.

28. Woolley to Roosevelt, February 12, 1932, Box 17, Woolley Papers.

29. Roosevelt to Woolley, February 25, 1932, Box 17, Woolley Papers; Daniel C. Roper to William E. Dodd, August 29, 1932, Box 39, Dodd Papers.

30. Memorandum from Miss Dewson to Mr. Howe, February 16, 1932, Box 54, Howe Papers; Josephus Daniels to Jonathan Daniels, February 26, 1932, Box 660, Daniels Papers; Thomas J. Walsh to Hon. Henry B. Mitchell, February 8, 1932, Box 384, Thomas Walsh Papers.

31. Cordell Hull to Josephus Daniels, February 28, 1932, Box 661, Daniels Papers.

32. Louis Brownlow to Ralph Hayes, April 15, 1932, and Hayes to Baker, April 18, 1932, Box 116, Baker Papers. There is added confirmation of Hull's willingness to desert Roosevelt from a source well outside of the immediate contest between the Wilsonians and the Albany advisers. Quite aloof from the scene, but well informed, was the brilliant rather conservative newspaperman-historian George Fort Milton, editor of the highly regarded *Chattanooga Times*. Hull's announcement for Roosevelt, Milton explained to William Gibbs McAdoo, stemmed from Roosevelt's assistance "in stopping the Smith–Raskob program" in 1931. But his fellow Tennesseean, Milton believed, was no last ditch supporter of Roosevelt. "I judge that it [the Tennessee delegation] will leave Roosevelt when Hull thinks it expedient to do so, and for the person Hull would like to see get the vote." See George Fort Milton to William Gibbs McAdoo, February 28, 1932, Box 366, McAdoo Papers.

33. House to Woolley, February 24, 1932, Box 125, folder 4386, ser. 1, Selected Correspondence, House Papers.

34. Moley interviews, tape recorded, author's possession.

35. Samuel I. Rosenman, *Working With Roosevelt* (New York, Harper, 1952), pp. 56–58.

6. The Brains Trust 1:
Moley and Politics

1. Arthur Schlesinger Jr., *The Politics of Upheaval* (Boston: Houghton Mifflin, 1960), especially parts 2 and 3.

2. Basil Rauch, *The History of the New Deal, 1933–1938* (New York: Creative

Age Press, 1944); Raymond Moley, *After Seven Years* (New York: Harpers, 1939), ch. 8; Otis L. Graham Jr., "Historians and the New Deals: 1944–1960," *The Social Studies*, 54 (1963), 133–40; *Richard Hofstadter, The Age of Reform: From Bryan to FDR* (New York: Knopf, 1956); William E. Leuchtenburg, *Franklin D. Roosevelt and the New Deal* (New York: Harper, 1963), 149–50, 163–66; Felix Frankfurter to Arthur Schlesinger Jr., June 18, 1963, Box 101, Frankfurter Papers. Rosen, "Roosevelt and the Brains Trust," *Political Science Quarterly*, 87 (December 1972), 533–37.

3. Raymond Moley to Franklin D. Roosevelt, May 19, 1932, and memorandum attached, Moley Papers. The Moley Papers were researched when they were in his possession.

4. Raymond Moley to Franklin D. Roosevelt, November 30, 1935, quoted in *After Seven Years*, p. 323; also interviews with Moley and Herbert Feis.

5. Leuchtenburg, p. 349 (bibliography). Schlesinger sent Moley a manuscript copy of his second volume, *The Coming of the New Deal* (Boston: Houghton Mifflin, 1959), and Moley responded with a memorandum which he believed had little impact on Schlesinger's views. The result was his decision to publish *The First New Deal* (New York: Harcourt, Brace, 1966).

6. Barton J. Bernstein, "The New Deal: The Conservative Achievements of Liberal Reform," in Bernstein, ed., *Towards A New Past: Dissenting Essays in American History* (New York: Vintage edition, 1969), pp. 264–65.

7. Ernest Lindley, *The Roosevelt Revolution: First Phase* (New York: Viking, 1933), p. 298. This impression was gathered through incidental contacts with Columbia faculty and in my interview with Adolf Berle in 1966. It is repeated in Arthur Schlesinger Jr., *The Crisis of the Old Order* (Boston: Houghton Mifflin, 1957), pp. 399–400. See also William E. Dodd to Daniel Roper, November 18, 1932, Box 39, Dodd Papers, in which he questions Moley's qualifications. Moley interviews.

8. Jack P. Greene, "The Sixty-Fourth Annual Meeting of the Organization of American Historians," *The Journal of American History*, 58 (December 1971), 710–11. By way of contrast, see Felix Frankfurter to Ernest Gruening, editor, *The Nation*, June 21, 1933, Box 60, Frankfurter Papers.

9. Paul K. Conkin, *The New Deal* (New York: Crowell, 1967), ch. 1 and p. 107.

10. R. C. Moley, "Why I Am A Democrat." College theme, n.d., ca. 1902, copy in author's possession; Tom L. Johnson, *My Story* (New York: Huebsch, 1913), pp. xxxv–xxxvi, 108–9.

11. Frank Freidel, Foreword, in Moley, *The First New Deal*, p. x.

12. Moley interviews, 1st ser., September 1963, pp. 1–3. Also see his fuller recollection of Beard as a teacher in Moley, *27 Masters of Politics* New York; Funk & Wagnalls, 1949), pp. 11 ff.

13. Interviews with Raymond Moley, June 3, 1963, and January 4, 1964.

14. Moley interviews, 1st ser., September 1963, pp. 1–4; Moley, *27 Masters of Politics*, p. 4.

15. Moley interviews, 1st ser., September 1963, pp. 3–4.

16. Moley interviews, 3d ser., June 1969, pp. 1–3; Alfred B. Rollins Jr., *Roosevelt and Howe* (New York: Knopf, 1962), pp. 201–2; "Campaign Addresses (Excerpts), Bronx, N.Y., October 30, 1928," in *The Public Papers and Addresses of Franklin D. Roosevelt* (New York: Random House, 1938), I, 62–66.

17. Moley's appointment is discussed in Lindsay Rogers to Moley, November 19, November 20, and November 21, 1930, and in Moley to Rogers, November 13, and November 24, 1930, Moley Papers; memorandum of conversation with Raymond Moley, June 21, 1960, in author's possession; the investigation of the New York City Magistrates' Courts is summarized in Raymond Moley, *Tribunes of the People* (New Haven: Yale University Press, 1932).

18. Moley interviews, 1st ser., September 1963, p. 6; Moley interviews, 3d ser., June 1969, pp. 4–6; Moley, *After Seven Years*, p. 1; Moley to Roosevelt, December 25, 1931, and "Statement for the Governor's Message . . ."; Roosevelt to Moley, December 29, 1931; and telegram, Guernsey Cross to Moley, January 6, 1932, Moley Papers.

19. Moley interviews, 1st ser., September 1963, pp. 5–7. Moley's initial speechwriting effort in Roosevelt's behalf in 1932 was the drafting of "Notes for Governor Roosevelt for Address to the Association of the [New York] Bar," March 12, 1932, Moley Papers.

20. Jouett Shouse to Franklin D. Roosevelt, March 11 and March 15, 1932, Box: Correspondence, 1930–1932, folder: FDR letters, 1932, Shouse Papers; Moley interviews, 1st ser., September 1963, p. 7.

21. *The Public Papers and Addresses of Franklin D. Roosevelt*, I, 624–27.

22. Herman Oliphant to Raymond Moley, May 20, 1932, Moley Papers.

23. Moley, *After Seven Years*, pp. 10–12.

24. Robert Woolley to Edward M. House, April 9 and April 12, 1932, Box 125, folder 4388, ser. 1, Selected Correspondence, House Papers.

25. Smith's speech is reprinted in the *New York Times*, April 14, 1932.

26. *Ibid.*, April 12, 1932; Matthew and Hannah Josephson, *Al Smith: Hero of the Cities* (Boston: Houghton Mifflin, 1969), p. 439.

27. *New York Times*, April 14, 1932.

28. Conkin, pp. 7–16.

29. See the initial drafts of the St. Paul address in the Moley Papers.

30. Edward M. House to Franklin D. Roosevelt, April 14, 1932, Box 95, folder 3287, ser. 1, Selected Correspondence, House Papers.

31. Memorandum, "Dictated by Mr. Howe, . . . Regarding Water Power—Interest," n.d., Moley Papers.

32. Franklin D. Roosevelt to Thomas J. Walsh, April 20, 1932, Box 384, Thomas Walsh Papers; Frank Freidel, *FDR: The Triumph* (Boston: Little, Brown, 1956), p. 271; Rexford Tugwell, *The Brains Trust* (New York: Viking, 1968), pp. 47–50.

33. This draft is in Box 54, Howe Papers.

34. Drafts of the St. Paul address with the notation "Hotel Lowry, St. P." are in Moley Papers. A copy of the address in the Moley Papers contains the famous sen-

tence hurled at the party's conservative interests (in Moley's hand): "If that be treason, make the most of it." It was not a platform interpolation.

35. Walter Lippmann, "Governor Roosevelt at St. Paul," *New York Herald-Tribune*, April 20, 1932.

36. The St. Paul address is reprinted in *The Public Papers and Addresses of Franklin D. Roosevelt*, I, 627–39.

37. Item 52A, Moley Papers.

38. Introduction, Moley memorandum, May 19, 1932, Moley Papers.

39. "Part I—Preliminary," Moley memorandum; folder: Memo of May 19, 1932; and Raymond Moley to Mrs. Malcolm L. McBride, May 11, 1932, Moley Papers.

40. Part 2, Item 1, Moley memorandum, May 19, 1932, Moley Papers.

41. Moley, *After Seven Years*, pp. 308–12; Rexford G. Tugwell to author, November 4, 1971; Moley to author, February 2, 1973; John Morton Blum, *From the Morgenthau Diaries: Years of Crisis, 1928–1938* (Boston: Houghton Mifflin, 1959), p. 309.

42. Raymond Moley to Franklin D. Roosevelt, May 19, 1932, Moley Papers; Jordan A. Schwarz, *The Interregnum of Despair: Hoover, Congress and the Depression* (Urbana, Chicago, London: University of Illinois Press, 1970), chs. 5 and 6; J. Joseph Huthmacher, *Senator Robert F. Wagner and the Rise of Urban Liberalism* (New York: Atheneum, 1968), pp. 89, 96–97.

43. Moley memorandum on relief, in May 19 memorandum, and rough notes, Moley Papers. Moley's notation on the need for a separate budget reads as follows: "Ordinary outlays should be balanced—But unusual relief—"

44. Van Hise, pp. 226–27, 277–78; and Maurice M. Vance, *Charles Richard Van Hise: Scientist Progressive* (Madison, Wisc.: State Historical Society, 1960), pp. 165–66.

45. Moley memorandum, May 19, 1932, Moley Papers.

46. *Idem.;* Moley to author, December 14, 1971.

47. Raymond Moley to E. R. A. Seligman, March 19, 1927, Seligman Papers; Moley to author, August 28, 1971.

48. Moley to Roosevelt, May 19, 1932, and Moley memorandum, Moley Papers.

49. Moley to author, August 28, 1971, and interview, September 1971.

50. Moley memorandum, May 19, 1932, and item marked "Intranationalism," in folder 53, Moley Papers.

7. The Brains Trust 2:
Tugwell and Agriculture

1. Rexford G. Tugwell, *The Brains Trust* (New York: Viking, 1968), pp. 12–20; Samuel I. Rosenman, *Working With Roosevelt* (New York: Harper, 1952), p. 59; Raymond Moley, *After Seven Years* (New York and London: Harper, 1939), p. 15; Moley interviews, 1st ser. September 1963, pp. 8–9; Tugwell Diary, Expanded

Form, 1932–1934, p. 3, Tugwell Papers; Tugwell to Willard E. Atkins, January 21, 1931, Box 1, Tugwell Papers; Tugwell, "Reminiscences," Oral History Research Office (OHRO), Columbia University, New York; Raymond Moley to George Creel, February 2, 1933, Moley Papers.

2. Tugwell, *The Brains Trust*, p. xxiv; Tugwell to Raymond Moley, January 29, 1965, Moley Papers.

3. See Elliot A. Rosen, "Roosevelt and the Brains Trust: An Historiographical Overview," *Political Science Quarterly*, 86 (December 1972); and Tugwell to Moley, February 4, 1964, Moley Papers.

4. Raymond Moley, "After Many a Summer," review of *The Brains Trust*, August 17, 1968. Released by the *Los Angeles Times* Syndicate.

5. Paul Conkin, *The New Deal* (New York: Crowell, 1967), p. 39.

6. Raymond Moley to author, December 14, 1971.

7. Tugwell, *The Brains Trust*, pp. xxiv–xxvi.

8. See especially Edgar E. Robinson, *The Roosevelt Leadership* (Philadelphia: Lippincott, 1955).

9. Edwin G. Nourse, *American Agriculture and the European Market* (New York: McGraw-Hill, 1924), p. 236.

10. Edwin R. A. Seligman, *The Economics of Farm Relief* (New York: Columbia University Press, 1929), p. 38.

11. National Industrial Conference Board, *The Agricultural Problem in the United States* (New York: NICB, 1926), pp. 142–44.

12. Editors' Introduction, John D. Hicks, *Republican Ascendancy, 1921–1933* (New York: Harper, 1960), pp. xi–xiii.

13. Tugwell, "Reminiscences," OHRO, Columbia University; Moley Memorandum, May 19, 1932, Moley Papers.

14. Moley Memorandum, May 19, 1932, Moley Papers.

15. Bernard Sternsher, *Rexford G. Tugwell and the New Deal* (New Brunswick, N.J.: Rutgers University Press, 1964), p. 3; Rexford G. Tugwell to Edwin R. A. Seligman, August 8, 1928, Seligman Papers.

16. Sternsher, pp. 5–6, 139; interview with Rexford G. Tugwell, August 1968; Tugwell to Wesley C. Mitchell, January 5, 1923, cited in Joseph Dorfman, *The Economic Mind in American Civilization* (New York: Viking, 1959), V, 503.

17. Rexford G. Tugwell to Willard E. Atkins, January 21, 1931, Box 1, Tugwell Papers.

18. For a complete bibliography of Tugwell's massive published and unpublished work, up to 1964, see Sternsher, *Rexford G. Tugwell*, pp. 413–24.

19. Dorfman, V, 505–7; Tugwell, *The Economic Basis of Public Interest* (Menasha, Wisc.: Banta, 1922; reprinted New York: A. M. Kelley, 1968), pp. v–viii, 100.

20. Dorfman, V, 510; American Trade Union Delegation to the Soviet Union, *Soviet Russia in the Second Decade: A Joint Survey by the Technical Staff of the First American Trade Union Delegation*, Stuart Chase, Robert Dunn, and Rexford Guy Tugwell, eds. (New York: John Day, 1928), ch. 3.

21. See, for instance, Henry T. Rainey to Earl C. Smith, April 4, 1931, in Box

3, Rainey Papers. Rainey, a leading Democrat in the House of Representatives, who succeeded John Nance Garner as Speaker, explained a planned visit to Soviet Russia in the summer of 1931: "What I want particularly to study is the subject of Russian Communal Farms. . . . I want to go there and see for myself what is going on in order to make my service in Congress more valuable. We are approaching a period of readjustments in industry and agriculture and some of these readjustments are going to be violent indeed. My impression is that a conscientious legislator ought to put himself in possession of the exact facts with reference to the five year program in Russia."

The Tugwell and Rainey visits were hardly unique. The Palmer raids of the post-World War I era which capitalized on fear of the Soviet experiment do not seem to be characteristic of American attitudes of the middle and later 1920s and the early 1930s, when there existed a more widespread attitude of inquiry and curiosity in connection with the Soviet Union. It was not unusual for conservative businessmen and politicians to acknowledge, especially with the onset of the Great Depression, that elements of the Soviet economic system might find application in our own society.

22. Rexford G. Tugwell, "Experimental Economics," in Tugwell, ed., *The Trend of Economics* (New York: Knopf, 1924), pp. 373–419.

23. Rexford G. Tugwell, "The End of Laissez-Faire," *The New Republic*, October 13, 1926; "America's War-Time Socialism," *The Nation*, April 6, 1927; and *Industry's Coming of Age* (New York: Harcourt Brace, 1927), pp. 208–11 and *passim*.

24. Raymond F. Mikesell, *United States Economic Policy and International Relations* (New York: McGraw-Hill, 1952), pp. 74–75; George Soule, *Prosperity Decade: From War to Depression, 1917–1929* (New York: Rinehart, 1947), pp. 139, 144–45; Hicks, p. 12.

25. Rexford G. Tugwell, "Experimental Control in Russian Industry," *Political Science Quarterly*, 43 (June 1928), 161–64.

26. *Ibid.*, pp. 165–87; see also, Edward H. Carr and R. W. Davies, *A History of Soviet Russia: Foundations of a Planned Economy, 1926–1929* (New York: Macmillan, 1971), ii, 787–808.

27. David Owen, Forward, in Keith Hutchison, *The Decline and Fall of British Capitalism* (Hamden, Conn.: Archon; reprinted 1966).

28. Roland Sarti, *Fascism and the Industrial Leadership in Italy, 1919–1940: A Study in the Expansion of Private Power under Fascism* (Berkeley: University of California Press, 1971), pp. 50–80, 136.

29. Sternsher, pp. 174–77; Tugwell, "Reminiscences," OHRO, Columbia University.

30. Tugwell, "Reminiscences," OHRO, Columbia University.

31. Tugwell, *The Brains Trust*, Introduction; Tugwell to Moley, January 29, 1965, copy in author's possession.

32. Rexford G. Tugwell, "An Engineer and the Price System: Mr. Hoover's Economic Policy," Box 1, Tugwell Papers.

33. Tugwell, "Mr. Hoover's Economic Policy," p. 19, Box 1, Tugwell Papers.

34. Frank O. Lowden to Rexford G. Tugwell, October 1 and October 12, 1931, and Tugwell to Lowden, October 5, 1931, Box 2, Tugwell Papers.

35. Walter H. Edson to Rexford G. Tugwell, February 5, 1932, and Tugwell to Edson, February 8, 1932, Box 1, Tugwell Papers.

36. Rexford G. Tugwell, "The Principle of Planning and the Institution of Laissez Faire," *The American Economic Review*, 22 (March 1932), Supplement, 75–92.

37. Rexford G. Tugwell, "Discourse in Depression," Box 2, Tugwell Papers. Tugwell's radio address, broadcast by NBC, is in Box 1, *ibid.*

38. The full text of the Oglethorpe University address may be found in the *New York Times*, May 23, 1932, as well as in *The Public Papers and Addresses of Franklin D. Roosevelt*, I (New York: Random House, 1938), 639–47.

39. Tugwell's interpretation of the Oglethorpe speech and his explanation of the hope it aroused in him that Roosevelt might embrace total planning for the economy is related in *The Brains Trust*, pp. 93–109.

40. Rexford G. Tugwell to Edwin R. A. Seligman, August 8, 1928, August 12, 1928, Seligman Papers.

41. Chester C. Davis to Milburn L. Wilson, March 15, 1932, and Wilson to Davis, March 26, 1932, M. L. Wilson Papers.

42. For the conservative view, see S. A. Gallier, Assistant Solicitor, Memorandum for R. R. Rogers, Assistant Secretary, October 14, 1932, in folder CD F40, Domestic Allotment Plan Material, M. L. Wilson Papers. Rogers, a supporter of domestic allotment, headed the Farm Mortgage Department of the Prudential Insurance Co., Newark, N.J. For the nationalistic view, see Fred Lee, McCracken & Lee, Washington, D.C., Memorandum on Legal Phases of the Emergency Agricultural Bill, Rainey-Norbeck Bill, 72d Cong., 1st Sess., July 14, 1932, M. L. Wilson Papers.

43. Address by L. S. Hulbert, Legal Department, Federal Farm Board, "Legal Status of Plans for Production Control," August 5, 1932, M. L. Wilson Papers.

44. Tugwell, "Reminiscences," OHRO, Columbia University.

45. M. L. Wilson to George Soule, April 12, 1932, M. L. Wilson Papers; Edward D. Duddy to Tugwell, May 16, 1932, and Tugwell to Duddy, May 19, 1932, Box 1, Tugwell Papers.

46. Tugwell, "Reminiscences," OHRO, Columbia University; Tugwell, *The Brains Trust*, pp. 206 ff.; Edward D. Duddy to Tugwell, June 11, 1932, Box 1, Tugwell Papers.

47. History Section Draft, "A Chronology of Selected Legislation and Proposals Relating to a Two-Price System for Agricultural Products," May 4, 1953, M. L. Wilson Papers.

48. The previous several paragraphs are based on a reading of the M. L. Wilson Papers; see also Mordecai Ezekiel to Rexford Tugwell, October 20, 1939, *ibid.*, and William D. Rowley, *M. L. Wilson and the Campaign for the Domestic Allotment* (Lincoln: University of Nebraska Press, 1970).

49. Rexford G. Tugwell to M. L. Wilson, August 30, 1932, M. L. Wilson Papers, explains his wish that planning should now be extended as a concept to industry; Raymond Moley to author, May 7, 1972, in author's possession, deals with Moley's conversion to intranationalist views at the urging of Tugwell.

50. Richard Kirkendall, *Social Scientists and Farm Politics in the Age of Roosevelt* (Columbia: University of Missouri Press, 1966), pp. 12–13; Rowley, pp. 1–4, 57–107.

51. M. L. Wilson to Ramsay Spillman, January 17, 1933, M. L. Wilson Papers. An earlier version of the domestic allotment idea was published by Spillman in *Farm, Stock and Home*, on February 1, 1926, as "Getting the Tariff to the Farmer."

52. John D. Black, *Agricultural Reform in the United States* (New York: McGraw-Hill, 1929), pp. 271–301; newspaper clipping (on Ruml), dated December 24, 1930, in Chester Davis Correspondence, CD F56, M. L. Wilson Papers; and John D. Black to M. L. Wilson, February 3, 1930, M. L. Wilson Papers.

53. Quoted in Rowley, p. 57.

54. M. L. Wilson to Frederick E. Murphy, July 24, 1931, M. L. Wilson to J. Robert Wiley, March 25, 1932, and M. L. Wilson to Chester C. Davis, March 10, 1932, M. L. Wilson Papers.

55. Kirkendall, pp. 3–4, 13.

56. M. L. Wilson to Bush W. Allen, August 27, 1931, M. L. Wilson Papers.

57. M. L. Wilson to James S. Milloy, April 1, 1932, M. L. Wilson to John Fabrick, May 19, 1932, M. L. Wilson to Frank R. Hammett, February 10, 1932, M. L. Wilson to J. Robert Wiley, March 25, 1932, M. L. Wilson Papers.

58. M. L. Wilson to Clarence Poe, November 7, 1932, M. L. Wilson Papers.

59. M. L. Wilson to Chester C. Davis, May 17, 1932, and M. L. Wilson to Rexford G. Tugwell, July 25, 1932, M. L. Wilson Papers; Tugwell, "Reminiscences," OHRO, Columbia University.

60. John D. Black to M. L. Wilson, October 20, 1932, M. L. Wilson Papers.

61. M. L. Wilson to John D. Black, October 25, 1932, M. L. Wilson Papers.

62. M. L. Wilson to Chester C. Davis, February 21, 1933, M. L. Wilson Papers.

63. Edward L. and Frederick H. Schapsmeier, *Henry A. Wallace: The Agrarian Years, 1910–1940* (Ames: Iowa State University Press, 1968), pp. 2–58.

64. Hoover's economic diplomacy as Commerce Secretary is described by Joseph Brandes, *Herbert Hoover and Economic Diplomacy* (Pittsburgh: University of Pittsburgh Press, 1962), especially pp. 213–20.

65. These developments, including Hoover's philosophy concerning government intervention on behalf of agriculture, are elaborated in Edward L. and Frederick H. Schapsmeier, "Disharmony in the Harding Cabinet: Hoover-Wallace Conflict," *Ohio History*, 75 (Spring-Summer 1966), 126–36, and in their Wallace biography, pp. 72–78. On the BAE and its significance see Rowley, pp. 3–4, 13–14.

66. Schapsmeier and Schapsmeier, *Henry A. Wallace of Iowa*, pp. 78–122;

Henry A. Wallace to George W. Norris, December 18, 1931, and January 23, 1932, Tray 7, Box 4, Norris Papers.

67. Henry A. Wallace to M. L. Wilson, March 24, 1930, Wilson to Wallace, April 21, 1930, and "Memo on Allotment Plan," in Wallace Correspondence, M. L. Wilson Papers.

68. M. L. Wilson to Henry A. Wallace, March 12, 1932, and Wallace to Wilson, April 20, 1932, M. L. Wilson Papers; Schapsmeier and Schapsmeier, *Henry A. Wallace of Iowa*, p. 80 and *passim*.

69. Henry A. Wallace, "Agriculture and National Planning," Voters Service Radio Program, M. L. Wilson Papers.

70. M. L. Wilson to "Dear Bozeman Folks," May 29, 1932, M. L. Wilson Papers.

71. Milliken and Ezekiel, Economics Division, "Readjustments in Our Foreign Trade," in folder: Domestic Allotment, CD F41, M. L. Wilson Papers.

72. Tugwell, "Reminiscences," OHRO, Columbia University; handwritten notation in Raymond Moley's copy of *The Public Papers and Addresses of Franklin D. Roosevelt*, I, 654–55, in author's possession.

8. The Brains Trust 3:
Berle and Industry

1. Raymond Moley, tape-recorded interviews, 1st, 2d, and 3d ser., in author's possession; Moley, *After Seven Years* (New York: Harper, 1939), p. 18; Moley to author, January 20, 1965.

2. Channing acknowledged the young man's contribution in the notes, p. 89, following ch. 3.

3. Max Ascoli, Introduction, Beatrice B. Berle and Travis B. Jacobs, eds., *Navigating the Rapids, 1918–1971* (New York: Harcourt, Brace, 1973), pp. xv–xix; "The Reminiscences of Adolf A. Berle Jr.," Oral History Research Office (OHRO), Columbia University, pp. 1–20, copy in Box 206, Berle Papers; Richard S. Kirkendall, "A. A. Berle Jr., Student of the Corporation, 1917–1932," *The Business History Review*, 35 (Spring 1961), 43–45; Adolf A. Berle Jr. to Louis D. Brandeis, February 19, 1932, folder: 1932, General Correspondence, Container S.C. 11, Brandeis Papers.

4. "The Reminiscences of Adolf A. Berle Jr.," p. 34 ff.

5. Kirkendall, "A. A. Berle Jr., Student of the Corporation," pp. 46–48.

6. "The Reminiscences of Adolf A. Berle Jr.," pp. 113–22.

7. Berle to Brandeis, February 19, 1932, Container S.C. 11, Brandeis Papers.

8. Adolf A. Berle Jr. and Gardiner C. Means, *The Modern Corporation and Private Property* (New York: Macmillan, 1933), preface.

9. *Ibid.*, pp. 1–44.

10. *Ibid.*, pp. 352–57; Joseph Dorfman, *The Economic Mind in American Civilization* (New York: Viking, 1959), V, 753–54; Kirkendall, pp. 47–48; Adolf A. Berle Jr., "Intellectuals and New Deals," *The New Republic*, March 7, 1964; Rex-

ford Tugwell, *The Brains Trust* (New York: Viking, 1968), pp. xxv–xvii, incorrectly ascribes to Moley rather than Berle a role as conservative in the Roosevelt–Brains Trust relationship; Arthur Schlesinger Jr., *The Coming of the New Deal* (Boston: Houghton Mifflin, 1959), pp. 183–84.

11. Kirkendall, pp. 52–53; Adolf A. Berle Jr. to George W. Anderson, December 16, 1931, Box 4, Berle Papers; Berle to Moley, February 3, 1966, copy in author's possession.

12. Berle to Moley, February 3, 1966, copy in author's possession; Berle, "The Reshaping of the American Economy," *The Centennial Review*, Spring 1965, in Berle and Jacobs, eds., *Navigating the Rapids, 1918–1971*, pp. 31–32.

13. Berle memorandum, "The Nature of the Difficulty," in Berle and Jacobs, eds., *Navigating the Rapids*, pp. 32–50.

14. Berle to Ralph Hayes, July 6, 1932, Box 8, Berle Papers; see also Hayes to Baker, April 8, 1932, Box 116, Baker Papers.

9. Stop Roosevelt Stage 2:
The Struggle for Control of the Party

1. Quoted in Edward J. Flynn, *You're the Boss* (New York: Viking, 1947), p. 89.

2. The most detailed examination of the state-by-state contest for delegates is made in Earland I. Carlson, "Franklin D. Roosevelt's Fight for the Presidential Nomination, 1928–1932," doctoral dissertation, University of Illinois, Urbana, 1955. The Carlson dissertation, indefatigable in its research and detail, appears to have shaped uncritical attitudes of historians who subsequently wrote on the subject. In curious fashion, it minimizes defeats and egregious blunders and emphasizes the attainments of the Albany advisers.

3. David Burner, *The Politics of Provincialism: The Democratic Party in Transition, 1918–1932* (New York: Knopf, 1968), ch. 2.

4. Jackson diary, January 26, 1932, author's possession.

5. James A. Farley, *Behind the Ballots* (New York: Harcourt Brace, 1938), pp. 94–96; Carlson, pp. 226–28.

6. Jackson diary, February 7, 1932.

7. Felix Frankfurter to Joseph M. Proskauer, February 22, 1932, and Proskauer to Frankfurter, February [?], 1932, Box 164, Frankfurter Papers.

8. Harlan B. Phillips, *Felix Frankfurter Reminisces* (New York: Reynal, 1960), pp. 238–39.

9. Belle Moskowitz to Felix Frankfurter, March 1 and March 6, 1932, Box 164, Frankfurter Papers.

10. Notation in Frankfurter's hand on Ellery Sedgwick to Felix Frankfurter, March 3, 1932; also Sedgwick to Frankfurter, February 4, and February 13, 1932, and Ralph Hayes to Frankfurter, March 23, 1932, in Box 164, Frankfurter Papers.

11. Jackson Diary, February 9 and February 19, 1932; Carlson, pp. 380–81; the results of the primary are analyzed in detail in Robert Jackson to Louis Howe,

March 15, 1932, Democratic National Committee (DNC) Papers (N.H.), and in Memorandum of Telephone Conversation between . . . Roosevelt . . . and Robert Jackson . . . , March 6, 1932, in author's possession.

12. Jackson diary, March 3, 1932.

13. Ralph Hayes to Newton D. Baker, March 25, 1932, and Hayes to John H. Clarke, April 2, 1932, Box 116, Baker Papers; Newton D. Baker to Jouett Shouse, March 11, 1932, Container: Correspondence, 1930–1932, Shouse Papers.

14. Robert Jackson to Louis Howe, Sunday night, n.d., probably March 1932, in DNC Papers (N.H.). A notation indicates that Roosevelt saw the letter.

15. Frank Freidel, *FDR: The Triumph* (Boston: Little, Brown, 1956); p. 291; Franklin D. Roosevelt to Josephus Daniels, April 2, 1932, Box 15, Daniels Papers.

16. Robert Jackson to author, December 17, 1965. Farley was ineligible to attend, since he was not a national party officer nor a member of the national committee. Cordell Hull attended as an invited, nonvoting member.

17. "Proceedings [of] Committee on Arrangements, Democratic National Committee," April 4, 1932, pp. 58–72. Copy in Shouse Papers.

18. Robert Jackson to author, December 17, 1965 and January 15, 1966; Jackson to Roosevelt, April 7, 1932, DNC Papers (N.H.).

19. "Proceedings, Committee on Arrangements," pp. 73–75; also interviews with Robert Jackson and Jouett Shouse. Both Jackson and Shouse, who differed on what was intended by the resolution three decades later, suggested Harry F. Byrd as an arbiter. Byrd, unfortunately, could not recall the details of the incident sufficiently to clarify the matter, in Harry F. Byrd to author, January 19, 1966.

20. Shouse is quoted in Charles Michelson, *The Ghost Talks* (New York: Putnam, 1944), p. 6; see the *New York Times*, April 5 and April 6, 1932.

21. Freidel, *The Triumph*, pp. 292–93.

22. Emily Smith Warner, *The Happy Warrior* (Garden City, N.Y.: Doubleday, 1956), p. 252; *New York Times*, April 7 and April 8, 1932.

23. *New York Times*, April 9, 1932; Joseph M. Proskauer, *A Segment of My Times* (New York: Farrar, Straus, 1950), p. 70.

24. Ralph Hayes to Newton D. Baker, March 21, 1932, Box 116, Baker Papers.

25. Ralph Hayes to Newton D. Baker, April 1, 1932, Box 116, Baker Papers.

26. Newton D. Baker to Stanley King, April 29, 1932, Box 5, Hayes–Baker Correspondence; and Baker to Mrs. Henry P. Talbot, June 25, 1932, Box 183, Baker Papers.

27. Ralph Hayes to Newton D. Baker, April 1 and April 12, 1932, Box 116, Baker Papers.

28. Jouett Shouse to author, December 6, 1965, author's possession, and Shouse to Frances Perkins, Memorandum, March 20, 1959, in Container: 1957– , Shouse Papers; Baker to Hayes, April 14, 1932, and Hayes to Baker, April 12, April 19, and June 7, 1932, Box 116, Baker Papers; Hayes to Baker, May 6, 1932, Box 5, Hayes–Baker Correspondence; Joseph Proskauer to Felix Frankfurter, February 26, March 2, 1932, and March 7, 1932, Box 164, Frankfurter Papers.

29. James Michael Curley to Carter Glass, September 11, 1931, Box 280, Glass

Papers; and Curley to Key Pittman, January 25, 1932, Box 11, Pittman Papers; Robert Jackson to Franklin D. Roosevelt, December 19, 1931, DNC Papers (N.H.); and Roosevelt to Jackson, December 21, 1931, copy in author's possession.

30. Robert Jackson to Franklin D. Roosevelt, February 2, 1932, DNC Papers (N.H.).

31. Carlson, pp. 387–89; Robert Jackson to author, November 16, 1966; Ralph Hayes to Newton D. Baker, June 8, 1932, Box 5, Hayes–Baker Correspondence. For a different version of this disastrous conference, which removes the onus from Louis Howe and James Roosevelt and places it solely on Curley see Elliott Roosevelt, editor, *FDR: His Personal Letters, 1928–1945* (New York: Duell, Sloan, and Pearce, 1950), I, 275.

32. Carlson, pp. 389–90; "Statement of Chairman Donahue" and Curley's statement are in Box 57, Howe Papers; the Curley–Smith exchanges are reported in the *New York Times*, March 11, 1932, and March 22, 1932.

33. Carlson, pp. 384–94.

34. William Gibbs McAdoo to Alben W. Barkley, March 23, 1931, Box XI: General File, 1930–1937 (Folder: Misc. and Personal, 1931), Barkley Collection.

35. William G. McAdoo, *Crowded Years* (Boston and New York: Houghton Mifflin, 1931), pp. 417–23.

36. *Ibid.*, pp. 111 and *passim;* William Gibbs McAdoo to Robert M. La Follette Jr., December 31, 1931, and McAdoo to Orlando Webber, January 2, 1932, Box 363, McAdoo Papers; and McAdoo to Webber, February 6, 1932, Box 364, McAdoo Papers.

37. For McAdoo's financial and economic views, see his correspondence with Robert M. La Follette and Orlando Webber in Boxes 363 and 364, McAdoo Papers; of some interest is his address on "Wheat and Cotton," delivered before the Salesmanship Club, Houston, Texas, March 19, 1932, item 29/2, Moley Papers.

38. William Gibs McAdoo to William E. Woodward, Deceber 29, 1931, and January 8, 1932; McAdoo to Carl Alex Johnson, January 8, 1932; McAdoo to A. W. McAlister, January 20, 1932; all in Boxes 363 and 364, McAdoo Papers. The generalizations are based in part on the McAdoo Papers as well as a reading of *Crowded Years.*

39. Quoted in Carlson, p. 282. See also Justus S. Wardell to James A. Farley, August 4, 1931, Box 42, folder 1326, ser. 1, Selected Correspondence, in House Papers, in which McAdoo's political power in California is casually dismissed. The forging of the Farley–Dockweiler–Wardell alliance is described in Report by James A. Farley to Louis Howe on California, labeled "Farley trip-1931-California," in Box 53, Howe Papers.

40. McAdoo to [?] Bertrand, March 31, 1931. Copy in DNC Papers (Calif.).

41. McAdoo to George W. Lynn, January 6, 1932; McAdoo to H. P. Wilson, January 5, 1932; McAdoo to Brice Clagett, January 23, 1932; McAdoo to Richard W. Lewis, January 26, 1932; McAdoo to Cordell Hull, January 26, 1932; McAdoo to William E. Woodward, February 10, 1932; William E. Woodward to McAdoo,

April 21, 1932; all in Boxes 363, 364, 365, and 367, McAdoo Papers. Also Press Release on Prohibition, June 9, 1932, in Box 568, *ibid.*

42. Louis Howe to Isidore Dockweiler, February 18, 1932, and Dockweiler to Howe, February 20, 1932, DNC Papers (Calif.).

43. "Memo," May 10, 1932, and clipping from the *San Francisco Examiner*, May 5, 1932, provide the primary results in detail, in Box 54, Howe Papers; Freidel, *The Triumph*, p. 287; A. O. Wharton, president, International Association of Machinists to Members, April 13, 1932, Box 366, McAdoo Papers; C. E. Elkins, legislative representative, Brotherhood of Railway Trainmen, to McAdoo, April 24, 1932, and Lyston B. Black, president, Texas State Society, to McAdoo, May 10, 1932, Box 367, McAdoo Papers; important, also, is a newspaper dispatch by [?] Aikman to *Baltimore Sun*, February 23, 1932, attached to Monroe Butler to McAdoo, February 23, 1932, in Box 365, McAdoo Papers.

44. William E. McAdoo to Anson B. Sams [Fla.], May 6, 1932, and Sams to McAdoo, May 5, 1932; William E. Woodward to McAdoo, May 5, 1932; John B. Elliott to McAdoo, telegram, May 6, 1932; in Box 367, McAdoo Papers.

45. Quoted in Ralph Hayes to Newton D. Baker, May 13, 1932, Box 116, Baker Papers.

46. Warner, *The Happy Warrior*, p. 253.

47. Bernard M. Baruch, *Baruch: The Public Years* (New York: Holt, Rinehart, and Winston, 1960), pp. 237–40; James F. Byrnes, *All in One Lifetime* (New York: Harper, 1958), pp. 63–64.

48. Ralph Hayes to Newton D. Baker, May 6, 1932, Box 5, Hayes–Baker Correspondence.

49. William Gibbs McAdoo to Bernard Baruch, telegram, June 10, 1932, in Selected Correspondence, Vol. 29, Baruch Papers; and McAdoo to Baruch telegram, June 16, 1932, Box 368, McAdoo Papers.

50. Justus S. Wardell to James A. Farley, June 4, 1932. Copy in Box 42, folder 1331, ser. 1, Selected Correspondence, House Papers.

51. Edward M. House to Walter Lippmann, April 30, 1932, and House to Ralph Hayes, May 4, 1932, Box 116, Baker Papers; Robert W. Woolley to House, October 6, 1931, Box 125, folder 4382, ser. 1, Selected Correspondence, House Papers; Thomas J. Walsh to James R. Bennett Jr., April 8, 1931, Box 382, Thomas Walsh Papers; Mary W. Dewson to Mrs. [?] Reed, July 13, 1931, Container VI, Political File, 1928–1932, Folder: 1931, Barkley Papers. These observations are further documented in Elliot A. Rosen, "Baker on the Fifth Ballot? The Democratic Alternative, 1932," *Ohio History*, Autumn 1966, pp. 226–46, 273–77. Roosevelt's general weakness in the South is confirmed in Frank Freidel interview with Burton K. Wheeler, July 8, 1954, copy in author's possession.

52. Newton D. Baker to Ralph Hayes, January 18, 1932, Box 4, Hayes–Baker Correspondence; Franklin D. Roosevelt to Josephus Daniels, May 14, 1932, Box 15, Daniels Papers.

53. Franklin D. Roosevelt to Robert Jackson, May 21, 1932, copy in author's possession; Freidel, *The Triumph*, p. 293 and interview with Senator Burton K.

Wheeler of Montana, Washington, D.C., July 8, 1954; Robert Jackson to author, April 29, 1965; mimeographed "Agenda," in Box 57, Howe Papers; Farley, *Behind the Ballots*, p. 106; Dudley Doolittle to Jouett Shouse, July 6, 1932, Container: Correspondence, 1930–1932, Shouse Papers; *New York Times*, June 6, 1932. I am obliged to Professor Freidel for a copy of the Wheeler interview.

54. Shouse's press statements on the issue are in Container: Democratic National Committee, 1932, Folder: Democratic National Convention, Shouse Papers; Jackson's position is stated in Jackson to John M. Comeford, June 11, 1932, Shouse Papers, and amplified in Jackson to author December 24, 1965 and January 15, 1966. See also: Bernard M. Baruch to William Gibbs McAdoo, June 9, 1932, and McAdoo to Baruch, June 10, 1932, Selected Correspondence, Vol. 29, Baruch Papers; Statement issued by John W. Davis, File 1917, Raskob Personal File, Raskob Papers; Newton D. Baker to W. P. Waggener, June 16, 1932, Box 226, Baker Papers; Herbert Bayard Swope to Jouett Shouse, June 9, 1932, Newton D. Baker to Shouse, June 29, 1932, Albert C. Ritchie to Shouse, July 6, 1932, Harry F. Byrd to Shouse, July 8, 1932, and Joseph Proskauer to Shouse, n.d., Container: Correspondence, 1930–1932, Shouse Papers.

55. Farley, *Behind the Ballots*, pp. 108–9.

56. Farley, *Behind the Ballots*, pp. 116–18; T. Harry Williams, *Huey Long* (New York: Knopf, 1969), p. 577.

57. Statement on two-thirds rule, untitled, Box 192, Baker Papers; Roosevelt's 1924 statement is quoted in Freidel, *The Triumph*, p. 299.

58. Flynn, p. 90; Freidel interview with Wheeler, June 8, 1954.

59. Copy of message in Folder: The Convention, June 27–July 2, 1932, Moley Papers.

60. Raskob's radio address may be found in File 1917, John J. Raskob Personal (Speech) File, Raskob Papers.

61. Newton D. Baker to Brand Whitlock, February 27, 1932, Box 233, Baker Papers; Newton D. Baker to Jesse T. Brillhart, April 24, 1932, Box 36, *ibid.*; Newton D. Baker to Frank Baker, August 23 and August 31, 1930, *ibid.*; Newton D. Baker to Mr. Patterson, Memorandum, May 27, 1932, Box 183, *ibid.*; and Baker to George Foster Peabody, July 22, 1932, Box 186, *ibid.*

10. The Roosevelt Nomination

1. On the drafting of the platform see Cordell Hull, *Memoirs* (New York: Macmillan, 1948), pp. 150–53. Because of his Senate responsibilities, Hull recommended Senator Gilbert M. Hitchcock of Nebraska as chairman of the convention's Committee on Platform and Resolutions. Also pertinent are: Ralph Hayes to Newton D. Baker, May 9, 1932, Baker to Hayes, May 11, 1932, and Hayes to Cordell Hull, June 15, 1932, Box 116, Baker Papers; Philip C. Jessup, Secretary, National World Court Committee, to Baker, May 19, 1932, Baker to Jouett Shouse, May 25, 1932 and Shouse to Baker, May 27, 1932, Box 85, Baker Papers; Walter Lippmann to Baker, May 9, 1932, with proposed foreign affairs plank and

Baker's revision attached, Hayes–Baker Correspondence; Norman Davis to Cordell Hull, June 23, 1932, Container 32, Series 1, Folder 56A, Hull Papers; Daniel C. Roper to Baker, May 16, 1932, and May 19, 1932, Box 200, Baker Papers; and generally the Newton Baker–A. Mitchell Palmer Correspondence in Box 183, Baker Papers. Brandeis' refusal to take a hand in platform drafting is in Container G-5, Brandeis Papers. A correct or "true" copy of the platform is appended to A. Mitchell Palmer to Baker, July 16, 1932, Box 183, Baker Papers.

2. Memorandum, labeled "Remarks," n.d., Box 568, McAdoo Papers. Evidently McAdoo intended the statement as a press release but was dissuaded by Bernard Baruch. See McAdoo to Baruch, n.d. [probably late November or early December 1932], and Baruch to McAdoo, December 3, 1932, telegram, in Selected Correspondence, vol. 29, Baruch Papers. I have made use in the text of sentences crossed out in the McAdoo Memorandum of the Blackstone Hotel luncheon.

3. W. E. Woodward to William G. McAdoo, November 18, 1932, p. 4, Box 377, McAdoo Papers; Frank R. Kent, "The Great Game of Politics," *Baltimore Sun*, November 18, 1932.

4. Belle Moskowitz to Mrs. Guy Montgomery, June [?] 1932, Moskowitz Papers, Connecticut College, New London.

5. Memorandum, labeled "Remarks," n.d., Box 568, McAdoo Papers.

6. Jouett Shouse to Newton D. Baker, July 7, 1932, Box 85, Baker Papers, and author's interview with Shouse; Norman Hapgood to Felix Frankfurter, July 8, 1932, Box 111, Baker Papers; and Shouse Memorandum (March 20, 1959), "The Chicago Convention of 1932," Shouse Papers.

7. Frank R. Kent, "The Great Game of Politics," *Baltimore Sun*, November 18, 1932.

8. William G. McAdoo to Bernard Baruch, n.d., vol. 29, Selected Correspondence, Baruch Papers; McAdoo to Charles E. Russell, November 26, 1932, Box 377, McAdoo Papers; and McAdoo Memorandum, "Remarks," Box 568, McAdoo Papers.

9. Brice Clagett, Memorandum, February 22, 1932, Box 380, McAdoo Papers.

10. James A. Farley, *Behind the Ballots* (New York: Harcourt, Brace, 1938), pp. 110–13, 120–21, 128–31; James Cox to Newton D. Baker, July 15, 1932, Box 79, Baker Papers; William W. Durbin to Josephus Daniels, August 12, 1932, Box 664, Daniels Papers; George F. Milton to Hinckley Lyon, June 17, 1932, Box 10, Milton Papers.

11. *Proceedings of the Democratic National Convention, 1932*, pp. 123–35.

12. Heywood Broun, "It Seems to Me," reprinted from the *Chicago Times* and *New York World-Telegram*, June 29, 1932. Copy in Box: Democratic National Convention: 1932, Shouse Papers.

13. Walter Lippmann, "Baker for President," June 29, 1932, reprinted from Cleveland *Plain Dealer*. Copy in Box 665, Daniels Papers.

14. Farley, *Behind the Ballots*, pp. 131–33.

15. Farley, *Behind the Ballots*, pp. 131–36; interview with James A. Farley, May 22, 1965.

16. Key Pittman and Harry B. Hawes to Tom Connally, June 27, 1932, Box 149, Pittman Papers.

17. As late as August 23, 1932, McAdoo, the Democratic nominee for the Senate, accused Dockweiler and Wardell of carrying on a "consistent defamatory campaign" against him. See McAdoo to William Randolph Hearst, August 23, 1932, Box 371, McAdoo Papers.

18. Breckinridge Long to Key Pittman, July 5, 1932, Box 12, Pittman Papers.

19. *Proceedings of the Democratic National Convention, 1932*, pp. 288–89.

20. Farley, *Behind the Ballots*, pp. 142–43, 314–15; Robert Jackson to author, October 20, 1966, and Jackson interview; *Proceedings of the Democratic National Convention, 1932*, pp. 301–2, 314–15; Thomas M. Storke, *California Editor* (Los Angeles: Westernlore Press, 1958), p. 310; Arthur F. Mullen, *Western Democrat* (New York: Funk & Wagnalls, 1940), pp. 275–76.

21. Mullen, pp. 276–77; *Proceedings of the Democratic National Convention, 1932*, pp. 319–20.

22. Ralph Hayes to John H. Clarke, July 6, 1932, Box 116, Baker Papers; Walter Lippmann to Norman Davis, telegram, from Chicago to Berne, Switzerland, n.d., and Davis to Lippmann, cable, n.d., Box 35, Norman Davis Papers.

23. Governor Martin Sennett Conner to Ralph Hayes, July 15, 1932, Box 116, Baker Papers. See also *Jackson* (Miss.) *Daily News*, July 1, 1932, and July 7, 1932, in which Conner confirmed that Mississippi planned to leave FDR for Baker on the fourth ballot, and Thomas J. Grayson to Roosevelt, July 5, 1932, Box 319, Democratic National Committee (DNC) Papers, 1932, Correspondence, 1928–1933. The author is obliged to Martha Swain for material from the DNC Papers (Miss.) and the *Jackson Daily News* gathered for her Vanderbilt University doctoral dissertation on Senator Harrison.

24. Ralph Hayes to John H. Clarke, July 6, 1932, Box 116, Baker Papers; Carter Glass to Newton D. Baker, September 2, 1932, Box 104, *ibid.;* and Baker to Glass, September 6, 1932, Box 299, Glass Papers; Raymond Moley, with the assistance of Elliot A. Rosen, *The First New Deal* (New York: Harcourt Brace, 1966), pp. 81–83.

25. Josephus Daniels to Bernard Baruch, June 17, 1932, vol. 28, Selected Correspondence, Baruch Papers; Daniels to Ralph Hayes, July 7, 1932, Box 665, Daniels Papers.

26. Ralph Hayes to John H. Clarke, July 6, 1932, Box 116, Baker Papers; Paul V. McNutt to Baker, July 15, 1932, W. Kann to Baker, telegram, July 1, 1932, and Herbert E. Wilson to Baker, July 20, 1932, Box 192, *ibid.,* in which it is posited that a majority of the Indiana vote was about to go to Baker; James Cox to Baker, July 15, 1932, Box 79, *ibid.;* W. D. Harris to Newton D. Baker, telegram, July 1, 1932, Box 192, *ibid.;* Fred Robertson (Kansas) to Baker, April 30, 1932, Box 199, *ibid.,* and H. K. Wells to Harley W. Johnson (Florida), June 24, 1932, copy in Box 192, *ibid.,* are indicative of the widespread sentiment that Roosevelt delegations should switch to Baker in the event of a stalemate. See also John W. Davis to Baker, July 5, 1932, Box 84, *ibid.,* Ralph Hayes to Baker, July 12, 1932, Box 5, Hayes–Baker Correspondence; Samuel Seabury to Baker, July 27, 1932, Box 226,

Baker Papers; Joseph Proskauer to Baker, n.d., Box 192, *Baker Papers;* John W. Davis to Randolph T. Shields, August 10, 1932, Box: 1932, John W. Davis Papers; and Samuel Seabury to Ralph Hayes, August 29, 1932, Box 116, Baker Papers. Roosevelt's weakness in a number of delegations, including New York, Minnesota, Mississippi, and Texas, is described also by Burton K. Wheeler in his interview with Frank Freidel, July 8, 1954, copy in author's possession.

27. Newton D. Baker to John Stewart Bryan, August 6, 1932, Box 47, Baker Papers; and Baker to John H. Clarke, July 9, 1932, Box 59, *ibid.* Roosevelt's attitude in the matter was apparently long held. In September, 1931, he confided to Robert Bingham, publisher of the *Louisville Courier-Journal,* "that he felt that Newton Baker was, in a sense, the heir of Wilson's spirit more than anyone else, and that if Newton Baker should consent to be a candidate he not only would not oppose him, but would do all in his power to aid him in bringing about his nomination and election." Robert Bingham to William E. Dodd, August 12, 1932, Box 39, Dodd Papers.

28. Judson King, Bulletin No. 156, National Popular Government League, August 18, 1932, Box 72, King Papers; William E. Dodd to Richard Crane, July 13, 1932, Box 39, Dodd Papers; Dodd to Baker, July 19, 1932, Box 87, Baker Papers; James Cox to Baker, July 15, 1932, Box 79, Baker Papers. An example of the state-by-state organization of the telegraphic campaign for Baker, in this case Kentucky, is to be found in Folder: January–September 1932, Box: 1930–1936, Democratic Party Papers, 50W28, Samuel Wilson Manuscript Collection, University of Kentucky, Lexington. Thomas M. Storke, a California delegate and editor of the *Santa Barbara News-Press,* a close friend of McAdoo's, recalled that California bankers promised funds for Baker's campaign if he were nominated as well as McAdoo's senatorial campaign. See Storke, *California Editor,* pp. 311–12. Ralph Hayes denied his deliberate involvement of utility interests in the telegraphic campaign in Hayes to William E. Dodd, July 25, 1932, Box 39, Dodd Papers.

29. Robert W. Woolley to Edward M. House, July 8, 1932, Box 125, folder 4393, ser. 1, Selected Correspondence, House Papers. Woolley may have been referring to Judge Martin T. Manton. In the famous O'Connor memorandum to Roosevelt, often quoted only in part, Roosevelt's law partner informed him as follows: "Of the 55,000 Democrats alleged to have been in Chicago for the recent Convention, unquestionably 62,000 of them arranged the McAdoo shift. Despite the foregoing, there was one in Chicago during the entire Convention who was in almost constant company with McAdoo and who, I believe, performed great service for you. That man was Judge Martin T. Manton. . . . ." Basil O'Connor, Memorandum for FDR, July 7, 1932, President's Personal File (PPF) 96.

30. Robert W. Woolley to William G. McAdoo, July 1, 1932, Box 12, Woolley Papers.

31. Oliver Carlson and Ernest Sutherland Bates, *Hearst, Lord of San Simeon* (New York: Viking, 1936), p. 246; W. A. Swanberg, *Citizen Hearst* (New York: Scribner, 1961), pp. 435–38.

32. The preceding account rests on Brice Clagett, Memorandum, February 22,

1933, Box 380, McAdoo Papers; and Daniel C. Roper, *Fifty Years of Public Life* (Durham, N.C.: Duke University Press, 1941), pp. 259–60. Minor differences in recollection have been reconciled in the text. Because of the Roper–McAdoo arrangement and McAdoo's later belief that Roosevelt had violated its terms, a conflict developed in late 1932–early 1933 involving also Cordell Hull and Edward M. House. McAdoo objected to Roosevelt's failure to consult him in the Treasury and State appointments (the setting in which the Clagett memorandum was written), then specifically to William Woodin's selection for the Treasury post. Woodin, he claimed, was identified with Wall Street interests and hardly qualified as a member of the party's progressive wing. House and Hull countered that the spirit of the agreement had been kept in these appointments despite the failure to consult McAdoo directly. See Daniel C. Roper to McAdoo, December 2, 1932, McAdoo to Roper, December 23, 1932, and Clagett to McAdoo, February 1, 1933, Boxes 377–79, McAdoo Papers; also McAdoo to Clagett and McAdoo to Roper, February 13, 1933, Box 380, *ibid*. Alfred E. Smith's and Herbert Bayard Swope's inability to reach McAdoo in these critical hours is related in Joseph M. Proskauer, *A Segment of My Times* (New York: Farrar, Straus, 1950), p. 72; and Emily Smith Warner, *The Happy Warrior* (Garden City, N.Y.: Doubleday, 1956), p. 261.

Breckinridge Long's role in these negotiations, involving also, Key Pittman and Garner, in Washington, is related in Long to Pittman, July 5, 1932, Box 149, Long Papers.

Arthur Mullen's belief that his negotiations with Senator Tom Connally of Texas were pivotal are related in his memoir, *Western Democrat*, pp. 276 ff.

33. "McAdoo at the last minute feared Baker," Frankfurter wrote Louis Brandeis, "so [Governor] Ely said—and moved quickly. It's characteristic of him." Frankfurter to Brandeis, July 6, 1932, Box S.C. 11, Folder: 1933, General Correspondence, June–December, Supreme Court, Brandeis Papers; also George Creel to Frank P. Walsh, July 6, 1932, Box 79, Frank Walsh Papers.

34. Storke, pp. 312–33. McAdoo's claim that the transfer of the California vote to Roosevelt was voted unanimously by the delegation is made in McAdoo to William Randolph Hearst, August 23, 1932, Box 371, McAdoo Papers.

35. Bascom N. Timmons, *Garner of Texas* (New York: Harper, 1948), pp. 165–67; R. G. Sucher (Washington Press Service) to Frank P. Walsh, July 6, 1932, Box 79, Frank Walsh Papers; Walsh to Sucher, July 29, 1932, Frank Walsh Papers. William E. Dodd to Henry Horner, July 8, 1932, Box 39, Dodd Papers; Raymond Moley to Mrs. Malcom McBride, July 22, 1932, Moley Papers; and Moley, *The First New Deal*, pp. 407–8. A year later, at Garner's request, Morrison was named as a delegate to the London Economic Conference despite the fact that no one in Washington knew his views on economic issues.

36. *Proceedings of the Democratic National Convention, 1932*, pp. 324–27.

37. Franklin D. Roosevelt to McAdoo, July 1, 1932, telegram, Box 369, McAdoo Papers; and Garner to McAdoo, July 3, 1932, *ibid*.

38. See Gerald W. Johnson's review of Richard Oulahan, *The Man Who . . . ;*

The Story of the 1932 Democratic Convention (New York: Dial, 1971), in the *Washington Post* book review section, March 14, 1972.

39. John J. Raskob to Harry F. Byrd, July 11, 1932, Box: DNC, 1932–33, Raskob Papers; Raskob to Jouett Shouse, July 7, 1932, Shouse Papers; John W. Davis to J. W. Johnston, July 11, 1932, Box: 1932, John W. Davis Papers; Newton D. Baker to Byron R. Newton, October 17, 1932, Box 162, Baker Papers; Jouett Shouse to Baker, July 7, 1932, Box 85, Baker Papers.

40. Baker to Byron Newton, October 17, 1932, Box 162, Baker Papers; Jouett Shouse to Josephine A. Kelley, July 7, 1932, Box: Correspondence, 1930–1932, Shouse Papers; John J. Raskob to James M. Cox, July 7, 1932, Raskob Papers. Most of the conservatives took refuge intellectually in the party platform; see especially Raskob to Cox, Raskob Papers.

41. Herbert Bayard Swope to Felix Frankfurter, September 15, 1932. Box 164, Frankfurter Papers.

42. Jouett Shouse to George S. May, June 15, 1953, Shouse Papers; George Wolfskill, *The Revolt of the Conservatives: A History of the American Liberty League, 1934–1940* (Boston: Houghton Mifflin, 1962); James T. Patterson, *Congressional Conservatism and the New Deal: The Growth of the Conservative Coalition in Congress, 1933–1939* (Lexington: University of Kentucky Press, 1967); and Jouett Shouse to Wendell L. Willkie, July 29, 1940, Shouse Papers.

43. Statement of Goodrich Murphy, n.d.; M. J. Pollett to Murphy, June 21, 1932; and Mrs. Arthur Patterson to Ed Plaut, February 4, 1964, Papers of Ed Plaut, RG 31-HH, FDRL.

44. Raymond Moley *After Seven Years* (New York: Harper, 1939), pp. 23–24 and reproduction following p. 146.

45. Schlesinger, *The Crisis of the Old Order, 1919–1933* (Boston: Houghton Mifflin, 1957), pp. 403, 532–33; based essentially on Samuel I. Rosenman, *Working With Roosevelt* (New York: Harper, 1952, pp. 70–79.

46. *New York Times,* June 25, 1973, p. 36.

47. See Roosevelt's handwritten notations on final Moley draft of Acceptance Speech, ca. June 28, 1932. This draft, in the Moley Papers, is identifiable by the inscription: "pp. 3–7 at S.E.P., 5/13/39" on the first page, since it was intended for publication in the May 13, 1939, issue of the *Saturday Evening Post* which serialized *After Seven Years.* See also final reading draft of "Acceptance Speech," Chicago, Illinois, 1932, and cover letter by Franklin D. Roosevelt, March 25, 1933, Speech File, FDRL.

11. The State of Hoover's Union

1. For contrary views see Murray N. Rothbard's essay in J. Joseph Huthmacher and Warren I. Susman, eds., *Herbert Hoover and the Crisis of American Capitalism* (Cambridge, Mass.; Schenkman, 1973), pp. 35–58, which pictures Hoover as the principal figure in "the twentieth-century shift from relatively laissez faire capitalism to the modern corporate state"; generally, the conclusions of Ellis W.

Hawley in *ibid.*, pp. 3–35, and in "Herbert Hoover, the Commerce Secretariat, and the Vision of an 'Associative State,' 1921–1928," *Journal of American History*, 61 (June 1974), 116–40, which suggest that Hoover's "associational progressivism" served to synthesize the New Freedom and the New Nationalism into a new species of progressivism, "ordered individualism"; and Joan Hoff Wilson, *Herbert Hoover: Forgotten Progressive* (Boston and Toronto: Little, Brown, 1975), which treats the Hoover policies as progressive. To the contrary, Herbert Hoover was not a progressive. Associational activity or voluntarism, part of his American system, were intended to preserve individualism and nineteenth-century antistatist, laissez faire attitudes. His economic policies as Secretary of Commerce, then as President, contributed substantially and directly to the Great Depression.

2. William Starr Myers, ed., *The State Papers and Other Public Writings of Herbert Hoover* (Garden City, N.Y.: Doubleday, Doran, 1934), II, 41–43.

3. Legislation of February 27, 1931, permitted the advance to war veterans of up to 50 percent of the face value of adjusted service certificates. Within four months loans totaled nearly $800 million. Milton Friedman and Anna Jacobson Schwartz, *The Great Contraction, 1929–1933* (Princeton, N.J.: Princeton University Press, 1965), fn. p. 17.

4. Myers, ed., *Hoover State Papers*, II, 43–50.

5. Friedman and Schwartz, pp. 3–21; Albert U. Romasco, *The Poverty of Abundance: Hoover, the Nation, the Depression* (New York: Oxford University Press, 1965), pp. 70–87; Broadus Mitchell, *Depression Decade: From New Era through New Deal, 1929–1941* (New York: Rinehart, 1947), pp. 127–29.

6. Friedman and Schwartz, p. 24; Romasco, pp. 87–94; Jordan A. Schwarz, *The Interregnum of Despair: Hoover, Congress, and the Depression* (Urbana, Chicago, London: University of Illinois Press, 1970), p. 80; Gerald D. Nash, "Herbert Hoover and the Origins of the Reconstruction Finance Corporation," *The Mississippi Valley Historical Review*, 46 (December 1959), 455–65; "Copy of Prepared Statement Read to Meeting of Nineteen New York Bankers held at Secretary Mellon's Apartment, Sunday, October 4, 1931," Herbert Hoover to George L. Harrison, October 5, 1931, and George Harrison to Hoover, October 7, 1931, Box 8, Harrison Papers.

7. Romasco, p. 89; John Hicks, *Republican Ascendancy, 1921–1933* (New York: Harper, 1960), p. 271; Mitchell, p. 77. Eugene Meyer was designated chairman of RFC and former Vice-President Charles Dawes as president and actual administrative head.

8. Friedman and Schwartz, p. 25, and pp. 34–35 fn.

9. These generalizations are based on my reading of the Ogden L. Mills Papers at the Library of Congress and those of George Leslie Harrison, Governor of the Federal Reserve Bank of New York, at the Columbia University Library. See especially Minutes of the Banking and Industrial Committee of the Second Federal Reserve District, May–October 1932, in Box 1, Harrison Papers.

10. Hoover, *Memoirs: The Great Depression, 1929–1941* (New York: Macmillan, 1952), pp. 30–31; Romasco, pp. 25–26, accepts the distinction drawn by

Hoover between his own policies and those of Mellon; Gene Smith, *The Shattered Dream* (New York: Morrow, 1970), pp. 73–74; "Mills of Washington," *Collier's*, December 19, 1931.

11. "Mills of Washington," *Collier's*, December 19, 1931; also *Time*, July 13, 1931; *The New Yorker*, December 12, 1931; and Mills to Arthur Krock, November 21, 1933. Containers 11 and 170, Mills Papers.

12. Ogden L. Mills to Ogden M. Reid, August 31, 1922; Mills to W. F. Jordan, December 21, 1923; Mills to Paul W. Bayard, March 14, 1924; Mills to Courtlandt Nicoll, January 3, 1923; Mills press release, printed in *New York Tribune*, January 14, 1931, in Container 1, Mills Papers; Mills to Ogden M. Reid, January 21, 1928, Container 7, *ibid.*; Mills to Eugene Meyer, May 15, 1928, and Hoover to Mills, May 26, 1928, and May 28, 1928, Container 6, *ibid.*

13. Minutes of Meetings of May 23, 1932, May 25, 1932, May 27, 1932, and June 2, 1932, Banking and Industrial Committee of the Second Federal Reserve District, Box 1, Harrison Papers; "Minutes of the Meeting of the Open Market Policy Conference [of the Federal Reserve Board]," Washington, D.C., November 30, 1931, Folder: Open Market (April 1931–June 1934), Box 13, *ibid.*; and George L. Harrison, Governor New York Federal Reserve Bank to other Governors, June 8, 1932, Box 18, *ibid.*

14. A copy of the Mills statement is in Container 169, Mills Papers.

15. Myers, ed., *Hoover State Papers*, II, 52, 57–72. Veterans' expenditures were actually increased by $124 million, amounting to a total of $1 billion or 25 percent of the proposed national budget for fiscal 1933.

16. Minutes of Meeting of October 18, 1932, Banking and Industrial Committee of the Second Federal Reserve District, Box 1, Harrison Papers; L. G. Galamba, Sonken-Galamba Corp., to Senator Arthur J. Capper, Kansas, April 23, 1932, Ralph Snyder, President, Kansas State Farm Bureau, to Capper, April 21, 1932, W. W. Finney, President, Emporia Telephone Co., to Capper, April 20, 1932, Herbert Hoover to George L. Harrison, April 26, 1932, and Harrison to Hoover, May 3, 1932, Box 8, *ibid.*; "Credit and Confidence," An Address by Ogden L. Mills, Annual Meeting of the American Acceptance Council, January 25, 1932, Box 12, *ibid.*; Harrison's Minutes of Meeting of Board of Directors, Federal Reserve Bank of New York, April 21, 1932, Binder 50, Harrison Papers, in which Harrison states "The federal reserve banks . . . cannot by themselves bring about inflation, or raise prices, or increase business activity. We may put out millions of dollars [in reference to the Open Market program], but if they merely pile up as excess reserves they have, at that point, no influence upon business or prices."

17. Ellis W. Hawley summarizes the prevailing view of most Hoover specialists, beginning with the emergence of the Hicks–Degler thesis, that "Hoover was indeed a type of collectivist planner, whose rejection of laissez-faire and development of associational activities paved the way for the New Deal," in Huthmacher and Susman, eds., *Herbert Hoover and the Crisis of American Capitalism*, p. 115.

18. Schwarz, pp. 99–101.

19. Meyers, ed., *Hoover State Papers*, II, 104–6; Hawley, in Huthmacher and Susman, eds., *Herbert Hoover and the Crisis of American Capitalism*, pp. 17, 25.

20. Ogden L. Mills to Charles R. Crisp, February 16, 1932, Mills Papers; Schwarz, ch. 5.

21. Schwarz, pp. 117–21; Bascom H. Timmons, *Garner of Texas* (New York: Harper, 1948), pp. 140–41.

22. Timmons, pp. 142–50; see Schwarz, pp. 115–39, for considerable detail and a differing interpretation; Myers, ed., *Hoover State Papers*, II, 206.

23. Myers, ed., *Hoover State Papers*, II, 187–88, and Schwarz, ch. 6.

24. Schwarz, ch. 6; Ogden L. Mills to Walter Lippmann, May 27, 1932, and June 6, 1932, Container 111, Mills Papers; Statement by Secretary of the Treasury Mills before the Committee on Banking and Currency of the Senate, June 2, 1932, Container 169, Mills Papers.

25. Myers, ed., *Hoover State Papers*, II, 222–26, 228–33.

26. Friedman and Schwartz, p. 24 fn.; "The Service of the Reconstruction Finance Corporation," Address of Arthur A. Ballantine, Undersecretary of the Treasury, October 21, 1932, Container 169, Mills Papers.

27. Correspondence of Thomas G. Corcoran and Felix Frankfurter, undated, ca. October–November 1932, Box 49, Frankfurter Papers.

28. Hawley, in Huthmacher and Susman, eds., *Herbert Hoover and the Crisis of American Capitalism*, p. 26, citing William A. Williams, *Tragedy of American Diplomacy* (rev. ed.; New York: Dell, 1962), pp. 127–37, and Paul K. Conkin, *The New Deal* (New York: Crowell, 1967), pp. 25–29.

29. Hoover, *Memoirs: The Great Depression, 1929–1941*, pp. 233–34; Myers, ed., *Hoover State Papers*, II, 247–65.

30. "Campaign Speech at Madison Square Garden, New York City, October 21, 1932. The Campaign a Contrast Between Two Philosophies of Government (Analysis of Democratic Proposals as dangerous to the foundations of American National Life)," Myers, ed., *Hoover State Papers*, II, 408–28.

31. Edmund E. Day, an official of the Rockefeller Foundation, and Professor John H. Williams of Harvard, had been appointed to the preparatory commission of experts to prepare an agenda for the forthcoming World Monetary and Economic Conference.

32. Ogden L. Mills to Owen D. Young and George Harrison, December 16, 1932, Container 9, Mills Papers; Box 12, Harrison Papers.

12. Defining the New Deal

1. Rexford G. Tugwell to author, May 5, 1964.

2. Howard Zinn, ed., *New Deal Thought* (Indianapolis, New York, and Kansas City: Bobbs-Merrill, 1966), pp. xv–xxxviii; Rexford Tugwell, *The Brains Trust* (New York: Viking, 1968), pp. xxi–xxiv.

3. Raymond Moley, *After Seven Years* (New York: Harper, 1939), pp. 35 ff.; Tugwell, *The Brains Trust*, pp. 268–75; Roosevelt to Baker, etc., August 30, 1932,

copy in Moley Papers, originals in Baruch, Baker, and Pittman Papers; Moley, tape recorded interviews, 2d ser. Roosevelt's letter to the party's luminaries informed them that Moley "is acting as a sort of clearing house for me. This part of my task has nothing to do with those who are engaged in the strictly political management of the campaign. . . . It would help me in a very practical sense if you would give me your thought from time to time, and if Professor Moley calls you or writes you on any specific point, I hope you will feel that it comes from me and that you will confer with him." It was further decided by Roosevelt and Moley that recognition would be accorded to the Soviet Union. They were advised, however, to avoid this issue in campaign discussion, since it would alienate party conservatives and be of no political value. See Henry Kittredge Norton to Moley, June 22, 1932, item 37/4, Moley Papers. Moley's notes of his discussion with Roosevelt are in the Moley Papers.

4. Moley interviews, 1st ser., September 1963; also interview with Moley, March 27, 1963, author's possession, and the New York Times, July 31 and August 1, 1932 (editorials).

5. "First draft speech 7/30/32 after acceptance speech. Corrections in handwriting FDR and me [Samuel Rosenman] and (I think) Tugwell," in FDR Speeches, Rosenman Papers; the later Moley drafts and notes are in "Platform Speech, July 30, 1932 (Radio)," Moley Papers. The platform address is reprinted in the New York Times, July 31, 1932, and in The Public Papers and Addresses of Franklin D. Roosevelt (New York: Random House, 1938), I, 659–69.

6. For an excellent summation of the conservative view on the dangers of an unbalanced budget, the flight from currency (the dollar) to gold, and willingness to accept bond issues for capital expenditures for relief, provided they were retired within a short period, see Owen D. Young to Newton D. Baker, June 8, 1932, Box 243, Baker Papers. Young's views, cautiously stated, enjoyed wide regard in the administration and on both sides of the aisle in the legislative branch.

7. Bernard Baruch to Franklin Roosevelt, December 8, 1931 and Roosevelt to Baruch, December 19, 1931, vol. 27, Selected Correspondence, Baruch Papers.

8. Bernard Baruch to Albert C. Ritchie, April 18, 1932; Baruch to Joe T. Robinson, Memorandum, May 1932, and generally Baruch–Rainey and Baruch–Robinson correspondence of 1932; Baruch to Herbert Hoover, April 11, 1932, May 10, 1932, and May 25, 1932, and Hoover to Baruch, May 13, 1932 and May 23, 1932; Baruch to Eugene Meyer, May 21, 1932; B. M. Baruch, "Chicago Convention, June 27, 1932," recapitulates his views; Baruch to Roosevelt, April 1, 1932, and memoranda for Roosevelt, May 27 and May 28, 1932; all in Volumes 27–30, Selected Correspondence, Baruch Papers. Also, Baruch to William G. McAdoo, March 3, 1932, Box 365, McAdoo Papers; Baruch to McAdoo, March 21, 1932, Box 366, McAdoo Papers; Baruch to Josephus Daniels, March 31, 1932, Box 663, Daniels Papers; Baruch to Thomas J. Walsh, October 10, 1931, Box 383, Thomas Walsh Papers.

9. Robert Jackson memorandum to author, February 24, 1966; Moley note attached to New York Times press clipping of July 19, 1932, Moley Papers.

10. Moley to Roosevelt, July 16, 1932, copy in vol. 30, Selected Correspondence, Baruch Papers; and Berle to Roosevelt, July 20, 1932, in Beatrice B. Berle and Travis B. Jacobs, eds., *Navigating the Rapids* (New York: Harcourt, Brace, 1973), pp. 51–52.

11. Baruch to John J. Raskob, July 22, 1932, and Raskob to Baruch, July 26, 1932; Raskob to James A. Farley, September 7, 1932; in vol. 29, Selected Correspondence, Baruch Papers; Moley, "Plans" for the campaign, Moley Papers.

12. Rexford Tugwell, *In Search of Roosevelt* (Cambridge: Harvard University Press, 1972), and *The Brains Trust*, pp. xxiv–xxvi, 270–278, and *passim;* Moley, *After Seven Years*, pp. 43–44; Moley interview, September, 1961; Moley, tape recorded interviews, 1st, 2d, and 3d ser., author's possession.

13. Bernard Baruch, draft of letter to Governor Roosevelt, November 25, 1932, vol. 30, Selected Correspondence, Baruch Papers.

14. Such devices, Tugwell had claimed earlier, could easily fall under the sway of the corporations.

15. Tugwell, *The Brains Trust*, pp. 525–28.

16. M. L. Wilson to Herman Kahn, January 17, 1956, and "Wilson Outline" attached, FDRL; Moley–Tugwell memorandum to Samuel I. Rosenman, July 11, 1932, Moley Papers; M. L. Wilson to Tugwell, July 12, 1932, and Wilson to Henry Morgenthau Jr., August 22, 1932, Moley Papers; Moley's "Plans," for the week beginning August 1, 1932, in Moley Papers; William D. Rowley, *M. L. Wilson and the Campaign for the Domestic Allotment* (Lincoln: University of Nebraska Press, 1970), pp. 151–53 and *passim;* M. L. Wilson to Ralph Budd, July 22, 1932, CD F30, M. L. Wilson Papers.

17. Moley–Tugwell Memorandum to Samuel I. Rosenman, July 11, 1932, Moley Papers.

18. Tugwell speech draft, folder C, Box 1, Tugwell Papers; Berle to Roosevelt, August 17, 1932, and memorandum attached, in folder: Roosevelt and Raymond Moley Correspondence, 1931–early 1932, Moley Papers.

19. See Lester G. Seligman and Elmer E. Cornwell Jr., editors, *New Deal Mosaic: Roosevelt Confers with His National Emergency Council, 1933–1936* (Eugene: University of Oregon Press, 1965).

20. Moley to Roosevelt, July 16, 1932, and accompanying memorandum, authored by Rexford G. Tugwell and Robert K. Straus, item 42/28, Moley Papers. See also Moley to Roosevelt, July 25, 1932, and attached Berle memorandum, which rejected inflationism and deficit spending. Wages of labor and salaried employees Berle argued could not keep pace with inflation. "There is a better way of doing this job. Where debtors cannot pay, the clean and decent way of accomplishing the result is not monkeying with the currency, but to scale down the debt to a point where it is within the debtor's capacity. Where interest charges are too high, bring them down to a decent relationship to the earning power of the person or business which has to pay them. Readjust where readjustment is necessary; but do not break the mass of wage earners and employees in the process."

21. Moley, "Plans—Week Beg. Aug. 1," Moley Papers.

22. These conclusions emerge from Raymond Moley, with the assistance of Elliot A. Rosen, *The First New Deal* (New York: Harcourt Brace, 1966).

23. See John A. Garraty, "The New Deal, National Socialism, and the Great Depression," *The American Historical Review*, 78 (October 1973), 907–44, for an interesting comparison of Roosevelt's techniques, support, and devices with those of Hitler. The argument is curious in its denial of what it then attempts to prove. Actually, economic currents and available mechanisms in advanced societies are similar in the contemporary world.

24. "Post-Mortem on Congress," July 19, 1932, *New York Herald-Tribune*.

25. See Tugwell Diary, December 24, 1932, FDRL; Leon Keyserling, review of Bernard Sternsher's *Rexford Tugwell and the New Deal* (New Brunswick, N.J.: Rutgers University Press, 1964) in the *American Historical Review*, 70 (April 1965), 824–27; the interesting exchange on the state of economic thought between Felix Frankfurter and Jacob Viner of the University of Chicago Economics department in Box 108, Frankfurter Papers; and Sternsher, "Tugwell's Appraisal of F.D.R.," *The Western Political Quarterly*, 15 (March 1962), 67–79; also Tugwell to Clyde H. King, January 23, 1933, Box 2, Tugwell Correspondence, Tugwell Papers; author's interview with Tugwell, summer 1968. For a different view, see James E. Sargent, "FDR and Lewis W. Douglas: Budget Balancing and the Early New Deal," *Prologue* (Spring 1974), pp. 33–43. Sargent's conclusion that neither Douglas nor Roosevelt "grasped the basic principle of compensatory spending that leading economists had started since the early 1930s," is contradicted by Keyserling. No American economist grasped the Keynesian dogma at that time. Professor Sargent's secondary conclusion, that the New Deal was an improvisation, is a paradigm of general scholarly belief on the subject.

26. Frankfurter to Geoffrey Parsons, April 17, 1933, Box 88, Frankfurter Papers; and generally the Frankfurter Papers for the conclusion.

13. Campaign Milestones 1932

1. Edgar Eugene Robinson, *The Presidential Vote, 1896–1932* (Stanford, Calif.: Stanford University Press, 1947), pp. 28–30; Robinson's *They Voted for Roosevelt: The Presidential Vote, 1932–1944* (Stanford, Calif.: Stanford University Press, 1947), pp. 7–8, 41 ff., demonstrates that Republican nominees after 1936 mustered surprisingly large totals. In 1940, Willkie polled 44.7 percent of the electorate; and Dewey, in 1944, won 45.9 percent. The reconstitution of the normally conservative majority in Congress is treated in James T. Patterson, *Congressional Conservatism and the New Deal: The Growth of the Conservative Coalition in Congress, 1933–1939* (Lexington: University Press of Kentucky, 1967).

2. Adolf A. Berle Jr. to Nicholas Murray Butler, October 4, 1932, Box 5, Berle Papers.

3. Rexford Tugwell, *The Brains Trust* (New York: Viking, 1968), p. 508.

4. Elise M. Wagner, "Inspired," stenographic transcript of the Western tour, Moley Papers.

5. Moley, *After Seven Years* (New York: Harper, 1939), pp. 52 ff.

6. Stenographic transcript of Western tour, Moley Papers.

7. E. G. Dunn to James A. Farley, August 9, 1932, and Farley to Moley, August 18, 1932, item 6/11, Moley Papers.

8. M. L. Wilson to Henry Morgenthau Jr., July 28, 1932, CD F73, M. L. Wilson Papers; Raymond Moley to M. L. Wilson, n.d. [telegram, August, 1932], Wilson to Moley, August 22, 1932, and Moley to Wilson, September 4, 1932, Moley Papers; Memorandum, author's attribution to Wilson, item 28/14, Moley Papers; M. L. Wilson, Memoranda [sic] Regarding Agriculture, n.d. [early September, 1932], Group 31, Accession 56–4, Papers of M. L. Wilson, FDRL. The initial Wilson outline for the Topeka Address is in Box 5, Democratic National Committee (DNC) Papers (Library and Research Bureau Papers, 1932–1933).

9. Harriman address, item 28/6, Moley Papers; of importance, also, was the valued advice of W. A. Shaeffer, the Fort Madison, Iowa, pen manufacturer, to FDR, September 11, 1932; see Roosevelt to Moley, September 14, 1932, item 20/34, Moley Papers.

10. M. L. Wilson's drafts of the Topeka address are in CD F36A, Roosevelt's Topeka Speech, M. L. Wilson Papers; Moley's drafts and the "Master Copy" of the speech are in the Topeka folder, Moley Papers. Also valuable are the contents of the folder labeled inappropriately, "Topeka—discarded stuff," Moley Papers; this last folder contains a Tugwell memorandum on the anticipated operation of the domestic allotment program, an indication of the Brains Trust's state of readiness in late 1932 for the task ahead. See also Roosevelt's reading copy of the Topeka speech and last-minute changes, in Speech File, 0498, FDRL.

11. Walter Lippmann, *New York Herald Tribune*, September 6, 1932, and *Tribune* editorial, October 2, 1932; M. L. Wilson to Mordecai Ezekiel, September 21, 1932, and Ezekiel to Wilson, September 24, 1932 and September 27, 1932, M. L. Wilson Papers; Ray P. Bowden to Wilson, CD F49, and Wilson to F. J. Wilmer, September 21, 1932, and generally Wilson Correspondence in CD F32 and CD F33, M. L. Wilson Papers.

12. Tugwell to Wilson, September 30, 1932, CD F90, M. L. Wilson Papers.

13. Recounted in M. L. Wilson to Moley, October 3, 1932, item 24/1, Moley Papers; see also Wilson to Moley, September 28, 1932, item 28/24, *ibid.*

14. William Starr Myers, ed., *The State Papers and Other Public Writings of Herbert Hoover* (Garden City, N.Y.: Doubleday, Doran, 1934), II, 293–318.

15. Address of Cordell Hull, Charlottesville, Va., July 14, 1932, copy in Moley Papers.

16. Notes in folder marked "Intranationalism," folder 53, Moley Papers.

17. Moley, *After Seven Years*, pp. 47 ff.; Raymond Moley to Cordell Hull, August 27, 1932, item 8/12, Moley Papers; Hull to Moley, September 5, 1932, draft of Moley telegram to Hull, n.d., and Hull to Moley, September 7, 1932, item 8/66, Moley Papers; Moley memo to Taussig *re* Tariff, August 28, 1932, and George Foster Peabody to Roosevelt, August 15, 1932, attached, in Box 27, Charles W. Taussig Papers; Taussig–Hull telegrams in folder G210, Box 32, Taus-

sig Papers; Taussig–Hull speech draft, in Box 29, Taussig Papers; and Taussig drafts, folder G127, Box 27, Taussig Papers.

18. Kemper Simpson to Raymond Moley, July 16, 1932, item 52/20, Moley Papers.

19. Moley, *After Seven Years*, p. 48; "Johnson [speech draft], annotated by Sen. [Thomas J.] Walsh," item 52/2, Moley Papers.

20. Moley to Lindsay Rogers, September 13, 1932, item 19/6, and Taussig speech draft labeled "Rogers on Taussig," Moley Papers.

21. Memorandum from Senator Swanson, 52/15, Moley Papers; Edward P. Costigan to Moley, September 17, 1932, 52/14, *ibid.* Roosevelt's suggestion to Moley that he reconcile the two statements for the Sioux City speech should not, in view of Moley's respect for Costigan, have left his adviser "speechless." Moley's recollection, part of a larger lesson of Roosevelt's tendency toward irresponsibility in international affairs, drawn in *After Seven Years*, seems *post hoc.*

22. Moley speech drafts, Butte, Mont., and Seattle, Wash. Moley Papers; Seattle, Wash., Address, September 20, 1932, transcript of Western tour, Moley Papers; M. L. Wilson to Moley, September 21, 1932, *ibid.*; Moley tape recorded interviews, 1st ser., September, 1963.

23. Mordecai Ezekiel to M. L. Wilson, September 28, 1932, and Wilson to Ezekiel, October 8, 1932; Wilson to Harry Owen, October 7, 1932, and to Dr. Bernard Ostrolenk, November 4, 1932, CD F33, all in M. L. Wilson Papers.

24. Moley memorandum to author, December 1964; Moley, *After Seven Years*, p. 50; speech drafts, Sioux City folder, Moley Papers; Tugwell, "International Economic and Financial Policies," item 52/4, Moley Papers; draft of Sioux City Speech, Box 385, Thomas J. Walsh Papers; official press release, Sioux City Speech, September 29, 1932, Speech File, 0544, FDRL.

25. Myers, ed., *Hoover State Papers*, II, 309–10; Telegram to 5 Farm Organizations, Speech File, 0585, Nov. 4 [?], 1932, FDRL; Moley, *After Seven Years*, p. 51.

26. Address of President Hoover, Dinner of the Indiana Republican Editorial Association, Indianapolis, June 15, 1931, Box 169, Mills Papers. It is questionable that Roosevelt considered the World Monetary and Economic Conference as an alternate route to recovery in the Hundred Days, as suggested in James R. Moore, "Sources of New Deal Economic Diplomacy: The International Dimension," *The Journal of American History*, 61 (December 1974), 728–44.

27. Ralph West Robey, Alexander Sachs, W. W. Cumberland, "An Approach to American Economic Problems," January 25, 1933, 53/1, Moley Papers; Robey summary of Sachs memorandum, January 31, 1933, *ibid.*; Alexander Sachs, "Intra-Nationalism As A Synthesis of Economic Nationalism and Internationalism," January 27–31, 1933, item 53/4, *ibid.*; Sachs, "Intra-Nationalism As A Program," 120/129, *ibid.*; Paul Mazur to Robert F. Wagner, December 5, 1932, attached to Mazur to Moley, January 24, 1933, item 113/16, *ibid.*; Rexford G. Tugwell to author, May 5, 1964; Moley Diary, winter, 1933, various entries.

28. "Text of Roosevelt's Outline of 'New Deal,' " *New York Herald-Tribune*, October 7, 1932; also Speech File, 0551, October 6, 1931, FDRL.

29. Broadus Mitchell, *Depression Decade: From New Era through New Deal, 1929–1941* (New York: Rinehart, 1947), p. 451; *The Public Papers and Addresses of Franklin D. Roosevelt* (New York: Random House, 1938), I, 771–95.

30. *The Public Papers and Addresses*, I, 771–812; Joan Hoff Wilson, *Herbert Hoover: Forgotten Progressive* (Boston and Toronto: Little, Brown, 1975), pp. 90–93, 149–51; J. Joseph Huthmacher, *Senator Robert F. Wagner and the Rise of Urban Liberalism* (New York: Atheneum, 1968), pp. 75–77, 89–90, 92–101; Jordan A. Schwarz, *The Interregnum of Despair: Hoover, Congress, and the Depression* (Urbana, Chicago, London: University of Illinois Press, 1970), chs. 2 and 6; Daniel R. Fusfeld, *The Economic Thought of Franklin D. Roosevelt and the Origins of the New Deal* (New York: Columbia University Press, 1956), pp. 173–74, 181, 246–48; memoranda, speech drafts, and reading copy of campaign addresses, Moley Papers and Speech File, FDRL.

31. *New York Times*, September 11, 1932.

32. Richard Lowitt, *George W. Norris, The Persistence of a Progressive, 1913–1933* (Urbana, Chicago, London: University of Illinois Press, 1971), pp. 549–53.

33. George W. Norris to Basil Manly, September 1, 1932, Tray 1, Box 4, Norris Papers.

34. Judson King to George W. Norris, September 13, 1932, Norris Papers.

35. Roosevelt's address on "Public Utilities and Development of Hydro Electric Power, Portland Oregon, September 21, 1932," is reprinted in *The Public Papers and Addresses*, I, 727–42. In drafting the address, Moley relied principally on the following: Donald R. Richberg, "Critical Issues in Public Utility Regulation, A Statement presented in testimony before the N.Y.S. Commission on Revision of Public Service Commission Law," January 13, 1930, item 45/7, Moley Papers; Richberg, "The Future of Power and the Public," published originally in *The Annals* of the American Academy of Political and Social Science, January 1932; material furnished by James C. Bonbright of Columbia University also in folder 45, Moley Papers; Adolf A. Berle to Moley, September 20, 1932, item 45/16, Moley Papers; Huston Thompson to Moley, August 1, 1932, and enclosures, item 45/18, Moley Papers; material furnished by Frank P. Walsh, Chairman of the Power Authority of the State of New York; Morris L. Cooke, "Planning for Power," *The Nation*, June 1, 1932; Leland Olds to Roosevelt and Moley, item 16/21, Moley Papers. Speech drafts containing Moley's and Roosevelt's holographic corrections are in the Moley Papers.

Roosevelt originally spelled out the "yardstick concept" in an article he published in *The Forum*, in December 1929. "One of the most important arguments in favor of their development [Muscle Shoals, St. Lawrence and Boulder Dam] by federal or state authorities is that, if so developed, they will remain forever as a yardstick with which to measure the cost of producing and transmitting electricity." This approach became FDR's alternative to public ownership of transmission lines.

36. The O'Fallon decision (St. Louis & O'Fallon Railway Company v. U.S., 279 U.S. 461) was an essential component in Roosevelt's determination to make use of

the contract method of regulation. It rendered ineffectual those few state utility regulatory bodies (e.g., Massachusetts and Wisconsin) which performed their function adequately, serving to buttress the arguments of those progressives who had concluded that the only effective regulation of utilities holding companies could come from the federal government. "Gas and waterworks socialists" believed that only through federal ownership of transmission lines could the small consumer expect cheap electricity.

The O'Fallon dispute originated in an attempt by the Interstate Commerce Commission to invoke the recapture clause of the Transportation Act of 1920 against the St. Louis & O'Fallon Railway Company for the years 1920 through 1923. The ICC contended that it had computed excess earnings for recapture in a manner which conformed with the "law of the land for rate making purposes" and that reproduction cost constituted only one element in determining fair value. Justice James McReynolds in the majority opinion (five to three) voided the ICC decision to recapture excess earnings under the 1920 law on the grounds that it had not taken reproduction cost into account. Justice Louis Brandeis shredded the majority opinion, with Holmes and Stone concurring, in a brilliant dissent which argued that in a period of inflated values current reproduction cost of assets did not necessarily prove a higher value. He demonstrated with cogency the actual impossibility of proper evaluation of a railroad's cost of reproduction even on a day-to-day basis.

A close study of the O'Fallon decision reveals not so much the clarity of McReynold's reasoning—since after all he had not decided that reproduction cost should serve exclusively as the basis for evaluation of a publicly controlled utility or railroad—but rather the warning that the Court expected reproduction cost to be considered seriously by regulatory bodies in rate making decisions. Since securities of railroads and utilities benefited from inflated valuation on Wall Street in the 1920s, reproduction cost as a basis for rate determination would result in high rates for consumers and extraordinary profits.

The Court's majority opinion alarmed progressives also because it represented the culmination of a series of decisions in the twenties by a conservative majority which tended more and more to emasculate state and federal regulatory bodies. Particularly important was Southwestern Bell Telephone Co. v. Public Service Commission of Missouri, 262 U.S. 276, decided in 1923. In this case the Court held that the rate base on which a private utility is entitled to earn a fair return was the then actual value of the property (reproduction cost) rather than the amount of cash prudently invested in the business. Progressives searched for ways to circumvent such decisions which all but sanctioned stock market manipulation as a means of raising the rates utilities charged consumers. Prudent investment, meaning the determination of rates by allowance for the prudent investment of cash in the construction and maintenance of a utilities system, was one possible solution if the courts would sustain it. If the court would not accept this approach one could turn to the contract method of regulation, the course advocated by Roosevelt. For a sophisticated discussion of the subject see: Franklin D. Roosevelt, "The Real Meaning of the Power Problem," *The Forum*, 82 (December 1929), 327–32.

37. Norris to Judson King, October 6, 1932, Tray 1, Box 3, Norris Papers; Norris' introductory remarks are in Tray 74, Box 5, *ibid.;* original drafts of the Roosevelt statement are in the Moley Papers; Roosevelt's final draft in Speech File, 0539, FDRL.; for vivid descriptions of the Roosevelt–Norris meeting I am indebted to Lowitt, pp. 557–58, and Moley tape-recorded interviews.

38. The discussion of the Commonwealth address and its significance is based on the following: Berle Memorandum, "The Nature of the Difficulty, and final Berle draft of the Commonwealth Address, reprinted in Beatrice B. Berle and Travis B. Jacobs, eds., *Navigating the Rapids,* (New York: Harcourt Brace, 1973), pp. 32–50, 62–70; Berle to Roosevelt, attention Professor Moley, telegrams and speech draft, September 19, 1932, item 2/3, Moley Papers, and Moley–Roosevelt revised draft, in Moley Papers; Berle to Roosevelt, attention Professor Moley, September 19, 1932, Box 15, and Berle speech drafts in folders "American Individualism—Romantic and Realistic," and "Progressive Government," in Boxes 17 and 18, Berle Papers; the speech is reprinted in *The Public Papers and Addresses of Franklin D. Roosevelt*, I, 742–56. Also valuable were: Adolf A. Berle and Gardiner C. Means, *The Modern Corporation and Private Property* (New York: Macmillan, 1933); Rexford G. Tugwell, *The Industrial Discipline and the Governmental Arts* (New York: Columbia University Press, 1933), pp. 199–219, 229, and *passim;* Bernard Sternsher, *Rexford Tugwell and the New Deal* (New Brunswick, N.J.: Rutgers University Press, 1964), pp. 96–98; Ellis W. Hawley, *The New Deal and the Problem of Monopoly* (Princeton, N.J.: Princeton University Press, 1966), pp. 472–94, and *passim;* Adolf A. Berle, "Memorandum, Investigation of Business Practices," [July 12, 1938], Box 11, Norman Davis Papers; ch. 43, "The Commonwealth Address," intended by Tugwell for publication in *The Brains Trust* and published, in modified form, in his *In Search of Roosevelt* (Cambridge: Harvard University Press, 1972); Tugwell to author, November 4, 1971 and December 21, 1971; Moley tape-recorded interviews and interview of September 28, 1966; Berle–George W. Anderson correspondence, Box 4, Berle Papers, and draft of an article on administration of corporations which appeared in the *Harvard Law Review* (June 1932), in Box 5, Berle Papers; and Felix Frankfurter to Walter Lippmann, September 22, 1932, Box 18, Frankfurter Papers.

39. Walton H. Hamilton, "The Control of Business," *The Nation*, May 25, 1932; Max F. Burger to Roosevelt, September 30, 1932, item 34/31, Moley Papers.

14. The Effort To Abort the New Deal

1. Rexford G. Tugwell to author, May 5, 1964; Adolf A. Berle Jr., Memorandum to R. Moley, November 10, 1932, in Beatrice B. Berle and Travis B. Jacobs, eds., *Navigating the Rapids, 1918–1971* (New York: Harcourt, Brace, 1973), pp. 77–79.

2. Department of State Press Release, June 25, 1932, 1-G/886, Hoover Papers.

3. L. Ethan Ellis, *Republican Foreign Policy, 1921–1933* (New Brunswick, N.J.: Rutgers University Press, 1968), pp. 187–88; Memorandum of transatlantic telephone conversation between the President [and Secretary Stimson], and Hugh Gibson and Norman Davis at Geneva, Sunday, June 19, 1932, at 10:20 A.M., 1-G/886, Hoover Papers.

4. Cable 260 from Gibson in Geneva to Secretary of State for the President and the Secretary, June 20, 1932, and Memorandum of transatlantic telephone conversation between Mr. Castle and Mr. Hugh Gibson and Norman Davis, from Geneva, July 1, 1932, 1-G/866, Hoover Papers.

5. Ellis, pp. 211–12.

6. Extract from Memorandum of transatlantic telephone conversation between Undersecretary of State Castle and Hugh Gibson and Norman Davis, "Lausanne Conference and Reparations," July 8, 1932, 1-G/886, Hoover Papers.

7. Stimson Diary, July 11 and July 12, 1932; Hoover, *Memoirs: The Great Depression, 1929–1941* (New York: Macmillan, 1952), pp. 172–73. The proposed statement, dated July 11, 1932, may be found in 1-G/886, Hoover Papers. The Hoover memoirs, it should be noted, give no indication of the President's shifting moods in the situation, which are accounted for, it seems, not as much by substantive questions, but by their potential impact on the presidential vote. This conclusion is drawn principally from numerous entries in the Stimson Diary for the period.

8. Stimson Diary, July 12, 1932; Jay Pierrepont Moffat Diary, July 12, 1932, Harvard University Library.

9. Stimson Diary, July 12–14, 1932, and July 26, 1932; *New York Times*, July 24, 1932.

10. Excerpts from "Address accepting the Republican nomination for President of the United States," 1-G/886, Hoover Papers; Harvey H. Bundy to Mr. Joslin, for the President, October 27, 1932, *ibid.*; Frank Freidel, *Franklin D. Roosevelt: Launching the New Deal* (Boston and Toronto: Little, Brown, 1973), pp. 44–45.

11. Ellis, pp. 188–89; Arnold J. Toynbee, ed., *Survey of International Affairs: 1932* (London: H. Milford, Oxford, 1933), pp. 258 ff.; William Starr Myers, ed., *The State Papers and Other Public Writings of Herbert Hoover* (Garden City, N.Y.: Doubleday, Doran, 1934), II, 260; Moffat Diary, June 27–30, 1932; Pierrepont Moffat to Mr. Secretary [Stimson], September 4, 1932, and memorandum "Left by Mr. Henry [France's Chargé] for consideration by the Secretary," vol. 22, Moffat Papers; Norman Davis, confidential memorandum, September 27, 1932, Box 3, Norman Davis Papers; Erich Eyck, *A History of the Weimar Republic* (Cambridge: Harvard University Press, 1962, 1963), II, 454. ·

12. Rexford G. Tugwell to author, May 5, 1964.

13. Ogden L. Mills to Dr. Foster Kennedy, July 7, 1932, Container 111 (vol. 3), Mills Papers.

14. Stimson Diary, May 20, May 21, and May 25, 1932; Moffat Diary, May 20–22, 1932; Herbert Feis to Felix Frankfurter, June 9, 1932, Box 54, Frankfurter Papers; Memorandum, Herbert Hoover, May 25, 1932, and Memorandum of tele-

phone conversation between Stimson and MacDonald, May 24, 1932, 1-G/886, Hoover Papers; William Starr Myers, *The Foreign Policies of Herbert Hoover 1929–1933* (New York and London: Scribners, 1940), pp. 202–3.

Herbert Feis's initial reluctance in the matter of U.S. participation in an international monetary and economic conference requires some explanation in view of general contemporary acceptance of the so-called William A. Williams or Marketplace thesis which purports this nation's dependence on economic expansion for resolution of its economic dilemmas. In a memorandum, "An Economically Independent United States," drafted in February 1932, the State Department's Economic Adviser concluded that the U.S. was the least dependent of the world's major nations on external sources of goods and raw materials. The Feis analysis, considered in tandem with the Brains Trust's adoption of intranationalism as the surest route to recovery, opens the Williams thesis to serious question as a viable interpretation of our economic diplomacy in the depression years, more broadly in the interwar period.

The Feis memorandum of February 1932 made the following assumptions: "that the export trade of the United States ceases altogether"; that imports would be restricted to a relatively few indispensible items paid for by interest on foreign loans and the profit on foreign investments; that consumption and production would be balanced, leaving this nation dependent basically on its own productivity. The nation's high standard of living could be maintained, he believed, because of its exceptional productivity, its skill, and its relatively abundant resources. He noted: "American farms, worked by machinery by one or two men, produce per man employed much greater quantities of foodstuffs than do European farms or the plots cultivated by Asiatics. American coal miners produce more coal per capita, American automobile factories produce more automobiles per worker, American railroads handle more freight per worker, American road-gangs build more roadway, et cetera. . . . The result, due partly to abundant resources and partly to skill, is that there is a greater quantity of material goods to be divided among 125,000,000 Americans than there is to be divided among any other 125,000,000 of the earth's population."

The economist took the year 1929 as his working model. Exports amounted to $5.1 billion or 10 percent of total production of agricultural products, manufactures, and mines. If they were cut off completely, Feis suggested, there might be a temporary decline of more than 10 percent in economic activity. But the net reduction in our standard of living would soon be less than that, once internal adjustments could be effected and a new balance struck based on an economically self-sufficient society. See Box 54, Frankfurter Papers.

15. Ogden L. Mills to S. Parker Gilbert, Jackson Reynolds, Walter Stewart, Melvin Traylor, Norman H. Davis, and Owen D. Young, August 29, 1932, Container 111 (vol. 3), Mills Papers; Memorandum, William Castle to Herbert Hoover, with Hoover's approval dated October 13, 1932, in 1-G/886, Hoover Papers; Felix Frankfurter to Walter Lippmann, October 13, 1932, Box 78, Frankfurter Papers.

16. Memorandum of transatlantic telephone conversation between Secretary

Stimson and Hugh Gibson and Norman Davis, at Geneva, Monday, July 25, 1932, 1-G/886, Hoover Papers.

17. Moffat Diary, September 7, 1932; Stimson Diary, September 7, 1932, and December 29, 1932.

18. Walter Lippmann to Norman Davis, August 25, 1932, Box 35, Norman H. Davis Papers; Memorandum from NHD [to FDR], August 22, 1932, and Davis to Roosevelt, October 13, 1932, Box 51, *ibid.*

19. Memorandum, Berle to Roosevelt, re Disarmament Conferences-Foreign Debts Settlement, November 4, 1932, Box 16, Berle Papers; Berle and Jacobs, eds., *Navigating the Rapids*, pp. 75–76.

20. Norman Davis to Governor Roosevelt, cable, n.d., ca. November 11, 1932; Davis to Roosevelt, November 15, 1932, and November 18, 1932; Roosevelt to Davis, November 26, 1932, Container 51, Norman H. Davis Papers.

21. Tugwell, "Notes from a New Deal Diary," December 20, 1932, Tugwell Papers; *New York Times*, December 23, 1932.

22. Tugwell, "Notes from a New Deal Diary," December 24, 25, 26, 27, 29, 1932, Tugwell Papers; see also *New York Times*, December 29, 1932.

23. Raymond Moley, *After Seven Years* (New York: Harper, 1939), p. 91.

24. Felix Frankfurter to Herbert Feis, May 27, 1932 and June 10, 1932, Box 54, Frankfurter Papers; Felix Frankfurter to Henry L. Stimson, December 9, 1932, Box 2, Frankfurter–Feis Correspondence.

25. Elting E. Morison, *Turmoil and Tradition: A Study of the Life and Times of Henry L. Stimson* (Boston: Houghton Mifflin, 1960), p. 438; Norman Davis to Henry L. Stimson, Dec. 28, 1932, Franklin D. Roosevelt to Henry L. Stimson, December 24, 1932, Stimson Collection. Stimson's "Mem. of notes of talk of Frankfurter" is in the Stimson Collection, December 22, 1932.

26. Stimson Diary, January 9, 1933 and January 19–20, 1933; Tugwell, "Notes from a New Deal Diary," January 17, 1933, Tugwell Papers.

27. Stimson Diary, January 20, 1933 and Memorandum of Conversation between President Hoover and Governor Roosevelt, January 20, 1933, written by President Hoover, following Stimson's entry; Moley Diary, January 21, 1933; Tugwell, "Notes from a New Deal Diary," January 22, 1933, Tugwell Papers.

28. Villard to Frankfurter, February 14, 1933, Box 108, Frankfurter Papers; Moley Diary, January 22, 1933, and, generally, entries of January and February 1933; Rosen, "Intranationalism vs. Internationalism," *Political Science Quarterly* (June 1966), contains a more detailed discussion, particularly of the debts issue.

29. "Original Notes, Inaugural Address," and Moley Notebook, Moley Papers; reproduced in Raymond Moley with the assistance of Elliot A. Rosen, *The First New Deal* (New York, Harcourt Brace, 1966), ch. 7.

30. Herbert Hoover to Senator David A. Reed, February 20, 1933, in William Starr Myers and Walter H. Newton, *The Hoover Administration: A Documented Narrative* (New York and London: Scribners, 1936), p. 341.

Index